ALSO BY MICHAEL KAMMEN

In the Past Lane: Historical Perspectives on American Culture (1997)

The Lively Arts: Gilbert Seldes and the Transformation of Cultural Criticism in the United States (1996)

Meadows of Memory: Images of Time and Tradition in American Art and Culture (1992)

Mystic Chords of Memory: The Transformation of Tradition in American Culture (1991)

Sovereignty and Liberty: Constitutional Discourse in American Culture (1988)

Selvages and Biases: The Fabric of History in American Culture (1987)

A Machine That Would Go of Itself: The Constitution in American Culture (1986)

Spheres of Liberty: Changing Perceptions of Liberty in American Culture (1986)

A Season of Youth: The American Revolution and the Historical Imagination (1978)

Colonial New York: A History (1975)

People of Paradox: An Inquiry Concerning the Origins of American Civilization (1972)

Empire and Interest: The American Colonies and the Politics of Mercantilism (1970)

Deputyes & Libertyes: The Origins of Representative Government in Colonial America (1969)

A Rope of Sand: The Colonial Agents, British Politics, and the American Revolution (1968)

EDITOR

The Origins of the American Constitution: A Documentary History (1986)

The Past Before Us: Contemporary Historical Writing in the United States (1980)

"What Is the Good of History?" Selected Letters of Carl L. Becker, 1900–1945 (1973)

The History of the Province of New-York, by William Smith, Jr. (1972)

The Contrapuntal Civilization: Essays Toward a New Understanding of the American Experience (1971)

Politics and Society in Colonial America: Democracy or Deference? (1967)

American Culture
American Tastes

American Culture
American Tastes

Social Change and the
20th Century

Michael Kammen

ALFRED A. KNOPF *New York* 1999

THIS IS A BORZOI BOOK
PUBLISHED BY ALFRED A. KNOPF, INC.

Copyright © 1999 by Michael Kammen

All rights reserved under International and Pan-American
Copyright Conventions. Published in the United States by
Alfred A. Knopf, Inc., New York, and simultaneously in Canada by
Random House of Canada Limited, Toronto. Distributed by
Random House, Inc., New York.

www.randomhouse.com

Knopf, Borzoi Books, and the colophon are registered trademarks
of Random House, Inc.

Grateful acknowledgment is made to *The Wilson Quarterly* and Mrs. Russell Lynes
for permission to reprint "A 1976 Commentary" by Russell Lynes
(*The Wilson Quarterly*, Vol. 1, Autumn 1976, pp. 158–160).

Library of Congress Cataloging-in-Publication Data

Kammen, Michael G.
American culture, American tastes: social change and the twentieth century /
Michael Kammen. — 1st ed.
p. cm.
Includes index.
ISBN 0-679-42740-6
1. United States—Social life and customs—20th century.
2. Popular culture—United States—History—20th century.
3. Social change—United States—History—20th century.
4. Aesthetics—Social aspects—United States—History—20th century.
5. Consumption (Economics)—Social aspects—
United States—History—20th century.
I. Title.
E169.04.K35   1999
306'.0973'0904—dc21   98-43155
CIP

Manufactured in the United States of America
Published August 22, 1999
Second Printing, October 1999

For Carol

Love consists in this, that two solitudes protect and touch,
and greet each other.

—RAINER MARIA RILKE, *Letters to a Young Poet*

Contents

Introduction   xiii

Selective Chronology   xxi

1. *Coming to Terms with Defining Terms*   3

2. *Culture Democratized: Distinction or Degradation?*   27

3. *Consumerism, Americanism, and the Phasing of Popular Culture*   47

4. *Popular Culture in Transition—and in Its Prime*   70

5. *Blurring the Boundaries Between Taste Levels*   95

6. *Cultural Criticism and the Transformation of Cultural Authority*   133

7. *The Gradual Emergence of Mass Culture and Its Critics*   162

8. *Mass Culture in More Recent Times: Passive and/or Participatory?*   190

9. *Historians and the Problem of Popular Culture in Recent Times*   219

10. *Meetings of the Minds? Moving Beyond Customary Categories*   242

Appendix: Symposia on Twentieth-Century Perceptions of Culture in the United States   261

Notes   263

Acknowledgments   305

Index   307

Illustrations

1. *Coney Island Beach* (1935) by Reginald Marsh (etching). The William Benton Museum of Art, The University of Connecticut, Storrs, Conn. Gift of Helen Benton Boley.   23

2. *H. L. Mencken and George Jean Nathan* (1947) by Irving Penn (platinum-palladium print). *Vogue*, February 1, 1948. National Portrait Gallery, Smithsonian Institution. Gift of Irving Penn. Courtesy *Vogue*. Copyright © 1948 (renewed 1976) by Condé Nast Publications, Inc.   39

3. *Tuesday Evening at the Savoy Ballroom* (1930) by Reginald Marsh (tempera on panel). Rose Art Museum, Brandeis University, Waltham, Mass. Gift of the Honorable William Benton, New York.   79

4. *Russell Lynes* (1949). Yale Collection of American Literature, Beinecke Rare Book and Manuscript Library, Yale University, New Haven, Conn.   96

5. Taste-level chart drawn by Tom Funk for *Life* magazine, April 11, 1949, pp. 100–01. Courtesy of Tom Funk.   98–99

6. *Arturo Toscanini* (1939) by Herbert Gehr (gelatin silver print). National Portrait Gallery, Smithsonian Institution.   112

7. *Edward L. Bernays* (1984) by Patricia Tate (oil on canvas). National Portrait Gallery, Smithsonian Institution. Gift of Richard Hinds.   112

8. Jeanne Gordon of the Metropolitan Opera crowning Paul Whiteman as the "King of Jazz" in 1926. From Paul Whiteman, *Jazz* (New York: J. H. Sears & Company, 1926), p. 206.   114

9. *Benny Goodman* (1960) by René Robert Bouché (oil on canvas). National Portrait Gallery, Smithsonian Institution. Gift of Benji Goodman Lasseau and Rachel Goodman Edelson.   115

10. Taste-level chart from *The New Republic*, March 2, 1992, p. 26. Courtesy of Tad Friend.   127

11. Taste-level chart from *The Utne Reader*, Sept.–Oct. 1992, p. 83. Courtesy of Tad Friend.   128

12. *H. L. Mencken* (1949) by Al Hirschfeld (gouache on board). National Portrait Gallery, Smithsonian Institution. Courtesy of Al Hirschfeld.   144

13. *Hollywood* (1937) by Thomas Hart Benton (tempera with oil on canvas). The Nelson-Atkins Museum of Art, Kansas City, Missouri (bequest of the artist). © T. H. Benton and R. P. Benton Testamentary Trusts/Licensed by VAGA, New York, N.Y.   154

14. *The New Television Set* (1949) by Norman Rockwell (oil on canvas). *Saturday Evening Post* cover, November 5, 1949. Los Angeles County Museum of Art, gift of Mrs. Ned Crowell.   184

15. *Andy Warhol* (1975) by James Browning Wyeth (gouache and pencil on paper). National Portrait Gallery, Smithsonian Institution. Gift of Coe-Kerr Gallery.   192

Ignatz Mouse says to Offisa Pup: Ignatz's ambitions go beyond the mere flat comic strip: the intricate plot of *Krazy Kat* encompasses Ignatz's diabolically contrived efforts to transcend the familiar two dimensions, the lowly flatland of popular culture, and attain to the roundness of high art. Ignatz explains his intentions to Offisa Pup: "Like other immigrants and their children . . . I'm ready to give America a big Chanukah present back—a new image of the self. But this time why lock ourselves up in the pop-culture ghetto? Why not strut uptown to the mansion of high art, of roundness, and say that our gift to America could rank with Eugene O'Neill's or Henry James's? America *needs* a truly *democratic* high art. America needs the round comic strip!"

—Jay Cantor, *Krazy Kat: A Novel in Five Panels* (1987)

Without tradition there can be no taste, and what is worse, there can be little for taste to act upon.

—John Erskine, *Democracy and Ideals: A Definition* (1920)

Good taste does pay off, without any question.

—Harry Scherman, founder of the Book-of-the-Month Club (1926), reminiscing in 1955

We need to recover the history of the concept of "popular culture." We have to understand the origins of certain sorts of judgements about popular culture: as debased, as bastion of authenticity, or as irrelevant. We have to see popular culture in its historically shifting relation to dominant cultural forms, in order to avoid the temptation to naturalize existing social and cultural relations. Above all, we must not lose sight of the fact that popular culture matters: it has clearly mattered to those who have sought to classify it or to control it.

—Morag Shiach, *Discourse on Popular Culture* (1989)

Introduction

This book is essentially an extended essay about changing views of leisure and American preferences concerning its growing array of uses. It also examines perceptions of popular and mass culture in the United States during the past century. "Popular" and "mass" have meant different things to different people at different times, however, so quite understandably the terms have commonly been interchanged and confused, often because they have not been viewed carefully in historical context. Such casual usage has been encouraged by our equally loose and occasionally frivolous invocations of highbrow, middlebrow, and lowbrow, those all-too-familiar yet elastic categories of cultural taste that have sometimes been applied with excessive (meaning undemonstrable) precision, but at other times with reckless (meaning unreliable) caprice. Just ask ten educated friends to differentiate between popular and mass culture. I predict that you will receive ten fairly divergent answers, and few of them will be historically informed.[1]

Although the author of this project is a practicing historian, we will not proceed decade by decade, or even generation by generation, which would be mechanical and perhaps lethal. Change over time matters immensely, and it must receive due attention. (Hence the Selective Chronology of landmarks in popular culture immediately following this Introduction.) But the organizational scheme that follows is fundamentally topical within a flexible chronological framework. Why? First, because this is an inquiry concerning the *problem* of popular culture and its contested meanings rather than a comprehensive history of popular culture. And second, because I can develop my assertions more clearly and economically through a thematic approach rather than a strictly sequential one. Although the book contains episodes, it is not a narrative. Rather, it is meant to be an explanation of numerous narratives or accounts that readers may already have encountered—many of them, because of their apparent implications, contradictory.

I do, however, take up my topics with this serial logic: they appear in the approximate order of their historical salience, that is, when they respectively began to influence or affect American understanding of taste levels and their role in twentieth-century leisure and desire. Chapter 2, therefore, will be devoted to the hesitant, conflicted search for a compelling rationale for leisure pursuits appropriate in a democratic culture with a very strong work ethic, a rationale that could achieve widespread appeal without being tainted by charges of coarseness or degradation—a quest most visible during the early decades of the twentieth century, but especially in the 1920s. Chapter 3 concerns commercialization and cultural consumerism, an important phenomenon from the turn of the century that has intensified apace ever since. That chapter will also take note of the relationship between popular culture and national identity, a nexus that involved shifting attitudes toward Old World cultures as well as reconsiderations and appropriations from the American past, particularly during the years from around 1900 through World War II.

Chapter 4 seeks to locate and define post-traditional, commercialized popular culture during its most effervescent and prominent period, the late nineteenth and first half of the twentieth century, with particular emphasis upon its interactive and participatory qualities and the culture of celebrity that emerged between the two world wars. Chapter 5 explores the gradual blurring of traditional boundaries between taste levels—the loss of meaning and the eventual irrelevance of strictly defined cultural strata correlated in people's minds with class, education, and degrees of affluence—mainly after midcentury. Chapter 6 will look at two distinct barometers of ambivalence and contestation: the Great Debate about mass culture that dominated the 1950s, and public opinion polls from the 1940s through the 1970s concerning attitudes toward the uses of leisure and toward popular as well as mass culture. That chapter also emphasizes the decline of cultural authority, especially that held by critics, in the later twentieth century, and the increasing importance of cultural power, usually sustained by corporate capital rather than by valorized critical authority. We will witness the rise and decline of respected cultural expertise between the 1920s and the 1980s.

Chapter 7 looks at what I perceive as the emergence of "proto-mass culture" during the interwar years, followed by the first problematic phase of overlap and fuzziness in marks of difference between popular and mass culture, circa 1930–60. (Chronological distinctions made throughout the book are only meant to be suggestive in order to clarify the inevitable messiness of such overlaps. They are *not* intended to be a new gospel or precise gauge of historical measurement.) In chapter 8 I describe and define mass culture as we have known it in our own time, by which I mean since the 1960s and '70s. The persistence of popular culture as a recognizable realm will not be ignored, however, and areas of intersection or convergence must be acknowledged.

Chapter 9 examines the curious and sometimes difficult relationship between historians and popular as well as mass culture, mainly since the 1980s, and does so using two case studies: Ken Burns's television documentary *The Civil War* (1990) and the Museum of Modern Art's extremely controversial exhibition *High & Low: Modern Art and Popular Culture* (1990–91). Finally, chapter 10 seeks to pull these various strands together by discussing the ongoing prevalence of cultural ambiguities and contestation in recent years; by making brief comparisons with trends overseas; and by assessing some rather apocalyptic claims quite recently asserted about the condition of American culture at the close of the century.

For several decades starting in the sixties, numerous scholars on the left sought to redefine the interactive relationship between high and popular culture, out of a desire to demonstrate the cultural autonomy and widening influence of taste preferences among working-class people. Depictions of the lifestyles of ordinary folk went from nearly nonexistent or else trivialized to "subaltern," or at least quite separate in their origins and evolution. More dynamic and complex theories, influenced by studies of European culture, stressed that "so-called high culture has been and will continue to be renewed from below, just as popular or even mass culture derives much of its energies from above. The boundaries shift and dissolve, the categories harden and soften."[2]

I am in full agreement with that, although the former (impact from the bottom up) is more difficult to demonstrate than the latter. It can be done, however—the MoMA exhibition *High & Low* being a case in point. A large number of art critics found fault with it for myriad reasons, but the viewing public, by and large, liked it and learned a great deal from it. Kirk Varnedoe, the curator, anticipated controversy but held fast to his convictions and survived a firestorm. "The relationship of high art to mass culture," he declared, "is one of the great subjects crucial to what made modern art modern." The inspiration for the show had been an article by Adam Gopnik, a writer for *The New Yorker*, showing the influence of cartoons and caricature on Picasso's portraits between 1905 and 1912.[3]

The critics' ultimate complaint, however, was that "the promised circuitry of exchange between art and popular culture is shown to go one way only: from low to high."[4] Although this objection was exaggerated, perhaps Varnedoe and Gopnik had overcompensated because for so long it has been much easier (or at least far more common) to demonstrate patterns of "trickle down" rather than gravity-defying pulsations of "filter up." The basic point, of course, is that the flow between cultural taste levels is not unidirectional. Rather, it is a process of interaction, and sometimes more like the continuous action of a circuit.

Be that as it may, I feel a certain envy for writers who describe and explain cultural phenomena at a particular taste level, whether it be highly cerebral, avant-garde, middlebrow, or mass culture.[5] Not that theirs is an easy task, by any means, but it is somewhat less complicated, perhaps, than presenting a story of permeability, where categories casually interpenetrate and conventional lines of stratification collapse into one another. The history of cultural taste levels in the twentieth century has increasingly been one of fluidity, blending, and the attendant blurring of boundaries. Because that is one of the central propositions of this book, it warrants some advance notice here, particularly as a preview for chapter 5 below.

At the turn of the century George Lyman Kittredge, a prestigious Shakespearean scholar and folklorist at Harvard, observed that educated Americans jumped back and forth from the "learned" to the "popular," a sentiment echoed by H. L. Mencken a generation later. In 1937 poet and playwright Archibald MacLeish made a determined effort to use radio as a bridge between high and popular culture. His play *The Fall of the City* (1937) called upon serious writers to recognize the cultural reach and possibilities of radio. The art of Thomas Hart Benton effectively and indissolubly integrated folk, high, and popular traditions. Consequently, an Omnibus television program in 1953 explicitly presented Benton's paintings as a fusion of cultural levels. And for more than a decade starting in 1964, Susan Sontag insisted that perceptions of a gulf existing between high and low art were illusory. The emergence of new media exemplified "not a conflict of cultures but the creation of a new kind of sensibility which is defiantly pluralistic and dedicated both to excruciating seriousness and to fun, wit, and nostalgia."[6]

This book seeks to explain how that kind of cultural pluralism came about and to describe some of its implications as a historical process. I will devote particular attention to the major sources of cultural authority, such as critics, and their increasingly conflicted relationship with major repositories of cultural power, such as corporate sponsors and media executives. The once delicate balance between these two forces has been markedly altered in the past three decades, thereby rendering many of the generalizations in the best of our analyses reductive and misleading. Here is an example from a pioneering study that belongs to the same genre of inquiry as the present work: "People pay much less attention to the media," wrote the sociologist Herbert J. Gans in 1974, "and are much less swayed by its content than the critics, who are highly sensitive to verbal and other symbolic materials, believe. They [ordinary people] use the media for diversion and would not think of applying its content to their own lives."[7] A wide range of national opinion studies made in the 1970s (examined in chapters 7 and 8 below), however, forcefully contradicts such assertions.

Ultimately, I hope that *American Culture, American Tastes* will convey to readers a sense of the swiftly expanded meanings and perceptions of "culture" in twentieth-century America. Back in 1914 the young Walter Lippmann, already a precocious pundit, offered a working definition that seemed remarkably inclusive for the time:

> Culture is the name for what people are interested in, their thoughts, their models, the books they read and the speeches they hear, their table-talk, gossip, controversies, historical sense and scientific training, the values they appreciate, the quality of life they admire. All communities have a culture. It is the climate of their civilization.[8]

Much of the swift and moving drama of modern American cultural history can be found in the myriad ways in which that description has perforce become even more expansive in recent decades—and has generated a disparate body of writings from students in many disciplines and from beyond the walls of academe as well. I have drawn quite heavily upon that literature: borrowing and agreeing in some areas, skeptical and offering alternative explanations elsewhere. I have relied a great deal upon public opinion polls concerning aspects of American culture, not because the polls are so accurate—indeed, they manifest numerous contradictions—but because they supply such abundant evidence of variable public perceptions of American culture and leisure, which is the core subject of this essay.

Almost a quarter of a century ago the British cultural critic Raymond Williams reminded us that the word-concept "culture" has undergone several major shifts in meaning over the past half a millennium. Its most common usage during the last century—as an abstract noun referring to music, literature, painting and sculpture, theater and film, and so forth—dates only from the later nineteenth century and emerged in the wake of discussions prompted by Matthew Arnold's *Culture and Anarchy* (1867). Arnold associated culture with authority. Doing so seemed inescapable to him because he regarded culture as "a principle of authority, to counteract the tendency to anarchy." Williams added, moreover, that the adjective "cultural" seems to date from the 1870s and only became common during the 1890s. As Williams observed, "the word is only available, in its modern sense, when the independent noun, in the artistic and intellectual or anthropological senses, has become familiar." He added that hostility to the word "culture" appears to date from the controversy provoked by Arnold's views.[9]

In sum, *American Culture, American Tastes* is written in response to an enormous (and constantly growing) corpus of writing that has appeared in recent years about taste levels, cultural stratification, and a process of "informalization" in the United States.[10] The creators of that corpus, needless to say, are usually well informed and thoughtful. Some of their work is outdated, however, in part because it was ahistorical to begin with—oblivious to complex changes wrought by time. Aspects of their work suffer from being excessively present-minded. But in addition, swift and unexpected developments during the past decade or so have made their conclusions vulnerable for reasons they could not readily have anticipated. The passage of time will undoubtedly wreak havoc with my own interpretations, too, yet I indulge a conceit that the historical perspective informing *American Culture, American Tastes* may supply it with some staying power. Although it is polemical in places, it is not meant to be a tract for our times. Rather, it is intended to serve simultaneously as a wraparound window and as a rearview mirror, as well as an ancillary side mirror, to assist those who need to negotiate the confusing cultural traffic of our century.

Whenever an interviewer asked Duke Ellington to categorize a musical mode, or inquired about music and race, or about the skills of a musician the Duke greatly admired, he liked to quote "the words of the Maestro, Mr. Toscanini, who said concerning singers, 'Either you're a good musician or you're not.' In terms of musicianship [for example], Ella Fitzgerald is 'Beyond Category.' "[11] Ellington's phrase is elegantly helpful in reminding us that pigeonholes are highly confining; but our scope will not be exclusively restricted to excellence. Americans now spend more than a trillion dollars a year in their pursuit of leisure—far more than they spend on health care, or cars and trucks, or on housing.[12] How that level of expenditure gradually came about, and *the diversity of preferences and attitudes that accompanies it*, warrants our attention.

Selective Chronology

1784   Charles Willson Peale creates a museum of miscellaneous attractions in Philadelphia.

1790s   Earliest American circuses begin to appear.

1811   The first American county fair is organized in Pittsfield, Mass.

1841   First state fair is held at Syracuse, N.Y., featuring domestic manufactures.

1841–43   P. T. Barnum takes over and transforms the American Museum in New York. Enjoys peak fame in the 1850s.

1843–44   Minstrel shows with urban-based troupes begin to achieve great popular success.

1850–51   P. T. Barnum brings singer Jenny Lind from Sweden for a national tour.

1871   Fisk Jubilee Singers make their pioneering tour in concert settings in border states and the North.

1872   Montgomery Ward issues the first mail-order catalogue.

1874–76   Chautauqua Lake, N.Y., becomes the site of an assembly for training Sunday school teachers, a program that gradually expands to include general education and popular entertainment, such as concerts.

1876   The National League is created, the beginning of modern professional baseball. American League created in 1901.

1881   Barnum and others begin to move their circuses by railroad.

1885   Sheet music begins to be produced for home use.

1885–86   Buffalo Bill Cody achieves popular success with his Wild West Show, first opened in Omaha in 1883.

1886   F. W. Woolworth creates the first 5-and-10-cent store. By 1900 there will be fifty-nine such stores.

1887   E. F. Albee and B. F. Keith reduce the cost of admission to their vaudeville show to 10 cents, the start of a price revolution in entertainment.

Thomas Edison invents a phonograph using cylindrical wax records.

1888   The Eastman Company introduces the Kodak, a simple box camera containing a 100-exposure roll of film: the beginning of modern amateur photography.

1893   World's Columbian Exposition held in Chicago's White City.

1894   The Sears catalogue begins to appear as a semi-annual.

1895   First amusement park opens at Coney Island, Brooklyn.

Advertising intensifies in low-cost magazines like *Munsey's*, which displayed 300 items per issue by 1895. Revenue from ads will become more important than subscriptions.

The first comic cartoon, "The Yellow Kid," appears in Joseph Pulitzer's *New York World*, and is stolen in 1896 by William Randolph Hearst for his paper, the *Journal*.

1896   Thomas Edison develops kinetoscope camera that can project pictures on a screen.

1900   Publication of *The Wonderful Wizard of Oz* by L. Frank Baum.

1902   National syndication of comic strips begins when Hearst sells the right to reproduce his strips to other newspapers.

1903   *The Great Train Robbery* is one of the first commercially successful story films.

The first box of Crayola crayons is produced: eight colors for 5 cents.

First baseball World Series (Boston defeats Pittsburgh).

1905   Penny arcades begin to appear.

1905–10   Rise of the nickelodeon to popularity.

1907–32   *Ziegfeld's Follies* enjoys great appeal and emulation.

1911   *Photoplay* appears, the first movie fan magazine. The genesis of celebrity culture.

1913   Arthur Wynne creates the first crossword puzzle. It appears in the *New York World* on Sunday, Dec. 21.

1914   The first transcontinental telephone line is completed.

ASCAP (American Society of Composers, Authors and Publishers) founded. It enjoys a monopoly on fees for twenty-five years.

1915   *Birth of a Nation*, D. W. Griffith's innovative and influential—and subsequently controversial—film, appears.

"Highbrow and Lowbrow" published by Van Wyck Brooks in his *America Comes of Age*.

1919   Johnston McCulley's serialized novel *The Curse of Capistrano* introduces the character Zorro, who later serves as the prototype for Superman, Batman, and other heroes with alter egos.

Jack Dempsey wins the heavyweight championship from Jess Willard, loses it to Gene Tunney in 1926, and loses the rematch to Tunney in 1927 in the controversial "Long Count" in Chicago. Dempsey becomes the first fighter to draw a $1 million gate.

1919–20   Wax recordings are introduced.

The first tabloid newspapers are published in New York City.

1920   Radio as a public enterprise begins in Pittsburgh.

1923   *Time* magazine is started by Henry Luce and Brit Hadden.

1926   Book-of-the-Month Club is created.

Dempsey loses to Tunney in Philadelphia on Sept. 23. Charlie Chaplin, Al Jolson, and William Randolph Hearst are at ringside in a huge crowd. Eight hundred correspondents devote two million words to the match. The age of the modern newspaper sports department has begun.

1926–28   NBC and CBS emerge as national networks; large numbers of local affiliates by 1935.

1927   *The Jazz Singer* with Al Jolson becomes the first widely distributed film with sound.

Charles Lindbergh makes the first solo flight across the Atlantic.

1928   The *Amos 'n' Andy* radio comedy series makes its debut.

1930   "Mickey Mouse" and "Blondie" become syndicated comic strips.

1931   The Crossley system for rating the size of radio program audiences is established, followed in 1935 by the Hooper system.

1931–34   Miguel Covarrubias's caricatures, "Impossible Interviews," appear in *Vanity Fair.*

1933   Walt Disney's film *The Three Little Pigs* creates a sensation.

First baseball All-Star game, won by the American League.

1934   Colonial Williamsburg opens to the public.

1934–35   *Major Bowes' Amateur Hour* becomes the most popular radio program, and is much imitated.

1935   George Gallup establishes the American Institute of Public Opinion, the beginning of polling.

1936   Jesse Owens wins four gold medals at the Berlin Olympic Games as Hitler watches.

1936–37   Luce launches *Life* magazine, a swift success.

1937   Disney's *Snow White and the Seven Dwarfs*, the first feature-length animated cartoon appears; another success.

Joe Louis defeats James J. Braddock in Chicago for the heavyweight championship, and holds the title for twelve years.

1938   Orson Welles's alarming radio broadcast on Oct. 30, "War of the Worlds," creates a nationwide scare.

Benny Goodman and his swing band perform at Carnegie Hall.

1939   Pocket Books begins to publish inexpensive soft-cover editions.

Clement Greenberg publishes "Avant-Garde and Kitsch," an attack upon the advent of vulgar popular culture.

1940   Syndication of "Superman" as a comic book hero.

1941   BMI (Broadcast Music Inc.) challenges ASCAP as a performance rights organization, ending ASCAP's monopoly.

1944   Jerome Robbins and Leonard Bernstein collaborate on *Fancy Free*, Robbins's first ballet: three sailors on the town.

1945   The Grand Ole Opry is broadcast live from Ryman Auditorium in Nashville on Dec. 8. Performers include Roy Acuff, Minnie Pearl, Eddy Arnold, and the Fruit Jar Drinkers.

1946   More than 200 new mass-oriented magazines appear.

1947   Jackie Robinson becomes the first African-American to play major-league baseball since blacks were expelled in the late 1870s.

1948   The emergence of commercial television.

        Invention of the long-playing record.

1949   "Highbrow, Lowbrow, Middlebrow" by Russell Lynes appears in *Harper's* (February) and is abridged in *Life* (April).

1949–56   TV moves from 6% penetration of American homes to 76%. It will rise to nearly 90% by 1960.

1950   Diners Club issues the first credit card.

1951   The coaxial cable makes possible transcontinental transmission of telecasts.

1952   Presidential nominating conventions receive television coverage for the first time.

        Harry Smith issues *Anthology of American Folk Music*, which helps to inspire the folk revival of the 1950s.

1952–53   *Victory at Sea*, U.S. naval history during World War II, is a big hit on television.

1952–60   The Great Debate among intellectuals concerning the "problem" of mass culture takes place.

1953   *TV Guide* first published, an instant success.

1953–54   Soap operas dominate afternoons on all networks.

mid-1950s   Large shopping centers (malls) emerge in the mid-1950s.

1954   McDonald's has twenty-one franchises and in 1955 Ray Kroc opens his first McDonald's in Des Plaines, Ill.

        Davy Crockett is serialized on Disney's weekly TV show and becomes a nationwide sensation.

1955   Disneyland opens in Anaheim, Calif.

1956   Elvis Presley appears for the first time on *The Ed Sullivan Show*.

1957   *West Side Story*, a hit musical with classical roots, appears on Broadway.

1960   Seventy million people watch the first presidential debate on television (Sept. 26): Kennedy vs. Nixon.

"Masscult & Midcult," an attack on middlebrow and mass culture by Dwight Macdonald, appears.

1964   Marshall McLuhan publishes *Understanding Media: The Extensions of Man.*

Cassius Clay wins the heavyweight championship from Sonny Liston in Miami and changes his name to Muhammad Ali.

"Notes on Camp" by Susan Sontag identifies a new mode of kitsch in a neutral way (unlike Greenberg in 1939).

1965   *Time* cover story (April 2) devoted to "The Computer in Society."

1967   The first football Super Bowl: Green Bay defeats Kansas City.

The Popular Culture Association is founded and the *Journal of Popular Culture* begins publication.

1967   Satellite transmission from Tokyo to New York begins.

1969   Apollo 11 arrives at the moon. On July 20, Neil Armstrong becomes the first human to walk on the moon.

The Woodstock Music Festival is held in upstate New York.

1970   "Talk radio" begins in Boston with telephone calls to fill dead spots. Participatory programs on TV follow in the 1980s.

1970s Satellites begin to speed the transmission of TV programs around the world.

1972   Home Box Office (HBO) begins modestly; by 1997 it will have 23 million subscribers.

1975   Muhammad Ali beats Joe Frazier in Manila, an epic fight with an international television audience.

1976–77 Alex Haley's book *Roots* enjoys success and then becomes a surprise hit as an eight-part TV series on ABC (January 1977).

1977   Elvis Presley dies at Graceland, age forty-two.

1980   MTV first appears.
CNN begins.

1983   *Time* cover story (Jan. 3) celebrates the "Machine of the Year" (the computer) rather than a Man of the Year.

1990   Ken Burns's *The Civil War,* an eleven-part documentary, appears on PBS.

1990–91   *High & Low: Modern Art and Popular Culture* exhibition is shown at the Museum of Modern Art in New York, and then at venues in Chicago and Los Angeles.

1993   A plan to locate a Disney theme park near a Civil War battlefield in Virginia is defeated by a coalition wielding indictments of Disney's versions of American history and of commercialism encroaching on historic preservation.

American Culture
American Tastes

1

Coming to Terms with Defining Terms

∞

A decade ago, when I began to teach courses on the evolution of taste levels and cultural stratification in the United States—courses concerned with culture in a democratic society, the commodification of culture, the changing nature and uses of leisure, culture and national identity, those kinds of issues—a troublesome lack of definitional clarity and precision in the pertinent literature quickly became apparent. Since then this disarray has become a genuine challenge, not just to me personally, I believe, but to anyone seriously interested in understanding popular culture. Adding to my perplexity, this lack of clarity even appeared evident among the best and brightest—sociologists, historians, literary scholars, art historians, those working in cultural studies, American Studies, and journalism; the problem looked to be ubiquitous.

The most obvious puzzles, in my view, arose from the habit of using the phrases "popular culture" and "mass culture" interchangeably, as though there were and are no discernible differences. I shall offer only a few representative examples on the grounds that giving excessive evidence of bad habits may only encourage them. (A batting coach shows players what to do rather than what not to do.) In 1984, for instance, an innovative cultural historian wrote the following in an otherwise brilliant essay titled "Books and Culture": "The 1930s joined the European voice to the American perception in a situation where the fear and distaste of modern *mass or popular* culture seemed justified by the twin totalitarian viciousness of fascism and communism [emphasis

3

added]."[1] We even have serious writers who casually refer to "mass popular culture"; and National Public Radio now has a Popular Culture commentator who mostly seems to report on mass culture phenomena, such as film.[2]

It must be acknowledged that sometimes the conflation of mass and popular culture occurs in the context of (or with reference to) the Great Debate over the evils of mass culture that occurred primarily during the mid- and later 1950s. In these instances, it is frequently unclear whether the author is directly at fault or simply repeating the muddled usage of predecessors. Either way, however, the reader who needs definitional clarity gets fuzziness instead.[3]

Yet another cause for confusion occurs when a writer chooses to discuss popular culture within the framework of something casually labeled "mass society" in which "mass communication" has begun to occur. Mass society is a demographic phenomenon (dramatic population growth) once commonly associated with vulnerability to charismatic demagogues capable of swaying the masses toward either socialism or fascism, particularly during the second quarter of the twentieth century. Mass communication involves a technological transformation once identified with universal access to newspapers, magazines, radio, and television, but now more frequently identified with satellites, computers, and the Internet. Mass society may very well serve as a host or context for mass culture; but historically the former antedated the latter in ordinary usage, whereas the latter seems to have outlived the former in common parlance. Mass communication certainly facilitates the dissemination of mass culture; and both are undeniably dependent upon the venturesomeness of innovative entrepreneurs. Yet to intermingle the two only confuses the vehicle with the voluminous load it is supposed to distribute. The one has wheels, wires, and wavelengths. The other has comic books, cartoons, sitcoms, and videocassettes.[4]

A few writers have bothered to differentiate thoughtfully, but they have not done so systematically or in depth. Almost four decades ago Oscar Handlin remarked that mass culture—by which he meant culture disseminated through the mass media—had a "disturbing" effect upon both popular and refined cultures, each of which predates mass culture. He wisely noted a common misconception that the mass culture of 1960 was merely an extension of popular cultures of the past.[5]

Richard Slotkin, whose discipline is American Studies and whose specialty has long been the role of dominant myths in the United States, acknowledges the need for discrimination. "The productions of the cultural industries are indeed varied and ubiquitous," he writes,

> from the newspapers and mass entertainment to the textbooks that teach our children the authorized versions of American history and literature—but the authority of these "mass culture" productions has been and is offset by the influence of other forms of culture and expression that are genuinely "popular": produced by and for specific cultural communities like the ethnic group, the family-clan, a town, neighborhood, or region, the workplace, or the street corner. Although few of these subcultural entities are now isolated from the influence of mass media, they are still capable of generating their own myths and their own unique ways of interpreting the productions of the media.[6]

Historian Jackson Lears adamantly refuses to mix the two, and does so for a reason sensibly separate from Slotkin's yet altogether congruent with it: "one cannot after all maintain a coherent or sophisticated notion of class and still equate mass culture with 'popular culture.' "[7]

The disposition to confuse or conflate the two phenomena is due, at least in part, to disciplinary allegiances and ideological commitments. Because, for example, the phrase "mass culture" is commonly perceived as carrying pejorative connotations, many of those who really enjoy it and write positively about it prefer to use the term "popular culture," almost as a synonym, when they actually do mean mass culture: record-breaking attendance for films and television shows, compact discs that sell in the millions, apparel like jeans and sneakers, fast-food chains, standardized products sold at Wal-Mart and Kmart, and so forth.[8] The use of euphemism in this context has increased in recent years, but it certainly is not new. More than a generation ago an astute young cultural critic, Robert Warshow, casually used "popular" and "mass" interchangeably, but also referred with almost clinical care to a transformation given explicit recognition following World War II. "The mass culture of the educated classes," he observed, "the culture of the 'middle-brow,' as it has sometimes been called—had come into existence."[9]

A British cultural critic has called attention to a similar paradox in the realm of film reviews. It is not unusual for writers to praise intellectually unpretentious popular movies for reasons that are not merely unrelated to their apparent appeal but even seem inimical to it. According to C. W. E. Bigsby, "Popular culture, then, can apparently be transformed into 'high' art by a simple critical act of appropriation. Indeed so insecure are these categories that the popular culture of one generation can become the high culture of the next and vice versa—a fact which applies not only to individual artists but to genres (theatre, novel, film), subgenres (farce, science fiction, detective fiction) and styles (romanticism, realism)."[10]

Needless to say, popular culture not only existed but thrived for centuries prior to the period from 1885 to 1935 that I shall highlight. I draw a marked distinction between what British scholars refer to as "traditional" popular culture (flourishing in the sixteenth to nineteenth centuries) and the considerably more commercialized and technologically transformed popular culture that emerged at the close of the nineteenth century and then blossomed exuberantly early in the twentieth. Traditional popular culture has also been called pretechnological and preindustrial. A fine example from the United States is the dime museum, which flourished during the nineteenth century but disappeared after 1900 because of the emergence of nickelodeons, film, and mechanized amusement parks.[11]

When we turn to folk culture and contemplate its advocates over a historical span of, say, seventy years, notable changes and even more diversity become apparent. Back in the 1930s Constance Rourke made an ardent yet isolated case for folk culture as the very essence, not merely of popular culture, but of national identity in the United States. Despite the plaudits her work received, her particular emphasis did not gain many adherents for more than a generation.[12] In recent years we have professional students of folk culture deeply concerned to maintain a clear distance between handwrought folk traditions that they cherish and a mass consumer culture that they dislike.[13] And we have historians of popular culture who perceive its roots deeply embedded in folk culture, who find agency rather than victimization in popular culture because they do not believe that consumers are helpless in the hands of producers and entrepreneurs.[14]

By now the nonspecialist reader may very well feel overwhelmed by a surfeit of citations and contradictory points of view. If such browsers are still bearing with me, they surely must sense that the study of popular culture is clearly thriving in institutions of higher learning. Scholars may not be all of one mind, but they certainly are single-minded if not downright feisty in their pursuit of popular culture. Paradoxically, however, that is not the impression that one gets from casual browsing, particularly in the press or even among the cognoscenti. In 1974 Herbert Gans declared that "popular culture is not studied much these days either by social scientists or humanists. . . ." Twenty years later the retiring Secretary (director) of the Smithsonian Institution threw his hands up in despair at rising interest in popular and mass culture displays at the National Museum of American History. "How the hell do you define pop culture anyway?" he demanded.[15]

Much of this book will be devoted to answering that question from various angles of vision. Here at the start it seems prudent to begin with an even more basic question on which there is no consensus respecting inclusiveness: What is culture? If we look at two famous responses to that query (offered well after Walter Lippmann's) which share a common point of departure, we will gain from the second one a definition of popular culture by negative reference: culture is ordinary rather than rarefied, a matter of quotidian meanings rather than the gleanings of formal education. Both definitions still have their devotees today, though the balance of opinion has surely shifted from T. S. Eliot's elitist view to Raymond Williams's more populist view. Let's begin with Eliot in 1948:

By "culture," then, I mean first of all what anthropologists mean: the way of life of particular people living together in one place. That culture is made visible in their arts, in their social system, in their habits and customs, in their religion. But these things added together do not constitute the culture, though we often speak for convenience as if they did. These things are simply the parts into which a culture can be anatomised, as a human body can. But just as a man is something more than an assemblage of the various constituent parts of his body, so a culture is more than the assemblage of its arts, customs and religious beliefs. These things all act upon each other, and fully to understand one you have to understand all. Now there are of course higher cultures and lower cultures, and the higher cultures in general are distinguished by differentiation of function, so that

7

you can speak of the less cultured and the more cultured strata of society, and finally, you can speak of individuals as being exceptionally cultured. The culture of an artist or a philosopher is distinct from that of a mine worker or field labourer; the culture of a poet will be somewhat different from that of a politician; but in a healthy society these are all parts of the same culture; and the artist, the poet, the philosopher, the politician and the labourer will have a culture in common, which they do not share with other people of the same occupations in other countries.[16]

Although Eliot acknowledges the existence of mine workers and field laborers, he assumes that in some mysterious way they will share the national cultural identity of those with more education and money and higher social status than themselves. How they choose to use their leisure and what distinctive pleasures they may enjoy are beyond his realm of concern.*

Twenty years later, in 1968, Raymond Williams did not repudiate Eliot so much as find his definition incomplete:

> In talking of a common culture, then, one was saying first that culture was the way of life of a people, as well as the vital and indispensable contributions of specially gifted and identifiable persons, and one was using the idea of the *common* element of the culture—its community—as a way of criticizing that divided and fragmented culture we actually have.
>
> If it is at all true that the creation of meanings is an activity which engages all men, then one is bound to be shocked by any society which, in its most explicit culture, either suppresses the meanings and values of whole groups, or which fails to extend to these groups the possibility of articulating and communicating those meanings.[17]

At the close of that extract, writing just when the study of popular culture began to require recognition if not outright legitimacy in academe, Williams anticipated the inclusiveness that would occur in

---

* For an unusual indication of Eliot's enthusiasm for popular culture, see his essay "Marie Lloyd" in *Selected Essays* (New York, 1932).

progressive stages during the 1970s and '80s. Meanwhile the historian E. P. Thompson, Williams's contemporary, made a useful distinction (in writing about the eighteenth century) between the "polite culture" of more genteel folk and a "customary popular culture" of ordinary people so different that it would lie beyond the recognition of even pious or affluent members of the middle class who had no aspirations for learned culture yet longed for the gentility of "polite culture."[18]

Students of colonial and nineteenth-century America, however, examining a less traditional and less rigidly stratified society, have narrowed the distance between book learning and collective beliefs. David D. Hall has warned against the presumption that ordinary people possess a culture totally separate from that of an educated elite, and has argued that there were always intermediaries able and ready to interpret one segment of society to another. Bridging the nineteenth into the twentieth century, David Grimsted has discovered common ground for bookish and popular culture; but even more important, he has punctured the customary distinction that elite culture was untainted by pecuniary ambitions, unlike popular culture, which was not merely tarnished but downright mercenary. Grimsted has suggested that "a desire to create, and a need to live, and a yen for money or recognition are not warring but joined elements in human beings. Such a gross truism would hardly be worth making did it not relate to one of the most popular explanatory put-downs of popular culture. To decry popular culture because it's involved with profit motives is to disparage all levels of culture, all similarly tinged with personal adulterated motives."[19]

Both Grimsted and Hall acknowledge the existence of diverse levels of cultural taste, while minimizing their distinctiveness or the distance that separates them. The process of change over time, however, has not been neatly linear but more nearly cyclical, with widely shared cultural tastes more noticeable early (seventeenth to mid-nineteenth centuries) and late (since the 1960s), whereas the segmentation of cultural tastes was more prominent in between. Inquiries have certainly demonstrated that sharp distinctions between high culture and low did not yet obtain during the first half of the nineteenth century, whether one looks at museums, carnivals, the audiences for painting or for Shakespeare.[20]

The situation in Victorian America is more complex, and there is considerably less consensus among students of the later nineteenth century. One's preferences depend a great deal upon the modes of cultural experience one chooses to examine. Looking at museums, symphonic music, and opera, for example, Lawrence W. Levine finds cultural hierarchy becoming much more pronounced in this period. Genteel taste, exclusiveness contrary to museum and zoo charters that proclaimed an educational mission to the masses, an emphasis upon decorum within the hallowed precincts of temples devoted to art and music, admission fees that fended off the working classes, all contributed to a marked increase in segmentation and stratification.[21]

Those who concentrate more on books and reading habits, however, are impressed by the broad appeal across taste-level lines of such writers as Harriet Beecher Stowe, Horace Bushnell, Henry Wadsworth Longfellow, and Henry Ward Beecher. Hence their belief that clear dichotomies between high and popular culture did not yet exist even in Victorian America.[22]

An intermediate position can be found if one examines the controls over magazine content exercised by Victorian editors who carefully monitored the propriety of public taste. Or the way American folk heroes, such as Kit Carson, displayed notable variations in their diction depending upon whether their venue was a dime novel or a play directed to the middle class, not to mention diverse regional audiences. After looking at a variety of cultural institutions in the United States during the later nineteenth century, Neil Harris reached a multifaceted conclusion: Functioning within those institutions he found "unstable mixtures of preservation and popularization, dogmatism and tolerance, opposition to and acquiescence in mass taste." He saw a surprising blend of "high and popular culture in unlikely places.... Whether the popular was acknowledged out of respect for its integrity or from a desire to reshape it is not always clear." Yet Harris concludes that these institutions "adopted a stance toward modernity that was both more skeptical and more probing than easy wisdom would suggest."[23]

Harris and others have noted that popular as well as high culture programs and exhibitions occurred at the numerous world fairs that took place in the United States between 1876 and 1915. Entrepreneurs recognized the need for both and provided for them—but in carefully controlled ways, such as noncontiguous locations. At Chicago's Columbian Exposition in 1893, for example, Frederick Jackson Turner addressed the American Historical Association about the frontier West within the pristine confines of the sparkling White City while Buffalo Bill and his philistine Wild West Show performed on the Midway Plaisance. Cultural segregation, plain and simple.[24]

As late as the 1870s, taste levels and stratification had not yet become rigid or inflexible; but they were perceptibly hardening. In 1871, for example, Ralph Waldo Emerson and William Roscoe Thayer (a proper Bostonian who published extensively on Italian history and politics) made a transcontinental trip by railroad (riding in a private car) and enjoyed a look at Yosemite. In Salt Lake City the two preeminent intellectuals attended a melodrama, *Marriage by Moonlight; or the Wildcat's Revenge*, and were not impressed. A month later they went to a "notorious theater" in San Francisco, one said to be a favorite of gold miners. It must have been a kind of burlesque–opera house. In any case, Emerson and Thayer found it "flat and dreary." As American society became more heterogeneous, crossing cultural boundaries became increasingly problematic.[25]

One year later, yet another old-line New Englander puzzled over the big question, though this time quite publicly in *Scribner's*. Presumably others shared his concern about the optimal connections between high culture and the working class. "What are the relations of culture to common life," asked Charles Dudley Warner, "of the scholar to the day-laborer? What is the value of this vast accumulation of higher learning, what is its point of contact with the mass of humanity...." Warner suggested that public intellectuals had civic responsibilities; but few among his contemporaries shared that concern, and his cri de coeur would hardly be heard again for almost a century.[26]

It is undeniably true that T. S. Eliot wanted a larger reading public for poetry, but mainly because he also hoped to have a bigger audience for his social and religious ideas. "I believe that the poet naturally prefers to write for as large and miscellaneous an audience as possible," he once wrote, but then continued enigmatically: "it is the half-educated and ill-educated, rather than the uneducated, who stand in his way: I myself should like an audience which could neither read nor write." Eliot later modified that oddly patronizing notion into a theory highly representative of the tripartite "brow level" doctrine that dominated American thinking during the middle third of the twentieth century. He explained that a writer really needed three concentric publics: "a small public of substantially the same education as himself, as well as the same tastes; a larger public with some common background with him; and finally he should have something in common with everyone who has intelligence and sensibility and can read his language."[27]

Other cultural critics tended to follow a tripartite division while using different labels and varying grounds for differentiation. Leslie Fiedler, for example, with a more whimsical wisdom than Eliot's, defined taste levels in terms of what people preferred to read. His correlations were clear-cut and made no allowance for overlap. Highbrows read the little reviews. The philistine middle class read "the slicks." And the masses were consumers of the pulps. Whereas Fiedler's masses simply took what was available, affordable, and comprehensible, Michael Denning has offered a very different vision of working-class cultural autonomy in which the writers of dime novels were sympathetic to working-class culture and readers from that culture interpreted dime novels in a highly particular way that coincided sensibly with the actual world they inhabited. "The cultural formation of the dime novel," Denning writes, "derives its energy and crudity from the conjuncture of the birth of a culture industry with the emergence of an American working class. Its narrative formulas gain their resonance largely from their closeness to working class ideologies, from the mechanic accents of the producer culture to which its readers, writers, and earliest publishers belonged."[28]

In 1984 the American historian Warren Susman wondered (and asked) whether popular culture operated according to formulas while high culture functioned in response to conventions. The question is important though difficult, but perhaps we can respond to it in terms of the varied patterns of repetition that may be observed at different taste levels.[29] In high culture, repetition occurs because participants fully expect to see different stagings of the Ring Cycle or *Hamlet* and then compare them, always with certain conventions in mind though not feeling bound by them until, perhaps, *Hamlet* is set in Houston with redneck guards or *Die Götterdämmerung* features Hell's Angels.

Most newspapers read by middlebrows presume that you have not followed a story faithfully, so repetition is built into each installment as background. In the realm of popular culture, a great many people never seem to tire of old favorites like Lawrence Welk, formulaic romance fiction, certain beverages, and cartoon characters. Familiarity and reliability are more desirable than novelty.[30] With mass culture, by contrast, novelty is necessary in order to maximize sales, initiate fads, and excite audiences. Repetition is also inevitable, nonetheless, for two reasons. First, nothing is copied so quickly as a success, so that a hit program elicits a multimirrored hall of look-alikes. And second, the secret of effective advertising is repetition with minor variations. Hence we see certain ads so often that we come to learn them by rote.

Departing too radically from convention runs the risk of rejection and abject failure. Yet rigid adherence to convention also entails the risk of stagnation and alienation. Only the avant-garde, by definition, seek to flout convention. In fact, their most prominent convention is their unconventionality.

Having acknowledged the historical existence of "brow levels" used as a kind of shorthand for cultural stratification by taste levels, and also having indicated that I want to differentiate between mass and popular culture, perhaps I may appropriately recognize that what appears to be a current trend—the mixing and consequent blurring of taste levels— has historical roots that date back roughly four decades. The recent vogue is highly visible. In 1996 the cultural historian Ann Douglas published an essay titled "High Is Low" in which she announced that a wall dividing the art world had disintegrated. Some of her particulars, however, suggested that it had been heading toward collapse for much of the twentieth century. Early in 1997 Michiko Kakutani's "Culture Zone" column for the *New York Times* called attention to a blurring of preferences in apparel across class and racial lines. As she provocatively put it, "why are homeboys and suburbanites wearing each other's clothes?" A few months later an essay observed that "deconstruction" had entered the lexicon of daily life. Although it may often be used improperly, that word-concept has curiously entered the realm of popular writing.[31]

Taken together, do those examples begin to suggest that some sort of cultural Mixmaster has been activated? Forsooth, perhaps even a paradigm shift? Let's scroll back to 1955 and read John Berger, art critic at that time for the *New Statesman* in England and *The Nation* in the United States. He ridiculed the notion that an iron divider loomed large between highbrows and lowbrows. He insisted that "a great deal of highbrow and lowbrow culture derive from exactly the same attitude of life and differ only in their degree of self-consciousness." Berger acknowledged the existence of "different standards of appreciation": Some people with an "unusually developed visual sensibility" see works from the perspective of the artist; they appreciate how the artist has solved certain aesthetic and technical problems. A majority, meanwhile, identify not with the artist but with the content of the art. "They will applaud not the process of creation but the result. This difference, however, is not the same as that between highbrow and lowbrow. Both these attitudes of appreciation are necessary to one another."[32] What Berger saw as an arbitrary and wrongheaded division between highbrow and lowbrow was, in his view, "based on a misreading of history."

We may or may not agree with Berger; many of his contemporaries in 1955 did not. But eventually, during the decades that followed, his rejection of strict lines of demarcation would be reiterated by critics in diverse fields. His attack on cultural snobbery was only an opening salvo, and what we have read in recent years is mainly an insistent elaboration.

For myself, as Supreme Court justices say, I concur in part and dissent in part. I dissent from Berger because for most of a century, from the 1870s until the 1960s, a great many Americans did in fact believe that cultural stratification existed and they responded accordingly. In 1949 the editor of *Harper's* magazine received the following handwritten letter from a man in Bard, New Mexico: "Just a line to let you know that I do not think your magazine is what it used to be. It seems to me evry [sic] thing you print is too much high brow, or it may be that I am just low brow." Already in 1892, a literary reviewer was noting the irony that Walt Whitman celebrated the masses and yearned for their approval, yet was chiefly read by the "cultivated few."[33] Countless examples of taste-level awareness will appear in the chapters that follow.

But I also concur with Berger because many of those who read and invoke history in order to elucidate taste levels in the United States do so in such a variety of ways that "history" gets to be a grab bag, ransacked almost randomly in support of often contradictory conclusions. A few examples should suffice. Richard Ohmann, a historian of American literature, sought to answer the question: "Where did mass culture come from?" He found his answer in the transformation of American journalistic publishing (newspapers and magazines) at the end of the nineteenth and during the early years of the twentieth century. In 1880s, he explained, "editors and publishers first succeeded in basing their business on low prices, large circulations, and advertising revenues. And the great editors of the 1890s, who turned this principle into even greater profits, understood it well." Consequently, enterprising publishers blended two business practices that were already effective but had until then been independent of each other. They borrowed from the women's magazines and the cheap weeklies the concept of making a large group of consumers more accessible to advertisers, and they took from the most prominent monthlies the idea of appealing to people who wanted to be part of a newly emerging national audience. By about 1905, according to Ohmann, monthly magazines had become "the major form of repeated cultural experience" for Americans.[34]

The difficulty here, symptomatic of problems posed by so much of the material treated in this book, is that the clientele for these magazines can be (and has been) viewed in highly variable ways. During the decades examined intensively by Ohmann, 1885 to 1905, the most influential national monthlies were *Harper's* and *The Century*. Scarcely anyone regards these as progenitors of mass culture. A few students even place them in the highbrow category, but most consider them what subsequently came to be called middle- or upper-middlebrow. The same is true of *Scribner's*, founded in 1887. The *Atlantic Monthly* underwent a revival after 1898, when Walter Hines Page took over as editor. It must be acknowledged, however, that sales of the *Ladies Home Journal* rose from 600,000 in 1891 to a million by 1903. And by 1900 *Munsey's Magazine* had become the first general-interest illustrated magazine to achieve a genuinely high circulation. But, again, do any of these publications qualify as products of *mass* culture? Judging by their contents, and by other kinds of attractive reading material (like gazettes) that would have had their greatest appeal for working-class Americans, I would prefer to categorize them—except perhaps for *Munsey's*—as manifestations of popular culture, aimed mainly at the protean and capacious middle class.[35]

Richard Ohmann even acknowledges that *Munsey's* went mainly to middle-class people rather than to farmers and workers, and therefore that configuration is less inclusive than what we mean by mass culture. Yet Ohmann nevertheless claims that an "integrated mass culture" emerged in the 1890s, though the meaning of "integrated" remains unclear.[36]

The same kinds of difficulties arise when we turn to other criteria of cultural stratification in search of the genesis of mass culture. The historian Kathy Peiss looks at the diversions pursued by working women in New York at the turn of the century and finds what she calls the emergence of "mass leisure."[37] Because the paid vacation did not become a reality for working-class Americans until well after World War II, however, mass leisure surely did not mean in 1900 what it would come to mean by the 1960s. Moreover, can mass leisure of any kind imply the existence of full-scale mass culture in the absence of such mass media as radio and television?

Similarly, Lary May locates the birth of mass culture between 1911 and 1929, but especially during the 1920s because of the appearance then of large and gaudy movie palaces. He cites "an unprecedented mass audience centered in the growing cities." But his operative meaning of mass culture remains elusive because he is really describing the uses of leisure in urban settings primarily for middle- and lower-middle-income Americans. These glitzy movie palaces cost more and were less physically accessible than the much smaller and unadorned neighborhood structures patronized by nearby working-class folk, especially the newer immigrants.[38] Consequently, the film audience in the United States during the first three decades of the twentieth century remained more segmented by class and taste levels than some observers have been willing to recognize.

Writing about the emergence of the Book-of-the-Month Club in the later 1920s, Janice Radway explains that controversies generated by this entrepreneurial innovation occurred as part of the "American attempt to come to terms with the process of massification." She frequently refers to a "huge mass audience" and to a "modern mass society." Radway believes that Henry Seidel Canby, a professor of English at Yale who served as chairman of the club's selection committee, included the masses in his assessment of cultural markets and their dynamics in the United States. Yet Radway and others acknowledge that the Book-of-the-Month Club is best described by a new category (or label) that made its first appearance during the 1920s: middlebrow.[39] No one can plausibly claim the BOMC and its imitators as exemplars of mass culture. Popular, perhaps, and middlebrow surely, but not mass. Its subscribers were numerous though hardly vast—tens of thousands but not yet millions.

Two more illustrations should suffice. In noting the popularity of "auto-camping" by the end of the 1920s—automobile holidays accompanied by camping in the out-of-doors—historian Warren Belasco designates this protean activity (its modus operandi changed every few years) as a "mass institution." Although it is true that Henry Ford had democratized access to the automobile by the end of the 1920s, ownership remained particularly an upper- and middle-income phenomenon. Neither the urban masses nor the rural poor went auto-camping. Meanwhile historians of feminism as an ideology, and of the changing role of women in American society, tend to place the emergence of mass culture in the 1940s.[40]

Clearly, then, there is no agreement among students of American culture in the twentieth century as to when mass culture either began or achieved full flower. One of the principal purposes of this book is to clarify that uncertainty. I am persuaded that the appearance of newspaper and then radio syndication (ca. 1908–38), along with many other developments, including those just mentioned, comprise an era that might properly be categorized as proto-mass culture; but I believe that the nature and uses of mass leisure prior to the 1960s, along with the technologies that served mass leisure, differed appreciably from mass culture as we have known it since the later 1950s.

Because the availability of leisure and widening access to it have undergone such a dramatic transformation during the past century, my concern with mass and popular culture in this book will focus particularly upon changing American attitudes toward leisure and their uses of it. The rise of recreation in its broadest possible sense and changing modes of entertainment will be at the heart of my story: how Americans have amused themselves and how they have felt about their amusements are central to our understanding of the so-called American Century. Indeed, the growing legitimacy of amusement itself in manifest ways is crucial.

For example, the law creating the National Zoo in Washington, D.C., enacted by Congress in 1888–89, rationalized its existence by emphasizing that it would be "for the advancement of science and the instruction and recreation of the people." But realities and the recognition of change brought new priorities to the fore. In 1891 a staff member pleaded with the Secretary (director) of the Smithsonian Institution that exotic animals be added to North American wildlife at the zoo "for the *amusement* and instruction of the people." By 1901, as the new century opened, the secretary acknowledged to his diary that the new National Zoo offered "an admirable place for health, *recreation* and *entertainment*." So an institution intended for the advancement of science had, within a decade, become vastly more important as a source of entertainment.[41] That transformation is highly symptomatic, and it provides an essential context for my focus throughout this book upon popular culture during the past century as entertainment, first and foremost. Hence my emphasis upon the changing nature and uses of leisure as matters of degree as well as kind in distinguishing between mass and popular culture.

Its most enthusiastic advocates have defined mass culture as "everything that members of an industrialized society share with all other members. Anything not universally shared may be less than 'mass,' an aspect of a 'minority' or 'sub'-culture."[42] Fine. Let us bear in mind that as late as the 1930s many Americans, especially in the South and West, did not yet live in a fully industrialized society; and up until midcentury there were a great many aspects of American culture that most certainly were *not* universally shared. Consequently, according to their own criteria, devotees ought to acknowledge that mass culture could not become truly pervasive until well after World War II. Mass culture, then, must be nonregional, highly standardized, and completely commercial. Handmade quilts, for example, do not qualify as mass culture, not because they lack commercial value (for they most certainly possess that), but because they vary so much by region or locale, sometimes by religious sect, and also in the reasons for their making.

For the sake of clarification, then, let me suggest some of the characteristics of mass culture as we have known it for about four decades so that readers can understand why I consider the significant developments just described, along with others, as being better perceived either as popular culture or as proto-mass culture.

We must begin with television, which went from being expensive and therefore exclusive to being perceived as an affordable necessity during the mid- to later 1950s. Afternoon soap operas did not become standard fare on all of the major networks until 1954, when NBC reluctantly capitulated because it could not compete with the huge success enjoyed by soap operas on CBS. By the early 1960s television executives systematically started to "dumb down" their programs for a mass, undifferentiated audience—far more than radio had ever done. For that reason, the presumed or potential homogenization of American viewers, TV would contribute considerably more to the shaping of mass culture than radio had. Keep in mind, also, the sheer number of local radio stations along with stations that targeted particular clienteles compared with the severely limited number of dominant, national television networks.[43]

Fast-food chains like McDonald's got started in the mid-1950s but did not "take off" until the sixties or become ubiquitous until the seventies. They should not be considered a true component of mass culture until the early 1970s, because initially they targeted a large but specific clientele: suburban families rather than urban workers, the customary habitués of White Tower and White Castle hamburger houses. Unlike their predecessors, McDonald's featured cleanliness. They were not "joints" and had neither jukeboxes nor vending machines. They aimed to please the baby boom middle class rather than the urban workingman and -woman. All of that changed during the 1970s and '80s when McDonald's rapidly began to add downtown locations for teenagers and busy single people who did not have time to cook and who ate on the run.[44]

When regional shopping centers started to emerge in the mid- and later 1950s, the community marketplace characterized by personal relationships shifted from the old "downtown" to the more anonymous suburban shopping center, anchored by major national chain stores with standardized products, such as Sears, Penneys, and Montgomery Ward. The preponderance of chain stores and national franchises brought shoppers all of the latest national trends, not only in products but in merchandising techniques as well. Standardization was also perceived as the key to success for national motel chains beginning in the 1960s. Franchising meant local ownership but predictable nationwide similarities. A national name conveyed reliability and security to potential patrons.[45]

On September 26, 1960, seventy million people watched the presidential debate between John F. Kennedy and Richard M. Nixon—an unprecedented number of viewers who could exchange reactions the next day about what they had seen. And then there is Monday night football, a newly routinized mass phenomenon in which people in many thousands of cities and towns watch two teams from some other part of the country compete. All sorts of rituals developed in response to the magnetic attraction of Monday night football, such as places where women with no interest in football could gather and socialize. Not until 1967 was it possible to relay film by satellite from Tokyo to

New York, and then at a very high cost. By 1970, however, we know that a majority of Americans received their news coverage from television, most notably news about the war in Vietnam.[46]

Finally, to round out a selective menu of mass culture's distinguishing features in our own time, we have the inundation of bulk mail catalogues, special promotions for credit cards and life insurance, tele-advertising and direct sales, philanthropic and medical research solicitations—mostly made possible by the sale of computerized membership lists. It has to be mass culture when the process depends upon targeting zip codes and census data based upon household incomes, all from vast electronic data banks. We can call 1-800 numbers seven days a week, twenty-four hours a day, and be answered by a recorded voice that presents us with a list of options we can only opt if we have a touch-tone telephone.[47]

All of that and more, compounded of pixels, adds up to mass culture of a character unknown and unimagined by most people prior to the later 1950s. (On April 2, 1965, *Time* magazine devoted its cover story to "The Computer in Society." On January 3, 1983, *Time* chose to celebrate the "Machine of the Year" rather than a Man of the Year. Its cover story was entitled "The Computer Moves In" and the lead visual featured a man and a woman sitting at tables staring at computers.) Writing in 1965, when mass culture as we know it was relatively new, two notably influential British writers, Stuart Hall and Paddy Whannel, produced a sophisticated text that predictably mingled mass and popular culture into a multi-ingredient omelet. They defined mass culture as art that is machine-produced according to a formula. They devoted a closing chapter to critics and defenders of mass culture, and like most of the aggressively defensive partisans of popular and mass culture at that time, they rejected any spurious distinction between the serious and the popular or between entertainment and high culture values. They took mass and popular culture quite seriously themselves and resented those critics and scholars who regarded their own chosen meat as poison.[48]

There is a striking contrast between their upbeat perception of mass culture and that of Clement Greenberg in 1939 and Dwight Macdonald's two decades later (building upon Greenberg's). Hall and Whannel highlighted technology and the formulaic element—mass production moving ahead in a manner independent of older models or art forms. To its advocates, mass culture was capable of innovation or even novelty. It could produce repetition but not uniqueness; yet the production of repetition was altogether appropriate if one subscribed to egalitarian values.[49]

An important reason why Greenberg and Macdonald so despised mass culture derived from their belief that it imitated and thereby degraded high culture—a pattern of reasoning that made less and less sense with the passage of time as polls demonstrated that ordinary Americans had little interest in high culture, never mind its send-ups. But as Greenberg wrote in one of his most celebrated essays: "The precondition for *kitsch* . . . is the availability close at hand of a fully matured cultural tradition, whose discoveries, acquisitions, and per-fected self-consciousness kitsch can take advantage of for its own ends." Macdonald put it even more simply, albeit more perversely: "Masscult is a parody of High Culture."[50]

I shall have much more to say about mass culture in chapter 8— critical, albeit not for the reasons that prompted Greenberg and Mac-donald to be. In closing this introductory chapter, however, I want to alert the reader to several other central themes of the book. First, I regard the half century from 1885 to 1935 as the heyday of commer-cialized popular culture in the United States, from Buffalo Bill's Wild West Show to the demise of burlesque and vaudeville, with a great deal more ululating in between.

Second, I see a crucial and vital period of overlap involving what I have called proto-mass culture and the prime of popular culture, an overlap that I date from approximately 1930 to 1965. The word "over-lap" (rather than "transition") is deliberately chosen because there was, undeniably, a great deal of simultaneity. How does one categorize a Norman Rockwell illustration on the cover of the *Saturday Evening Post* when its circulation edged close to three million—popular culture or mass? The answer must be both, of course, because Rockwell's illus-trations are, in their own curious way, beyond category.[51]

Why then do I reject the word "transition"? Because popular cul-ture did not die and is not ready for interment. It remains very much with us, albeit more easily observed in smaller towns than in large cities, in rural America more than urban or suburban, yet ubiquitous nonetheless in revivals as well as in some new TV shows and radio pro-grams, for example. Moreover, because of technological changes, pop-ular culture always has been and remains more ephemeral and evanescent than mass culture. Although Mae West's distinctive humor survives on film from the 1930s and '40s, for example, her many years in vaudeville and nightclubs can never be recaptured or reproduced.

What then of the criteria that I use for differentiating between popular and mass culture? The somewhat less important criteria involve matters of scale—such as thousands of people at an amusement park as opposed to many tens of millions worldwide watching the Super Bowl in January, for example—and increasing dependence upon technologies of visual access, entertainment, and information rather than avenues of personal access, self-instruction or amusement, and knowledge for its own sake rather than practical utility. To make the abstract more concrete (albeit reductive), it's the difference between games of skill at the state fair and video games, or between "scoping" the boardwalk at Coney Island or Atlantic City and surfing the Web at home.[52]

Which leads to the distinction that matters most. I regard popular culture—*not always but more often than not*—as participatory and interactive, whereas mass culture (until the 1980s, when computers caused significant changes that have yet to be fully charted),[53] *more often than not* induced passivity and the privatization of culture. In writing about P. T. Barnum and his public in the nineteenth century, Neil Harris described a degree of responsiveness on the part of patrons who delighted in disentangling issues of validity and deception. Hence the participatory aspect of popular culture. In 1870 the famous landscape architect Frederick Law Olmsted described two capacities or qualities latent in all people: the "exertive" and the "receptive." I am persuaded that popular culture calls forth the exertive while mass culture can rely far more upon the receptive.[54]

Being "exertive" or participatory may occur either in the making *or* in the consuming of a product or a pleasure. (A quilting bee provides a good example.) How people used or responded to what was offered them matters a great deal. It once was common for kids to create their own toys, combining vivid imaginations with miscellaneous materials at hand. That pattern is much less true today; not absolutely, of course, but significantly so. Now, they are more likely to want particular manufactured items seen on TV or at the mall. Particularity means authenticity: just like Johnny's or Judy's.

The cultural historian Alan Trachtenberg has made a useful distinction between experience and information. Needless to say, they are not mutually exclusive—we act upon information, and new knowledge may prompt us to seek experience.[55] Nonetheless, when popular cul-

1. *Coney Island Beach* (1935) by Reginald Marsh (etching)

ture was in its prime, Americans seemed to *search* for experience, whereas in recent decades they have had cause to privilege information above experience, a parallel in symmetry with the relative shift that I perceive from participatory to more passive.[56]

At the close of the 1870s, the major cultural tension that seemed to attract the attention of journalists, preachers, and social critics got subsumed under the polarized rubric "Vulgarity and Gentility," which became the subject of a major editorial in the *New York Times*. Remarkably egalitarian in tone, the essay sought to minimize any inevitable connection between class and taste, between social status and brow levels—a sure sign that this very issue had become vexing in Victorian America.

There are people who are coarse and vulgar, and there are others who are refined and gentle; but they cannot be distinguished from each other by any garb or circumstance apart from character. It is true that a certain leisure, with opportunity for the cultivation of taste and for the pursuit of social satisfactions, favors a life that may be called gentle, and that hard work and rough competition tend to coarsen the manners and take the patrician tone from the speech. Yet it will not do to say that they who get their own living are the vulgar, and that they who do not work at all, or who work only for pleasure or for honor, are the only gentlefolks.[57]

A century later that widely noticed dualism had been supplanted by a very different one: "Narcissism and Altruism." The social critic and historian Christopher Lasch caused quite a stir in 1978–79 with his provocative book *The Culture of Narcissism*, a work that prompted President Jimmy Carter to invite Lasch to the White House. Lasch derided wrongheaded critics of narcissism for their naïveté in failing

> to make connections between the narcissistic personality type and certain characteristic patterns of contemporary culture, such as the intense fear of old age and death, altered sense of time, fascination with celebrity, fear of competition, decline of the play spirit, deteriorating relations between men and women. For these critics, narcissism remains at its loosest a synonym for selfishness and at its most precise a metaphor, and nothing more, that describes the state of mind in which the world appears as a mirror of the self.[58]

The problem of passivity and privatization in a new guise with new manifestations! Within the span of a century a dominant lifestyle among Americans had come full circle, but with a troublesome twist. People had shifted from a culture of domesticity centered on hearth and home to a culture of entertainment in public places, made possible in wondrous ways by urban electrification at the close of the nineteenth century. By 1910–20 "going out" meant more than the customary fare of popular culture: the circus and the carnival, the minstrel show and the Wild West show, Barnum and burlesque. It meant illuminated amusement parks and trolley parks, nickelodeons and movie houses, vaudeville and musical reviews, dance halls and cabarets. Stepping out made popular culture lively, and vice versa, during the first half of the twentieth century.[59]

Then came television and suburbia, almost simultaneously, and within a quarter of a century a remarkable shift back to privatized leisure occurred with astonishing speed. In 1951 a Gallup poll asked: "Which do you enjoy most—radio, television or the movies?" Radio got 50%, TV 24%, and movies 21%. Late in 1975 a Roper poll of 2,007 Americans pursued a more complex but intriguing issue:

> People have been talking recently about the fact that they are changing some of their living habits. I'd like to ask you about this list of things which you are doing more than you were a year ago and which you are doing less than a year ago.[60]

Here are some of the responses to what people were doing *more* than they used to. (The answers total more than 100% owing to multiple responses.)

Spending time at home	54%
Watching television	42
Reading books	34
Entertaining friends in your home	22
Going out to places of public entertainment	16

In terms of public places and private spaces, it almost seemed as though the clock had been turned back one hundred years. But not quite. We had achieved an interesting mix of mass and popular culture; but above all, a partial retreat from the public sector to the haven of home and even specific spaces within the home. The privatization of leisure. A retro process that, all in all, seems to have transcended customary patterns of categorization.[61]

I certainly do not believe that television is exclusively a passive experience, nor do I deny that it can have participatory and interactive consequences. Television gave a genuine lift to the civil rights movement, 1963–65, and to opposition against the war in Vietnam, 1968–73. Some people still watch television together, and they may very well discuss what they watch. But if the program is really important (such as a nominating convention or a State of the Union address), the audience at home is most likely to watch *other* people discuss what they have just seen and heard.

It seems clear that we can invoke a historical orthodoxy that still persisted less than half a century ago, so long as we acknowledge that it never went entirely unchallenged. The template for that orthodoxy looked something like this: High culture is expected to connect humankind to its finest past achievements, whereas popular culture provides more ephemeral access to amusement and experience across class lines in the here and now. High culture is meant to create as well as preserve. Popular and mass culture function in more transitory ways within a contemporary time frame. Their principal objective is not enduring excellence but pleasure and commercial appeal.

How those orthodoxies underwent modifications and transformations will concern us in the chapters ahead.

2

Culture Democratized: Distinction or Degradation?

∞

A madcap episode that occurred on the edge of New York's Greenwich Village in October 1963 can serve as an allegory of the ongoing tensions arising from the practice of cultural populism in the United States. Three agents of the Internal Revenue Service tried to close down a second-floor loft that served as home to the Living Theatre, an avant-garde drama company run by Julian Beck and his wife, Judith Malina. Over its seventeen years of existence, the company had achieved international renown for staging controversial, populist plays. But the company also happened to be flat broke, behind in its rent, and $28,000 in arrears on federal tax payments—considerably less than the interest payment deductions claimed by many wealthy Americans. Be that as it may, Beck and Malina recruited friends and fans to stage a sit-in designed to frustrate the IRS's intentions. What then ensued most closely resembled an early film farce featuring the Keystone Kops.

A banner strung from the Living Theatre's office window (at the same venue) charged: "U.S. government stops art!" Reporters and television crews arrived on the scene to cover the story. Food and supplies were "airlifted" up from the street in a wastebasket lowered from the windows. The next day, Beck and Malina decided to stage a final performance of *The Brig* by Kenneth W. Brown, assuming after a series of telephone calls that rippled out like a chain letter that their audience could be admitted through two unsealed firedoors. The revenue agents responded by pulling a fuse and plunging the theater into darkness. When the TV crews raised a fierce protest, the IRS relented and restored the lights. Meanwhile, an audience managed to assemble by climbing ladders and crossing over the rooftop of an adjacent building. The play went on, but by 1:30 a.m. some performers and attendees who refused to leave were arrested. The Living Theatre was then closed.[1]

End of the saga? Of course not. Within days a real estate operator and theater owner had offered Beck and Malina the use free of charge of another, better theater. Within a few weeks the Living Theatre had reorganized, rising like a phoenix from the ashes. *The Brig* was back onstage. All the prisoners had been released within twenty-four hours of the donnybrook at Sixth Avenue and 14th Street. Beck and Malina alone stood trial, and not for tax evasion but rather for impeding federal officers in the exercise of their duty! The whole episode represented a perhaps inevitable clash between governmental authority and cultural forces so radically democratized that they refused to recognize that authority. Yet however bizarre the story may sound, it had antecedents in the cabarets and speakeasies of the Prohibition years, 1919 to 1933.

I. Popular Culture and Democratic Values

The complex relationship between popular culture and a progressive or democratic ethos seems to have followed a distinctive path in the United States, in part because democratic values enjoyed such rhetorical prominence from the 1830s onward and in part because a society at least formally committed to such values offered unusual opportunities for entrepreneurs eager to maximize the potential of broad market opportunities. Walt Whitman's assertion that "to have great poets, there must be great audiences, too" is ambiguous for interesting reasons. What did he mean by the second "great"? Large? Perhaps. Qualitatively great, remarkably discerning? Possibly. Eagerly appreciative? Very likely, though without excluding the first two possibilities. In any case, Whitman surely understood that cultural excellence would be defined in new and different ways in a democracy, yet his response to the qualitative character of taste levels in mid-nineteenth-century America clearly must have been more complex than we might casually assume.

Harking back almost half a century to his cultural enthusiasms as a young man in the 1840s, Whitman's fascinating recollection includes a clear sense of stratification despite our recent emphasis upon an accessible, shared public culture in the antebellum years. "I spent much of my time in the theatres then," he remarked, "going everywhere, seeing everything, high, low, middling—absorbing theatres at every pore."[2] He explicitly recalled a degree of segmentation that we do not customarily associate with mid-nineteenth-century America. His most recent biographer emphasizes the existence at that time of a "participatory culture" that deeply influenced Whitman, who wanted his verse to dissolve the boundaries between taste levels. "I think of art as something to serve the people," he wrote, "the mass: when it fails to do that it's false to its promises."[3]

That is exactly the attitude that we associate with Whitman, of course, and in his later years he railed against the growing tendency to telescope the concept of culture into high culture, a response entirely consistent with our sense of increasing hierarchy during the last three decades of the nineteenth century. Referring to "the enemy, this word Culture," Whitman advocated "a programme of culture, drawn out, not for a single class alone, or for the parlors or lecture rooms. . . ."[4]

As many have noted, however, Whitman never achieved the large, appreciative audience among the masses that he yearned for and, at times, eagerly expected. The adoring admirers of his poetry came largely from the more educated strata and from those whom we regard in retrospect as avant-garde. It is entirely possible, therefore, that Whitman's memory and sensibility played tricks on him in his declining years, and that he projected back to the 1840s and '50s a degree of stratification in taste that did not really emerge until the 1870s. We know, for example, that art union competitions and exhibitions during the 1830s and 1840s were open to talent and well attended by a cross section of the population. We have also learned that oil paintings as well as prints enjoyed broad appeal because of a "democratic drive to lower the barriers of high culture." Art leagues, exhibitions, and galleries emphasized nationalistic pictures to highlight a sense of cohesive identity that transcended class lines.[5]

To the extent that a shared public culture existed in America during the middle decades of the nineteenth century, nationalism may very well have been at its core. But other stimuli were present and potent as well. A goodly number of workingmen's associations, for example, following the example of Franklin's Junto a century earlier, had self-help and cultural uplift as primary objectives. Their activities, moreover, often went well beyond the mundane or the rudimentary. In March

1853, for instance, the Metropolitan Mechanics' Institute of Washington, D.C., assembled to hear an address from Joseph Henry, Secretary of the Smithsonian Institution and the most distinguished scientist in America. Such organizations did not just exist in major cities. We need only look to the Institute's counterpart in tiny New Harmony, Indiana, at midcentury.[6]

On the other hand, many of the Shakespearean productions in the United States during the middle third of the nineteenth century pandered to the lowest common denominators of public attention by interspersing songs, slapstick, and melodrama unrelated to plays written by the bard of Avon. From an affirmative perspective, those people responsible for such productions thereby democratized them by maximizing their accessibility.[7] From a more critical perspective, however, the entrepreneurs only anticipated the corniness and coarseness of kitsch by almost a century.

A sculptor named John Rogers provides a less ambiguous example of intensely popular art that cut vertically through Victorian taste levels. Working with clay, Rogers modeled famous American figures as well as sentimental domestic scenes. People admired his "documentaries" for their patriotic authenticity and his family groups for their humanity. Standing sixteen to twenty inches in height, these works enjoyed instant recognition and broad appeal as icons for the home. Rogers always insisted that he did not wish to attempt "any high art"; and James Jackson Jarves, a prominent art critic, meant to compliment Rogers with the observation that "his is not high art."[8]

In various ways and for multiple reasons, however, the appearance of democratization in Victorian America can be quite deceptive. Manufacturers of sporting goods, for example, responded with alacrity during the 1880s and '90s to new enthusiasms for physical exercise and the growing leisure to pursue it. The marketing efforts of these firms certainly did expand interest in and opportunities for organized play. Participation in sports became an important component of popular culture. But the manufacturers also recognized their commercial stake in the development of standardized products for games with clear-cut rules. Consequently, participatory innovation by the competitors became a casualty of alliances between sporting goods firms and coaches, professional athletes, journalists, and the administrators of leagues and associations. The sale of guidebooks, often making a spurious claim to be "official," became especially lucrative. As one authority has written, however, "every successful partnership *inside* the industry established firmer boundaries on the range and styles of sports offered to consumers on the outside." The commercialization of sport diminished democratization because the manufacturers and professionals wanted authority and control over this burgeoning area of popular culture and enthusiasm.[9]

A very different illustration of the desire for control had comparable consequences in another sphere. During the last quarter of the nineteenth century authorities used newspapers, brochures, and guidebooks to inform audiences of the behavior expected at theatrical and musical events. The attentiveness, restraint, and polite appreciation that were inculcated seemed constraining and undemocratic to some in the middle class and to many "below" them. The requisite gentility and passivity may very well have been as offputting as the actual substance of the performance.[10] Here we encounter quiescence as a required quality of refined culture—in contrast to the commonly criticized passivity that would later accompany mass culture, especially following the advent of television. Historically considered, then, passivity has been demanded as well as deplored, but in quite different contexts and for very different reasons.

Overlapping with that increased demand for civility at refined entertainments, an extraordinary convergence of developments starting in the later 1880s greatly expanded audiences for popular culture, thereby democratizing amusements for the working class, especially, but also for many in the "middling" classes as well. The most essential feature facilitating this new inclusiveness was a dramatic drop in "popular prices," a phrase associated with the name of Benjamin Franklin Keith, the most famous of all the vaudeville and early cinema pioneers. Keith's so-called dime museum in Boston (expanding from an array of human oddities to a small theatrical troupe) tapped the come-and-go transient market in a respectable venue that he called "refined vaudeville." He thereby seemed to offer democratic distinction while attracting the middle class as well as the working class. He succeeded in drawing a mixed audience that included women and children.

The simultaneity and wide range of this "entertainment discount revolution" is truly astonishing. The war between William Randolph Hearst and Joseph Pulitzer to dominate the penny press at the end of the century is well known. So is the availability of *Munsey's* illustrated magazine for fifteen cents. In 1887 Keith and Edward F. Albee decided to charge only ten cents for their performances. The so-called 10-20-30 price scale emerged at the turn of the century and drew large crowds for melodrama in particular. (The upper balcony cost a dime.) Frederic Thompson's Hippodrome, a massive theater in New York City, offered seats at 25 cents to a dollar, rather than up to the two dollars demanded by the competition.[11]

This price revolution was not confined to the lowest tastes and the tightest budgets. In 1894 Walter Morosco cut prices dramatically at the Grand Opera House in New York. Within a decade, affordable entertainment of every conceivable sort was available to all. In 1903–04, Kohn and Zukor opened their Automatic One Cent Vaudeville Emporium, where a penny operated every viewing machine. By 1905, admission to amusement parks across the country had leveled down to ten cents. The earliest nickelodeons, having started in Pittsburgh, spread rapidly in the years following 1905. The 5-and-10-cent stores begun by Frank W. Woolworth in 1886 proliferated by 1900, when there were fifty-nine. Penny arcades began to appear in 1905, and within a few years became a socially inclusive term referring to amusements affordable by all.[12]

Several key points must be kept in mind here. First, this democratization of entertainment was not confined exclusively to large urban areas, and cheap did not necessarily mean tawdry. In small American towns movie theaters were filled with respectable middle-class citizens, just as they were increasingly in big cities after World War I. Second, the simultaneity of this swift and easy access to so many modes of popular culture would not be repeated until 1946, when more than two hundred brand-new mass-oriented magazines appeared, helping to mark the onset of mass culture as we know it.[13]

Boosters of the nickelodeon early in the twentieth century liked to call it "democracy's theater." And the speed with which nickelodeons attracted enthusiastic patrons in the century's first decade would be replicated (and then some) by the rocketing success of television after 1948.[14] In fact, the pattern is deceptively simple: moving pictures became the most appealing form of commercial entertainment during the first half of the twentieth century, rapidly replaced by television as the most successful in the second half. In 1971 a Louis Harris poll of 1,600 Americans indicated a preference for watching films *on television* over going to a movie house, and an even more positive response (66%) to this statement: "Movies on television have taken the place of going to a movie theatre for us." A Roper poll of more than 2,000 persons in 1977 found only 21% "very interested" in moviegoing and 36% not very or not at all interested. The remaining 43% felt "moderately interested."[15]

That problematic era for film during the 1950s to 1970s provides an arresting basis for comparison—and a notable sense of change over time—even though it projects us rather far ahead of our focus here, which is the early democratization of entertainment. When film was all the rage during the 1920s, one observer called the glittering new movie palaces "shrines to democracy" because all seats were equal: none was reserved, there were no privileged tiers, and chairs on the balcony were exactly the same as those on the main floor. Lloyd Lewis, a well-known Chicago journalist, put it this way in 1929: "In this suave atmosphere, the differences of cunning, charm, and wealth, that determine our lives outside, are forgotten. All men enter these portals equal, and thus the movies are perhaps a symbol of democracy. Let us take heart from this, and not be downcast because our democratic nation prudently reserves its democracy for the temple of day dreams."[16]

Just as notable, though less evident than the contrast between public attitudes toward moviegoing before and after 1950, is the altered view of critics toward films during the fifteen years prior to 1929, when Lewis wrote "The De Luxe Picture Palace." William Dean Howells warmly admired the technology that made film possible but lamented what movies could not do: "convince the taste and console the spirit." Brander Matthews, a prominent though highly traditional theater critic, wondered in 1917 whether cinema was a "menace to the drama." The very same tension and polarization of attitudes—genteel "thoughtful laughter" versus the "New Humor" (comic realism)—existed at that time concerning vaudeville.[17]

Most arresting of all, however, was the complex response of the critic Randolph Bourne, as culturally radical in 1915 as Howells and Matthews were genteel and conservative. Although Bourne recognized that film assuredly democratized because it was the art of the people, its poor substantive quality as culture caused him profound concern, which he expressed in a fascinating way—by acknowledging a hierarchy of taste levels and institutions serving them, yet despising them just the same. He generalized his deep disappointment with film in this way, an indictment of cultural standards old and new:

I feel even a certain unholy glee at this wholesale rejection of what our fathers reverenced as culture. But I don't feel any glee about what is substituted for it. We seem to be witnessing a low-brow snobbery. In a thousand ways it is as tyrannical and arrogant as the other culture of universities and millionaires and museums. . . . It looks as if we should have to resist the stale culture of the masses as we resist the stale culture of the aristocrat.[18]

Bourne's reaction is significant for several reasons. It not only recognized the existence of a cultural hierarchy in America, but condemned the quality of *all* levels at the very same moment, 1915, when Van Wyck Brooks, his fellow radical critic, did so in the famous essay titled "Highbrow and Lowbrow." Although these Young Turks certainly considered themselves cultural democrats, they were fully prepared to impose their own agenda upon ordinary Americans: what Brooks would call a "usable past" and what Bourne would call a transnational America, that is, the meaningful importance of history when the public mood could not have been more present-minded and the necessity for cosmopolitanism when the public mood could not have been more nationalistic and parochial.[19] Democratic cultural critics can be stridently out of touch with the temper of ordinary Americans; and their desire to see their own values prevail could be just as arch as the attitudes of the cultural aristocrats they so hotly repudiated and hoped to replace.

The development of serious film criticism required a full generation to emerge because for several decades, even through the 1920s, many publishers and editors mistakenly perceived moviegoing as primarily a vulgar mindless phenomenon. When Nunnally Johnson asked to review films for *The New Yorker*, Harold Ross, its founder and editor, dismissed the proposal archly by declaring that "movies are for old ladies and fairies." Eventually, however, Ross reconciled himself to this upstart industry and decades later some of the best-known film criticism in the nation, written by Pauline Kael, appeared regularly in *The New Yorker*, providing yet another compelling litmus of cultural change.[20]

II. The Sources and Social Dimensions of Democratic Change

The influence of critics and journals of opinion as well as artistic organizations raises a related yet different aspect of cultural democratization. Throughout the nineteenth century a dominant impression prevailed at the upper levels of the social pyramid that cultural values and appreciation trickled down from higher to lower social strata, from critics and "tastemakers" down to ordinary folk who took their cues from their betters. That was equally true of art unions during the 1840s, the founders of museums in the 1870s, and powerful editors like Edward Bok of the *Ladies' Home Journal* at the close of the century. Edith Wharton and Louis Comfort Tiffany both shared that assumption.[21]

They were not entirely wrong, either. The United States Sanitary Commission, created during the Civil War, emerged as the largest and most highly organized philanthropic activity ever known in the United States. It was run by members of the northern social elite who successfully instilled in the popular mind an acceptance of principles of order and stability along with enhanced reverence for cultural institutions. The commission exemplified an altruistic organization that had a profound impact upon both popular and national culture. As George M. Fredrickson has written, the commission's success encouraged conservative activists to believe that a greater reverence for the entities they favored "could be instilled in the popular mind by an aristocratic elite operating in a private or semi-official capacity."[22]

Very few viewers seemed to recognize that the ways in which people enjoyed their leisure time, even when they were being entertained by song-and-dance men in music halls, often filtered up from the folk rather than trickled down from a handful at the top. Thomas D. Rice, for instance, along with other founders of minstrel acts in antebellum America, borrowed heavily from close observations of African-American styles of singing and dancing, especially during the decade following 1828 in the South and the border states. The same would be true a century later with jazz, of course, when elements of black folk culture filtered up in significant ways and profoundly altered the trajectory of popular music in the United States, starting notably in the 1920s and '30s. The demand for black fiddlers and banjo players during the nineteenth century, important as it was, would be surpassed by the impact of figures like Louis Armstrong and Duke Ellington in the twentieth.[23]

It really should be no surprise, of course, that the dissemination of culture occurs, at least partially, through the process of filter up; yet many of us still need to be reminded that trickle down does have its democratic inversion. Nor is the bottom-up process at all new or even

American. Looking at children's stories in early modern France, for example, Robert Darnton found that elite and popular culture did not occupy discrete realms. The audiences for Racine's plays had imbibed folklore with their mother's milk; and Mother Goose tales circulated from nurses and nannies to bourgeois and aristocratic parents.[24] A considerable amount of classical music written in nineteenth-century Europe built upon or incorporated traditional folk tunes. And in 1900 Claude Debussy wrote "Golliwog's Cakewalk" after visiting the Paris Exposition and being inspired by Scott Joplin playing his own lively ragtime compositions on the piano.

Joplin's presence in Paris and his impact upon Debussy leads us to yet another complex aspect of the relationship between democracy and cultural preferences. Very clearly, new forms of popular culture flourished during the half century following 1890 because technology and entrepreneurial innovations made them so much more affordable than they had ever been. Consequently, popular culture also became more socially inclusive, though the basis for that inclusiveness is not entirely clear. David Nasaw has argued that race (as a negative reference) mattered considerably more than class as the basis for bonding socially diverse audiences. That is, so long as blacks were excluded or segregated—the intolerant rejection of a presence—whites from assorted socioeconomic backgrounds felt comfortable sitting and laughing side by side. Nasaw insists that the exclusion or segregation of people of color was a necessary condition for the "democratization" of theatrical and movie audiences.[25]

Other scholars are less impressed than Nasaw by the degree of class integration among whites at leisure entertainments ranging from film to burlesque and vaudeville. Instead, Lary May and Robert C. Allen are struck by the way that producers and entrepreneurs skillfully aimed their programs at middle-class audiences with self-consciously middle-class values. In the case of *Ziegfeld's Follies*, that even made the illusion of seminudity by the showgirls acceptable to both the police and the gender-mixed audience. In the case of film stars, Hollywood studios presented them in the 1920s as "ordinary folks whose lavish lifestyles could be democratized." In this way, the stars might be perceived as heroic models rather than sources of resentment for the middle class.[26]

III. The Meanings of Democratization to Contemporaries

Even as the concept of "democracy" unaccompanied by modifiers can be a vague and muddled term, readily deployed in various ways, there is no definitional consensus about the meaning of cultural democracy or a democratic culture. Cultural democracy may imply the repudiation of cultural stratification and the belief that no taste level or preference is any more worthy than another. More radically, it can mean the rejection or elimination of all sources of cultural authority. Or it may simply refer to the most inclusive conditions of access and participation in whatever the members of a society deem culturally worthwhile, ranging from entertainment to Chautauqua-type instruction to leisure activities in places of natural beauty. As Walter Lippmann remarked in *Drift and Mastery:* "Before you can begin to have a democracy you need a country in which everyone has some stake and some taste of its promise."[27]

Thus far we have concentrated on the changing realities of access, inclusiveness, and diversity in American culture during the generations prior to the 1920s. We need to turn next to the explicit meanings that contemporaries ascribed to the democratization of culture in the United States. Not surprisingly, those perceptions range from simplistic to complex and from ambivalent to affirmative. Needless to say, the ambivalent and complex reactions are not only more interesting but most revealing about the impact of cultural change as well.

If we begin at the dawn of the century, we find both simplicity and complexity, though responding to fairly diverse concerns. Edward F. Albee, for instance, regarded vaudeville as very democratic because it offered something for everyone. Addressing quite different matters, Harvard's first faculty member to "profess" American literature, Barrett Wendell, explained why he idealized writers of the American Renaissance (ca. 1840 to 1870), a view echoed one generation later by Lewis Mumford. Literature in the age of Emerson, Hawthorne, and Melville was not aristocratic or even elitist. Rather, wrote Wendell, in their generation "the warring ideals of democracy and of excellence were once reconciled." George E. Woodberry, Wendell's contemporary at Columbia, felt absolute nostalgia for that era when democracy combined and merged with excellence, by which he meant high ideals.[28]

That kind of concern with excellence persisted for several decades, notably until the close of the 1920s and most often articulated by American writers and critics still influenced by the cultural standards of Matthew Arnold. For some, complexity lay in the challenge of demonstrating that culture in the Germanic sense of *Kultur*—high, polite, and not at all mediocre as Tocqueville had predicted—could actually be achieved in a democracy. As the playwright George Cram Cook said of himself and his peers: "It is for us to prove that the finest culture is a possibility of democracy." Writing of "Democracy and Public Taste" in 1927, Percy Holmes Boynton of the University of Chicago managed to reveal a preference for high culture and described middlebrow culture in pejorative terms. Yet he concluded on a hopeful note by expressing the belief that Americans would be able to level up. Somehow, democratization would occur when as many people as possible acquired an appreciation for the finer things.[29]

The most curious of these complicated elitists who made a half-hearted effort to adjust following a full generation of dramatic change was William C. Brownell, the most prominently devout disciple of Matthew Arnold in the United States. In a 1927 essay for *Scribner's* concerning "Popular Culture," the aging Brownell tried to put the best face possible on developments whose implications he really did not comprehend. Commenting on "the promise of our cultural progress," Brownell proclaimed it to be bright because "the formal addition of popular culture to formal education is the salient contribution of our time to the democratic distinction no doubt obscured but not obliterated by current tendencies that are curable because contagious rather than intrinsic." Brownell liked the phrase "democratic distinction," used it often, and, despite his obvious elitism, did not seem to regard it as a potential oxymoron.[30]

Like Wendell and Mumford, Brownell could be optimistic because he saw class as much less of a barrier to extended education and cultural uplift in the United States than in Great Britain. What he meant by "popular culture" when he used the term in a positive way is exemplified by the uninformed concertgoer who carefully reads program notes prepared by a professional—in sum, an ordinary person who defers to cultural authority. Hence the satisfaction Brownell derived from a perceived trend: "the readiness with which popular responds to professional culture [which] should tend to allay alarm as to the vulgarizing effects of popularization. . . ." He acknowledged that Americans held to an undefined democratic ideal, and then made an unelaborated

2. *H. L. Mencken and George Jean Nathan*
(1947) by Irving Penn (platinum-palladium print)

distinction between "the popularization of culture and its vulgariza-
tion." Ultimately he seemed to find solace in the breadth of American
education and consequently the capacity for wide-ranging uplift. "Our
general culture is probably more general—general enough at all events
to hold out the promise both of becoming more so and at the same
time rising to a higher level."[31]

As late as the end of the 1920s, then, relics from another era, like
Brownell, could only envision a process of trickle down and then level
up; but at least they did not ordinarily verbalize an overt contempt for
democratic culture as did H. L. Mencken and George Jean Nathan.
Democratic distinction seems to have been a less progressive concept
than Thomas Jefferson's aristocracy of talent rather than birth. Both
required education, the more the better; but Jefferson did not expect
that those with natural abilities would constantly defer to the judgment of professional cultural authorities. Their talent and initiative

would make them self-reliant. Right or wrong, their taste would be their own.[32]

The decade following World War I would be the last time when men and women considered reasonable and progressive could candidly express doubts about democracy. And when they did so, their concerns invariably connected with culture and social relations rather than the political system or process. *The Education of Henry Adams*, a national best-seller in 1919, conveyed anxiety about the diminution of cultural energy that might result from complete democracy. "Art is something for the few," Adams remarked, "and who those few are is unpredictable." He yearned for a "critically alert culture," and feared that that objective could not be realized in a total democracy. Edith Alvord, a Progressive and prominent social reformer in Detroit, recorded this entry in her journal after visiting a neighborhood movie house in 1919: "I am democratic but I hate the odors of democracy." Although women's clubs grew rapidly during the 1920s and became more inclusive, older members tended to regret that change. They complained that many women wanted the social prestige "but are not willing to work for culture."[33]

During the 1920s a genuine dialogue occurred, which occasionally burst into open debate, over the potential role of traditionally understood culture in a modern democracy and in what some critics also regarded as the emergence of mass society. Edward L. Bernays, known as the founder of public relations, seemed to view democracy rather cynically—not as a political philosophy regarding the ethics of power but as a form of social organization that maximized opportunities for persuasion if not manipulation. Such an outlook was commonplace among intellectuals during the 1920s.[34]

Other critics, writers, and influential editors during the interwar years developed less ambiguous and more affirmative sentiments concerning cultural democratization than the likes of Bernays, Brownell, and Boynton. The most exemplary and important of these may have been Stuart Pratt Sherman, a prolific writer on American literature who left the University of Illinois in 1924 to become editor of the *New York Herald Tribune*'s new literary supplement, a position in which he genuinely shaped opinions about writing in the United States. His essays in *Americans* (1922) and *The Genius of America* (1923), along with his extensive correspondence, reveal his strongly felt desire not only to recover the native literary tradition but to do so in a way that would meet the challenge of a truly democratic culture. "The line I have

taken and intend to follow," he wrote to Brownell, "is the encourage-
ment of the native tradition, with all its imperfections on its head, the
Puritan, the pioneer, the Jacksonian strain, the adventurous, daring,
exploring spirit, democracy—whatever it can be made to mean, and
including, at any rate, a growing fraternity." In 1923 Sherman made
the following declaration to a colleague who had commented on "the
democracy of a man of letters": "There is no question at the present
time requiring more thinking, calling for a more definite stand, and
demanding more *explicit* expression for a man of letters than precisely
the question: What does democracy mean to me?"[35]

Sherman would not have been hostile to leveling up and to some
operative meaning for a culture of "democratic distinction"; but his
deep commitment to public education and to the intelligentsia's
responsibility for outreach to a broad audience meant that his advocacy was a lot less arch and disdainful than Brownell's—even though
Sherman himself became just the kind of professional *vade mecum* for
the unenlightened that Brownell had envisioned. The key difference—
generational as well at temperamental—lay in Sherman's strong commitment to "a genuinely democratic diffusion of standards." His role
as a cultural authority would be gentle rather than genteel, deliberative
rather than didactic, cajoling rather than condescending.[36]

Like so many during the interwar years, Sherman's ideal of cultural
democracy was inseparable from a form of nationalism that had more
to do with shaping a clearer sense of national identity than it did with
blatant national chauvinism. Paul Rosenfeld, for example, a versatile
critic who wrote about music, art, and literature, observed that artists
could "help enormously to create a democratic society in America. In
investing American essences with worth and presenting them with
beauty, they help to convey the national idea. . . ." During the later
1930s, many participants in the Popular Front coalition felt deeply
committed to the democratization of culture, as did thousands upon
thousands of participants in the various Works Progress Administration programs that supported artists, writers, and theater people. Holger Cahill, director of the Federal Arts Project, remarked in its
operating manual that "the aim of the project will be to work toward
an integration of the fine arts and the practical arts."[37]

Even before the Popular Front emerged in 1935 as an unexpected
amalgam of cultural democracy, a phenomenon affecting many more
Americans empowered the people, ordinary people, as cultural
authorities—indeed, provided them with the illusion that surely *they*

must be the ultimate cultural authority. I have in mind *Major Bowes' Amateur Hour*, a radio program that utterly surprised the networks in 1934–37 by becoming the most successful broadcast in the United States. It followed the genuine popularity of vaudeville's amateur nights, and featured nonprofessional unknowns performing for the acclaim of highly diverse, nonspecialist audiences. The immense appeal of this populist broadcast eventually inspired as many as eight hundred national and local radio programs that found some sort of role for amateur talent.[38]

To reinforce the democratization fostered by that participatory phenomenon, many of the necessarily affordable fads and crazes of the 1930s, such as dance marathons and walkathons, added to the sense that cultural activities arose from the grass roots and were accessible to anyone with energy and few inhibitions.[39] The creation and development of the Gallup Poll also occurred in the later 1930s, underwritten financially by newspapers that bought George Gallup's service. His regular reports on "what America thinks" became available to millions of readers through the press. It gave those readers a sense that what they thought really mattered.* By 1940 America felt that it was able to take its own pulse and blood pressure. That gave new meaning to Walter Lippmann's notion of public opinion. Public opinion was becoming a democratic force in an empirical way rather than merely an impressionistic one. To some people, that made it seem more certain. By midcentury, however, others began to wonder whether the advent of cultural democracy would undermine all forms of intellectual and cultural authority.[40]

IV. Democracy and Cultural Stratification

Toward the middle decades of the twentieth century an interesting contrast emerged between the taste levels people felt most comfortable being identified with (*not* high) and the cultural aspirations conveyed by critics for the society as a whole (*upward*). The former was certainly not a new phenomenon. Evangelist Billy Sunday had received warm praise from an Iowa newspaper early in the century because he seemed down-to-earth, a man of the people: "He is not in favor of higher culture and higher criticism." During World War I the Committee on

---

* This is when columnist and commentator Walter Winchell quipped that "Democracy is where everybody can kick everybody else's ass."

Public Information designated "Kultur" as a socially unacceptable word (1917–18), not merely because Kultur was emblematic of the evil Prussian society, but because it represented hierarchical values undesirable in a democratic society.[41]

Woody Guthrie, the legendary folksong writer and performer, resisted any pressure to "level up" for commercial motives or to please the banal tastes of upscale folks. As he wrote to a friend early in the 1940s, referring to folk singers Pete Seeger and Lee Hays: "Don't let Pete and Lee go highbrow on you." He also asked John Lomax how "to get some of our upper crusts to listen to the real thing." A very different sort of person, the entertainment mogul William S. Paley of CBS, declared: "I am not a highbrow. I do not look down on popular taste. Oftentimes popular taste is my taste." In 1957, after Charlie Chaplin made *A King in New York*, a film critical of the anti-Communist Red Scare, Edward R. Murrow asked Chaplin why his treatment of the United States was so one-sided. "If you give both sides," Chaplin replied, "it becomes bloody dull. I'm not a highbrow— I'm an instinctive artist." Repudiating the identity (and even the category) of highbrow had become a mantra for many by midcentury.[42]

During the decades that spanned 1936 to 1966, we even find diverse, learned cultural critics, individuals recognized for their good taste and discriminating high standards concerning all forms of cultural creativity, deprecating the pretentious snobberies of would-be highbrows. In 1936 Gilbert Seldes criticized writers who only hoped to please a cultured elite, and who felt that they had failed if they somehow achieved broad popularity. Joseph Wood Krutch would echo that sentiment in 1966, damning the snobbery of those, like Dwight Macdonald, who scorned middlebrow culture precisely because of its wide appeal.[43]

Public opinion by then seems to have been very much on Krutch's side and unsympathetic to highbrow taste. A Gallup poll (the topic being "Taste") taken in 1975 asked 1,561 Americans "Which ONE of the categories on this card would you say best describes your own interests and tastes?" Here are the responses:

High brow	9%
Upper-middle brow	46
Lower-middle brow	35
Low brow	7
Don't know	4

The vast majority saw themselves as some kind of middlebrow. The only surprise, for 1975, is that even fewer people saw themselves as lowbrows than as highbrows.[44] We do not know the margin of error on this sample; and as we shall see, by 1975 most Americans did not feel very comfortable being asked to identify exclusively with any single category. By then the postwar obsession with discrete and meaningful cultural pigeonholes seemed not merely blurry but even silly to large numbers of Americans.

Yet more often than not the cultural aspirations of critics—above all those who observed and commented on the media—hoped (and in some cases genuinely believed) that it would be possible to "level up" the taste and cultural consumption desires of people in the United States. They nurtured no secret wish to make everyone a highbrow, nor did they scorn whatever seemed creative and engaging in popular culture. And they did not believe that popular culture and its audiences were inevitably doomed to mediocrity and banality. "A steady infiltration of cultural elements into the commercial program can be accomplished," Gilbert Seldes predicted in 1951. The following year Joseph Frank asserted that "democratic society does not necessarily lead to a leveling of culture so long as one does not confuse political democracy with majority rule in cultural matters."[45]

In 1956 Daniel Bell published in *Commentary* a widely noticed essay titled "America as a Mass Society: A Critique." In it he responded to the fretful Cassandras warning against "mass society," ranging from José Ortega y Gasset to Hannah Arendt. In Bell's sanguine assessment, a greater proportion of the population than ever before was participating in what he deemed worthwhile cultural activities—a consequence, in part, of doubling the American standard of living since the early twentieth century. Bell found it "curious that in these 'aristocratic' critiques of modern society, refracted as they are through the glass of an idealized feudal past, democracy is identified with equality alone." The depiction of modern culture, he declared, "as debauched by concessions to popular taste—a picture that leaves out the great rise in the general appreciation of culture—is equally overdrawn."[46]

Unlike so many intellectuals during the 1950s, Bell did not find himself distressed by the prospect of a "vast middlebrow society." He acknowledged that broad-gauge participation in cultural activities was the inevitable concomitant of democratic citizenship and increasing affluence. Bell even assailed the basic assumptions of the mass-society critique by citing the vigor of ethnic subcultures and voluntary associations in the United States. He challenged the notion that a rootless mass existed. "The rising levels of education," he insisted, "have meant a rising appreciation of culture."[47]

Other cultural critics with a more intimate knowledge of the media and their spokesmen attacked the sophistry of those who defended "leveling down" with the rationale of reconciling democratic practice and theory. Frank Stanton, the president of CBS, provided a prime example of this casuistry when he testified before a congressional committee. "A mass media can only achieve its great audience," he declared, "by practicing . . . cultural democracy . . . by giving the majority of the people what they want. . . . We find that most of the people, most of the time, want entertainment from their mass media."[48]

Gilbert Seldes, by the 1950s primarily an analyst of television and radio, answered Stanton with scorn. "When a broadcaster says, 'We give the people what they want,' the translation should be, 'The people would rather have something than nothing, so we give them something,' and 'The people don't dislike what we give them. . . .' " Seldes offered a more extended riposte to the media moguls in 1956: "The physical properties of the public arts give to their managers certain social powers, but the managers do not generally accept responsibility for the creation of audiences; they say they satisfy public demand. To abridge a long argument, let us say they cannot pretend, as they do, that they create audiences for Shakespeare and symphonic music but do not create an audience for crime serials."[49]

Starting in the 1960s, other students of the mass media and major institutions of popular culture offered occasional defenses or explanations on their behalf on the grounds that they contributed to cultural democratization. But none appeared as thoughtful or compelling as Bell's arguments had been, and most seemed either specious or simply impressionistic. Example: television democratized what traditionally had been an elitist, box-seat view of theatrical spectacle by giving everyone the same view of an event or performance regardless of wealth or status. Or, Groucho Marx democratized entertainment by interacting with ordinary people on television.[50]

These kinds of arguments at the level of *reductio ad absurdum* came from writers considerably more sympathetic to popular and mass culture than the fierce critics of the 1940s and '50s had been. As we shall see, they would be supplanted in the last quarter of the twentieth century by numerous writers, most often in the new field of cultural studies or the emerging subdiscipline of popular culture studies, who presented a fairly positive picture of mass culture as a means of empowerment rather than, as Theodor Adorno and his Frankfurt School colleagues had insisted during the 1940s, a dastardly narcotic. Most recently one observer has plausibly declared that the major media "make possible the free flow and clash of opinions essential to the functioning of democracy."[51] Others might dispute that view as simplistic, but it is widely shared.

The ongoing democratization of culture has unquestionably accelerated over the past three or four decades, if we mean that the rubric or category of "culture" itself has arguably become more inclusive. Accepting that point, one must concede that major changes have occurred if Graceland in Memphis attracts almost as many tourists per year as the White House and many more people visit museums and historic sites than attend sporting events. If, on the other hand, visitation figures for Mount Vernon and Colonial Williamsburg have declined while those for Disney World and assorted theme parks have risen, that suggests that entertainment enjoys greater cultural appeal than educational experiences, and that amusement outranks enrichment in desirability.[52]

However one prioritizes such experiences, we are obliged to acknowledge changes in the balance of what the public expects and supports. For better or for worse, we have not achieved Brownell's democratic distinction—at least not with any consistency. Meanwhile, some of our cultural heritage seems to be headed for extinction, and those who lament that trend are likely to be labeled as snobs. As Alexis de Tocqueville wrote to a close friend in 1831, the leveling tendency "is either in full progress in some states or in its fullest possible development in others. It is in the customs, in the laws, in the opinions of the majority. Those who are opposed to it hide themselves and are reduced to adopting its own colours in order to advance."[53] The validity of that assertion became much more meaningful a century later, when those who felt concern about trends legitimized in the name of democracy had to be very careful lest their concerns expose them to charges of elitism.

3

Consumerism, Americanism, and the Phasing of Popular Culture

∞

Quite a few of the most innovative and engaged students of mass society and culture have been neo-Marxists who place a prominent emphasis upon the commodification of culture. Although they agree on many things, their views are not necessarily interchangeable and significant differences exist among them. On the British side, for example, there is a tendency to locate the genesis of commercialization in cities as a major impetus for popular culture much earlier in time than Americanists do for the United States. Other radical critics, irrespective of nationality, take an almost conspiratorial view of cultural entrepreneurs, painting them in manipulative and even malevolent tones. Still others are willing to acknowledge the powerful role of cultural entrepreneurs but ascribe unintended benefits to their activities, such as the democratization of leisure and the affordable pleasures that it makes possible.[1]

The most pervasive problem that I encounter among neo-Marxist interpretations of culture, however, involves their tendency to telescope time. From a historian's perspective, progressive sociologists, members of the cultural studies guild, and literary historian/critics do not allow sufficiently for nuanced periodization based upon gradual transformations. Alan Swingewood, for instance, a British sociologist, believes that popular culture had its social basis in material production. Consequently, he and others call it "commercial culture." He appears, at times, to differentiate between popular and mass culture in nineteenth-century Britain; but the grounds for distinction are not made clear.

Swingewood does imply that popular (commercial) culture emerged first, and that mass culture was still in embryo when the English novelist Wilkie Collins wrote his famous essay "The Unknown Public" in 1858. The unknown public, Collins wrote, is "hardly beginning, as yet, to learn to read. The members of it are evidently, in the mass, from no fault of theirs still ignorant of almost everything which is generally known and understood among readers whom circumstances have placed, socially and intellectually, in the rank above them." In Swingewood's treatment of *The Myth of Mass Culture*, we get crude distinctions between the nineteenth and twentieth centuries, but because his provocative Marxist approach is totally topical, chronological subtleties and nuances of change are minimized.[2]

Turning to American sociologists on the left, Elizabeth and Stuart Ewen, in their study of the social basis of consumer society, *Channels of Desire: Mass Images and the Shaping of American Consciousness*, also telescope time problematically in describing an American trajectory that skips almost overnight from agrarian simplicity to industrial complexity. According to the Ewens, mass culture in the United States—by which they mean a social landscape marked by consumer industries, mass media, and intensive merchandising—"developed just when a formerly rural or otherwise non-industrial people were being transformed into a permanent, mass industrial population. The panorama of a mass culture was a bridge between the aspirations of an old culture and the priorities of a new one."[3] No, I say: Too fast and unhistorical. The transformation that they refer to was, in my view, ever so gradual rather than swift. Moreover, because the transformation occurred in stages between the 1880s and the 1960s, and because it connects premodern with contemporary America, the transformation itself is fascinating, worth more than just an allusion. The transformation, in fact, with particular reference to the uses of leisure, is primarily what *this* book is all about.

Because it is possible to point to the broad dissemination of Sears, Roebuck and Montgomery Ward catalogues by 1910, it becomes all the more necessary to distinguish between mass culture and proto-mass culture beyond the obvious difference of sheer scale. Lines of distinction can be too readily overdrawn; but some basic contrasts nevertheless seem evident as between, say, 1910 and a half century later. A strong and entirely appropriate emphasis in recent writing has diverted our attention to the rise of department stores and mail-order companies, which of course had nationalizing implications. What has unfortunately been lost for the period from 1870 to 1930 is the continuing importance of face-to-face commerce by means of general stores and traveling salesmen. In a world when face-to-face commercial relations still mattered, personal selling strategies remained extremely important. (At the end of the nineteenth century, just before publishing *The Wonderful Wizard of Oz* [1900], L. Frank Baum earned his living as a door-to-door salesman.) Because door-to-door canvassers and "drummers" who sold to the trade still played a vital role, the commercial landscape was more decentralized than most recent literature has acknowledged. That has been the price paid for a preoccupation with determining the genesis of our highly rationalized, bureaucratized, and impersonal consumer culture.[4]

Let us then, for the sake of convenience and succinctness, use the abbreviations PMC (for proto-mass culture) and MC (for mass culture). PMC featured the procurement of affordable goods to fulfill basic family needs, whereas MC facilitated the consumption of information and extensive entertainment from mass media barely imagined in 1910. PMC involved a culture of aspiration that still required a great deal of delayed gratification, whereas MC involved a culture of fulfillment that minimized delayed gratification by means of unprecedented affluence and extensive credit schemes. During PMC, taste was heavily determined by means of finite resources, whereas the ethos of possession in MC made it commonplace to own more than one actually needed as well as more than one could afford. Daniel Horowitz has demonstrated that prior to the 1930s, data from household budgets do not point to a world in which mass culture and commercialized leisure predominated in the lives of most families with low to moderate incomes. Susan Porter Benson has also shown that prior to World War II, most working-class families in the United States "remained on the margins of the emerging world of consumption because their incomes were neither large enough nor steady enough to allow the wide range of discretionary spending usually associated with mass consumption." Until the 1920s, moreover, traditional moralistic assumptions remained prevalent in the realm of working-class consumption.[5]

During PMC, travel for most Americans remained limited rather than extensive, whereas MC witnessed travel on a scale that would have been inconceivable at the turn of the century. During PMC, regional and local identity remained extremely important, almost primary in the lives of most Americans, whereas both of those considerations became less crucial in MC, when a sense of national identity became more pervasive and meaningful. By the 1970s, for example, more than half of the people living in New Hampshire had not been born there, a first in the state's history.

Despite the conventional wisdom, I suspect that standardization of basic products may have been greater in 1910 than later in the century. Certainly the range of choices (and the array of specialized catalogues) is far more extensive in our own time. In 1910 a potential customer might have been delightfully overwhelmed by innovation and the affordability of mail-order items. Several generations later novelty had come to be expected as the norm (every Christmas a totally new craze for the kids), and basic affordability felt more negotiable because of the eagerness of commercial enterprises to extend credit.

Prior to the full national impact of radio during the mid-1930s and the advent of television some fifteen years later, magazines had been the primary locus of modern, widespread advertising. With electronic media, ads simply flow at and over the listeners. They become literal "receivers" despite their potential capacity to respond positively, negatively, or not at all. Magazine ads, however, are much easier to ignore. A person must make some sort of effort to look them over, consider them, perhaps even clip a few out as reminders. Responding to magazine ads, therefore, is a more proactive process. Whereas television advertising is more insistent, people are not likely to get angry at magazine ads unless they are tasteless or exploitative. Radio and television commercials are far more likely to become one or both; but they do not demand the attentiveness that magazine ads call for. Television ads, by comparison, normally elicit an inactive response except for special situations like pledge drives or channels devoted exclusively to sales for buyers at home, a recent phenomenon.

The full emergence and impact of mass media after midcentury diminished regionalism and increased the simultaneity with which products (ranging from goods to entertainment) could be exposed to a nationwide audience. By the time Daniel J. Boorstin first coined the phrase and wrote about "consumption communities" in 1967, their distribution and configuration had become more pervasive than Edward Bernays or anyone who pioneered in marketing might have envisioned half a century earlier. Foreign as well as American scholars have effectively demonstrated the prodigious and swift spread of mass media and the dramatic expansion of consumer culture starting in the mid-1950s. That helps us to comprehend some of the basic differences of degree between mass culture and what I have designated as proto-mass culture earlier in the twentieth century.[6]

In this chapter, therefore, we will look at the commodification of culture, a process that has proceeded apace, albeit with acceleration after World War I, and compare that process with the influence of nationalism upon American culture, a pattern that has pulsated at an irregular pace over the past 120 years.

I. Promoting Consumerism and Popular Culture

During the last years of the nineteenth century, advertising suddenly became crucial for the sustenance of commercially ambitious American magazines and helped to make some of them affordable to a far broader audience. In most instances advertising revenue became more important to publishers than counter sales and subscriptions. That shift was symptomatic of the advent of a new era. Advertising as a vocation gained immensely in sophistication and impact during the decade between 1905 and 1915. Earnest Elmo Calkins first published *Modern Advertising* in 1905, a benchmark and a handbook for those who sought to shape and even dominate the nascent consumer society. When he published a revised edition ten years later, Calkins could point to new contributions by others in this budding field and declare that advertising had become "more scientific and more certain than it was."[7]

As we have already seen, the marketing efforts of sporting goods manufacturers became truly intense during the last two decades of the nineteenth century. Extensive advertising campaigns used deceptive techniques to promote the sale of equipment, manuals, and guide-books that they designated as "official" in order to enhance desirability. The manufacturers also worked collusively with coaches, trainers, and sports entrepreneurs in an effort to increase demand for their goods. Misleading advertising, devised for other kinds of products, became standard usage in connection with so-called medicines and health products. Between 1885 and 1910 the commodification of exercise, competitive sport, and health cures became major manifestations of popular culture in the United States.[8] Why do I deliberately use popular rather than mass? Because the numbers of people we are talking about are significant but not yet vast compared with, say, the 1970s and 1980s. Moreover, the mechanisms for reaching audiences with information and then actually making sales were cumbersome compared with television advertising, national distribution, and sales on credit during the later decades of the twentieth century.[9]

We have diverse indications along with illustrative material from historians that the commercialization of leisure did not cause an immediate or direct transition to mass culture. We know, for example, that beyond the big cities audiences for vaudeville during its halcyon days were segmented by geography, by their ability to pay, often by ethnicity, and by access to transportation and mobility. Between 1880 and 1920 most promoters of vaudeville accepted and catered to that diversity. During the interwar years, slowly but steadily, touring acts began to set more consistent standards of performance, and consequently to raise expectations. Acts became less regional, less ethnic, less rooted in a particular sense of place. As Robert W. Snyder has written, when companies took their acts on the road, "performers made popular culture less a part of a place and more dependent on the portable offerings of an entertainment industry." Snyder then adds a crucial distinction, however, one that reminds us of the extent to which we are now three full generations removed from the 1920s. "Although vaudeville paved the way for forces of centralization and standardization in American culture," he observes, "it was itself far more attentive to cultural particularities than the electronic forms that followed it."[10]

Looking carefully at the Cold War years following World War II, Jackson Lears has even remarked that casual assumptions that the United States became covered by a seamless web of consumer culture not only ignore psychological complexities but also obscure the variety and vitality of subordinate cultures flourishing outside or beneath the mainstream.[11]

Major responsibility for this presumptive cultural homogenization of the United States—and particularly for the perception of homogenization—rests with those who controlled the mass media at midcentury. In 1950–51 cultural critics Gilbert Seldes and Charles A. Siepmann independently yet simultaneously called attention to a self-serving conception of the masses convenient (indeed necessary) for the moguls who preferred to think of the United States as providing a uniform audience with a limited number of identical interests rather than a plural society composed of diverse groups. Men such as Frank Stanton, the longtime president of CBS, cherished the ideal of a single great audience.[12] From the 1960s through the 1980s they programmed accordingly and enjoyed considerable success in making their ideal a reality. During that period the major networks contributed mightily to the standardization of media fare and thereby helped move the country toward mass culture as we know it.

Far too much of the serious writing about the advent of commercial culture around the turn of the century implies that more traditional forms of popular culture simply disappeared or else became inconsequential. A more comprehensive look at the evidence (and at the entire United States, not just a few large cities) reveals that organized recreation (by entrepreneurs as well as by social reformers) did not dramatically displace the customary, informal uses of leisure. Commercial activities did not entirely supplant noncommercial ones. Social dances of all kinds remained widely popular through the 1910s and 1920s, including square dances, barn dances, and open air dances. That may have been the great age of vaudeville and of Ziegfeld's Follies—the latter from 1907 to 1932, when our image of the American showgirl was created—but commercial and more traditional popular culture coexisted on an equal footing through the 1930s, especially when we consider the country as a whole.[13] Popular culture and PMC *both* were manifestations and expressions of increased leisure and the rise of American recreation.

What scholars from a broad range of disciplines do seem to agree upon, however, is that the flowering of consumer culture dates from the 1920s. That is the pivotal period when commerce and culture could no longer be tidily compartmentalized, a trend that threatened the social security and convictions of America's traditional cultural elite. As Stuart Ewen has correctly observed, "consumerism, the mass participation in the values of the mass industrial market, thus emerged in the 1920s not as a smooth progression from earlier and less 'developed' patterns of consumption, but rather as an aggressive device of corporate survival." Manufacturers and entrepreneurs wanted high wages in the 1920s so that workers could become viable and reliable consumers. The ethos of consumption did not just emerge because wages and desires rose in tandem. It happened as a consequence of intense and conscious manipulation.[14]

And it happened because advertising and public relations achieved prominence as well as respectability during the 1920s. They received the official blessings of Calvin Coolidge and Herbert Hoover. Advertising targeted young people as never before, and in ways that made young people arbiters of taste. Many of them therefore became more knowledgeable about the new world of commodities than their parents—particularly if the latter were immigrants. Henceforth the consumer preferences of youth would be respected as never before. By 1963, just to peek ahead once again, American adolescents spent $22 billion, an amount double the gross national product of Austria.[15]

That familiar phrase, "the man in the street," first surfaced during the 1920s. It is symptomatic of the intensified (and often newfound) determination of people engaged in marketing to learn more about and reach ordinary people. Nevertheless, although we associate a full surge of mass *production* with the 1920s, we must be careful not to confuse that development with the full-blown emergence of mass culture. Not everyone in the United States worked in a factory. Not everyone shared a common taste in music or other leisure entertainments; and as the social philosophers Louis Adamic and Horace Kallen demonstrated at the time, many distinctive enclaves of traditional culture persisted.[16] Moreover, the author of a brilliant historical study of General Electric has provided this persuasive observation:

> It is not possible to survey the forms of mass culture in the twentieth century with the assumptions [of the nineteenth]. The corporation creates patterns of meaning wholesale and sells them to the public. It divides society into markets while ignoring fundamental divisions between workers and white-collar personnel, between regions, and between ethnic groups.[17]

Stuart Ewen has shrewdly noticed that during the quarter century between the 1920s and the later 1940s, the ability of American capitalism to expand markets commensurate with its growing productive capacity was limited in many ways. Not until the 1950s, in fact, did the dreams of entrepreneurs and marketers back in the 1920s really begin to be fully realized. And only after midcentury would the pervasive extension of credit and the maximization of advertising potential be fully realized. Before 1950, for example, radio and television generally stopped broadcasting at ten o'clock in the evening. Soon after 1950, ventures into late-night broadcasting would expand and open potential markets with simultaneous and memorably conveyed messages.[18] Hence my strong preference for differentiating between proto-mass culture in the decades prior to 1950 and mass culture since then. As we shall see, there are numerous other reasons as well.

II. Commercialization and the Transition to Mass Culture

What needs to be kept uppermost in mind, I believe, is that consumerism and its implications for mass culture occurred in discernible increments rather than all at once in 1900 or 1925 or 1950. John Dewey observed in 1930 that the need to buy had become as much an American "duty" as saving had once been. The Lynds' book *Middletown* (1929) quotes from the leading newspaper in Muncie, Indiana: "The American citizen's first importance to his country is no longer that of citizen but that of consumer. Consumption is a new necessity." By the mid- and later 1930s the Depression reinforced that pervasive ethic as a new notion in political economy took hold: namely, that the productive capacity of the United States could only be restored if people purchased what manufacturing plants produced.[19]

Needless to say, not many people had very much disposable income during the 1930s, so self-help books started to emerge and enjoyed wide-ranging popularity—a trend that has grown dramatically in our own time. Some of these guidebooks aimed to make a person more successful through self-improvement; but others were primarily concerned with personal self-fulfillment. As Frederick Lewis Allen told his sister in 1937, his wife was writing such a book, but unlike Dorothea Brande's *Wake Up and Live* (1936), a best-seller, Agnes Allen "isn't interested in helping people to make more money, to become popular, or to achieve virtue: she is merely dispensing suggestions on how to make your life more satisfactory to you yourself."[20]

Other manifestations of self-help during the mid- and later 1930s reveal resistance to the advent and potential implications of mass culture. The convenient monthly publication *Consumer Reports* would eventually have international counterparts; but the American version turned out to be the prototype—just what one might expect in a straitened consumer culture in which brand-name goods appeared on a broad scale. When the journal began publication in 1936 as *Consumers Union Reports*, it advocated consumer action in order to pressure manufacturers to improve factory working conditions as well as the quality of goods produced and sold.[21]

When Pocket Books started to publish inexpensive paperbacks in 1939, and then accelerated production through the next two decades, such books could readily reach millions rather than thousands of readers—which augmented a major breakthrough to the emergence of mass culture at midcentury. Unlike previous books, cheap paperbacks were handled by periodical distributors and sold in drug stores, chain stores, bus stations, and airport terminals—mass market publication sales as we understand that concept. The paperback revolution at midcentury most certainly helped to democratize culture in terms of access to books. And the dynamics of that process did not simply "level down" in terms of mysteries, romances, self-help, and do-it-yourself books. Trade books and quality paperbacks also flourished during the 1950s and '60s, sold mainly through college and general bookstores rather than drug store and transportation terminal racks. Eventually the distinction between mass market and quality paperbacks became increasingly blurred when both types became available in many of the same places—a symptomatic phenomenon affecting our perception of cultural stratification as being in decline ever since the 1960s.[22]

Coinciding with inexpensive paperback books in the 1940s, a parallel trend appeared that had important implications for our own time: corporate sponsorship of public service events that conveyed a highly positive image for big business. In 1940, for example, a Manhattan-based public relations firm arranged for one of its clients, Pepsi-Cola, to sponsor a Peace Luncheon "dedicated on behalf of American business to the hope of the world again at peace." The designated day for this festive luncheon, June 17, coincided with the anniversary of the first Geneva Peace Conference in 1905. Announcements explained that celebrities of today and yesteryear would be present, including Teddy Roosevelt, Mark Twain, Lillian Russell, Anna Held, and Thomas A. Edison. "Masks are now being modeled in the physiognomy of each of the above and many others . . . with the greatest possible accuracy in connection with this 35 year celebration of the bottling of Pepsi-Cola."[23]

Aside from the curious blend of altruism and commercialism (in this instance the commodification of international peace efforts), the configuration of historical celebrities supports a fascinating finding made by the sociologist Leo Lowenthal in 1944—a revealing one in terms of changes in popular taste levels during the first four decades of the twentieth century. Using biographical articles that appeared in *Collier's* and the *Saturday Evening Post*, Lowenthal found that even in these popular magazines—mass-circulation by the standards of the day—most biographical attention concentrated on men in politics, captains of industry, or people from the serious arts. Entertainers and sports figures did not become prominent subjects until the later 1920s and especially the 1930s. Before that time, biographical essays, even in popular magazines, were mainly presented in order to provide educational models. They did not become "frivolous" and anticipate the likes of *People* magazine until the second quarter of the twentieth century. This transformation supplies an interesting challenge to those who would locate the perceived emergence of celebrity-oriented mass culture in the decade 1895–1905.[24]

Moreover, looking at the substantive content of these articles, Lowenthal found a striking shift in the most admired attributes of American heroes from "agents of social production" to "agents and methods of social and individual consumption." In addition, irrespective of the heroes' walk of life or vocation, Lowenthal's content analysis found increasing emphasis upon the private lives of heroes rather than their public personae, and more particularly on what these people liked to consume: their personal taste preferences. By the later 1920s and '30s, according to Lowenthal, "these new heroes represent a craving for having and taking things for granted. They seem to stand for a phantasmagoria of world-wide social security; for an attitude which asks for no more than to be served with the things needed for reproduction and recreation. . . ."[25]

The World War II years played an absolutely crucial (and hitherto underestimated) role in accelerating the transition from proto-mass culture to the "real thing." Employment skyrocketed, and up with it went disposable income. Moreover, because certain kinds of commodities, like cars and clothing, were not readily available, Americans spent unprecedented amounts on entertainment and recreation of all sorts. War workers flocked to see films, and the movie industry flourished as never before. Nightclubs and cafés were consistently crowded despite rising prices. Markets for music and books shot up also, most notably for murder mysteries, self-help books, and books about health.[26]

There were just 3,900 supermarkets in the United States in 1939, but more than 16,000 by 1944. In the closing years of the war the advertising industry achieved the largest budget in its history and began to prepare the public for postwar goods. Robert W. Woodruff (long-time chairman of the board) used World War II to establish a global thirst for Coca-Cola. The *Saturday Evening Post* enjoyed declaring, with a rhetorical flourish directed at the despised Japanese: "Your people are giving their lives in useless sacrifice. Ours are fighting for a glorious future of mass employment, mass production, and mass distribution and ownership."[27]

Most observers with a historical orientation seem to agree that the commercialization of culture accelerated rapidly after World War II. As the sense of national and international crisis caused by fascism waned, commitment to altruistic goals diminished accordingly. The media gradually lowered their standards and traditional criteria of cultural stratification were relaxed as a consequence. Mass leisure and mass communication, which are essential for the intensive commodification of popular culture, became increasingly normative and pervasive for large numbers of Americans beginning in the 1950s. Warren Susman observed that for many families the culmination of a visit to Disneyland after 1955 was a special exhibit called "American Journeys," a selective, nostalgic reprise of the American past. "Immobilized and passive," Susman remarked, "having visited a world in which one can consume to the presumed satisfaction of all desires," visitors confirmed the sense of well-being that accompanied constant reminders that they enjoyed the world's highest standard of living.[28]

Similarly, looking at the 1950s, Victoria de Grazia contends that "a universal language of commodities now connected America's vast empire of goods." That decade marked the true beginning of mass consumption as we know it, and henceforth mass markets swiftly became a "real fixture" in national life. Simultaneously de Grazia also sees a marketing revolution taking place in Europe during the 1950s and '60s, when changes in marketing techniques were accompanied by a dramatic increase in consumer spending. In sum, similar things were happening in non-Communist Europe, but at a more hesitant pace than in the United States.[29]

From the perspective of a historian, it is essential that we recognize these gradations of change even within such a concentrated phase as the post–World War II generation. That happens to be exactly the period, a genuinely pivotal era, when the chrysalis of proto-mass culture broke open and the mature form emerged, not merely liberated but quickly ubiquitous. Lizabeth Cohen has shown that the new suburbanites of the 1940s and '50s still depended upon the city for all sorts of major purchases, and they used small, locally owned commercial outlets in nearby towns to serve their minor needs. A new market structure dependent upon regional shopping centers (so-called malls) and aimed at the suburban mass consumption society did not begin to emerge until the mid-1950s. Within a decade the community marketplace shifted from city and town centers to privately owned suburban shopping centers. By the 1960s and 1970s, the uses of leisure time and the process and places of consumption were becoming inseparably intertwined, thereby arranging a great many community experiences (simultaneous though not ordinarily interactive—the "herd of independent minds" again) according to the cultural tastes of predominantly white, middle-class suburbanites.[30]

When journalist-turned-social critic Vance Packard published his runaway best-seller *The Hidden Persuaders* (1957), he popularized the notion (and the perception) of a mass of consumers being constantly, gullibly manipulated by corporate schemers. By the end of the 1950s, critic Paul Coates observes, "enhanced purchasing power and a massive extension of the educational system—among other factors—had rendered the products of mass culture so pervasive as to secrete the dubious antidote of a new sensibility: that of camp."[31]

Advertisements by sponsors of television programs during the fifties swiftly began to exercise an increasing amount of control over not merely the kind of program they made possible, but its content as well as its manner of presentation. Camel cigarettes sponsored *Man Against Crime* on CBS. Writers for that program received in mimeographed form detailed instructions, such as: never show a disreputable person smoking a cigarette. And John Cameron Swayze, the most popular television newscaster of the 1950s, had a lighted cigarette burning on his desk throughout the broadcast with a pack prominently displayed so that the camera could not fail to reveal the sponsor's brand.[32]

The separation and subsequent segmentation of youth culture played a significant part in the commercial enhancement of mass culture. Once again, this was a gradual process that occurred over a period of several decades at midcentury. The creation of *Seventeen* magazine in 1944 highlighted the fact that teenagers had developed an identifiable, discrete subculture with attendant dress, behavior, styles of leisure—and therefore marketing possibilities. Well over a decade after that, mainly in the 1950s and 1960s, television brought intense (rather than casual) commercialization into the lives of children. The full emergence of "kidvid" on Saturday mornings in the 1960s, for instance, facilitated an overwhelming variety of ads for child-oriented toys and food.[33]

Although much attention has been devoted to the growing importance of young people as consumers with considerable amounts of money available to spend, especially since the 1960s, the entrepreneurial impulses of young people during the countercultural intensity of the later 1960s have been virtually ignored. Yet they too played a key role in bringing the commercialization of popular and mass culture to new levels, not to mention adding new dimensions. The famous Woodstock Festival held in upstate New York in August 1969, for example, owed its conception and precisely calculated development to four young entrepreneurs who intended from the outset to make a great deal of money from the project. Two of them might be called proto-yuppies who supplied the necessary capital for development. The other two were genuinely anti-establishment young men, Michael Lang and Artie Kornfeld, who envisioned a scenario of love and peace—along with wondrous wealth for themselves. The most thorough history of Woodstock puts their activities under a candid spotlight.

> The two were "movers" in a microcosm of followers, young men full of confidence and purpose who could lay back and unwind over a joint and still take care of business with unyielding tenacity. Here was that beautiful irony indicative of the generation's anti-Establishment heroes who wallowed in the splendors of cutthroat capitalism—fighting to excel in the very thing the movement rejected. They masqueraded as hippies although they also shared an affection for spending large sums of other people's money.[34]

Ever since the 1960s there has been an increasingly complex, contested relationship in the United States between capital and culture broadly conceived, that is, between powerful corporations and their opponents in what amounts to a series of conflicts over the control of rampant consumerism. In 1965 the Highway Beautification Act, commonly known as the billboard law, passed in the Congress by a single vote. No other legislation that session caused so much heated controversy and required so much effort to persuade senators to support it. Commercial America seemed to believe that the use of advertising on billboards surely must be a right protected by the First Amendment.[35]

By the 1970s, on the other hand, corporations increasingly regarded the acquisition and display of art as well as support for exhibitions as good public relations. Robert Kingsley, Exxon executive and founder as well as chairman of the Arts and Business Council, explained that Exxon's "support of the arts serves as a social lubricant. And if business is to continue in big cities, it needs a lubricated environment." David Rockefeller put it even more explicitly. "From an economic standpoint, such involvement in the arts can mean direct and tangible benefits. It can provide a company with extensive publicity and advertising, a brighter public reputation, and an improved corporate image. It can build better customer relations, a readier acceptance of company products, and a superior appraisal of their quality. Promotion of the arts can improve the morale of employees and help attract qualified personnel."[36]

By the mid-1980s the commercialization of aggregate information, such as membership lists of museums and professional organizations, had become a dominant feature of the United States economy—driven in so many ways by the need for gross quantities of information about potential consumers. In 1985 the Council on Library Resources, a private organization, issued an extraordinary and highly symptomatic statement:

> Ways must be found to assure continuing attention for those aspects of culture and learning that are important but, in a commercial sense, not necessarily in fashion.... Uncritical adherence to the concept of information as a commodity will distort the agendas of institutions and disciplines alike.... Public interest in the principle of open access must appropriately influence the structure of the information system and its components. It is certain that the information needs of society cannot be defined by the marketplace alone.[37]

Nevertheless, in an age of declining resources, universities became increasingly dependent on corporate America for money, equipment, laboratories, and other research facilities. As the *Chronicle of Higher*

Education put it in 1985: "the relation between academe and business is more cordial than it has been in decades."[38]

The same pattern applies to what are now called "megachurches," congregations that have grown exceedingly large because enterprising ministers have carefully observed techniques successful in the world of entertainment, studied the transient tastes of middle-class America, and learned from the secular institutions that appeal to it. Such enterprising clergymen study the writings of Peter F. Drucker, the leading theorist of corporate management and leadership, and hang posters by their pastoral doors that highlight provocative questions raised in Drucker's writings: "What is our business? Who is our customer? What does the customer consider value?" The phenomenon of megachurches, along with the immense monetary success of televangelists in recent years, demonstrates the commercialization of culture in yet another realm of American life, religion.[39]

In 1986 a federal judge refused to "sell" the exclusive coverage of a major naturalization ceremony to ABC-TV for $10 million.[40] Examples of such resistance to commercialization of a public process, or of cultural events that do not *require* a corporate sponsor in order to occur at all, are increasingly rare. We have long known that artifacts produced in the private sector can be bought and sold, including the books that authors write, the pictures that artists paint, and the music that composers create. But attempts at the commodification of civic life still come as a shock—at least for some of us.

It must be acknowledged that a revisionist perception of consumerism has emerged since the mid-1980s. I find this view only partially persuasive and will return to it when we consider contemporary mass culture in chapter 8. The reader should be forewarned, however, that cultural critics of a certain populist persuasion insist that consumers are formative participants in the culture of consumption (rather than simply passive victims), selecting goods that please them and endowing them with a significance not necessarily anticipated by those who sell them.[41]

III. Promoting Americanism and Popular Culture

The felt desire by citizens of the United States for identifiably American manifestations and expressions of culture dates back to the early decades of the nineteenth century. For some people, the need simply reflected an expression of national pride (and a modicum of cultural insecurity). For others, by midcentury and later, the desire also meant an opportunity to peddle books and magazines, songs and theatrical entertainments that proclaimed a distinctive national identity in a world that did not believe that a democracy was capable of "genuine" culture and that the United States, in particular, had a population too heterogeneous to produce a distinctive culture or identity in any case. At midcentury Walt Whitman felt that American literature seemed too imitative of polite culture in Europe. It lacked sufficient "Americanness."[42]

Numerous writers have observed that from the 1830s through the 1890s notions of popular culture (exemplified by theatrical entertainments, minstrel shows, and affordable writing in booklets and magazines) were strongly tinged by nationalistic hues. That was equally true of tales of Davy Crockett and the Alamo, dime novels about Buffalo Bill's exploits as a scout, and Edwin Booth's cerebral Shakespearean performances. Each figure became legendary, in fact, precisely because he embodied the Americanness for which Whitman had yearned.[43]

What complicated matters, however, as Eric Lott has observed, is that popular culture in nineteenth-century America was contested and consequently unstable, "a site of conflicting interests, appropriations, impersonations, indeed 'nationalities,' even in its allegedly national forms." Competing vernaculars existed in the United States because of regional, racial, and class differences. As Lott has written of the minstrel show, "one sees a constant struggle for control—encompassing black, white, immigrant Irish, and other cultures—within blackface forms themselves."[44] Yet another reason why I am unwilling to apply the label of "mass culture" to nineteenth-century America, therefore, is because major differences of class and race remained so powerful (and combustible) throughout the century. Many factors were required to make mass culture genuinely "mass," and one of them was a waning and resultant diminution of class consciousness, class distinctions, and class-related tastes. So long as those distinctions persisted in palpable ways—and they did until the second half of the twentieth century—we could not have a truly mass society, never mind a singularly mass culture.

Every so often during the later nineteenth century some poet, preacher, editor, or politician would proclaim a sentiment seemingly indicative of cultural or social homogeneity on a vast scale—pejoratively on occasion, yet sometimes with approval. "It is not a trifling matter," wrote James Russell Lowell, "that thirty millions of men should be thinking the same thought and feeling the same pang at a single moment of time, and that these vast parallels of latitude should become a neighborhood more intimate than many a country village."[45] That assertion might be valid as an allusion to veterans of the Grand Army of the Republic, perhaps, but not to the great mélange of new immigrants, farmers migrating beyond the Mississippi, and young people leaving rural areas to seek their fortunes in the burgeoning cities. Most Americans did not yet respond to the same news at the same time and think the same thoughts "at a single moment." As late as 1930, Joy Elmer Morgan anticipated radio as the basis for establishing a truly "national culture" and called for government regulation in order to achieve the "public enlightenment" that radio had the potential to foster. By then the prospect did exist, though it had not become a reality quite yet.[46]

By the first decades of the twentieth century an ironic development had occurred, though virtually no one perceived it as ironic at the time. That recognition would come some fifty years later. Throughout the nineteenth century Americans had yearned for genuinely distinctive forms of art, literature, and music in the United States. If they did not always have high culture specifically in mind, they certainly envisioned elevated forms of expression. On the eve of World War I, however, when Europeans began to take note of American creativity, it would be innovations in popular culture that caught their attention and prompted their admiration. A long editorial essay in *Scribner's* offered this highly revealing observation in 1913: "Every [American] traveller to Europe in recent days has had the opportunity of observing the interest shown in American tunes and dance rhythms which, as associated in his mind with forms of amusement not necessarily of the highest class, certainly do not strike him as very worthy of being thought representatively American."[47] The author/editor did not believe that Americans took sufficient or particular pride in their "rag-time artists," yet acknowledged that musicians and audiences in Europe had a surprisingly different perspective. "They don't regard American popular music as being any nobler in tone than we do ourselves; but they do find it technically new; they do find that it is original, that it leads in a fresh direction." Then came the reluctant acknowledgment that jazz might even be a distinctive and valued native contribution: "We may have in these vulgar [musical] measures something more valuable than we grasp; something which belongs peculiarly to us, and which may contain the germs of a greater development—something, in short, to be called national."[48]

The writer went on to observe that recent visitors to the United States were most eager to discover "the 'popular' note of America," the lively and distinctive products of Tin Pan Alley, which was then productively pulsing with new music, and theatrical entertainments. The editorial recognized the need to reconsider, in less snobbish ways, the humbler sources of national cultural expression. "Folk-songs, folk-lore, national dances, national epics, the full-flavored welling up from the soil of the love and joy of life—these, we were reminded, were the heritage of the older, artistic peoples, whence all great national art had sprung."[49]

This was not the first time cultural critics in the United States had been obliged to acknowledge that European perceptions of American popular culture did not coincide with native sentiments and self-awareness. But it may well have brought a shock of recognition: namely, that American culture as a national concern might be valued more highly for its popular contributions than for its "serious" or highbrow aspirations. In 1908 that same column (magazine department), perhaps written by the very same editor, had quoted an English critic who remarked that "while there may be less erudition in America, there is conspicuously more culture." More meant popular, fresh, and diverse rather than high; entertainment rather than the advancement of knowledge. That critic's observation would raise a curtain for the century to come.[50]

Meanwhile, during the early decades of the twentieth century, connections between Americanism and commercial culture appeared in several new ways. Film companies promoted and even celebrated their novel role as chroniclers of contemporary events and history. Within weeks of Woodrow Wilson's death in 1924, the first film tribute to him was in production. The film consisted of motion picture footage taken during Wilson's presidency and retirement interspersed with title frames extolling his virtues in effusive and pious terms. The producers hoped to present the film "reverently" each day, somewhere, forever. In sum, they hoped that the film would prove to be profitable as well as inspirational![51]

During World War I, and especially in 1915–16, intensive public discussions of "Americanism" took place, with notable contributions from attorney Louis D. Brandeis (not yet on the Supreme Court), philosopher Horace Kallen, critic Randolph Bourne, socialist Elizabeth Gurley Flynn, and others. Dissenters like Flynn and Bourne called for cultural pluralism and internationalism as the best (least chauvinistic) definition of patriotism. But theirs was distinctly a minority position and lacked broad appeal. In 1916 "Americanism" meant compliant assimilation and Americanization to most people who considered themselves to be of native stock. Once the United States became directly involved as a combatant in 1917–18, George Creel's Committee on Public Information rolled into high gear as a pro-Allies propaganda bureau that effectively manipulated and even commodified public perceptions held by Americans. The distribution of treatises and posters had a powerfully cohesive impact upon public opinion. Creel's efforts were considerably enhanced by lessons learned from developments in commercial advertising during the previous two decades. Failure to support the war effort became tantamount to treason.[52]

Back in 1897, when the commercialization of culture in the United States was still immature (by comparison with half a century later), the critic Brander Matthews had defined "Americanism" in social and civic terms. The word meant patriotism and acceptance of the principles underpinning the U.S. government. "It frowns upon all appeals to the former allegiance of naturalized citizens of this country; and it thinks that it ought to be enough for any man to be an American without the aid of the hyphen."[53]

By the 1920s, however, four decades of intensive immigration had opened the eyes of manufacturers and marketing people to the process of Americanization as an opportunity for expansive consumerism. Masses of new Americans meant far more than patriotism, which had been Matthews's emphasis twenty-five years earlier. Frances Alice Keller, an advertising woman who placed ads in the foreign-language press, viewed advertising in the 1920s as a vital opportunity for social integration—and sales. Here is the pitch that she made to businessmen, many of them unaccustomed to thinking about newcomers as worthwhile targets for consumerism.

National advertising is the great Americanizer. American ideals and institutions, law, order, and prosperity, have not yet been sold to all our immigrants. American products and standards of living have not yet been bought by the foreign born in America. . . . If Americans want to combine business and patriotism, they should advertise products, industry and American institutions in the American Foreign Language press.

That refrain would be reiterated by many others throughout the decade.[54]

For Americans of "older stock," that is, not recent immigrants, the interwar years witnessed a parallel but perhaps equally lucrative phenomenon: the sale of "history" as patriotic culture. Or, put differently and crudely, the American past got commodified during the 1920s and '30s. By the spring of 1922, the *Saturday Evening Post* decided to devote a weekly section to the subject of collecting Americana. The colonial revival in home furnishings and the decorative arts enjoyed considerable popular appeal by then, and it increased steadily over the next four decades. Many well-publicized events contributed to this blend of consumerism and Americanism: Henry Ford's purchase and restoration of the Wayside Inn in Sudbury, Massachusetts; the opening of the American Wing of the Metropolitan Museum of Art in 1924; and the opening of the restored Colonial Williamsburg less than a decade later. First, the demand for reproductions of early American furniture seemed to be insatiable; and it persists to this day, though it may have peaked during the most intense Cold War years, 1947–67. Second, slavish copies of Williamsburg homes appeared pictorially in ladies' magazines and in solid reality in gentrified suburbs. Hence the home of George Wythe, who taught Thomas Jefferson law, would be reproduced in places like Scarsdale, New York; and the U.S. Embassy in Helsinki would be an adapted replica of another Williamsburg residence. The elite bought originals while the middle class acquired reproductions. The taste ethic was the same, however. Colonial revival Americana reigned supreme.[55]

In 1933 a massive survey of American society and cultural trends, commissioned by President Herbert Hoover four years earlier, summarized in highly positive ways many of the developments that have been described in this chapter. A long section devoted to "The Arts in Social Life" included a segment entitled "Art and Business." It noted that national advertising exerted an immediate influence throughout the country: "millions see its work as against thousands who visit museums and exhibitions." The essay proudly proclaimed that ever since 1920 art had become "an active factor in our business life." A special accolade was aimed at the proliferation of murals that now beautified America despite their commercial stimuli. "Not so long ago," the author explained, "there was little to see in mural painting in America outside the Library of Congress and the Boston Public Library. Today there are admirable examples all over the country, nearly all of them directly attributable to the advertising value of a handsome bank or office building or department store. A trend which at least in part touches indirect advertising is the conscious attention to the architecture and surroundings of manufacturing plants."[56]

The British historian J. H. Plumb has observed that "personal ownership of the past has always been a vital strand in the ideology of all ruling classes."[57] The social and economic elite in the United States controlled interpretations as well as visions of history during the first two thirds of the twentieth century. Consequently, the American past became a carefully filtered part of popular culture, yet entered mass culture only partially, belatedly, and then manipulatively.[58]

By the beginning of 1942, when the United States became fully engaged on the side of the Allies in World War II, manipulation of patriotism by the government—ranging from the sale of war bonds to the dissemination of propaganda posters and the mobilization of Hollywood studios to make anti-Axis films—owed much to advertising and public relations techniques that had been refined ever since the 1920s.[59] Back in 1915, Walter Lippmann had related patriotism in a direct, uncomplicated way to national prestige and pride. Three decades later the linkages had become more complex because they owed a great deal to the sophisticated commercialization of popular culture that emerged in the years following World War I.* Robert K. Merton's intensive, quantitative and qualitative analysis of a war bond drive conducted on the radio by Kate Smith in 1944 not only provides a basis for comparison with Creel's less immediate, less personalized Committee on Public Information (1917–19), but anticipates the full impact of nationwide network radio on mass culture.[60]

---

* In Frank Capra films made during the later 1930s, Americanism meant "the rewards of social stability—wealth, success and the girl for the hero; fellowship, happiness and trustworthy leaders for the rest of us. It was a religious faith in a secular social myth that found its embodiment in patriotism and American democracy." Robert Sklar, *Movie-Made America: A Cultural History of American Movies* (New York, 1975), 212.

In the decades following the war, film companies and subsequently television would increasingly be regarded as chroniclers of contemporary history. The route from the monthly newsreel of the thirties and forties *The March of Time* to Oliver Stone's *JFK* and *Nixon* is by no means direct, but the commercial presentation of national and international events fed a hunger that grew relentlessly from the 1930s onward. To a lesser degree, yet surely significant, we have in the realm of popular culture successful books that can be called instant history, ranging from Theodore H. White's *Making of the President* series (1961–73) to Norman Mailer's *Armies of the Night: History as a Novel, the Novel as History* (1968). Americana had become, as never before, a simultaneous component of mass *and* popular culture—powerful testimony to the fact that one did not supplant the other. They coexist, albeit with lines of demarcation that are less and less distinct.[61]

By the middle of the twentieth century, as Jackson Lears has remarked, the essence of the American Way of Life had shifted from an ambiguous populism during the 1930s to categorical affirmations of free enterprise. What remained fairly constant was a pervasive belief in national uniqueness and homogeneity sustained by the world's highest standard of living. That degree of affluence, underpinned by capitalism (elevated on a pedestal of ideology if not religion), pervaded postwar social thought and helped to pave the way for mass culture as we know it.[62]

4

Popular Culture in Transition—and in Its Prime

∽

I. Changing Perceptions of Cultural Stratification

Popular culture in manifold forms has been a prominent part of the human experience for quite a long time. It developed in the American colonies among congregations of the faithful and at seasonal festivities, at taverns and inns, in vernacular songs and superstitions. During the past century, however, the phrase "popular culture" has increasingly meant very different things to different people, partially because it has been invoked in such diverse ways—sometimes with populist affirmation but often with snobbish disdain.[1] From the particular perspective of this book, it is helpful to pin the matter down chronologically: I contend that popular culture enjoyed its most flamboyant heyday during the half century that followed the mid-1880s. In order to make that claim persuasive, I must clear away a tangled briarpatch of misconceptions. But let me begin in a schematic yet historically informed manner. Why do I designate the period, roughly from 1885 to 1935, as an era when popular culture was in its prime in the United States?

First, because it was during this period that a notable growth of leisure time occurred. Second, because the commercialization of organized entertainment reached a whole new plateau previously unknown. Third, because innovations in transportation and technology made it possible for entrepreneurial amusements to reach audiences on an expanded scale. Fourth, because a gradual repudiation of the genteel tradition created opportunities for modes of social behavior and interaction that would have been unthinkable to most middle-class Americans in the age of Victorian polite culture. Fifth, because the distinctiveness of regional and local lifestyles still retained enough strength to resist the powerful surge of homogenization that accompanied what so many people in the later 1920s referred to as "standardization." And sixth, because the pervasive manifestations of popular culture in that era remained largely participatory and interactive, based upon certain modes of sociability that began to fade in the decades following World War II when mass culture as we know it emerged fully and subordinated popular culture by supplanting or else overwhelming much of it and then replicating it for audiences on a numerical scale previously unimagined.

If these six criteria for differentiation are valid—though I anticipate that some critics will surely dispute them—then why is there so much confusion associated with this perplexing subject? A part of the answer may be found in casual conceptual usage, as we saw in chapter 1. Part of the explanation can also be found in the chronological untidiness that is inherent and inevitable in historical inquiry. Popular and mass culture did not appear in a neat sequence; they overlapped in time by as much as a generation, as I intend to show here and in chapter 7 below. But their overlap is most notable and therefore difficult to disentangle during the 1930s and '40s, a time of transition that I prefer to designate as the pivotal era of proto-mass culture, whose characteristics I will say more about in the third section of this chapter. The roots of mass culture, as we have noted earlier, were most certainly present at the beginning of the twentieth century; but it takes time for roots to nourish sturdy organisms that not only grow to maturity, but do so with sufficient vigor that other organisms are either crowded out or else eclipsed in the shadows cast by such vigorous new species. That analogy seems especially well suited to the historical relationship between popular and mass culture during the latter half of the twentieth century.

A second cause for confusion arises from the fact that we have had in common usage for a long time now two *sets* of terms that get melded together casually, even though they really are not interchangeable. I have in mind mass, popular, and elite culture as one scale of measurement, and lowbrow, middlebrow, and highbrow as the second. There clearly are instances, it is true, where mass culture and lowbrow taste coincide, but I insist quite strenuously that as the twentieth century progressed, close correspondence between the two "scales" diminished.

Highbrows and middlebrows not only consume mass culture; in crucial ways they are also individually instrumental in creating new innovations in mass culture. Popular culture, in turn, has profoundly influenced modern art, especially in some of its more avant-garde manifestations. And at one time or another so-called middlebrows have been avid consumers of all three cultural taste levels: mass, popular, and elite. I may watch the Super Bowl faithfully for three decades; go to the county fair each year to hear bluegrass music; but also listen with rapt attention to baroque music played on period instruments. The diversity of our tastes has not been well served (or explained) by the extensive litany of terminological options that we use.

A third source of confusion might be called ideological. Writers and critics who dislike or disapprove of middlebrow or mass culture will use those labels explicitly and pejoratively. Writers and critics who have a positive attitude toward such taste levels, however, are more likely to designate as popular culture, or even folk culture, what I mean by mass culture. John Fiske, for example, one of our leading authorities on mass culture, titles his book on the subject *Understanding Popular Culture* (1989), and shifts the leverage of agency from successfully manipulative commercializers to clever consumers. The creativity of popular culture, he insists, "lies not in the production of commodities so much as in the productive use of industrial commodities. The art of the people is the art of 'making do.' The culture of everyday life lies in the creative, discriminating use of the resources that capitalism provides."[2]

Our terminological menu has also been extended by the widely used phrase "vernacular culture," which may or may not be a euphemism for popular culture, mass culture, or even folk culture. All that we can say with assurance is that vernacular does *not* mean elite or highbrow. It does imply something native or distinctive to popular taste, such as everyday, ordinary language, or a style of architecture distinctive to a particular class of people in a specific region. When that is the case, vernacular conveys a meaning quite different from popular or mass culture—it suggests something closer to folk—yet there has been a tendency simply to blend it with popular or mass culture, however inappropriate.

The complexities and limitations of all these labels are easily illuminated. How should we categorize what happens when Aaron Copland takes a traditional Shaker tune and works it into a haunting melody called "Simple Gifts" for *Appalachian Spring* (1944), a melody subsequently played on the concert stage and most famously as the theme for the prestigious TV documentary series *CBS Reports*—a melody so widely recognized that many listeners who know nothing about Shakers or Copland can hum it perfectly? How do we categorize the career of Leonard Bernstein, a man who helped young people understand and enjoy classical music, who composed the score for the film *On the Waterfront* and for *West Side Story*, and also wrote a mass? How do we categorize William Faulkner when *The Sound and the Fury* (1929), *The Reivers* (1962), and *Sanctuary* (1931) could conceivably be designated when they first appeared as highbrow, middlebrow, and lowbrow, respectively? The solution lies in Duke Ellington's favorite phrase, "Beyond Category."[3]

Perhaps the single most important lesson to be learned from the history of cultural stratification in the United States is that distinct taste levels have indeed existed, yet they have been permeable and increasingly subject to being shared across lines of class, race, and degrees of education. From Van Wyck Brooks in 1915 to Lawrence W. Levine in 1988, a series of distinguished observers has insisted upon the unattractive presence of cultural hierarchy in America, most notably for two full generations starting in the 1870s. They argue persuasively that ordinary folks were discouraged or driven away from theaters, concerts, and museums, which is undeniably true.[4]

What also has to be remembered, however, is that that time span is exactly when so many alternative modes of entertainment became available to the middling and working classes—an array of leisure-time options from amusement parks to concert saloons, from vaudeville to silent film, from sheet music for communal singing to organized sports. There was even a new assortment of museums with much broader appeal than places like the Metropolitan Museum of Art in Manhattan. The crucial point, therefore, is that the emergence of cultural stratification did not leave ordinary Americans with nowhere to go in search of pleasure. Their new options cost less, were considered more fun and better suited to their educational levels than the more elitist entertainments and edifications that did not exactly welcome the great unwashed with open arms. That is yet another reason why popular culture flourished as never before and with greater variety between 1885 and 1935.[5]

Quite a few cultural entrepreneurs recognized early on that more money could be made providing inexpensive amusements for the many than by contriving costly diversions for the few. E. Z. C. Judson, who created dime novels and western novelettes as "Ned Buntline," wrote to a friend in 1885: "I found that to make a living I must write 'trash' for the masses, for he who endeavors to write for the critical few, and do his genius justice, will go hungry if he has no other means of support."[6] By the turn of the century, inevitably, some entrepreneurs invested in producing cheaper imitations of what the elite wanted, thereby demonstrating that the perception of cultural hierarchy was indeed derived from reality. A sarcastic observer remarked in 1900 that "culturine is a typical American product of the present day. . . . Indications are that in the very near future it will become fully as popular and costly as the genuine article which it was originally designed to imitate. Culturine may be described as a substance that bears the same relation to culture that velveteen does to velvet, oleomargarine to butter, or plush to sealskin."[7]

The terms "highbrow" and "lowbrow" derived from the mid-Victorian fascination with cranial capacity, a curiously racist outlook that equated one with high intelligence and the other with very limited mental ability. Edward A. Ross, a Progressive sociologist, perpetuated such notions well into the twentieth century when he published *The Old World in the New* (1914), in which he ascribed a lowbrow mentality to immigrants from Eastern Europe. It is noteworthy, however, that highbrows did not invariably enjoy an august status during the first half of the twentieth century, when the sacralization of culture is supposed to have been most potent and lowbrow culture despised. A 1915 editorial in *Scribner's* lamented that no highbrow could possibly write a best-seller; and that same year Van Wyck Brooks complained that both brow levels were "equally undesirable, and they are incompatible; but they divide American life between them." The elitist stance taken by Walter Lippmann in 1920 was unusual. American artists and writers, he remarked, "are not being suffocated by the perfection of the past, but by the scorn of excellence in the present. . . . We have a public opinion that quakes before the word highbrow as if it denoted a secret sin."[8]

By midcentury the public perception of highbrows was in confused disarray and commonly cynical, whether one looked at photo-essays in *Life* magazine or comments by the likes of Lionel Trilling in *Partisan Review*. It did not help that Adlai Stevenson's presidential candidacies in 1952 and 1956 popularized the image of an egghead as someone too cerebral to be effective in the so-called real world. Even highly creative and intellectual individuals, such as writers, cultural critics, and people in theater or the arts, were more likely to identify themselves as upper-middlebrow. That label seemed to have better connotations of being a normal, functional human being. Few people other than academics were likely to identify themselves as highbrows without embarrassment or self-consciousness. Outside of academe the dominant perception of highbrow was a person whose existence and effort made no difference in the world. Ezra Pound put it bluntly in 1930: "The highbrow can't poss. have any immediate effect on the mass."[9]

There is no lack of evidence that cultural stratification and entrenched perceptions of it persisted throughout the first half of the twentieth century. In the early 1930s NBC Radio had a Red Network that aired popular entertainment and a Blue Network which featured more refined and sophisticated programs. The *Partisan Review* crowd made sharp distinctions when discussing content for the journal: painting was high art, theater was middlebrow, and the movies were lowbrow. In 1937 the young Orson Welles took Marc Blitzstein's pro-labor opera *The Cradle Will Rock* to Bethlehem, Pennsylvania, in order to perform for the factory workers there. Only two hundred showed up for the opera, which featured a strike set to music. The bulk of Bethlehem's labor force opted for a steel company picnic that had been deliberately arranged to compete with the opera. The workers preferred sunshine and beer. Taste levels in food also remained stratified by class and education.[10]

The witty playwright S. J. Perelman (1904–1979) did not want to be remembered as a man who wrote scripts for Marx Brothers movies. Why? Because they were lowbrow. He hoped to achieve lasting recognition instead as an essayist for *The New Yorker* and as a successful writer of Broadway plays, both of which he regarded as upper-middlebrow. The great irony of Perelman's career is that he delighted readers with his zany but cerebral prose, yet rarely satisfied his employers. After Perelman co-authored the screenplay for *Monkey Business* in 1931, Groucho Marx complained that Perelman's humor was too literary and convoluted for a popular audience. That began a lifelong debate between the two friends about whether or not screen comedy could afford to be "intelligent." The producer Mike Todd, on the other hand, remarked in the 1950s that Perelman "writes great dialogue, but it's strictly *New Yorker.* The circulation of *The New Yorker* is three hundred and fifty thousand. I want this picture [*Around the World in Eighty Days*] to be seen by over a hundred million." That anecdote is symptomatic of the difference in scale that entertainment people envisioned when they distinguished between popular and mass culture: hundreds of thousands of "customers" versus hundreds of millions.[11]

During the 1930s Walt Disney developed an adoring cult following for his cartoons, and then for his feature-length animated films, such as *Snow White and the Seven Dwarfs* and (in the forties) *Bambi.* But when he released *Fantasia* in 1940, it turned out to be, despite his heretofore unbroken string of huge box office successes, a commercial failure. The crowds he had become accustomed to stayed away because the reviews made *Fantasia* sound too highbrow. For most Americans that was a pejorative designation. More than half a century later, evidence still indicates that stratification has not entirely disappeared, even though it is much diminished. Shelly Garrett, the most successful impresario of the Chitlin Circuit (popular touring theatricals aimed at an African-American audience), has never met August Wilson, the most illustrious black playwright of our time. Wilson, in turn, has never heard of Shelly Garrett! As Henry Louis Gates, Jr., puts it: "They are as unacquainted with each other as art and commerce are said to be."[12]

What we have seen thus far suggests that cultural hierarchy certainly persisted on through the 1940s, and that more than mere traces remain to this day. Although popular and mass culture became increasingly difficult to differentiate, the career of S. J. Perelman, along with numerous others, indicates that distinctions between them remained quite clear in the minds of many from the 1920s well past midcentury. The isolation of highbrow pursuits along with a popular aversion to highbrow culture lingered even longer. But we need to take a closer look at popular culture in its halcyon days, 1885 to the eve of World War II, because more than Mike Todd's optimal audience size separated popular from mass culture, though that numerical distinction is hardly inconsequential.

II. Popular Culture in Its Prime

In my view, one of the most basic differences between popular and mass culture hinges upon the more participatory and interactive qualities of the former in contrast to the more spectatorial and passive qualities of the latter. *The contrast is not intended to be absolute. It cannot be.* And quite arguably mass culture has recently become more interactive, at least in key respects, than it was during the 1950s, '60s, and '70s. (More on that later.) I also believe that local and regional variations gave popular culture during the first half of the twentieth century certain identifiable characteristics that became considerably less apparent in the second half. In sum, popular culture required a greater degree of personal engagement by individuals, and initiative as well. People were more likely to take themselves to places of entertainment, rather than privately receiving electronic entertainment in their homes. Therefore popular culture meant being in public spaces and places to a greater degree proportionately than mass culture does. The latter is more likely to occur in a residential place with attention focused on a television set, a screen for home movies, or increasingly and most recently a computer.

These comparisons are necessarily approximate rather than categorical, and there is a considerable amount of coinciding chronology, most notably for a quarter century starting in the mid-thirties. Nevertheless, the distinctions enable us to make a start in attempting to understand how the uses of leisure in 1890 differed qualitatively as well as quantitatively from 1940 and then, let us say, from 1990. The qualitative and the quantitative aspects of experience are not so neatly compartmentalized either, by the way. Whereas the vast Columbian Exposition at Chicago in 1893 was a relatively anonymous, impersonal, and spectatorial event (at least within the White City as opposed to the bustling Midway Plaisance outside the enclosure), state and county fairs at that time provided more engaging and participatory activities. As Alan Trachtenberg has noted, the White City was designed "in the mode of theatrical display, of *spectacle*. . . . Visitors to the Fair found themselves as *spectators*, witnesses to an unanswerable performance which they had no hand in producing or maintaining."[13] Here we have an anticipation of what mass culture would increasingly offer more than half a century later. That is why I prefer to call the Columbian Exposition proto-mass culture. It was an astonishing but early harbinger of things to come.

The most familiar forms of popular culture during the late nineteenth and early twentieth centuries ordinarily traveled from one city to the next, which meant that communities literally invested themselves in preparing for exciting events that were high spots on the annual calendar, such as the day (or days) when the circus came to town. When P. T. Barnum began to use railroads in 1881 to make his circus more mobile, it could reach a greater number of communities more quickly. Circus day became a very special occasion when people of all ages and classes gathered together to watch not merely the performance itself but every step from unloading to setting up to participation in the inevitable community cleanup that followed the circus's departure. Circus-time retained that spellbinding mystique for many decades, and restless youngsters yearned to run away and join the circus. It had a unique allure.

The success of Buffalo Bill's Wild West Show starting in the mid-1880s endured for almost a quarter of a century, and prompted the emergence of countless other Wild West shows that achieved much less acclaim but reached the smaller communities where most Americans still lived. The same was true of minstrel shows, which by the 1880s and 1890s, the waning phase of their popularity, meant more generalized entertainment than the raucous and racially caricatured performances of the antebellum period when the minstrel show had its genesis. Burlesque, vaudeville, and musical revues were starting their climb to widespread popularity as the new century opened, gradually supplanting the Wild West and minstrel shows as top attractions.[14]

Less organized and schematized but equally entrepreneurial were the amusement parks that began to open during the 1890s and flourished until the 1940s. Coney Island in Brooklyn is merely the most famous of these. But when electric trolley lines appeared early in the twentieth century all across the United States, traction companies paid by the month for the power that energized their trolleys. Because they needed to fill their trolleys on the weekends when many fewer people used them to go to work, they built what were called "trolley parks" at the end of the lines on the edge of the city. Those parks became magnets for families, but especially for young adults who wanted to escape parental supervision. Many of the events at these places of amusement were participatory and interactive, ranging from competitive feats of strength to hitting the clown's face with a hurled ball and winning a prize. Amusement parks were places to see and be seen, but also places to go, do, compete, and meet people, especially young people, who might otherwise be inaccessible. Hence the poignant but bittersweet nostalgia of the musical *Carousel*, first performed in the 1940s.[15]

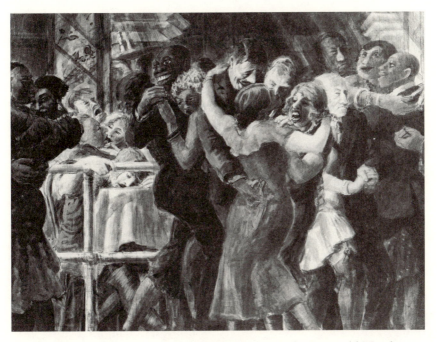

3. *Tuesday Evening at the Savoy Ballroom* (1930) by Reginald Marsh
(tempera on panel)

Saloons served many functions during the later nineteenth century, and not just as places for imbibing alcoholic beverages. Political activities and patronage transactions occurred there, as well as the organization of community assistance for those in need. The social dynamics of saloon life are indispensable to an understanding of what was most distinctively participatory about popular culture in its prime. From providing a venue for playing cards to planning for the next local election, saloons were a major focus of community life, despite the disapproval of Carry Nation and the Woman's Christian Temperance Union starting in the 1890s.[16]

Around 1910, just as saloon culture was starting to decline in respectability, larger American cities began to show a rapid increase in the number of dance halls. The so-called "taxi-dance halls" had been associated with vice and the availability of sexual services; but the newer, brighter commercial dance halls were perceived as a relatively safe environment in which to meet strangers away from the prying eyes of chaperones. Obviously, the principal activity at dance halls could not have been more participatory and interactive. (See fig. 3.) In small-town America, even in the heartland where churches exercised considerable power over social mores, square dancing and newer forms of social dancing enjoyed immense popularity straight through the age of swing in the later 1930s and World War II.[17]

Cabarets did *not* meet with local approval in smaller communities; but in large cities they provided an intimate space that encouraged performer-customer interaction. Comedians recruited or assimilated unsuspecting members of the audience into their acts. Singers circulated among the tables, mainly in order to increase their tips but thereby bringing the audience into greater contact with the performer.[18]

This was also the takeoff time for Tin Pan Alley, the commercial source of new popular music widely disseminated through the sale of inexpensive sheet music. Around 1885, music publishers had begun to produce sheet music for home use; and by the turn of the century, pianos started to be manufactured in large numbers and at affordable prices, so that increasing numbers of people could play and sing at home. Prior to the advent of radio and quality phonographs, purchased sheet music meant someone playing the piano while others gathered around to sing, or perhaps even dance. In rural America communal singing became an immensely popular pastime, especially at church suppers but in totally secular settings as well.[19] By the 1920s annual production of phonographs rose dramatically, but the quality of their sound was still not very good.

Between 1905 and 1920 Billy Sunday sped athletically out of Iowa and became the most popular urban evangelist in American history prior to Billy Graham. Sunday required that a special tabernacle be built in every city where he conducted a revival; and, equally important, he insisted upon interactive cooperation among all the churches co-hosting his stay in a particular city. His revivals were notably participatory because every member of his ad hoc congregation was urged to "hit the sawdust trail," that is, make a decision for Christ, walk forward to the stage, and shake Billy Sunday's hand. Moreover, his revivals provided a prime example of broad-gauge consumer culture because at the back of the tabernacle commercialized religion ran amuck: sales of tracts, signed photographs of Sunday, revival memorabilia, gospel sheet music—the whole gamut. Evangelical religion as popular culture was a thriving enterprise between the 1890s and the 1920s.[20]

I suspect that quite a substantial portion of middle-class and affluent America had very affirmative feelings about religious revivals and church-related activities, but especially with the working class in mind. The Lynds have a notably striking observation that pertains to "Middletown" from the 1890s through the 1930s. One interviewee told them that "it is desirable to *spend* leisure *profitably.*" Therefore, they conclude "that group welfare is measured in terms of money prosperity; and that too much leisure for the 'common man' is to be feared as deleterious to his character and retarding to the welfare of the whole group."[21] The business class wanted to keep the working class occupied, decent, and orderly.

Rereading *Middletown* also serves as a healthy reminder that from about 1910 until the 1930s the automobile was so much of a novelty that a popular and common leisure activity for more affluent Americans was simply taking a local ride to no particular destination. Most "common" men and women could not afford a car until well into the 1920s; but for those who could, the auto meant that two to six people might enjoy an exuberantly interactive experience. Going somewhere by car meant doing spontaneous things along the way. And auto-camping began to enjoy considerable appeal during the 1920s. The numbers were not yet vast, but the venture was proactive and participatory. The Lynds also show us, persuasively, that most leisure activities in middle America during the 1920s took place in groups, with dancing and playing cards (especially bridge) topping the list in terms of appeal to what they call the "business class," meaning the higher social echelon. By 1926–27 moviegoing had begun to make serious inroads in attendance at lodges, saloons, and union meetings.[22]

Despite these perceptible shifts in popular culture, however, the Lynds offer a warning against overemphasizing the nature and pace of change. The newer forms of leisure, they note, "must be viewed against an underlying groundwork of folk-play and folk-talk that makes up a relatively less changing human tradition. Middletown has always delighted in talk. . . . Much of its leisure time it spends in talking or listening to talk." And talk, of course, is supremely interactive—unless it takes the form of a monologue. People did listen to the radio quite a bit, especially by the mid-1930s when most folks owned one, an activity that has been described by many (though certainly not all) scholars as passive.[23]

The Lynds' allusion to "folk-play," which may sound rather vague to us, is actually quite meaningful. The sending of valentines, for example, started to enjoy great popularity in the mid-nineteenth century. When commercially printed cards became available, traditionalists voiced their criticism that "Cupid's manufactory" was being neglected. They felt strongly that authentic valentines should be hand-made.[24] Turning to a very different illustration, Thanksgiving Day football games emerged in the 1880s and 1890s as a ritual, swiftly joined by the highly participatory Thanksgiving Day parade prior to the game. It was local; it was not electronic; it had spectatorial as well as interactive aspects.

The persistence of regionalism, both in reality and in marketing strategies, provides yet another significant distinction between popular and mass culture. Early in the twentieth century, for example, department stores, chain stores (such as they were at that time), and mail-order houses started to organize the flow of large quantities of merchandise. They engaged in advertising on an unprecedented scale, yet even the largest department stores remained fundamentally local or regional entities.[25]

Casual or light reading, an important aspect of popular culture, also underwent notable changes during the late nineteenth century, partially owing to changes in technology, to new assumptions about communication and its audiences, and to the initial stirrings of enthusiasm for celebrity. (*Photoplay* appeared in 1911, the first movie fan magazine.) As newspapers increasingly became sources of entertainment as well as basic information at the turn of the century, decades before the advent of radio and television, reporters developed much more visual and even auditory styles of writing that barely have any counterpart in popular journalism today. In a sense they anticipated the sports broadcaster on the radio during the 1930s and 1940s who had to recreate for his listeners an entire baseball game on the basis of limited information received by telegraph.[26]

As we have already noted, the number and accessibility of popular magazines increased dramatically during the first decades of the twentieth century. The *Illustrated Daily News* began to appear in New York in 1919, featuring large photographs, short news stories written in punchy prose that emphasized crime, sex, movies, and sports. The very first tabloids, the *Graphic* and the *Mirror*, soon followed. But New York City was not representative of the nation at large. Consequently, these were tantalizing foretastes, but not as yet the norm. Far from it. Be that as it may, according to the advocates of reader response theory (and also what is called appropriation theory), reading is not necessarily a passive activity, especially when popular literature is being consumed. Richard Hoggart, Michel de Certeau, Janice Radway, and others have insisted that readers project all sorts of personal ideas into what they read. They do more than simply receive and absorb messages. They invest themselves. That often appears to have been true in the United States.[27]

III. *The Pivotal Decade: The 1930s*

I regard the 1930s as the pivotal decade because it was the last one when popular culture as I have defined it remained the centerpiece of American social life—already encroached upon but not yet supplanted by mass culture as we now know it. For the range of reasons why I believe that is true, let us continue for a moment with reading. One of the Lynds' most intriguing discoveries when they revisited Muncie, Indiana, during the Great Depression is that reading increased sharply in hard times. Using very precise circulation figures for books borrowed from the public libraries, they found that people read less during the affluent twenties and much more during the grim thirties. In part, of course, people read more when there is enforced leisure; but also, borrowing books from the public library is a free, or very low-cost, entertainment. In any case, public libraries played an enhanced role in American popular culture during the 1930s.[28]

We also know that pulp confession magazines enjoyed the peak of their popularity during the 1930s. Moreover, the pulp formula proved so attractive and successful that more genteel magazines subsequently picked it up and adapted it to the taste of their own readers. In *True Story, True Confessions, True Romance, True Detective,* and then even in *Harper's* and *Atlantic Monthly* by the mid-thirties, personal problem-solving became an appealing, highly anticipated staple. Tales of passion were paramount: romance, rape, murder, and revenge; but occasionally there would also be narratives with social as well as human interest. A prime example is Robert E. Burns's *I Am a Fugitive from a Georgia Chain Gang!,* which first appeared as a serial in *True Detective Mysteries* in 1931 and was partially based upon authentic documentary material.[29]

The Book-of-the-Month Club, created in 1926 to increase consumer demand for books and fill a need caused by the paucity of bookstores in the United States, distributed promotional literature that claimed getting and reading these carefully chosen selections would make a person more attractively interactive and therefore more participatory in any social setting. Just knowing about such important new books could improve a person's public performance. Moreover, the subscriber would even become an active participant in shaping contemporary culture! Critics of the club, on the other hand, usually self-styled highbrows who were appalled by these kinds of attempts to commodify traditional culture, declared that such schemes only encouraged passivity and were bound to cause a decline in taste among the reading public.[30]

Still other critics castigated book clubs as well as their customers on grounds that would become commonplace several decades later: contributing to the dastardly phenomenon of standardization. "The reader who takes advantage of this innovation in bookselling," one critic wrote, "will be adding to the process of standardization which has invaded every department of American life." Henry Seidel Canby, chairman of the Book-of-the-Month Club's selection committee, offered a withering rebuttal to anxious snobs who believed that the United States was "being fed a standardized education from standardized text-books by teachers so standardized that a breach of the conventions of doctrine may lead to penalties." "Standardized" became a favorite smear word for those who disdained middlebrow culture.[31] The debate persisted for decades, but without any resolution. The advent of comprehensive mass culture in the 1950s and '60s, however, gave those who loathed standardization a much larger target: lowbrows as well as middlebrows.

Other prominent aspects of popular culture during the thirties enjoyed particular attractiveness because of their low-to-minimal cost, such as gardening, for example, which achieved great appeal and stimulated the dramatic increase in garden clubs, primarily among women. The passion for well-defined hobbies in the 1930s ranged from mah-jongg at the start of the decade to the jigsaw puzzle craze in 1932–34 (a time-consuming family pursuit), to roller-skating and bicycling by 1933–34, to bingo at church socials, to Monopoly which Parker introduced in 1935, to contract bridge, to social dancing, dance marathons and kissathons (to win money). As Warren Susman has summarized the era: "The 1930s was *the* decade of participation and belonging."[32]

When the Lynds revisited Muncie in the mid-thirties, they remained very impressed by the thriving nature of club life there, especially women's study clubs, and by the fact that while club life was stratified, it did include people from all walks of life and social groups. By 1935, moreover, the Community Fund made possible a wide range of athletic programs, a hobby show, a doll show, a pet show, handicrafts, group singing, and training in dramatics as well as theatrical productions. The Lynds regretted that listening to the radio seemed to have supplanted the extensive communal singing that had once characterized assorted social occasions and family reunions. Muncie had very few radios in 1925, many more by 1930 (46 percent of all homes), and near-saturation by 1935. They concluded that "radio is now almost entirely a passive form of leisure in Middletown." More recent studies suggest that by the later thirties Muncie was highly representative in that respect.[33]

Nevertheless, perceiving and defining the role of radio in American cultural life is exceedingly elusive, in part because the medium's reach as well as the variable responses it generated changed so swiftly. National networks did emerge—NBC in 1926, CBS two years later, and Mutual in the mid-1930s—yet purely local stations continued to thrive during the 1930s and even the 1940s. We know that by 1930 radio reached about twelve million homes, yet there is no consensus whether that figure seems modest or impressive. We do know that sales of radios dropped precipitously during the early thirties and that the advent of cheap radios, affordable by almost everyone, did not occur until the mid-thirties. Even more important from our perspective is the contested issue of passive listening versus active engagement. One partisan who wrote for radio during the 1930s and '40s offered this perspective: "The thing that you were able to achieve in radio was involvement. Participation. Because you didn't have all the pieces to the puzzle. The person coming to the radio set had to bring some of the pieces to fill in."[34] As we have just seen, however, not everyone agreed.

Moreover, the first ever taped program on network radio did not occur until 1946 (Bing Crosby's *Philco Radio Time*), fully a quarter century after radio began. So long as radio remained live, it offered a sense of intimacy, particularly if the program had a live audience, which was common until well after World War II. Despite the sheer size of the listening audience, live broadcasts created at least an illusion of intimacy: the voices were speaking to *you* in your home. That feeling kept radio at least partially within the realm of popular culture.[35]

By 1935 a large number of radio stations were affiliated with national networks. One cannot avoid acknowledging that after fifteen years radio had become, at the very least, a proto–mass culture phenomenon. We can specify in particular ways how its imperatives differed from those of popular culture. A touring vaudeville routine was good for a year; the performers repeated the same acts in one place after another. A single radio program, by contrast, was obsolete after one performance. (Summer reruns developed later and became cause for complaint.) And the perceived passivity prompted by certain radio programs marked yet another element in its preview of mass culture. A 1938 advertisement in *Life* for listening to radio stressed its convenience because the listener could stay at home and enjoy a play rather than going out to a theater, hear an orchestra without going to a concert hall, or listen to a religious service without having to dress for church or see anyone. The advertisement emphasized convenient inertia and the absence of human interaction as virtues of radio.[36]

The claims of advertising, however, did not coincide with everyone's actual experience. In such a large and heterogeneous society, monolithic responses to nationally accessible media would have been improbable. "The real split in movie audiences," according to numerous critics, "was not between mass and class [lowbrows and the elite] but between *active* and *passive* viewers. The active viewer saw, took in, responded. Whether his final reaction was pleasure or disgust, he knew he had been through something. The passive viewer responded with nothing."*[37]

Clearly, one's perspective on the advent of mass culture and the degree of interaction it inspired depends on where a person is situated in time. By the end of the 1930s, obviously, radio did not stand alone with its large and growing audience. Cinema enjoyed immense popularity also, and so did syndicated comic strips: Buck Rogers (1929) in science fiction, Mickey Mouse and Blondie in 1930, L'il Abner (1934), Donald Duck (1936), and then Tarzan, Little Orphan Annie, the Gumps, and Dick Tracy. Every child and many an adult couldn't wait for tomorrow's paper in order to find out what would happen next.

Soon after television arrived in 1948, however, perspectives changed and the impact of radio seemed less impressive than it had a dozen years earlier. By midcentury the revolutionary impact of television made the influence of radio pale by comparison. "In radio,"

---

* It has recently been argued that silent film theaters, 1905–20, were "filled with talking, yelling, fighting, singing, and lots of laughter. . . . Neighborhood theaters were not like churches or museums where people spoke in hushed whispers. They were boisterous social centers in which multiple messages could be heard." Steven J. Ross, *Working-Class Hollywood: Silent Film and the Shaping of Class in America* (Princeton, 1998), 24–25.

remarked the shrewd comedian Fred Allen, "even a moron could visualize things his way; an intelligent man his way. It was a custom-made suit. Television is a ready-made suit. Everyone has to wear the same one." Uniformity and conformity seemed maximized in response to television as a mass medium. No one had said that about radio because in retrospect it possessed a diversity (and perhaps a vitality) not present in television. Writing in 1951, Arthur M. Schlesinger, Jr., put it this way: "We have had the mass media of entertainment for a long time now, the radio for a generation and movies nearly two; but it has taken the rise of television to drive home in a frightening way the implications of mass communications for our culture."[38]

Film, radio, and then television emerged in sequence, each one a little more than twenty years farther along. The careers of many popular entertainers and forms of entertainment spanned all three. Consequently, it is interesting to note that some of them made a series of successful transitions from one medium to another, thereby enhancing popular culture to levels that appealed even more broadly. Eddie Cantor, Groucho Marx, Orson Welles, and soap operas come to mind as examples of highly successful adaptation patterns. For others, however, making only one transition turned out to be impossible, though for diverse reasons. "Amos 'n' Andy," Fred Allen, symphony orchestras, and amateur performers had enjoyed immense appeal on radio, but none succeeded on commercial television.[39]

Each medium had its own social dynamic and required its own distinctive style of presentation. Curiously enough, the men who ran network television did not seem to realize that initially and assumed, for example, that popular radio programs would not require a revised type of presentation for a visual audience. They gradually learned, but often it required several years with sad costs in wasted talent and disillusioned sponsors. That is why quite a few cultural critics who had been enthusiastic supporters of what they called "the lively arts" during the 1920s, meaning popular culture, became disappointed or disillusioned with the mass media (mostly television and film), and raised their voices to express growing concern about the "great audience" becoming an excessively passive audience. Even Marshall McLuhan acknowledged that our "presence" in the electronic age is a fact of "passive rather than active experience."[40]

Serious concern about television (as the ultimate mass medium) causing Americans to become passive and increasingly isolated from one another was first expressed during the 1950s and has persisted ever since. Studies by social scientists of the impact of television on family life found that relationships became less interactive. People might sit in the same room but often did not really connect with one another. As children grew older, they became more likely to watch silently, or even in separate rooms. Writing about family life and television, Lynn Spigel emphasizes the privatization of leisure and entertainment. Watching programs on weekend evenings meant a "night out at home." As an authority on soccer has written after watching global telecasts of a World Cup championship competition: "today the stadium is a gigantic TV studio. The game is played for television so you can watch it at home." Critic Robert Hughes has lamented "passive submission to the bright icons of television, which come complete and overwhelming, and tend to burn out the tender wiring of a child's imagination because they allow no re-working."[41]

All of which must seem very familiar by now; but what has not been recognized explicitly is that concerns about passive responses to entertainment and the uses of leisure have increased incrementally over the past hundred years. Audiences for classical music in the later nineteenth century had attentiveness imposed upon them, which is not the same thing as passivity. Others, however, lamented that the massive increase in church membership early in the twentieth century encouraged the congregation to be passive. The service was regarded as a professional performance that showcased the power of the minister and choir rather than participation by the congregation. In 1932 one clergyman asked: "Are we going to become a nation of spectators . . . ?"[42]

In 1927 Aldous Huxley, who eventually emigrated to the United States in 1937, published an essay in *Harper's* in which he ascribed an increase in passivity to technology in general and to the pervasiveness of machinery in particular.

> It removes man's incentive to amuse himself. In the past when people needed recreation they were compelled to a great extent to provide it for themselves. If you needed music you had to sing or play an instrument. If you wanted a pictorial record of some person or scene you had to draw and paint. If you lived in a village or out of the way town and wanted drama you had to act, yourself. To-day you need do none of these things. You turn on the gramophone or the radio when you need music; you click

your Kodak when you want a picture; you go to the village movies when you want drama. Recreation is provided ready-made by enormous joint-stock companies. The play-instinct, which found active expression in the past, is now passive.[43]

An ailment called "spectatoritis" was first designated in 1932, though it is not clear whether it appeared as a result of unwanted free time because people were unemployed and had excessive leisure or because going to the movies had acquired such appeal. Around the same time complaints were also voiced that jazz was meant for dancing, yet it had become a concert phenomenon, in some venues at least, for passive listening. In 1934 a critic commented that George Gershwin "now composes to be heard, not to be sung. He is lucky because we are becoming a nation of listeners, thanks to the radio." By 1946 Seldes's lament about a transformation that he had witnessed during the previous fifteen years reached a popular culture audience via *Esquire*, a men's magazine too expensive for the masses. He disliked the way pop music was being styled by the entertainers in search of distinctive identity. "There was a time when our popular songs seemed to be like us," he wrote. "That time ended when people stopped singing songs and began to listen to them."[44]

By the 1950s such expressions of concern about the coming of mass culture and its impact upon human initiative and engagement with others became commonplace in American discourse, articulated at all levels, ranging from interviews published in *Life* to elegant essays composed by the leading literati. In 1952 Allen Tate declared that the man of letters "must discriminate and defend the difference between mass communication for the control of men, and the knowledge of man which literature offers us for human participation." Dwight Macdonald's litany throughout the fifties insisted that what he called "Midcult" as well as mass culture both increased American passivity rather than creativity, and contributed significantly to the growth of consumerism as well.[45]

Following the Great Debate during the 1950s concerning the negative consequences of mass culture, a dialogue that persisted into the early sixties, several observers and critics came forward to defend ordinary Americans against the harsh litany of complaints about their passivity. Almost without exception, however, these writers have been journalists, sociologists, literary critics with a professional investment in reader response theory, or apologists for American advertising who passionately insist that advertising is neither manipulative nor primarily responsible for consumerism. James B. Twitchell, for example, believes that advertising has created a "conversation" in which consumers are on an equal footing with sponsors and the consequence is a "generative human activity."[46]

But there have been equally vigorous responses to such claims. Herbert I. Schiller, an expert in communications and commerce, offers this reaction to the modern situation when mass culture undeniably dominates: "The audience does count. But not in the way the active-audience theory explains. The managers of the cultural industries are acutely sensitive to the moods and feelings of the nation's many publics. It is their job, for which they are paid handsomely, to make day-by-day, if not hour-by-hour, assessments of these feelings. When they are mistaken, as they frequently are, they lose their jobs."[47]

As a historian, I find three considerations missing in the writings of those who are reluctant to accept that passivity has shown a steady increase with the advent of mass culture. First, by failing to make historical comparisons, they lack any gauge with which to measure change over time. Take as just one example of what gets overlooked this account of the truly active audience early in the twentieth century when vaudeville (and popular culture) was in its prime:

> When Eddie Cantor appeared at a 1908 Miner's Bowery Theater amateur night, the gallery gods shouted, "Take the muzzler off! . . . Go to work you bum!" And when he won them over, "there was a rumble of stamping feet, shrill whistling, and a thin shower of coins that pelted the backdrop and rolled toward the gutter of footlights. This was their way of applause, with leather, metal and siren shrieks; they scorned the effeminate clapping of hands." Losers were yanked off with a long hook. At the end of the show the survivors were lined up on stage, and the master of ceremonies walked down the line, holding a five-dollar bill over each performer's head. The one who received the loudest applause won the money.[48]

Second, participants in this "dialogue" concerning passivity fail to acknowledge that "passive" can be used in several different ways. In relation to high culture it may mean nothing more than decorum, for example, not talking while a symphony or an opera is being performed. Passivity in relation to mass culture, however, customarily implies a lack of initiative, undiscriminating acceptance of mediocre films or programs, escapism and the isolated privatization of leisure time. Even *Life* magazine, hardly a hostile critic of mass culture, published the results of an inquiry at the onset of commercial television showing a marked decline in alternative forms of relaxation, ranging from automobile driving to nightclubbing, from reading to filmgoing.[49]

A third consideration that is commonly ignored concerns the degree of genuine diversity within radio and movie audiences. The most meaningful distinction may very well be between active and passive audiences for a particular medium rather than between lowbrow and elite—the latter a lingering distinction from the era of Van Wyck Brooks that has lost much of its viability. The American public has not shifted during the course of this century from being entirely empowered to being altogether passive. Any claim for such a complete transformation would be simplistic. As one observer remarked of radio during the 1930s, "as soon as he buys his set" any listener has the potential to become a critic, "tuning out this, tuning in that, preferring, disliking. . . . What he says is law." As John Erskine put it, "radio is the easiest of all the arts to walk out on." When James Agee wrote his astute film criticism during the 1940s, he declared that Hollywood's "worst mistake was in its persistent catering to the passive audience; the one that goes and goes, but is equally empty of enthusiasm or indignation. . . . Hollywood is neglecting its active audience and catering hardest to the habitual, passive audience which does it least good, and will be the first to desert it for television."[50]

I shall return to this sharply contested distinction between agency and passivity in chapter 8, devoted entirely to mass culture since mid-century. Here it may be sufficient to acknowledge my belief that popular culture and proto-mass culture co-existed and overlapped during the 1930s and '40s. The latter was gaining strength, a broader public, new marketing strategies (such as the paperback revolution), and technological breakthroughs that vastly expanded simultaneous viewing audiences across the nation (such as the coaxial cable in 1951 and later satellites and cable television). Next, however, we must ask what has become of popular culture after its heyday ended in the 1940s.

IV. The Persistence of Popular Culture

Popular culture as I have perceived and designated it certainly did not disappear following World War II. (Indeed, the term "pop" as a casual allusion to popular culture did not appear until *after* the war.)[51] It may have been gradually surpassed in quantitative terms (audience size, modes of communication, dollars spent, etc.), but it retained its distinguishing attributes and vitality during the middle third of the twentieth century and has persisted beyond that, especially in rural and small-town America as well as in some suburban areas. I have in mind such exemplars of enduring popular culture as county fairs and flea markets; dish-to-pass suppers at community centers and the fellowship halls of churches; local theatrical groups who make an immense effort to delight their neighbors rather than turn a profit, though each successful production helps to make the next one possible; quilting groups; military re-enactments obsessed with authenticity; farmers' markets; the renaissance of interest in local history and historical societies; square dancing and folk dancing; bluegrass festivals; sacred harp singing (a fascinating mode of organized spontaneity); and the passionate involvement in high school football and basketball games, where so many devoted supporters attend every single game, at home and away, come rain or come shine.

In 1947 the United States had 18,500,000 participants in 33,000 bowling leagues. Many Americans also bowled competitively for their lodges or clubs (Elks or Kiwanis). *Life* proclaimed that "bowling had become a way of life." A year later bowling emerged as a $200-million-a-year sport. *Life* considered it "the most popular participant sport" in the United States. The primary reason was not the lure of tournament championships or prize money, but sociability, friendly competition, and team spirit for people of almost any age. Leisure time at baseball games and beaches also perpetuated forms of entertainment that enjoyed great appeal during the postwar years. In the 1940s and '50s, a passion emerged among young males who did not blandly accept the automobiles produced by Detroit. Instead, participants in the "hot rod" culture actively redesigned, redecorated, and in some instances even reengineered cars to suit their own sense of display and their needs for racing. The ethos of hot rod culture at midcentury, according to one writer, was not passivity but commitment "to labour, to strive, to plan, to exercise skill, to compete, to succeed, to risk." A book titled *Best Hot Rods* (1953) exemplifies this ethos throughout.[52]

Middlebrow culture, moreover, expanded its base and its audience dramatically as educational levels rose and leisure time increased. In 1941 the *Saturday Review* had a very modest readership of 23,000 and had to be heavily subsidized by an "angel"; by 1961 it had become one of the nation's leading magazines in advertising revenues and was taken over by the McCall Corporation. By that time cultural centers of various kinds were opening all over the United States, in communities large and small. Editorials appeared in mass and popular magazines praising "the new role for culture" in the United States. Recordings of classical music sold surprisingly well, as did serious books in soft-cover editions.[53]

This trend agitated a self-styled upper-middlebrow writer like S. J. Perelman, who directed his wicked satire in 1961–62 against the apparent (widely noted) American obsession with "getting cultured." He told an interviewer that "it seems incumbent on everyone to express themselves in words and paint." Perelman's play *The Beauty Part* opened late in 1962 and revealed a degree of snobbery on his part that seemed out of touch with the expansive democratization of culture. Perelman's snide vision of an unsophisticated country scoffed at Americans as ignorant culture vultures. One critic called attention to the author's "acidic scorn for society's debasement of art and culture into bogus fabrications of their pure selves. In Perelman's vision of culture-consuming America, the acclaimed artist is he who prostitutes his principles to become a pseudo-artist. Success descends not on the creator of pure art, but on the dilettante practitioner of pseudo-arts, like interior decorators and designers, and on the cultural scavengers like agents, editors, and producers who batten off the talents of true creators."[54] Despite some favorable notices from critics, the play closed in 1963 after only eighty-four performances. It was the wrong message at the wrong time.

It is readily assumed that mass culture has grown exponentially since the 1960s, and that is correct. But the less recognized (certainly the less written about) reality is that the audience for middlebrow and popular culture has also grown. Who attends all of those blockbuster exhibitions at art museums, listens to a diverse range of radio stations, and is grateful that several decades ago the Federal Communications Commission (FCC) demanded that radio and television devote specific amounts of time to public interest programs? The network moguls were certainly not happy with that requirement at the time.[55] When the philosopher Abraham Kaplan wrote his "Aesthetics of Popular Culture" in 1966, he carefully insisted that his subject lay in between highbrow and lowbrow, and that popular culture had yet to achieve its greatest potential. The popular arts, he explained, "may very well appeal to a mass audience, but they have characteristics that distinguish them from other varieties of mass art, and distinctive patterns of presentation."[56]

I believe that Kaplan was correct; yet the irony is that by the time he wrote those words, numerous observers and authorities had begun to emphasize a very different development: what they called the collapse or the blurring of taste levels in the United States. We turn to that development next, noting as we do so a benchmark observation made by Gilbert Seldes in 1953. He commented that Americans had come to regard entertainment as a right rather than a privilege, the latter meaning something that had to be earned. They assumed that amusement should be continuously on tap, rather than a reward for diligence in the workplace, the community, and the domestic sphere.[57] Having a television set in virtually every American home by the end of the 1950s did much to legitimize such expectations. For that reason, I view the transformative impact of television on American uses of leisure as more important than that of any other medium or technological innovation.

5

Blurring the Boundaries Between Taste Levels

∞

I. The Deceptive Appearance of Increasing Stratification

In February 1949 Russell Lynes, the managing editor of *Harper's* magazine, published an essay in *Harper's* called "Highbrow, Lowbrow, Middlebrow." Its subtitle engaged the reader directly: "Which are you?" Mildly satirical and tongue-in-cheek though it may have been, the article aroused immense interest. Readers of this middlebrow magazine took the piece seriously to the point where they began to speculate about the configuration of their own taste preferences, and the reasons for those preferences. However humorous or facetious Lynes intended to be, he said enough about the attitudes of people at any given level toward those at other levels to seem convincing. Or at least to seem that he had the courage of his convictions. And the essay conveyed sufficient common sense and sociological "truth" to be regarded intently by anyone so disposed. Lynes remarked, for example, that "only the lowbrows can be found in about equal percentages at all financial levels."[1]

Life magazine, ever attuned to trends in public interest, produced a feature two months later that not only summarized Lynes's bemused conclusions about American taste, but captured a huge public for his views by doing what *Life* did best: making an event or an issue into a highly visual and visible phenomenon. Designer Tom Funk drew a broad two-page "chart" that classified and exemplified the public's taste levels in everything from clothes, entertainment, and drinks to

4. *Russell Lynes* (1949)

reading, phonograph records, and games (fig. 5). Lynes cooperated in this amusing exercise because he had supplied a few of these examples in his essay, but not forty-four of them arranged in eleven categories.[2]

The popular impact of *Life*'s article, and especially its spreadsheet, surely exceeded anyone's expectations because for many months to come it seemed that the favorite parlor game in the United States, or topic of conversation at parties, involved people asking one another about their taste preferences in order to pigeonhole them at a particular brow level. Moreover, the essay and its chart prompted a fair amount of introspection. If I actually prefer bourbon and ginger ale to a very dry martini, or musical extravaganza films to legitimate theater, am I really the sort of person that I thought I was? Are my tastes consistent with my educational background? With my social aspirations?

In addition, people could converse forever, it seemed, about Lynes's conclusions. Was it true that highbrows disliked middlebrows and their tastes, yet enjoyed many of the lowbrow's preferences? Lynes specified jazz as an enthusiasm shared high and low, which may have been a miscategorization, but that is not the crucial point here. He prompted speculation. Was it true that the lowbrow was really tolerant of the highbrow, "whom he regards as somewhat odd and out-of-place in a world in which people do things and enjoy them without analyzing why or worrying about their cultural implications"? Between Lynes's original essay and *Life's* pictorial rendition of it, Americans living through the Age of Anxiety (W. H. Auden's phrase) now had a distraction from nuclear anxieties to social amenities.

During the early summer of 1949 the nationally popular television program *Kukla, Fran, and Ollie* devoted an entire installment to a dialogue about taste levels (brows) in the United States. In May 1950 Vassar College offered a carefully planned performance of dance, music, and caricature concerning "Lowbrow, Middlebrow, Highbrow." And in October 1952 the erudite Bergen Evans hosted a television program on which Lynes discussed the distinguishing characteristics of his "brow people" with etiquette expert Amy Vanderbilt and anthropologist Willard Park. Intended to be facetiously serious, it succeeded.[3]

Lynes had not merely captivated the national imagination, he had apparently touched a sensitive nerve. He thereupon wrote a series of closely related essays which appeared sporadically over the following eighteen months: "Intellectuals v. Philistines"; "The Age of Taste"; and "The New Snobbism," which became a slim and amusing tome called *Snobs: A Guidebook to Your Friends, Your Enemies, Your Colleagues and Yourself* (1950).[4]

One of the most striking features of Lynes's "Highbrow, Lowbrow, Middlebrow" essay from early in 1949, however, is that he actually divided Americans into four rather than just three levels of cultural stratification. He differentiated the middle group into upper and lower middlebrows, casually referring to them both as "pests," a pejorative label that he may have borrowed from Virginia Woolf's 1930s essay "Middlebrow," a wicked diatribe in the form of a letter to the *New Statesman* that she never actually sent but that was published posthumously in 1942.[5] The significance of Lynes's unprecedented quadripartite scale is that it made American taste levels seem more stratified than ever before and also made the levels look more discrete and compartmentalized than ever before.

In so doing, Lynes received reinforcement during the early and mid-1950s from cultural critics like Dwight Macdonald, Clement Greenberg, and many others who poured out numerous essays, most of them more strident and opinionated in tone than Lynes's work, proclaiming that, indeed, the United States was plagued by multiple taste

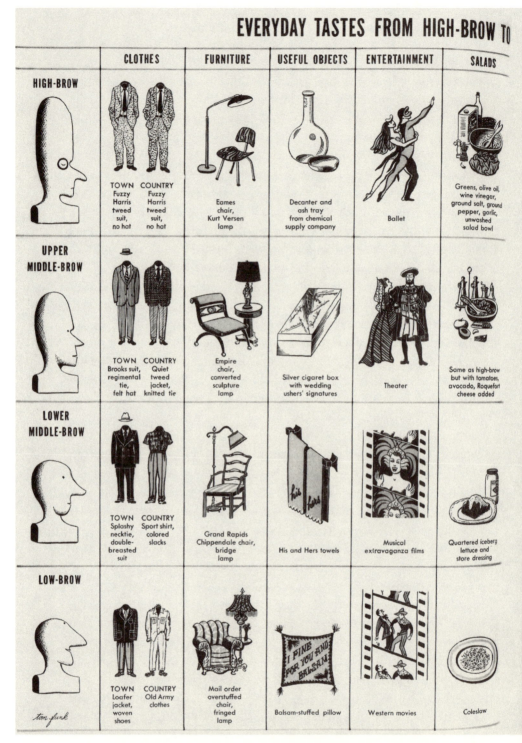

5. Taste-level chart drawn by Tom Funk for *Life* magazine,
April 11, 1949, pp. 100–1

DRINKS	READING	SCULPTURE	RECORDS	GAMES	CAUSES
A glass of "adequate little" red wine	"Little magazines," criticism of criticism, avant garde literature	Calder	Bach and before, Ives and after	Go	Art
A very dry Martini with lemon peel	Solid nonfiction, the better novels, quality magazines	Maillol	Symphonies, concertos, operas	The Game	Planned parenthood
Bourbon and ginger ale	Book club selections, mass circulation magazines	Front yard sculpture	Light opera, popular favorites	Bridge	P. T. A.
Beer	Pulps, comic books	Parlor sculpture	Jukebox	Craps	The Lodge

levels, each of them problematic in its own way. Greenberg, at least, made the following acknowledgment:

> "Highbrow," "middlebrow," and "lowbrow" are terms of brutal simplification. Nor were they coined to denote types of culture so much as types of social personality, and all three in an invidious sense—as if any kind of personal culture were a foible, and all the more a legitimate object of ridicule because revealed in one's physiognomy. But I am afraid that no other terms available fit the realities I am trying to deal with as well as these three. And the reader, I feel sure, will understand immediately what they mean, and at the same time realize that the distinctions they make are not hard and fast ones.[6]

Other writers were more willing to indicate that the distinctions really did reflect social and cultural realities, and therein lies a major anomaly in this entire narrative, because in actuality the distinctions among American preferences, and among the options available to them, were starting to be less stratified and less clear-cut by midcentury rather than more so. Just when Russell Lynes and so many other observers were emphasizing ladders and scaffolds of taste, abundant evidence shows that the ladders were insecurely positioned and the scaffolds precarious.

There seems to be a fairly broad consensus, encompassing people with otherwise divergent perspectives, that ever since midcentury, and especially since the dominant role of television became evident around 1960, cultural stratification and the existence of distinct brow levels have become blurred where they haven't been overtly blended. Some cultural critics, like John A. Walker (who is British but writes about the Anglo-American scene), are fairly cautious on this point. "Although it may seem at times that cultural hierarchies, such as highbrow, middlebrow and lowbrow, have broken down altogether," he writes, "this is not the case. It is simply that the situation has become more complex and that a more sophisticated analysis is needed to explain the relationships between styles, tastes and economic factors."[7]

Arguments for ignoring the conventional distinctions, however, can be found as early as 1948, when Sidney Finkelstein wrote about jazz in the context of international rather than exclusively American music. He rejected the high/low dichotomy (which invariably pegged jazz as lowbrow) and criticized the nostalgia of jazz critics who try to limit the work of popular musicians to the realm of folk practices, ignoring the influence of classical music upon them and vice versa.* Marshall McLuhan, writing in 1964, was the first prominent critic to reject systematically the customary categories in a way that caused a wide range of readers to take notice. Writing about changes in the phonograph, both its technology and its audience, he said:

> When a medium becomes a means of depth experience the old categories of "classical" and "popular" or of "highbrow" and "lowbrow" no longer obtain. . . . When l.p. and hi-fi and stereo arrived, a depth approach to musical experience also came in. Everybody lost his inhibitions about "highbrow," and the serious people lost their qualms about popular music and culture. Anything that is approached in depth acquires as much interest as the greatest matters. Because "depth" means "in interrelation," not in isolation.[8]

By 1975, the sociologist and cultural critic Daniel Bell was sounding a chord that echoed through many minds and texts written by others. He felt that the rapid growth of cultural homogeneity marked a new "crisis of consciousness" in the United States.

> We have become, for the first time, a common people in the hallmarks of culture. Even the old distinction of "highbrow" and "lowbrow," which Van Wyck Brooks installed sixty years ago and which was pursued so vigorously twenty years ago by Dwight Macdonald . . . has lost its meaning today. Are *M*A*S*H* and *Nashville* highbrow or lowbrow? In fact, neither: they are Middle America mocking itself in the accents of the highbrow and the lowbrow.[9]

I will return to sentiments of that sort in section four of this chapter and once again later in the book. We have already seen the ways in which popular and mass culture can overlap and interpenetrate one

---

* In a widely noted 1933 essay in the *Daily Worker,* Marxist critic Mike Gold had rejected jazz as too bourgeois and asserted that a proletarian revolution needed music like Beethoven's!

another's presumptive spheres. With the passage of time and developments after the 1930s, in fact, their spheres become less and less discrete. So chronological distinctions are immensely important in the history of blurred or collapsing taste levels, and in this chapter we will pay special attention to nuances of timing—acknowledging nevertheless that students of American culture in the twentieth century do not agree over matters of timing.

Finally, the reader should note that as we take an overview of cultural blending in modern American history, we can find it prominently evident in the early and middle nineteenth century, and then once again in the later twentieth century. Charles Willson Peale's museum in Philadelphia, the first in America, was open to all and was patronized by all. Norman Vincent Peale (a very distant relation), and a key figure in the popularization of religion in the United States during his ministry at Manhattan's Marble Collegiate Church (1932–84), was also an ecumenical figure whose appeal cut across brow lines in much the same way.[10] Although our story may seem cyclical, then, the reasons why cultural stratification was less important early on and then again more recently are not the same. They range from the conflict between elitism and a democratic ethos in earlier years to the impact of mass media, heightened social mobility, and the general increase in both leisure time and disposable income, as we shall see.

II. Perceptions of Persistence in Taste Levels

We must begin by acknowledging the historical persistence of perceptions that distinct cultural audiences existed from the 1850s to the 1950s, and that the diversity of those audiences can be found in what they were willing to acquire in the way of entertainment. In the mid-nineteenth century Nathaniel Hawthorne, discouraged by his modest sales compared to the broad appeal of such writers as Sarah Josepha Hale, Fanny Fern, Maria Cummins, Susan B. Warner, Mary Jane Holmes, and Augusta Jane Evans, complained wistfully about the commercial success of "a d——d mob of scribbling women." A generation later, when Edward Eggleston sought to produce serious historical volumes about the American past, he too gave vent to his frustration at the undeserved success of mediocre popularizers.[11]

Our most sophisticated historian of burlesque in the later nineteenth and early twentieth centuries, Robert C. Allen, carefully calls attention to those situations when popular and high culture converged, yet his story is primarily one of stratified tastes and divergent audiences in the half century following 1870. Moreover, he shrewdly uses such designations as bourgeois culture and working-class commercial culture in order to connect cultural stratification more meaningfully to differences in class, affluence, and moral values.[12]

When George Seldes wrote his autobiographical narrative of a very long and distinguished career in American journalism, he recalled his apprenticeship years in Pittsburgh from 1909 to 1916. How did it happen that he was able to get opening-night tickets for the farewell appearance of Sarah Bernhardt, universally regarded as the world's greatest actress? No one else at his newspaper wanted them. "In those journalistic days everything damned by the word 'highbrow' was the subject of laughter in the city rooms of all seven papers, the word 'culture' was pejorative, the word 'art'—in a city that held an international exhibit every two years—joined four letter unprintable words. Not one evening paper in my time ever mentioned a book."[13]

During the early 1930s, when Walter Winchell achieved fame as a gossip columnist who seemed oblivious to customary standards of good taste and criteria for genuinely significant news, drama critic and radio pundit Alexander Woollcott proclaimed it "the Age of the Two Walters" because the trashy Winchell and the elegant Walter Lippmann were emblematic of a divide between patrician journalism and writing that pandered to the lowest common denominator. As Winchell's biographer has explained, "because he both effected and symbolized the changing of the cultural guard in this century, examining his life enables us to understand better the challenge that mass culture issued to high culture in America."[14]

Writing about the 1930s and '40s, the historian Gary Cross is attentive to the complexity of change during those decades. On the one hand, large-scale production and increasingly national networks of communication tended to reduce the distance between high and popular culture in reality. Yet the more that appeared to be happening, the more self-styled guardians of high culture either went into self-imposed isolation or else determined to uplift mass taste. Intellectuals like Clement Greenberg and Dwight Macdonald fought a losing battle against advertisers and media entrepreneurs to perpetuate cherished markers between high- and lowbrow boundaries even as they were becoming more and more permeable. Stephen Whitfield likes to point to the 1956 marriage of Marilyn Monroe to Arthur Miller as a notable symbolic turning point when high culture and popular culture quite literally were joined. The marriage may not have endured, but the convergence became ever more apparent.[15]

The sheer celebrity status of Miller and Monroe reminds us that irrespective of historical time and circumstance, there are at least three kinds of provocations that have accounted for popular appeals that cut across all taste levels, and celebrity is only the most recent. The first and most important is creative genius capable of conveying messages that are at least multiple if not universal. Productions of Shakespearean plays in antebellum America come to mind. So do Charlie Chaplin films in the first three decades of the twentieth century, and then Walt Disney cartoons and feature-length films during the next three decades. Chaplin and Disney offered something for everyone and their art was appreciated at all levels, including the most arch highbrow critics.[16]

The third provocation is sheer curiosity. The 1913 Armory Show of post-Impressionist (and mostly European) art may have scandalized the art critics, but it attracted large and diverse crowds to the 69th Regimental Armory in New York: actors and musicians, butlers and shopgirls, even schoolchildren. On the night the show closed before moving on to Chicago, an artist who was present observed that "it was the wildest, maddest, most intensely excited crowd that ever broke decorum. The huge Armory was packed with the elite of New York—and many not so elite." D. W. Griffith also successfully combined innovative genius with sheer novelty. As a consequence he expanded the class range of film enthusiasts in the United States. A medium that began primarily as a working-class phenomenon broadened its appeal steadily after 1915. Griffith had as much to do with that expansion of interest and patronage as anyone.[17]

Finally, the elaborate municipal pageants that enjoyed widespread local appeal during the first decades of the twentieth century owed much of their success to civic aspirations and pride, but also to a carefully contrived blend of elite, popular, and ethnic cultural forms. Percy MacKaye, one of the most creative and successful pageant masters, specifically designed the St. Louis pageant of 1914 for the widest possible audience, but because he relied excessively upon allegorical elements, the pageant was perceived as "highbrow." Pageant masters soon learned that an excess of symbolism would diminish the attractiveness of their dramatic creations. The most successful pageants combined potentially contradictory considerations in order to reach the widest possible audience: progressivism *and* antimodernism, traditional civic religious ritual *and* the promise of artistic innovation. Above all, evocations of a common past, however spurious, could dissolve social and cultural barriers among local residents, thereby "triggering the release of their underlying emotions and the revitalization of their overarching civic commitments."[18]

Before moving on to a closer look at the process of blurring boundaries between high and popular as well as popular and mass culture, we should recognize that during the past quarter of a century efforts to keep recognizing cultural strata as necessary and viable classifications have mainly come from academic scholars and cultural critics, but for diverse professional reasons. The Popular Culture Association was founded in 1967, for example, by teachers and writers disaffected from the pervasive appeal of intellectual history (the history of ideas) during the previous thirty years. It seemed too elitist because it ignored the cultural lives and tastes of ordinary Americans.

When Herbert J. Gans, a liberal sociologist, published *Popular Culture and High Culture* in 1974, he sought to be as nonjudgmental as possible. Hence this declaration of nonpartisanship presented explicitly in the guise of a value judgment: "that the evaluation of any taste culture must also take its taste public into account, that the evaluation of any item of cultural content must be related to the aesthetic standards and background characteristics of the relevant public, and that to the extent that all taste cultures reflect the characteristics and standards of their publics, they are equal in value." Well, that's remarkably neutral, but equally notable because as late as 1974 a shrewd analyst like Gans was trying to subdivide discrete "taste publics" more categorically than Russell Lynes had done in 1949. In retrospect, that marks Gans as even more of a maverick than he seemed twenty-five years ago.[19]

Writing an interpretive overview of the 1940s and '50s, the historian John P. Diggins made an interesting and in several respects persuasive distinction between an optimistic popular culture and a pessimistic high culture during those decades; and he ascribed the latter, especially, to the archly critical role of refugee intellectuals like

Adorno and Horkheimer. Diggins's emphasis on optimism, however, seems to have ignored the Age of Anxiety syndrome that persisted after 1946/47, and his ascribed pessimism seems to have bypassed the rather inclusive and surprisingly sanguine 1952 symposium in *Partisan Review*, "Our Country and Our Culture." Nevertheless, what matters here is that Diggins in 1988 was still stressing stratification rather than conflation or the blurring of taste levels. For more than a decade now, moreover, custom-oriented critics like Hilton Kramer have been very outspoken about the need to maintain standards, which means perpetuating the protection of high culture from the philistine contagions beneath it.[20]

Others who do not share the historical or polemical positions of Diggins and Kramer have simply looked at a particular genre, like novels about the American West, and wondered about the viability of traditional distinctions between high and low art. Still others, attracted by the theoretical possibilities of poststructuralism for cultural analysis, have resonated to suggestions like this one from Hayden White: "The linguistic model provides us with a basis for dissolving the distinction, hierarchical and essentialist in nature, between high culture on the one side and low, folk, or popular culture on the other. This distinction, as long as it exists as a value judgment rather than as a simple description of a distinction peculiar to literate cultures, or civilizations, precludes the possibility of a genuine science of culture."[21]

Near the end of this chapter we shall return to observers in recent years who do not doubt that traditional distinctions among cultural strata have collapsed almost beyond recognition.

III. Diminishing the Distance Between High and Popular Culture

Blurring the lines between high and popular culture is actually an old and by now familiar story in Europe. In his persuasive work on eighteenth-century France, for example, Robert Darnton not only minimizes the distance between patrician and plebeian culture, he also does not choose to differentiate between folk and popular culture. The Italian historian Carlo Poni has observed that while popular culture in Italy (seventeenth to the nineteenth centuries) had its own sources and autonomous traditions, there continued to be a great deal of interaction and mutual influence between elite and popular culture. In Georgian London, 1780 marked the first year that debating societies left their semiprivate, clublike sites. Their new settings were large commercial venues, seating up to twelve hundred people, where men and women could come to speak and listen, enjoying an evening of enlightened entertainment at a modest price.[22]

It is possible to list countless artists, writers, and composers who are customarily categorized as highbrow, but whose creativity encompassed material from all levels of their society's cultural heritage. Mozart's *Magic Flute*, for example, strikes a remarkable balance between the high tradition of classical music and staging designed to be attractive to a popular audience. Throughout his career as a poet William Butler Yeats incorporated both the sonnet (a court tradition) and the ballad (a folk tradition), combining them in a manner that he made distinctively his own. Although other societies admired and were influenced by Germanic culture in the nineteenth century, I am aware of no other that went so far not merely in equating culture with high culture (*Kultur*), but doing so almost entirely on aesthetic rather than religious or moral grounds. *Kultur* was defined in terms of beauty, whereas popular culture, the existence of which they acknowledged, was defined in terms of entertainment. That sharp distinction had a clear influence in the Anglo-American world during the later nineteenth century, but it would not have much staying power in the United States after the first few decades of the twentieth.[23]

An influential study of literacy in early modern Europe, from the sixteenth century to the nineteenth, found that as literacy steadily increased, official and high culture penetrated popular culture all the more readily. In the process, illiteracy more rapidly came to be recognized as a social disability.[24] That is an important pattern to bear in mind when looking at the permeability of taste levels in the United States, where the growth and pervasiveness of literacy outstripped the norm at any given time in most nineteenth- and twentieth-century European societies.

Students of early American history have found some striking examples of taste levels either converging or following patterns of behavior set by one another. In Puritan New England, lay and clerical thought corresponded more closely than we assumed a few decades ago. A brotherhood organization like the White Oaks of Philadelphia organized an annual fishery festivity modelled directly on the more elaborate festival celebrated by the gentry of the city. Yet instances such as these exemplified the process of "trickle down" more than they anticipated what I have been referring to as the actual blurring of taste levels.[25]

By the second quarter of the nineteenth century, however, we begin to encounter numerous and striking illustrations of taste publics and preferences that clearly transcended class lines and levels of formal education. The Hudson River school of painting enjoyed broad appeal to the whole spectrum of northeastern society from critical connoisseurs to ordinary citizens. A contemporary who did not belong to that "school," William Sidney Mount, a genre specialist, explained that "it is not necessary for one to be gifted in language to understand a painting if the story is well-told—It speaks all the languages—is understood by the illiterate and enjoyed still more by the learned."[26]

During the 1840s and 1850s, especially, boundaries between modes of performance and public taste levels proved to be extremely permeable. The American lyceum flourished at midcentury, blending elite and popular culture by offering lecturers and subjects attractive to heterogeneous audiences. The line between professional and popular science is also difficult to draw in that time period. And Stephen Foster's songs enjoyed an appeal that not only cut across taste levels but sectional lines of separation as well.[27]

The contrast between Charles Eliot Norton, a Boston Brahmin and self-styled highbrow, and his contemporary Walt Whitman, who wished to contain multitudes, is symptomatic of the wide range of possibilities in nineteenth-century America. Norton once called Whitman "a compound of New England transcendentalist and New York rowdy." It is certainly true that Whitman's poetry mingled images from elite and popular culture precisely because he wished to dissolve the boundaries between taste levels that Norton sought so desperately to preserve. It is especially noteworthy that in mid-nineteenth-century America books were published in multiple formats, variously priced, in order to attract as many audiences as possible. *Leaves of Grass*, for instance, was available in $2, $1, and 75¢ versions.[28]

Even during the last three decades of the nineteenth century, when we are most likely to envision the sacralization of culture in the United States, and consequently a notable degree of stratification, there are numerous instances of lines being blurred between high culture and what later would be called middlebrow. In 1869 an entrepreneur organized a Peace Jubilee in Boston to celebrate the end of the Civil War. A structure large enough to accommodate thirty thousand people was built and prominent instrumentalists and vocalists were hired to perform with an orchestra of one thousand members and a chorus of ten thousand. For its finale, the orchestra played Verdi's anvil chorus with accompaniment from a squadron of firemen beating anvils, and the firing of live cannon. How does one categorize such an event in terms of brow levels or crowd appeal?[29]

When the Museum of Fine Arts opened on the very same site seven years later, Boston's Mayor Cobb predicted that this embryonic museum would become "a favorite resort of the cultured few who find a supreme delight in the finer creations of art; and, what is more important, all classes of people will derive benefit and pleasure from barely looking upon objects that appeal to the sense of the beautiful. Even the least favored and least cultivated persons cannot fail to derive some refining and elevating influences from the sight of beautiful things."[30] That rhetoric turned out to be more fanciful and less realistic than the clientele that actually materialized. Yet the possibility that such rhetoric might even be voiced in 1876 is not consistent with our stereotypical view of patrician-led New England at that time.

Looking toward the close of the nineteenth century, we hear people observing that the brand-new phonograph and its music appealed to all classes in the United States. We find historian Neil Harris noting a "surprising blending of high and popular culture in unlikely places such as Carnegie Hall, the Chicago Art Institute, and the Library of Congress." Harris also points out that John Philip Sousa deliberately created a repertoire that would cut across diverse levels of taste. Reaching "the masses" mattered greatly to Sousa and the symphonic band did, in fact, enjoy a very inclusive appeal. The extent to which audiences blended can also be seen at century's end when tin cans of food, such as Pilgrim strawberries, bore labels on which fine art was reproduced (a picture entitled *Pilgrims Going to Church in Colonial Times*). The label carried no direct attribution, but we have to assume that the success of such an advertisement depended upon some degree of ordinary consumer familiarity with the painting.[31]

We know that William Dean Howells, a powerful arbiter of genteel taste, was an avowed fan of vaudeville. In 1896, moreover, a New York paper asserted that vaudeville enjoyed popularity with the masses *and* the well-to-do classes, "who seem to prefer them to performers of a higher and more serious character." Alexander Bakshy, drama critic for *The Nation*, never doubted the validity of vaudeville as an art form. Mary Cass Canfield, a prominent playwright and drama critic, praised vaudeville and placed it among the great American art forms. Edward Reed, a professor of English literature at Yale, wrote about vaudeville with genuine affection and appreciation.[32]

In 1909, as part of the Hudson-Fulton Tercentenary celebration, New York's Metropolitan Museum of Art put together the first exhibition devoted entirely to Americana, especially the decorative arts and material culture. To the surprise of many, this show became a popular success and attracted large crowds. Those who loaned most of the objects may have belonged to old families and the New York–New England elite, but the audience for that show turned out to be far more inclusive than anyone envisioned. By 1922 the Annual Exhibition of American Industrial Art had some critics pleading with viewers not to snub machine-made art. Going beyond that, some even wanted to eradicate the distinction between fine art and industrial art, a radical notion in terms of traditional taste levels.[33]

The decade of the 1920s witnessed more than its predictable share of audiences participating in multiple taste levels. In 1927 the *Saturday Evening Post* carried a series of articles about collecting rare books, written by A. S. W. Rosenbach, an authoritative snob but also a highly successful dealer. The series achieved immense popularity and brought the *Post* a burst of mail as ordinary readers ransacked their attics for hidden treasures. Recently, moreover, innovative experts on American reading habits have concluded that the content of middlebrow magazines during the 1920s actually leveled up and attracted a goodly number of well-educated readers. That is exactly what Gilbert Seldes not only hoped for, but helped to make possible. He began the 1920s as managing editor of *The Dial*, the most prestigious highbrow magazine in the United States. He genuinely loved popular culture, however, and after publishing *The Seven Lively Arts* in 1924, Seldes left *The Dial* and wrote for *The New Republic* and *The Nation*, but most notably for the *Saturday Evening Post* for five years beginning in 1926. During the 1930s he undertook a monthly column for *Esquire*, a new popular magazine, as well as a daily column for the *New York Evening Journal*. His topics were largely middlebrow, a cut above the average reader of that paper.[34]

The advent of radio during the 1920s contributed to the blurring of high and popular culture as separate taste levels in ways that no one had anticipated. In 1923 David Sarnoff, the presiding figure at RCA and eventually at NBC, eloquently announced that "the greatest advantage for broadcasting lies in its universality, in its ability to reach everybody, everywhere, anywhere, in giving free entertainment, culture, [and] instruction. . . ." During the 1920s more than 60 percent of broadcast time was devoted to music, and a considerable portion of that was classical. In 1925, for example, the Atwater Kent Program provided classical music over a chain of thirteen stations. When NBC made its premiere broadcast in 1926, it mixed classical and popular music in an extravagant production that cost the new network $50,000 but reached an estimated audience of twelve million people. The New York Symphony, the New York Oratorio Society, and several opera stars participated. In 1929, however, *The Rudy Vallee Show*, which gained a very wide audience, made a significant break by avoiding the serious music that had been standard fare for most of the decade. It aimed exclusively at middle-class listeners who preferred popular music.[35]

During the mid-1930s, though, classical music made a remarkable comeback on radio. Although it never regained the high proportion of total broadcast time that it enjoyed in the 1920s, NBC created a symphony orchestra for Arturo Toscanini when he returned to the United States in 1936 following his disillusionment with Mussolini. His programs achieved a large and devoted listenership; some believe that he became a kind of "culture god" in the United States. According to an eight-page spread in *Life* magazine: "Never before in history has man had at his fingertips the gift of so many priceless treasures of music, education, drama," and so on. Edward Bernays, the founder of public relations in the United States during the 1920s, had especially hoped to assemble a multiclass audience for serious music and opera in the United States. It is astonishing how swiftly Bernays saw his dream realized, and creation of the NBC Symphony Orchestra brought it to fulfillment.[36]

During the mid- and later 1930s, most notably in 1937–38, the major networks made a serious commitment to quality dramatic productions for adults. That meant a notable infusion of Shakespeare, but also Victor Hugo, Ibsen, Marlowe, Gogol, Corneille, Tolstoy, T. S. Eliot, and many others. To achieve that goal, the networks themselves had to serve as sponsors, and for a while they were glad to do so. Radio had achieved immense popularity by then and advertising for other programs brought in abundant revenue.[37]

6. *Arturo Toscanini* (1939)
by Herbert Gehr
(gelatin silver print)

7. *Edward L. Bernays* (1984)
by Patricia Tate
(oil on canvas)

The blending of taste levels occurred in other ways and through other media during the 1930s. The films of Walt Disney and Frank Capra captivated moviegoers from all walks of life. Capra's hugely successful 1934 comedy *It Happened One Night*, starring Clark Gable and Claudette Colbert, set the standard for comedies throughout the thirties. It swept the Oscars, appealing to middlebrows especially, but as one critic noted, it pleased "highbrow and lowbrow alike." In that same year an essay in *Woman's Home Companion* noted with delight that Disney "was discovered by the mob before he was discovered by the art world . . . [as] the masses gave a lesson in art appreciation to the intelligentsia."[38]

Meanwhile, Miguel Covarrubias, a brilliant Mexican artist who first came to the United States in 1923, designed an uproarious series of caricatures called "Impossible Interviews." Appearing in *Vanity Fair* between 1931 and 1934, they juxtaposed Sigmund Freud vs. Jean Harlow, Greta Garbo vs. Calvin Coolidge, Martha Graham vs. Sally Rand, John D. Rockefeller, Sr., vs. Josef Stalin, Aimee Semple McPherson vs. Mahatma Gandhi, Huey Long vs. Benito Mussolini, and Eugene O'Neill vs. Jimmy Durante, to cite only some of the most provocative examples. The cleverness of the contrasting personality types and the absurdity of their inconceivable dialogues diverted attention some- what from Covarrubias's ingenious artistry. The appeal of these carica- tures crossed the boundaries between high and popular culture also, in part because one person in each pair represented sobriety and the other one celebrity, or one represented mental creativity while the other displayed impudent beauty. Studies in differentiation, they obliged viewers to violate norms of categorization—at least in these fantasies.[39]

One of the pioneering caricaturists, Al Frueh (1880–1968), had drawn celebrities ranging from grand opera to vaudeville. His draw- ings, which appeared in Joseph Pulitzer's newspaper, the *New York World*, depended for their success on instant recognition. Therefore we have reason to believe that readers recognized Enrico Caruso as well as comedians Weber and Fields. When some of his prints appeared in 1915 at the Salon of American Humorists exhibition, a critic from the *New York American* praised Frueh's work lavishly, "for here is evidence of an intellectualizing process that not only regulates the style but also nerves the humor with ironic vim." Like Covarrubias, Frueh managed to cross boundaries and appeal to viewers whose tastes, according to Van Wyck Brooks's prediction, could never con- verge. As one scholar has observed, "lower art aping higher forms would be a recurrent comic motif in caricature."[40]

In January 1938 the first of two notable turning points took place in the conjunction of popular with high culture. Ever since 1924 Paul Whiteman had presented symphonic jazz in concert, often to large and delighted audiences in venues like Aeolian Hall; but such auditoriums were not considered special; they were notable for their size rather than their distinction as places where serious people went to listen to great music. Benny Goodman received credit for breaking that barrier in 1938 when he performed at Carnegie Hall.* Doing so seized the popular imagination and meant a new degree of respectability for swing and jazz. Moreover, Goodman's orchestra had both black and white musicians, thereby publicly displaying a pattern of reciprocal influence that had long been important to the development of jazz. For

---

* It was not well remembered in 1938 that ten years earlier W. C. Handy had pre- sented a concert of African-American music at Carnegie Hall.

8. Jeanne Gordon of the Metropolitan Opera crowning
Paul Whiteman as the "King of Jazz" in 1926

Goodman's musicians, who were ethnically diverse, to perform with
men from Count Basie's band, one of the great black aggregations of
that era, broke down boundaries once again, adding the racial mix to
the novelty of swing being heard with wild enthusiasm in Carnegie
Hall.[41]

A second notable turning point took place on March 1, 1942, when
Walt Disney spoke to the audience by radio hookup at intermission
during a performance of the Metropolitan Opera in New York. Disney's topic was singular but sweeping: "Our American Culture." He
began with a modest disclaimer: "Dopey is as well qualified as I am to
discuss culture in America." He went on to say that the very word "cul-

9. *Benny Goodman* (1960) by René Robert Bouché
(oil on canvas)

ture" had an "un-American connotation" about it that seemed "snobbish and affected. As if it thought it was better than the next fellow."
That sort of attitude, said Disney, might lead to a form of tyranny
where self-appointed guardians of traditional "culture" could put a
"fence around painting or art or music or literature." In Disney's view,
such elitism was intolerable because culture belonged "equally to all
of us."[42]

In the United States, Disney insisted, easy access to cultural opportunities existed for "rich and poor alike in great abundance" through
radio and the movies, magazines and newspapers, symphonies and ballets, poetry and painting, writing and the diversified world of illustration. Those remarks epitomized the optimism, inclusiveness, and
democratizing impulses of Disney's Depression-era populism. They
echoed the message of *The Seven Lively Arts*, published by Seldes in
1924, and all of his prolific writing thereafter. Thus Disney, a consum-
mate middlebrow, addressed the audience at a high culture event and

told them that a status hierarchy of taste publics was inappropriate for the United States of America.[43]

Blurring of the distinctions between high and popular culture increased predictably in the years following World War II, and what had often remained only hortatory during the previous two decades began to emerge as reality. The war itself turned out to be a remarkable equalizer that attenuated class lines as determinants of taste in foods. A degree of leveling in eating habits occurred, resulting from rising expectations by some, more egalitarian desires by others, but especially from wartime rationing of certain foods. In 1946 all sorts of people concerned with the radio industry began urging "socially responsible" broadcasting—that is, more meaningful programming. They wanted radio to "level up," and they did have FCC support for more broadcasts concerned with public affairs. In a different realm, the invention of the long-playing record in 1947–48 became an important milestone in the merging of high and popular culture. The LP could contain a 25-minute orchestral movement or one of Duke Ellington's extended jazz compositions. The well-received Folkways Anthology released in 1952 meant that what had been the little-known music of the rural poor entered and influenced avant-garde as well as proletarian circles.[44]

Meanwhile, *Life* magazine continued to issue reports for its broad audience on the growing appeal of ballet in the United States, on operas by Gian Carlo Menotti becoming "high brow smash hits" on Broadway, on the release of a film of the opera *Tales of Hoffmann* by a director-writer team who had made a number of movies with high-brow motifs or themes. When *A Tree Grows in Brooklyn* opened as a musical in 1951, *Life* took note of an apparent trend: "Broadway musicals are tackling more dramatic (or even operatic) subjects." Theater in general seemed willing to be concerned with serious issues, and as a consequence audiences were being attracted rather than driven away.[45]

From the mid-1950s onward the blurring of lines between high and popular culture became manifest in additional ways and in unexpected venues. Early in the fifties a few executives at NBC Television decided to inject some "high culture" into their programming, an initiative designated as Project XX. The inaugural venture, immensely successful and durable, was *Victory at Sea*, a twenty-six-part history of U.S. naval action during World War II. Yet even though *Victory at Sea* became the most frequently repeated television series of the 1950s, attracting large foreign and school sales, potential advertisers avoided it and NBC had to consign the program to its Sunday afternoon "intellectual ghetto." NBC shifted in subsequent years to biography (Washington and Lincoln) along with semihistorical portraits of particular decades (the 1920s and 1930s). These achieved a mixed degree of success, revealing considerable uncertainty on the part of the network about the audience it meant to target with historical and nonfiction programs. As Daniel Marcus has observed, "NBC rhetoric regarding Project XX reflected a tension between high culture and mass entertainment—and the network hoped that the series would be perceived as both."[46] That goal swiftly became symptomatic of aspirations for television generally, with inevitable consequences. Whereas *Victory at Sea* managed to achieve appeal at all levels, its successors tried to please several and in the process remained not very satisfactory to any.

In 1954 the noted film critic Robert Warshow expressed his desire to minimize the customary polarity between high and popular. He believed that he could and should do justice to the claims of art and popular culture even though he recognized that those claims did not always or consistently coincide. By 1954 museum attendance per year in the United States reached the astonishing figure of 55 million persons, just about equal to the number of moviegoers per annum, a surprising symmetry. When the *Mona Lisa* was displayed at the Metropolitan Museum of Art and the National Gallery in 1963, the lines of people who waited for hours to catch a brief glimpse broke all attendance records and amazed everyone in the museum world. Then Thomas P. Hoving became director of the Metropolitan in 1966 and brought with him a philosophy that great art should not be the exclusive preserve of a social and intellectual elite. Some of his outreach exhibitions during the later 1960s grew heatedly controversial, either because their subject areas seemed too trendy or because their material scarcely seemed to be art as traditionalists understood it. Be that as it may, attendance at the Met reached six million visitors per year by 1970.[47]

A pivotal moment occurred in the winter and spring of 1963–64 when *Playboy* magazine, in its eleventh year, began to enrich (leaven?) its customary content with a Bertrand Russell interview of India's Prime Minister Nehru and a piece by literary historian and critic John W. Aldridge on the subject of "Highbrow Authors and Middlebrow Books." Essentially an essay on the changing nature of American fiction since the 1920s, it declared that there had been a decline of mid-dlebrow writing (once well represented by Dreiser, Sherwood Ander-son, Sinclair Lewis, F. Scott Fitzgerald, and Hemingway), whereas highbrow fiction seemed alive and well, along with serious criticism. Curiously enough, however, responding to a query in the wake of World War II, critic Leslie Fiedler had anticipated a blurring of taste-level offerings because of a short supply of popular writing:

> The opening of the super-slicks to more serious writing, the flirtation of the *Cosmopolitan* with belles-lettres, the association of large commercial publishers with little magazines, the frantic excursions of editors up and down the countryside are not so much tokens of some radical change of heart, as of an incipient panic at a growing discrepancy between mass production meth-ods of distribution and the low supply of popular literature; publishers and editors, abhorring a vacuum, turn in desperation, if not in love, to the more serious writer. This mild revolution will doubtless increase the pressures toward accommodation as well as opportunities for publication.[48]

That particular explanation of the "mixed media" (or mingled con-tents) phenomenon did not turn out to be the optimal one in the long run, but it indicates the growing recognition that tidy categorizations of packaging for particular taste levels would become less and less appropriate in the future. As John Cawelti put it in 1968, noting the increasingly ambiguous relationship of Americans to culture, "we are confronted, for perhaps the first time in history, with a real and contin-ual choice between such cultural alternatives as the traditional forms and ideals of high culture, the formulas of mass culture, and the com-plex and evasive strategies of the new art."[49]

Meanwhile, the enhanced attractiveness during the 1950s of his-toric site museums like Colonial Williamsburg, Old Sturbridge Vil-lage, and the Henry Ford Museum defied simplistic categorization. One could, I suppose, call them middlebrow; but they spent liberally on research and placed a very strong emphasis upon authenticity and public education. Moreover, by training apprentices in the presenta-tion of early crafts, they encouraged the recovery of older American arts and traditions. It seems meaningless, therefore, to compartmen-talize these historic sites and museums as exclusively elitist or middlebrow or popular culture. Turning to comparable phenomena, by the early 1960s symphony orchestras in the United States gave more sold-out concerts to more diverse audiences than at any previous time; and folk music presentations during the 1960s and '70s occurred just as frequently in concert halls as in coffeehouses. Taste publics had become genuinely intermixed.[50]

On the last day of the 1954 televised hearings involving Senator Joseph R. McCarthy and the U.S. Army, a Chicago dealer in TV sets tried an interesting experiment in order to satisfy his curiosity. He owned a corner store with two windows. In one window he placed a TV set tuned to the hearings. In the other he put a TV set tuned to a White Sox game at a time when baseball fever ran high in Chicago. Despite that fact, only three viewers watched the game while thirty-six jammed the sidewalk to observe the McCarthy hearings. Television sets were not yet universally owned at that time, and repeat coverage in the evening was much less likely to occur than it is today. The results of both events could be read about in the next day's newspapers. Nevertheless, the line between middlebrow and mass culture seemed fuzzy indeed, an important harbinger of things to come.[51]

IV. Bridging the Gap Between High Culture and Low

Bridging the traditional gap between highbrow and middling to lowbrow taste levels developed later than the high/middle or high/popular convergence, and for understandable reasons. High and low started out much farther apart. Moreover, until the years following World War II, going to college (never mind postgraduate education) had not been the norm for most Americans. During the 1930s, however, evidence emerged that highbrows tended to be far more tolerant of lowbrow taste than they were of middlebrow. Note the critic and composer Virgil Thomson's reaction to George Gershwin, expressed in 1935: "I don't mind his being a light composer, and I don't mind his trying to be a serious one. But I do mind his falling between two stools." And note Virginia Woolf's arch pronouncement, written at about the same time. She defined a lowbrow as a person "of thorough-bred vitality who rides his body in pursuit of a living at a gallop across life. That is why I honour and respect lowbrows—and I have never known a highbrow who did not. In so far as I am a highbrow . . . I love lowbrows." In 1949 Raymond Chandler, the prolific American author of detective thrillers, grumbled that "I am at home with the avant garde magazines and with the rough tough vernacular. The company I really cannot get along with is the pseudo-literate pretentiousness of, let us say, the *Saturday Review of Literature*. That sums up everything I despise in our culture. . . ."[52]

Manifold attempts by the mass media, starting notably in the later 1930s, played a major role in calling the arts to the attention of very large numbers of Americans. The actual impact of these efforts is difficult to measure and may not have achieved widespread uplift. But national chauvinism clearly provided an important stimulus. When *Life* magazine presented special features on American art in 1937 and 1938, it did so with a strongly nationalistic tone. It boasted that painting was being pursued more actively in the United States than anywhere else in the world and rejected the view ascribed to foreign critics that "American art is entirely derived from European sources." Quite the contrary, "it is in America, not war-torn Europe, that the world's art future lies."*[53]

A feature story about the rapidly growing interest in music at all levels, but especially classical music, gave special credit to the impact of radio and offered a judgment concerning passivity at odds with several that we have noted earlier. "When radio came," *Life* observed, "it was feared that America would become a nation of passive music lovers, content to listen rather than play. But the rise of classical radio music has been accompanied by a great rise in amateur orchestras." Five months later an essay devoted to the maturation of culture in the United States, especially music and art, commented that so much of this new interest occurred in the realm of high culture. Two weeks after that a feature on amateur theatricals insisted that drama played a key role in American culture and titled one section, perhaps with some hyperbole, "High Schools Going High Brow." One week later, pundit Walter Lippmann had an essay in *Life* titled "American Destiny" which offered high hopes for American culture *if* citizens would only display a more positive attitude toward the importance of enrichment in their lives.[54]

---

* Another Henry Luce publication, *Time* magazine, once reproduced a Jackson Pollock painting upside down. See William Phillips, ed., *Partisan Review: The 50th Anniversary Edition* (New York, 1985), 291.

Following the war *Life* ran a feature entitled "Broadway Goes Highbrow," an upbeat discussion of the revival of classics by Shakespeare, Ibsen, and O'Neill on the Great White Way. For years the chief function of theater had been to provide escapist entertainment. Now, "in a world of confused values, playgoers are more inclined to seek satisfaction in the enduring works of established authors." In 1947 an essay about Martha Graham and her dance company proclaimed that interpretive dance was a highbrow art and an expression of the subtleties of the human mind. Two years later yet another *Life* essay reported that performances by a ballet company in Chicago were breaking all attendance records. Later in 1949, *Life* acknowledged that two ballets were New York's biggest box office hits. Referring to the ballet version of *Carmen*, the essay observed that it "attracted audiences new to ballet but delighted by the lively and low-comedy numbers which made it as easy to take as a Broadway musical." Clearly, highbrow genres had to make major compromises in order to attract a larger and more diverse clientele. But equally clearly, that is exactly what was happening by midcentury.[55]

The reasons why bridging was both necessary and possible varied considerably from one art form to another and from one situation to the next. In 1949–50 James T. Flexner found that his high-toned histories of American art were not selling well in trade editions, so he made a swift and smooth transition to Pocket Books and reached a new and much broader audience than he ever imagined possible. Blurring also occurred for reasons that might be called entrepreneurial/political. During the later 1950s and early '60s the commercial music establishment gave a great deal of reluctant support to recording and promoting folk music. Why? Because its management personally did not like and felt genuinely frightened by rock 'n' roll, especially its "lascivious" lyrics, and because of the unconventional personal lives of some of the leading performers. Without really wanting to, record company executives succeeded in transforming folk music from a left-wing exotic form with limited appeal into a pop culture commodity that by 1965 had reached the realm of mass culture.[56]

During the 1960s the pace of convergence between high and mass culture accelerated. Artists like Andy Warhol and Roy Lichtenstein made mass production both a subject and an object of their work. At that point art and commerce entered into an open, self-aware symbiotic relationship so obvious that Warhol and others could parody the connection with impunity and profit. Where advertising had exploited fine art on labels for tin cans at the turn of the century, now art exploited mass culture (like the comics) and turned mass media and advertising into tools of their trade—a reversal that initially seemed bizarre, but one that we now take for granted. By the 1960s, moreover, many commercial artists had been insisting for quite some time that advertising and commercial culture were themselves legitimate art forms. Some declared that an ad could be just as authentically impressive as a painting or a statue.[57]

During the 1960s *Television Quarterly* (Journal of the National Academy of Television Arts and Sciences) intensified the ambiguity between art and industry by publishing speculative articles written by such prominent people as André Malraux and Richard W. Jencks, president of the CBS/Broadcast group, on topics like "taste" and "the meaning of culture." By the later 1960s the commercial networks were scrambling (once again—a reprise of the mid-1950s) to produce "serious" programs in museums around the world: the Louvre, the Hermitage, and so on.[58] These documentaries in living color promoted the museum as an icon, as an emblem of nationalism and of national treasures. It would not be long before pop appropriations of notable artworks, like *The Scream* by Edvard Munch, became overworked clichés. Nor would a student of this trend be surprised when the "Three Tenors" (Pavarotti, Domingo, and Carreras) provided a musical spectacle in 1990 at the World Cup soccer games in Rome. High culture at the Caracalla Baths! The recording of that concert sold more than ten million copies, the video more than a million. The event had such appeal across all taste levels that the Three Tenors combined again in 1994 at Los Angeles and then once more in 1998 at Paris. Who is to say whether the high had been coarsened and made low, or that philistinism had expropriated elite culture? By the close of the twentieth century that had become a moot point.[59]

Ever since the 1920s, actually, there have been cultural critics who lament this process—what Dwight Macdonald called in 1945 "that present-day tendency toward a merging of commercialized culture and serious (or 'high-brow') culture." William Phillips and Hilton Kramer have perpetuated the tradition of deploring that conflation in our own time.[60] Theirs is a minority position, I believe, though the majority is not intellectually cohesive and does not offer a clear alternative. Look at the range of related but divergent responses. In an interview that she gave in 1975, Susan Sontag was asked whether it was useful to draw a distinction between "the cultural elite" and "the instinctual mass." She responded with a firm no, insisting that the distinction "is a vulgar one. By ignoring the difference between the descriptive and prescriptive senses of culture, it can't give a properly specific meaning to either. There are several senses in which 'culture' doesn't equal 'elite.' (Anyway, there are elites—not one, but many.)"[61]

A year later, Daniel Bell sounded wistful yet resigned in a statement whose tone is more than simply descriptive:

> High art itself is in disarray, if not "decadent" (though that term has never been adequately defined); the "public" is now so culturally voracious that the avant-garde, far from needing defenders among the critics, is in the public domain. The serious critic, then, must either turn against high art itself, thereby pleasing its political enemies, or, in John Gross's phrase, "resign himself to being the doorman at the discothèque." This is the trajectory of the democratization of cultural genius.[62]

Less than a decade after that, in 1985, Bell's fellow sociologist Herbert Gans sounded the same negative theme but without the rueful tone. He clearly described the declining strength and critical mass of high culture because it seemed "more marginal than ever, becoming a culture almost exclusively of the expert and dominated by cultural professionals: creators, critics, and especially academics. . . . The upper class 'aesthetes,' the self-educated socialist working-class intellectuals, and the Central and Eastern European refugees of the 1930s and 1940s are all disappearing." Replacement did not seem forthcoming to Gans.[63]

It has become commonplace to say that postmodernism, and more specifically postmodern theoretical endeavors in fields ranging from cultural studies to philosophy, have contributed to the decline of cultural authority because these critics and their lodestar gurus do not write in a manner that is readily comprehensible even to educated people who have no expertise or interest in postmodern theory. However valid that may be, we still must provide an explicit elaboration (or validation) for the claim that postmodernism contributes to the blurring or even the flattening of taste levels.

The logical response is not at all obscure. Postmodernism has, in fact, prioritized the need to break down or even reject conventional categories of knowledge or perception. At the very least, most post-modernists prefer to regard the truth of "texts" as elusively relative rather than acknowledge that they somehow possess an objective reality that can ultimately be determined with assurance. Postmodernists delight in mingling categories rather than respecting the integrity of ones that have been handed down from on high. An obvious example might be Andy Warhol moving from an early career in commercial design to one in creative art that made commodification simultaneously the subject as well as an object of his art. Warhol and the many Pop artists that he influenced went a very long way during the 1960s in demonstrating the irrelevance of traditional taste levels in a society that had come to be so dominated and driven by commercial imperatives.[64]

One might say, I suppose, that within academe postmodernist conceptualizations became authoritative—a new neo-orthodoxy if you will. But beyond university circles a tentative awareness of postmodernism has largely served to augment mistrust for cultural authority in general. Ever since the early 1980s, those who work in the subdiscipline called cultural studies have insistently denied that there is any meaningful distinction between high and low culture. Populists with leftist politics affirm this development. Artists create works that challenge us with semifacetious titles like *Is It Still High Art?* By expanding the range of texts, objects, and artifacts considered suitable for cultural analysis because they contain expressive meaning, scholars in cultural studies deliberately blur distinctions between elite and popular but also between "text" and "reality."[65]

Some of these populists seem almost overtly anti-intellectual, others are lost in empyrean clouds of theoretical vapor, but still others are objectively descriptive of major changes that have occurred as commercialization has gradually shrunk what once seemed a firm fabric of cultural garments suitable for diverse clienteles. The heterogeneity of the clienteles may still remain, actually, but the authority of elites has diminished (as we shall see in the next chapter), leaving all participants looking more and more alike because they are now viewing and listening to so many of the same things. The democratization of culture may have diminished diversity in the process of empowering those who once lacked much of a say in what they wanted for their leisure or edification.

At the very least, however, some of the populists lack a sense of history concerning their own predilections. Otherwise they would realize that mockery of the hollowness of highbrow culture and its capacity for pretentiousness could be heard at the very start of the twentieth century. Political orientations have assuredly changed, but the satirizing of highbrow aspirations harks back to the second decade of this century. Such satire, moreover, appeared in middlebrow magazines like *The Century* (1914) and in those a step lower on the status ladder, like *Munsey's* (1911). In the latter instance the mockery was sexist as well. Walter Prichard Eaton, a respected cultural critic, commented that behind the hordes who labor in the arts (a close paraphrase) come the camp followers, the scavengers of culture, the highbrow-hunters—usually women. "The reward of the chase for them is the exhibition at one of their 'afternoons' of a man who has written a play, roasted a play [a critic], painted a picture, or otherwise qualified as 'artistic.' " Eaton then added that "most of these women don't really know anything about art," and he concluded that "there is some hero-worship in highbrow-hunting, no doubt; but there is vastly more vanity."[66]

During the later 1920s and '30s, *Vanity Fair's* monthly "Hall of Fame" page loved to mock the mutual anxieties of high- and lowbrow culture. From the perspective of editor Frank Crowninshield and his remarkable corps of writers, mingling the comic and the serious, the avant-garde and the popular, rendered distinctions between high and low meaningless. From the middlebrow perspective of *Vanity Fair*, mingling taste levels seemed amusing and harmless. Crowninshield, moreover, was convinced that innovation in the popular arts could do much to revitalize more "elevated" efforts. A decade later, radio comedian Fred Allen enjoyed spoofing social respectability and cultural pretensions through his delightful characters in "Allen's Alley." It is noteworthy that Fred Allen was one of the most cerebral of all the great comedians of that era, a secret that he kept very carefully guarded from his public. His intellectual qualities might have killed his mystique as a master comic.[67]

V. Coda: Rejuvenating the Middlebrow's Reputation

The purpose and focus of this chapter have been to demonstrate the steady augmentation, over the past eighty years, of a process whereby the historically touted distinctions between high and popular culture have become less significant than they were, let us say, between 1880 and 1920—a pattern of change that has also emerged since midcentury in the blurred relationship between taste publics for high culture and mass culture.

Just by way of reprise, note that in 1918 Edward Renton's printed guide to running a vaudeville theater reminded his readers that "the theatre draws people from all sorts and conditions; in particular does the vaudeville house draw from both the classes and the masses." By 1923–24 the earliest variety shows presented on radio deliberately mixed all possible levels of entertainment in any single program. Salvador Dalí moved freely between popular culture, with his pavilion at the 1939 World's Fair in New York (Dalí's *Dream of Venus*), and high culture, with his design the very same year for *Bacchanale*, a ballet mounted by the Ballet Russe de Monte Carlo. The Ballet Russe also collaborated with Walt Disney in the dance sequences for *Fantasia* (1940). As a final example, Lynn Spigel has shown persuasively that television played an essential role in the postmodern blurring of high and low culture. Television's presentation of the modern visual arts gradually made it more and more difficult to distinguish between commercial art and high art, a development encouraged by the work of such prominent contemporary painters as Roy Lichtenstein.[68]

The following question then arises: If the distinctions between high and popular culture have steadily diminished, where does that leave the taste level that we have known as middlebrow ever since the 1920s? In a famous essay published in 1960, Dwight Macdonald made an observation that seems to turn my tale inside out. He remarked that the line between Masscult and high culture had been "blurred" by the rise of Midcult (his words and his capitalization).[69]

Well, Midcult—or middlebrow, as most of us call it—has not had countless champions among the cultural critics. Its most ardent devotees, actually, are to be found among the cultural entrepreneurs who are the beneficiaries of all that disposable income possessed by middlebrows. But there *have* been some thoughtful and interesting observations about the important role played by middlebrows in our system of cultural stratification. Here, for example, is what Clement Greenberg had to say in 1953, which is before the blurring of lines became fully evident:

> While the middlebrow's respect for culture may be too pious and undifferentiated, it has worked to save the traditional facili-

ITEM	HIGHBROW	HIGHLOWBROW	MIDDLEBROW	LOWBROW
TV	Nova	Twin Peaks	Bill Moyers	Studs
City	Trieste	Baltimore	Houston	Tulsa
Nighttime reading	Yellow Silk	Men's Fitness	Playboy	Juggs
Simpson	Lisa	Bart	Marge	Homer
Willie...	Mays	Sutton	Wonka	Smith
Hairy Creature	Yeti	Bigfoot	Sasquatch	Sam Kinison
Brunch music	Messiaen	Kronos Quartet	Gershwin	Pachelbel
Pop music	Elvis Costello	Deee-lite	Madonna	Metallica
Observer	Safire	Miss Manners	Keillor	Buchanan
Feathery cartoon figure	Daffy Duck	Road Runner	Tweety Bird	Dan Quayle
Participant sport	Fencing	Bowling	Jogging	Monster trucks
Spectator sport	Chess	Bullfighting	Football	Monster trucks
Mouse	Art Spiegelman's	Apple computer's	E.B. White's	Walt Disney's
Beefcake	Connery (as Bond)	Seagal	Schwarzenegger	Van Damme
Cheesecake	Iman	Divine	Claudia Schiffer	Jessica Hahn
Norman...	Thomas	Bates	Lear	conquest
Jackson	Shoeless Joe	Jesse	Michael	Action
Sgt.	Shriver	Slaughter	Bilko	Schultz
anti-...	disestablish-mentarianism	vivisectionism	pasto	freeze
Initials	EEC	JFK	AAA	KKK
Tea	Lapsang souchong	Long Island Iced	Earl Grey	Mr. T
'80s phenomenon	Reagan	Reagan	Reagan	Reagan

10. Taste-level chart from *The New Republic*, March 2, 1992, p. 26

ties of culture—the printed word, the concert, lecture, museum, etc.—from that complete debauching which the movies, radio, and television have suffered under lowbrow and advertising culture. And it would be hard to deny that some sort of enlightenment does seem to be spread on the broader levels of the industrial city by middlebrow culture, and certain avenues of taste opened.[70]

In 1992 an unusual and unexpected defense of middlebrow culture appeared in *The New Republic*, written (tongue-in-cheek?) by a contributing editor to *Vogue* and *Esquire*, and therefore an advocate with a real stake in middlebrow. The essay brings us full circle in this chapter because, like Russell Lynes's essay in 1949, this one also included a chart in order to make its categories very explicit—and also presumably to assert (against the grain of our time) that categories of taste really do matter (fig. 10). Comparing the two charts may give us a sense of difference and change between 1949 and 1992. The lead category in 1992 is preference in TV programs; TV was not a category at all in 1949. Other new categories in 1992: City, Brunch Music, Pop

ITEM	HIGHBROW	HIGHLOWBROW	MIDDLEBROW	LOWBROW
TV	Nova	Twin Peaks	Bill Moyers	Studs
City	Trieste	Baltimore	Indianapolis	Oklahoma City
Nighttime reading	Yellow Silk	True Detective	Playboy	Juggs
Simpson	Lisa	Bart	Marge	Homer
Feathery cartoon figure	Daffy Duck	Road Runner	Tweety Bird	Dan Quayle
Participant sport	Fencing	Bowling	Jogging	Monster trucks
Spectator sport	Chess	Bullfighting	Football	Monster trucks
Tea	Lapsang souchong	Long Island iced	Earl Grey	Mr. T
Car	Volvo	Gremlin	Honda Accord	Trans Am
Pet	Pug	Ferret	Golden retriever	Penthouse
Snack	Scones	Tater Tots	Brie & Bremer wafers	Cheez Whiz
Romantic getaway	Crete	Niagara Falls	Hawaii	Orlando
Kids' names	Paige/Carter	Max/Lucy	Jason/Stephanie	Roseanne/Tom
MC	Squared	Bob Barker	Escher	Hammer
Addiction	Sex & drugs	Vintage clothing stores	Sex & drugs	Sex & drugs
Dessert	Poached pears	Jell-O	Cheesecake	Jello-O & Cool Whip
Collection	Rare first editions	Elvis	Stamps	Beer cans
Drug	Ginkgo	Ecstasy	Advil	Tums
Pilgrimage	MOMA	CBGBs	Lake Wobegon	Graceland
Spiritual pilgrimage	Tibet	Divine's grave	Vatican City	Medjugorje
Designer label	Donna Karan	Bobbie Brooks	Liz Claiborne	Frederick's of Hollywood
Pop music	Youssou n' dour	Deee-Lite	Neil Young	Ozzy Osbourne
Brunch background music	Haydn	Kronos Quartet	Pachelbel	NFL Game of the Week

Adapted with permission from The New Republic (March 2, 1992)

11. Taste-level chart from *The Utne Reader*,
September–October 1992, p. 83

Music, Observer, Participant Sport and Spectator Sport, and Tea.
Present in 1949 but gone by 1992? Clothes, Furniture, Salads, Drinks,
Sculpture, and Causes.[71]

The Utne Reader was sufficiently bemused by Tad Friend's 1992
chart to produce its own hilarious adaptation six months later, keeping
some of the *New Republic* categories but adding Favorite Car, Pet,
Snack, Romantic Getaway, Kids' Names, Addiction, Dessert, Collection, Drug, Pilgrimage, and Designer Label (fig. 11).[72] The game of
pin-the-label on the brow level goes on; but the categories are infi-

nitely expandable and spoofable. It's not clear whether that is because our imaginations have been enlarged or our range of entertainments has expanded.

"The Case for Middlebrow" by Tad Friend is hostile toward "culture guardians" like Dwight Macdonald who did, indeed, heap scorn upon middlebrow taste back in the 1950s but had become uncommon and fairly toothless by 1992. Friend does make a useful distinction between high art, which is "work of complex passion," and highbrow, which is "merely a stance of complexity. It imputes and then fetishizes difficulty for its own sake, as a way of asserting cultural superiority over the less learned."[73]

Why does middlebrow deserve to be rescued? Why does it not deserve condescension? Because, says Friend, it entertains and educates, "pleasurably training us to appreciate high art." It is accessible, unlike highbrow objects of esteem, and it prompts without embarrassment such inescapable emotions as sadness and joy. Middlebrow also "reconnects the intellectual with the emotional. It provides some unity in a culture where political, social, and intellectual fragmentation is now the norm. To neglect middlebrow is to deal yet another blow to a civilized and informed discourse, one in which we can all participate and have some clue about what everybody else is talking about."[74]

All of which is fine. I can enjoy many of Friend's middlebrow pleasures without despising highbrow or needing to somehow recategorize as middle what customarily has been deemed high. But ultimately, I believe, Friend helps to reinforce this chapter's point about blurring. First when he acknowledges, at the outset, that "lowbrow has never so mesmerized the masses or carried such highbrow chic." Right. Having conquered, why *not* stoop? Hence our modern propensity to merge high and low. And second, Friend discards Lynes's fourth category, upper-middlebrow and replaces it with his own fourth category. He calls it highlowbrow, "in which highbrow condescendingly co-opts low."[75] I'm not sure that the co-opting does not happen the other way around. But in any case, Friend helps to make my point. An amount of mixing has occurred that few would have imagined two generations ago.[76]

Reliable confirmation of that comes from none other than Russell Lynes. In 1976 the soon-to-be defunct *Washington Star* asked him to write a kind of postscript to his still-famous 1949 essay for *Harper's:* what had changed and what, if anything, had remained constant?

Lynes's comments provide strong confirmation that brow levels had become much less significant after twenty-seven years, despite the fact that *taste* levels had not disappeared entirely. They just did not correlate very clearly with social status, levels of education, or affluence. The Lynes postscript follows in its entirety.[77]

A 1976 COMMENTARY*
by Russell Lynes

In the nearly 30 years since "Highbrow, Lowbrow, Middlebrow" was published, the highbrow has changed his costume and his whiskers several times, the middlebrows have hared off after a succession of "ops" and "pops" and "Decos" and "Mary Hartman" (twice), and the lowbrows have found Archie Bunker and CB radios and game shows with which to amuse and identify themselves. The lines of my arbitrary categories have become even more indistinct than they were in 1949. But, I believe, the basic pattern still has some validity, or, if not the pattern, at least the underlying bed of nails, which is taste. The adaption [*sic*] and exercise of taste will, I expect, always be a serious social game as long as taste is regarded as a guide to status and people are convinced that there are durable standards of "good taste" and that "bad taste" is what their inferiors have.

The highbrows in the 1950s, you will recall, had a rather rough time of it. It was the decade of the McCarthy investigations, of Adlai Stevenson's two defeats as a candidate for President, and, perhaps, worst of all, the arrival of television—a symbol of mass middlebrowism. It was, moreover, the era of Sputnik I and the shocked clamor for more scientific training. While that incident ultimately gave a good many intellectuals an improved bargaining position, it was not the humanists, the preceptors of taste, who benefited. The Eisenhower years did not supply the highbrows with the opportunities that the election of Kennedy seemed to offer, if only briefly. And, despite Lady Bird Johnson's efforts to continue to hold high the torch of culture, her husband was barely tolerant of what highbrows considered her well-intentioned flirtation with the arts.

* From the *Washington Star*, Oct. 24, 1976, sec. F, pp. 1, 4, and the *Wilson Quarterly*, 1 (Autumn 1976), 158–60. Reprinted with the permission of Mrs. Mildred Lynes and the *Wilson Quarterly*.

During the 1960s it was fashionable to take note of "the cultural explosion." Vastly expensive cultural centers burgeoned in cities across the land, and it was generally agreed that culture was good for the community and hence good for business. Culture, you might say, was regarded as civic Geritol. Community theaters popped up like toadstools, many with the beneficence of the Ford Foundation. Established art museums were crowded as never before; new ones appeared by the dozens, and commercial art galleries multiplied at a rate almost as breathtaking as the prices of the wares in which they dealt. High in the Berkshires (the home of Tanglewood, Music Mountain, Jacob's Pillow), where I was born and which used to be dairy country, there were suddenly more violinists than there were cows, or so it seemed.

The highbrows found all this confusing. Obviously they could not oppose public enthusiasm for the arts, at least not to the point of wishing to turn off the faucet that dripped gold into their pockets. They did not want to put a crimp in anything that supported the *avant garde*, though they persisted in passionate disputes about the problems of mass culture vs. high culture. Moreover, they now had to protect their flanks, not just from the middlebrows, but from the activist young, the members of the dissident counter-culture who thought that the highbrows were just as responsible for America's sins as the bankers. Some adult highbrows tried to identify themselves with the young radicals only to discover that they were not wanted and not considered trustworthy. And, since everybody now had beards and refused to dress according to the old rules, how could a poor highbrow tell who were friends and who were enemies, who was serious, who not?

The upper-middlebrows, on the other hand, felt a surge of aesthetic adrenalin. To serve on the board of the local opera company became every bit as socially desirable as being on the executive committee of the Community Chest. If anything, the caste structure of tastefulness that I adumbrated in my 1949 essay became strengthened. In some respects, the line between highbrows and upper-middlebrows became blurred; but the line between upper- and lower-middlebrows grew sharper and more social. As a result, service on the boards of artistic institutions has made new demands on their members. They are not only expected to be made of money (or know where to find it) but to be culturally "hip" as well. Keeping up with what's "in" is as important as being socially "in" oneself, and, now, when the arts change with a rapidity unknown before, being upper-middlebrow involves considerable psychic strain.

As I look at the chart, which a *Life* editor and I concocted over innumerable cups of coffee 27 years ago, it strikes me, as it must you, that what was highbrow then has become distinctly upper-middlebrow today. Who regards an Eames chair as highbrow now? Or ballet, or an unwashed salad bowl or a Calder "stabile"? They have all become thoroughly upper-middlebrow, and what was upper has become lower. Only the lowbrow line of the chart still makes spiritual if not literal sense. Today television would find itself at all levels of the chart in ways too obvious to define. The "pill" has taken glamor out of Planned Parenthood as an upper-middlebrow cause, and Art is now their cause instead, and so on. It is a game anyone can play. Even if the shapes of the pieces have changed, and the board looks quite different, the basic rules seem to me much the same as they always were—and as insolent.

6

Cultural Criticism and the Transformation of Cultural Authority

∞

Cultural expertise as a social force conveyed by people who function as authorities has the capacity to bestow legitimacy or respectability upon a cultural custom or "product" in the broadest sense of those terms. Cultural authority may also embody or manifest cultural power; but authority and power are not exactly the same, and it has not been commonplace for the two qualities to be combined. Cultural power involves the production, promotion, and dissemination of cultural artifacts. Whereas critics and museums, for example, are expected to have cultural authority (and historically they did more often than not), movie studios and advertising agencies are understood to exert cultural power. We cannot put too fine a point on the distinction, however. Organizations and individuals who nominate books, films, and performers for awards and prizes, for example, possess elements of both authority and power.

During the mid- and later Victorian era, Matthew Arnold and his disciples on both sides of the Atlantic associated the designation and legitimization of culture with social authority, that is, the well-established social order and its institutions. They believed that culture (meaning high culture) served as a function of social authority and would help to counteract the undesirable tendency toward anarchy.

Cultural authority is no longer the exclusive preserve of any single stratum of society or type of professional group. There are cultural authorities in the realm of rock music as well as classical music, in the fine arts and in film. With the passage of time, however, significant shifts have occurred. A professional class (or cadre?) of cultural authorities emerged before the turn of the century and by the period, say, 1910 to 1940, such people exercised and enjoyed a very considerable degree of clout. Their numbers included relatively few scholars. For about three decades following World War II, people from academe did enjoy a remarkable amount of visible cultural authority, but that trend has receded noticeably since the 1970s. Meanwhile, ordinary people—the consumers of cultural artifacts—have steadily increased their own cultural authority, especially in the past forty years or so. A film or a rock group or a play (musical or dramatic) may not be well received by critics, yet enjoy considerable success at the box office nevertheless. Moreover, it can also happen that movies admired by the critics may fail to achieve popular appeal. That is a significant aspect of the democratization of culture. Cultural expertise (in contrast to scientific or technical expertise) does not possess the influence that it did earlier in the twentieth century.

What emerged to help supplant cultural authority was more than just a role for public opinion that acquired increasing confidence after midcentury. Sources of cultural power strong enough to make a difference despite their lack of legitimizing authority pushed traditional forms of cultural expertise aside or rendered them far less influential than they had once been. I have in mind the usual suspects: national media (despite being mistrusted by the public), Hollywood, public relations and advertising agencies, large corporations, and even government. These entities, exercising considerable cultural power with very little concomitant authority, profoundly affected the ways in which Americans used their leisure and entertained themselves, especially from the later 1950s onward. When Russell Lynes published *The Tastemakers* in 1954, he had in mind certain kinds of individuals and social groups, particularly critics and persons with a special degree of cultural cachet. Within a decade the determination of what got published and read, whose art was exhibited and purchased, whose music got performed or played on the radio, where tourists went and what they did when they got there, was being made by entities unmentioned in *The Tastemakers*. That is yet another litmus of the transition from popular culture and diverse taste publics before the 1950s to mass culture and more homogeneous taste publics after that decade.

All of which means that, once again, close attention to chronology, to patterns of change over time, is vitally important to our understanding of these issues and developments. So, too, is the scorecard of American arbiters of taste: who acquired influence, who lost it, and why. Finally, we must also factor in the gradual shifts in American attitudes toward authority and power. Why were they more likely to defer to the former in the 1920s than they were half a century later? Why did they feel more manipulated and helpless in the face of power networks by the 1970s and 1980s than they had six or seven decades earlier—all with specific regard to their cultural pursuits? That is our agenda for this chapter.

I. Cultural Authority Embodied and Exercised

It is well known that European visitors to the United States during the second quarter of the nineteenth century were intrigued by a novel phenomenon, social as well as political, that nearly everyone designated by a single word for the sake of efficiency: democracy. Somewhat less obvious, however, was one of the most important developments sustaining democratic tendencies, namely, the leveling of authority. And that really meant political and social authority, for the most part, because cultural authority barely existed as a customary force in American life and had scarcely any institutional embodiment as yet. As the historian Robert Wiebe has phrased it, from a European perspective "the stakes were society itself: who set the rules in public? who had access to public spaces? who had priority there? who could take an initiative? who had the right to choreograph other people's movements (as in parades)? who made decisions about who spoke, about who spoke to whom, about what could be said? Status and manners, in the inclusive European sense of the term, meant power. They controlled the functioning of public life."[1]

By the mid-1850s the fractious nature of American public life, precipitated particularly by slavery, sectionalism, and party fragmentation, left men like Walt Whitman wondering about potential remedies and contemplating as the best solution "throwing off authority" and cultivating "countless breeds of great individuals, the eternal and only anchor of states." In the second edition of *Leaves of Grass* (1856), Whitman observed that man-made laws in the United States had proven to be corrupt. Consequently, he encouraged his readers to regard laws lightly and to follow "inside authority," meaning their own conscience. In such poems as "A Woman Waits for Me" and "Respondez!," moreover, Whitman offered the same guidance concerning social and cultural matters. Do not feel bound by social conventions. Be your own cultural authority. Follow your own gyroscope.[2]

After the turmoil of Civil War and Reconstruction, however, a very different ethos emerged concerning attitudes toward authority and custodians of it—especially in the realm of culture. The major journals of opinion that did so much to define and refine American taste—*The Nation*, the *North American Review*, *Atlantic Monthly*, and *The Century*—were managed by socially conservative men who prided themselves on being prudent arbiters of taste. The likes of E. L. Godkin, William Dean Howells, and Richard Watson Gilder swiftly came to be recognized as pillars of respectability and cultural authorities to be reckoned with. Defining and perpetuating the Genteel Tradition for almost four decades was their bewhiskered, buttoned-up achievement.[3]

That was also an era when socially prominent (though not necessarily elite) women achieved a modicum of cultural authority—some in philanthropy or as patrons of the arts, others in cooperation with clergymen as custodians of domestic life and the moral sphere, most often by means of temperance reform and (along with men) the so-called purity or anti-vice crusade.[4] The Woman's Christian Temperance Union became a genuine force for a full generation after its creation in 1892, as did women like Jane Addams and Florence Kelley in developing institutional networks to assist newcomers and the needy in industrialized America. Women could also achieve recognition as cultural authorities by leading educational institutions or publishing works about the American past, especially in the realm of state and local history.[5]

Mrs. Schuyler Van Rensselaer wrote copiously about the history of New York City, about the history of architecture in the Old World and the New, about painters and painting in all periods. Her hortatory essays are interesting because of their American chauvinism, because she included "household arts," industrial arts, and handicrafts along with her advocacy of the decorative arts, and because of her patronizing effort to make the audience for art in the United States broader and more inclusive. As she concluded one characteristic essay in *Scribner's:* "it is wise to try to develop a public for such artists as may be granted to us. And it is wise to try to . . . increase attentiveness, knowledge, and the sensitiveness that means good taste for the sake of our people as individuals wishing to lead interesting and happy lives."[6]

Judging by editorials and the content of "quality" magazines in the later nineteenth and early twentieth centuries, many Americans sought and valued the guidance of cultural authority. At the turn of the century *McClure's* magazine highlighted the authority of its writers by providing bylines (an innovation) and even biographical sketches of its contributors, including their university degrees, professional positions, and other public activities. A 1914 essay in *The Dial* disparaged the commonplace phrase, "there's no accounting for difference in taste." Such a permissive attitude revealed "our disbelief in intellect and in the importance of rigorous intellectual discipline." Worse still, acceptance of such a view would mean that Americans had "banished authority from our lives"—not a desirable outcome.[7]

Moving down from patrician levels of taste, we find in this same period attempts by the manufacturers of sporting goods to publish authoritative rulebooks and guidelines that would not only regularize athletic competition but require the use of particular equipment. Members of the public who wanted to play "the game" as it was supposed to be played welcomed such guidelines. Turning to a different venue, early in the twentieth century managers in manufacturing situations sought to diminish the "workplace authority of skilled hands while simultaneously increasing on all workers the disciplinary weight of machine-driven jobs, time-motion studies, and piece rates."[8]

Even in the realm of popular entertainment at the turn of the century, theatrical managers and entrepreneurs recognized that the diversity of their urban audiences (and the increased size that they hoped to achieve) required a fairly wide range of acts, some of which would please certain segments of the audience more than others. As one researcher has written of Sylvester Poli, an extremely successful theatrical manager, he "constructed cultural authority out of an intricate network of competing alliances for which his shows' multifaceted 'refinement' provided apt expression." Cultural authority for Poli emerged from his complex relationships with various civic leaders, the public, and the performers themselves. His advertisements for female performers were very carefully worded. "In skirting the border line of social wickedness and weakness," he would write, "Miss Thornton shows that rare ability of touch and sentiment, and withal that artistic delicacy that amount to positive genius. . . ." Poli walked a figurative tightrope that enabled him to appeal simultaneously to somewhat prurient interests as well as respectable ones. He had learned in the 1890s to carefully negotiate multiple meanings of "cultural refinement." Like B. F. Keith and Edward Albee, widely known for the prudish respectability of their distinctive "Sunday School Circuit," Poli remained an enterprising pseudo-cultural authority for successful vaudeville during a fiercely competitive generation.[9]

In the 1920s a remarkable number of entertainment entrepreneurs, many of them immigrants or the sons of immigrants, combined covert cultural authority with overt cultural power in developing Hollywood film studios, radio networks, and entities like the Book-of-the-Month Club (in the case of Harry Scherman), invariably successful because of their savvy in learning to straddle taste levels, a skill that would later be raised to a higher plane of expertise by those who ran mass media from the 1960s onwards. Edward Bernays acknowledged and adroitly finessed a crucial question that had been raised by mass psychology: "where exactly was cultural authority located?" Bernays admitted that "some mysterious alchemy" existed in the relationship between institutional power and popular desire—as historian of communications Steven Smith has remarked, "a vague interchange of elitist leadership modified and responsive to popular wants."[10]

Simultaneously, between 1922 and 1929 Walter Lippmann engaged a comparable issue—the nature, role, and power of public opinion in a democracy—from the perspective of a newspaperman who took his responsibilities as a cultural arbiter very seriously. In 1922, when he published his profoundly influential book *Public Opinion*, he wrestled philosophically with the role of the press as an effective agent of cultural authority.

> I argue that representative government, either in what is ordinarily called politics, or in industry, cannot be worked successfully, no matter what the basis of election, unless there is an independent, expert organization for making the unseen facts intelligible to those who have to make the decisions. I attempt, therefore, to argue that the serious acceptance of the principle that personal representation must be supplemented by representation of unseen facts would alone permit a satisfactory decentralization, and allow us to escape from the intolerable and unworkable fiction that each of us must acquire a competent opinion about all public affairs.

Later in the same very substantial work, Lippmann suggested that "in the present state of education, a public opinion is primarily a moralized and codified version of the facts."[11]

Never before had an American observer or critic considered public opinion itself as a semi-autonomous form of cultural authority. After 1935, when George Gallup established the American Institute of Public Opinion, polling surveys on a wide variety of subjects became commonplace—and gradually more noticed. Polls had not yet become overly influential, as they are today, but John Q. Public began to recognize himself, en masse, as a source of authority to be reckoned with. By the later 1930s, as market surveys and public opinion research accelerated, some social scientists began to worry about the impact of polling on opinion and behavior. What they referred to as "a sense of numbers" could sway convictions and cause people to think less independently. Polls would soon be perceived as more than just a measure of public opinion: they loomed as potential modes of persuasion in themselves.[12]

By 1928 Lippmann had become deeply concerned to curb the power and the authority of public opinion. He found the infamous Scopes Trial of 1925 scary, not because people in Tennessee rejected evolutionary theory in favor of literal belief in Scripture but because the legislature they elected had the constitutional right to determine what would and would not be taught in public schools. Lippmann wondered whether democracy had perhaps run amuck. Could the people really rule themselves? Were majorities truly the best judges of the public good? Perhaps public issues had become too complex for ordinary people to comprehend rationally. In *A Preface to Morals* (1929), Lippmann expressed his grave concern that the new technologies making it possible for popular culture to flourish disengaged facts from their causes and contexts, with the consequence that they are only "half-known." Lippmann must have been deeply dismayed by a 1945 poll in which 3,243 Americans were asked: "If you had to give up either reading the newspapers or listening to the radio, which one would you give up?" Sixty-four percent said newspapers and only 29 percent answered radio.[13]

Lippmann devoted the fifth chapter of *A Preface to Morals* to "The Breakdown of Authority." Basically, he had in mind both religious and governmental authority, because religion no longer enjoyed the universal dominion that it once did and because religious obligations had become less compelling, for example, than patriotism. Taken in the context of his other writings and the secularization of American life in the 1920s, Lippmann certainly intended to depict a crisis of cultural authority quite particular in nature.[14]

Meanwhile, a culture of professional expertise had emerged in the decade following World War I. It was exemplified, in general, by the swift ascent of the social sciences to prominence, and more particularly by Robert E. Park and his disciples in urban sociology at the University of Chicago; by Charles E. Merriam's behavioral approach to political science emphasizing social psychology; by in-depth studies of American communities conducted by the Lynds, W. Lloyd Warner, and other pioneers of an ethnographic approach to the lives and social structure of ordinary Americans. What these scholars shared was an emphasis upon the empirical rather than the theoretical, upon verifiable observations rather than impressionistic generalizations, upon in-depth case studies rather than blithely ignoring the differences that resulted from race, religion, ethnicity, and geographical diversity.[15]

The implications of their expertise had more to do with public policy than with culture as we have been examining it here. But they had exact contemporaries who received recognition as experts in the realms of literature, music, art, and even popular culture. When Stuart Pratt Sherman became the editor of "Books" for the *New York Herald Tribune* in 1924, he disavowed the notion that his new, nonacademic role made him a cultural authority even while he began to perform exactly that role as a literary arbiter. In 1926, when Edmund Wilson wrote his anonymous "All-Star Literary Vaudeville," a widely discussed essay, he observed that Sherman "now occupies what has perhaps become, from the popular point of view, the central desk of authority, to which each of the performers in the all-star circus, from Ben Hecht to Ring Lardner, steps up to receive his endorsement."[16]

In 1926, when Henry Seidel Canby, a professor of literature at Yale, became chairman of the selection committee for the Book-of-the-Month Club, he too achieved national recognition as a preeminent literary authority in the United States. The radio programs that enjoyed broad appeal among middlebrows during the 1930s because they discussed and recommended books to potential readers also received accolades as reliable sources of public authority. Interestingly enough, radio itself became a mode of cultural authority during the 1930s. Why? Public opinion polls taken during the later 1930s showed that thirty million Americans, nearly one adult in three, doubted the honesty or the fairness of the press in the United States. That perception resulted in part from the presidential campaign of 1936 which Roosevelt won in a landslide even though a majority of American newspapers opposed him. People decided that radio broadcasting of public affairs was a lot more reliable than newspaper coverage.[17]

The National Better Business Bureau, established in 1925 as a kind of privately operated Federal Trade Commission, had as one of its major responsibilities monitoring the integrity of national advertising. It could not become a major source of cultural authority, however, because it had no weapons of enforcement. Consequently, it played the role of referee, promoting voluntary codes of professionalism. It also faced a problem in trying to draw a line between borderline transgressions and serious ones: for example, when the American Tobacco Company advertised, "Reach for a Lucky instead of a sweet!" Even at the peak of its influence during the interwar years, the consumer movement consisted of too many disparate groups, ranging from clubwomen to organizations for consumer education to the testing agencies, like Consumer's Research and the Consumer's Union.

Because there have been so many exposures of false advertising, of phony quiz shows with "star" contestants who knew the questions in advance (and the answers), and controversies with so-called experts aligned on opposite sides, deference to expertise is clearly less compelling than it was for almost four decades starting in the 1920s. Nevertheless, striking manifestations persist and nowhere more than in the realm of culture. When an exhibition of photographs by Robert Mapplethorpe at Cincinnati's Center for Contemporary Art in 1990 resulted in a trial of the museum's director for displaying child pornography and for "pandering obscenity," defense attorneys called twelve museum curators as witnesses. Jurors acknowledged after the acquittal that they were persuaded by expert testimony that art did not have to be beautiful in order to qualify as art; and, moreover, that Mapplethorpe's photographs did have artistic merit. Here was a very clear instance where the culture of expertise remained quite potent, indeed, right into the 1990s.[18]

II. Cultural Criticism as Cultural Authority

Cultural critics have had a significant role to play in American society ever since early colonial times, but the kinds of people they were and the kinds of roles they played have changed over a span that is now nearly four centuries. For most of the prerevolutionary era, the role of cultural critic was performed primarily by the clergy. They gave jeremiad sermons warning the society against such evil ways as alcoholism, prostitution, excessive usury, fornication, and violations of the Sabbath. They also preached that only a society in accord with God's commandments would retain a special, covenanted relationship with the Almighty. Equally important, and valid beyond the bounds of cerebral New England, the clergy had expertise in interpreting Scripture, which meant explaining God's ordinances.[19]

During the nineteenth century an assortment of social reformers (especially temperance crusaders and abolitionists), romantic idealists like Ralph Waldo Emerson and Henry David Thoreau, lyceum lecturers and some theologians like William Ellery Channing and Horace Bushnell, served as the most prominent cultural critics. Like the colonial clergy, they had many other social roles to play as well, but their emphasis upon individualism, self-reliance, Christian nurture, and the moral equality of men (occasionally meaning women, too) became central components of the national creed. Critical essays about literature and art were written by people who were themselves professional writers and artists. But cultural criticism per se had not yet become a recognized vocation. It remained for the most part an avocation through the 1880s. Charles Eliot Norton, a conservative New England aesthete, described the office of critic as one of "public instructor." James Russell Lowell called it "a kind of priesthood."[20]

During the four decades from 1880 until around 1920, the first generation of professional cultural critics emerged. They enjoyed an unusual degree of authority because they not only had expertise but were fairly well specialized in broad areas, unlike the dilettantes of preceding generations who made pronouncements on just about anything, some more compelling than others. Thus James Gibbons Huneker in music, William C. Brownell in literature (Matthew Arnold's most ardent disciple in the United States), Montgomery Schuyler in architecture, and Royal Cortissoz in art told Americans what to value from the past and how to appreciate current productions and performances. They had refined tastes and genteel sensibilities. Curiously, however, the best-remembered cultural critic of that generation was a maverick, quite unlike the others in being a generalist, unrefined, a penetrating satirist, and consequently a man whose views did not achieve the same broad readership at the turn of the century:

Thorstein Veblen. Unlike his immediate contemporaries, Veblen enjoyed considerable influence on the ideas of the next generation of critics, such as John Dos Passos, and his writings are regarded as classics today, even though like so many canonical works, they are not so widely read as one might wish.[21]

The next generation of cultural critics, the most important for our purposes, had quite different characteristics. They were versatile non-specialists who wrote about many aspects of cultural productivity and performance, even though many of them had favorite areas of concentration. Most had college educations, but none had academic affiliations and most of them expressed overt contempt for the groves of academe—sterile places where trenchant cultural criticism barely existed and certainly did not flourish.[22] I. A. Richards, an Englishman who taught at the University of Cambridge and then at Harvard, was one of the very few academics with an impact. He enjoyed particular influence as a respected critic's critic—less reactive and more of a seminal thinker than most of his contemporaries. In *Practical Criticism*, Richards called for closer analysis of works of art. He also wanted to look more intensively at the reader's experience of a work of art and felt less interested than Brownell's generation in a biographical approach to people who created works of art. Richards encouraged the development of detailed descriptions of readers' responses to literature. Why? "First, to introduce a new kind of documentation to those who are interested in the contemporary state of culture, whether as critics, as philosophers, as teachers, as psychologists or mainly as curious persons." And he believed that the principal goal of all critical efforts, "of all interpretation, appreciation, exhortation, praise or abuse is improvement in communication." Richards's impact, especially in awakening the practice of cultural criticism in university circles, endured for well over a generation.[23]

This cohort of critics knew one another personally, often intimately, and they loved disputation—in part because they could be feisty and ideological but also because they believed that contestation advanced the cause of cultural creativity and growth. As H. L. Mencken wrote in 1922, cultural debate "melodramatizes the business of the critic, and so convinces thousands of bystanders, otherwise quite inert, that criticism is an amusing and instructive art, and that the problems it deals with are important." Mencken also welcomed as a sign of genuine enlightenment "the revival of acrimony in criticism—

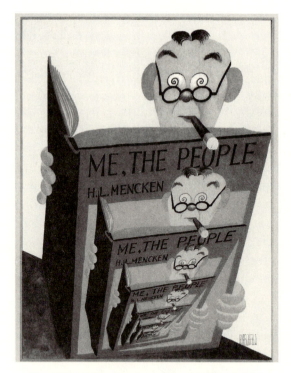

12. *H. L. Mencken* (1949) by Al Hirschfeld
(gouache on board)

the renaissance of the doctrine that aesthetic matters are important, and that it is worth the while of a healthy male to take them seriously, as he takes business, sport and amour."[24]

Despite close friendships and their often living in proximity, these critics did not pull any punches when they reviewed one another's work. So Edmund Wilson was a tough reviewer of Seldes's *Seven Lively Arts* (1924); Seldes could be harsh on the early fiction of F. Scott Fitzgerald; and Walter Lippmann attacked the well-known theater critic George Jean Nathan in 1928. Their collective world was like a carousel going around with men riding side by side in pairs, finding delight in the opportunity for dialogue, but all the while trying to unseat one another. Because they were cultural authorities, however, such activity transcended sheer pettiness and served a larger social purpose. Philip Rahv of the *Partisan Review* contextualized another writer with this provocative aperçu: "A close observer of the creative process once finely remarked that the honor of a literature lies in its capacity to develop 'a great quarrel in the national consciousness.' "[25]

The concerns of these critics ranged from recondite and arcane matters to issues of broad interest about which the general public welcomed the views of people whose vocation it was to have articulate opinions for open consumption. There was widespread concern about such questions as these: was a nation of producers becoming a nation of consumers? would advertising and consumerism create a nation of materialistic hedonists? The acceptance of cultural authority was not confined to literary and artistic questions with a limited constituency. Advertising and public relations people exercised considerable authority in telling consumers what they needed to know about lifestyle and entertainment. Harold Ross, Katharine Angell, and others at *The New Yorker* provided a *vade mecum* to literary taste. The *Reader's Digest* helped large numbers of Americans whom Dwight Macdonald would designate as lower middlebrow know what to think and even what subjects were currently being thought about. Duncan Hines's *Adventures in Good Eating for the Discriminating Motorist* (1936) and his *Food Odyssey* (1955) told Americans where to eat.[26]

During the 1930s new cultural authorities continued to appear. One notable innovation, moreover, involved the emergence of earnest and articulate experts who communicated with the public by means of new and popular media, such as radio. Milton Cross provides an ideal example as host of the Saturday afternoon live broadcasts of the Metropolitan Opera. Alexander Woollcott's weekly discussion of recent books also enjoyed considerable appeal.

Perhaps the most striking development during the 1930s, though not at all surprising, involved the democratization of cultural authority. Carl Becker helped to initiate this pattern in 1931 when he gave a widely noticed presidential address to the American Historical Association titled "Everyman His Own Historian." T. S. Eliot offered this similar and surprisingly nonelitist exhortation: "We should all try to be critics, and not leave criticism to the fellows who write reviews in the papers." The notion of the "participant observer" achieved prominence in American culture during the 1930s, an attractive concept to people who especially valued authenticity. In 1937 Gilbert Seldes wrote an essay about cultural totalitarianism (referring to Germany, Italy, and Russia) in which he saw a silver lining (or at least a lesson) in what dictators do about the arts: namely, demand that art be meaningful and popular. Seldes concluded with a plea that the avant-garde be creative in ways that could be accessible to popular audiences.[27]

Challenges to the dominance of cultural authorities began to be heard during the 1940s. "Culturally what we have," wrote William Phillips in *Horizon*, "is a democratic free-for-all in which every individual, being as good as every other one, has the right to question any form of intellectual authority."[28] For many Americans, that "free market" attitude toward cultural authority would persist right down to the present. As one critic observed in 1993, just because people choose different critics to "follow" doesn't mean that no standards exist any longer whatsoever. If a person prefers the television critics of the *New York Times* to those who write for *TV Guide*, it simply means that one generally agrees with and feels better advised by the judgment of the former. Experience becomes a guiding force. The reader who makes such choices thereby engages in a personal act of cultural authority that is egalitarian in nature. Each individual choice becomes a small statement in the larger discourse about cultural standards.[29]

An excess of egalitarianism, however, even in the absence of antiauthoritarian sentiment, can have the effect of diminishing the stature of and respect for cultural authority. When two intellectuals like John Dewey and Randolph Bourne had a serious disagreement, advocates of their respective positions may have joined the fray, but the contretemps did not have resounding consequences for the general public. During the 1930s and '40s, when modernists and antimodernists were at odds over taste in music, literature, and architecture, their debates had the overall effect of diminishing the stature of cultural authority. The public could not be sure who was "right," but it knew that taste, even the supposed arbiters of "good taste," were in disarray. The poet John Berryman confirmed that in his response to a query from *Partisan Review* in 1948. He specified a growing problem with cultural authority in the United States: Americans wanted more of it but could not readily determine which sources were reliable. The moralistic tone of cultural critics during the 1950s, ranging across a spectrum from Lionel Trilling to Vance Packard, ultimately added to the sense of anomie. And when the Great Debate over mass culture during the 1950s became notably shrill, even some of the harshest critics of mass culture were surprised by what seemed a kind of backlash. Ordinary people simply "tuned out" because the more hostile critics sounded like hopelessly nostalgic snobs. Dwight Macdonald acknowledged his surprise that British leftists regarded his critique as blindly elitist and out of touch with the times.[30]

As early as 1939, writing what became his classic essay "Avant-Garde and Kitsch," Clement Greenberg had expressed concern about the prospect that the general public might simply choose to ignore or bypass traditional cultural authority. Within a few years—throughout the 1940s, in fact—Fred Allen used Senator Claghorn in "Allen's Alley" as a weekly demonstration that authority figures could be utter fools. In 1954, Irving Howe's controversial dissenting essay "This Age of Conformity" closed with a strong expression of resentment directed toward "all the forms of authority . . . that press in upon modern life." During the mid- to later 1950s, when Walt Disney films and television programs enjoyed immense success, the cultural critics who had once admired his work so ardently turned harsh in response to his sentimentalism and banality. Disney responded: "To hell with the critics."[31]

Six years later, coming from the other end of the taste spectrum, Irving Kristol lamented that the great "Mandarins and Brahmins" of the intellectual elite had died. Now that they are gone, he asked, who would fill their role? "*Someone* has to be able to say, with assurance and a measure of authority, what is culture and what is not, what is decent and what is not. There must be some group or class that is admittedly competent to decide—not without error, but more wisely than anyone else—questions of moral and cultural value. Otherwise, a necessary and vital element of order in the life of a society will be lacking." Kristol's solution sounded like a clear echo of Walter Lippmann's in 1929: a democracy needed to be governed by a "natural aristocracy" of the virtuous and wise. Stewart Alsop, a respected and widely syndicated journalist who was the American aristocrat incarnate (educated at Groton and Yale), bemoaned near the end of his life in 1974 the decline of the old WASP elite because it meant the loss of political and cultural authority in general. He believed that their clout had started to wane in 1953, under Eisenhower, when non-elite people began to run the American government. Alsop hated to contemplate his beloved country as "a society without authority," meaning, of course, authority as he had known it in the guise of men like Dean Acheson.[32]

A smallish group of astute cultural critics, born about seven years either side of 1900, recognized not only that highbrow values and "competence" would not prevail much beyond the twenties and certainly not beyond midcentury, and therefore tried to bridge the gap between high and popular culture, between what had traditionally been viewed as refined and vulgar. They did so not to prevent what

Kristol and Alsop most feared—the collapse of civilization—but because they shared a commitment to democratic values and felt that popular culture contained pleasures for all who bothered to be open-minded. So critics like Edmund Wilson, Gilbert Seldes, and James Agee, each one widely respected in his own way as a cultural authority, tried valiantly to lessen the perceived distance between brow levels.[33]

I find Agee especially interesting in this regard. As a critic, he learned that he had to resist not one but two styles of cultural authority that he found distasteful. On the one hand, the avant-garde annoyed him because of their self-conscious proprietorship of modern literature, their overbearing seriousness about its fate in the United States, and the petty bickering among *Partisan Review* ideologues. He was equally vexed by the oppressive constraints of Henry Luce–style journalism (his employer at *Fortune* during the 1930s and *Time* in the 1940s), with its impersonal documentary techniques and its splashy displays of editorialized feature stories. Hence Agee's attraction to film and its possibilities as an art form that could break down the barriers between popular and elite culture.[34]

Unlike Wilson and Seldes, who empathized with Agee's ambivalence as well as his objectives, Agee was overtly hostile to the very concept of culture itself because—despite his love of classical music and great literature, Beethoven and Dostoyevsky, for example—the word inevitably seemed to connote high culture, which was at odds with his impassioned populism. In 1954 Agee wrote lyrics for several scenes in the musical comedy *Candide*, then being prepared by Leonard Bernstein and Lillian Hellman. His principal effort, which he could not complete because of personal despondency, was a "Culture Song" in which Martin, the governor of Buenos Aires, and Candide discuss art. In its derisive way this song, like the preface to *Let Us Now Praise Famous Men*, puts all "culture" on trial. Here is one extract from the lyrics that Agee struggled unsuccessfully to produce:

II Culture Song (*Variant*)

O Really?

I deplore the earthy buttock and the heavenly breast
    Of the overexplanatory nude.
Landscapes tire me, myths confuse, Madonnas I detest.
    I loathe homely portraits of Food.

Yet even I might love the Dauber's Art
If only it eschewed the Mind and Heart.

On blank canvas, if the Master, after long deliberation
    On precisely how to epitomize What is Not,
Would impose on virgin white in virgin white—what pigmentation—
    The ineffable, inevitable Dot!

O Really?

War is Wrong, they inform us; Futile. Misery Hurts. And Love is
    Grand.
    Our Human Fate is Hard; but God is Love.
Beauty is Beautiful. Pride Shall Fall. I *think* I understand:
    And Literature, I've had my surfeit of.

Yet even I might love the Loudmouthed Art.
If only it eschewed the Mind and Heart.

On new paper, if the Poet, as a Scientist uses Number,
    Placed the one exact, unarguable Word!
Not an orgiastic inkfest full of meanings which encumber;
    Just the Period's inevitable Surd!

O Really?

Bassoes grunt, tenors whinny, altoes moo, sopranoes snarl;
    And even if they didn't, there is Song.
The uterine strings, the bollicky brass, the woodwinds' swishy
    quarrel,
    Are Bloated Song, and equally long and wrong.

Yet even I might love the Yowling Art
If only it eschewed the Mind and Heart.

On pure silence, if the Maestro, after lifelong meditation,
    Killing every over-eloquent bleat and blat,
Would impinge the only note which charms a Man of Cultivation:
    The inaudible, ineffable F-Flat![35]

Agee's inability to close the gap between taste levels in 1954, just a year before his own premature death, seems symbolic of the expiring cultural authorities he had imbibed at Phillips Exeter and Harvard.

Others, like Leonard Bernstein, would successfully cross the divide; but Agee's incapacity to recognize the closing of an era early in the fifties speaks volumes—volumes it had long tortured him to try to write. A decade after he died, Susan Sontag put into words what Agee may have recognized but could not quite say: that the apparent gulf between high and low art is illusory, and that the new, cross-cultural media, like television, film noir, experimental fiction, and Pop art, showed "not a conflict of cultures but the creation of a new kind of sensibility which is defiantly pluralistic and dedicated both to excruciating seriousness and to fun, wit, and nostalgia." It was symptomatic that during the 1950s and '60s, Walter Cronkite conveyed a strong impression of cultural authority: trustworthy information, undistorted or editorialized in any way. Hence his success, for example, as host of the popular TV show *You Are There* (1953–57).[36]

During the 1940s, Agee had become a widely respected cultural authority on film. Although he earned a reputation as a maverick, as someone who told the *Partisan Review* crowd that the topic for their 1939 symposium ("The Situation in American Writing") was idiotic, he maintained a viable reputation as an intellectual who could communicate not only with middlebrows and highbrows but with ordinary people as well, even the most downtrodden denizens of rural Alabama. That kind of cerebral and personal versatility would not disappear in the United States altogether after Agee's death in 1955, but the prominence of cultural authority would steadily be supplanted by cultural power, which is a very different quality.

III. The Decline of Cultural Authority and the Rise of Cultural Power

From time to time in recent years, legislative initiatives have been taken to finance an expanded, noncommercial television system by levying taxes on (for example) the resale of stations or channels or on receiver equipment. An attempt of that sort reached the final phases of congressional action in the winter of 1987. At the very last moment, however, the proposal to levy such a tax was deleted from the bill. How did it happen? The chairman of the Senate committee proposing the measure acknowledged that the media owners were more powerful than Congress. "We had unanimity," he explained, "but the broadcasters are way more powerful."[37]

The reasons why overt expressions of cultural authority have given way to covert manifestations of cultural power are numerous, but they have much to do with the rise of full-scale mass culture, dominated by corporations, during the past forty years. Part of the explanation also lies in the inability of popular culture (as we have defined it in the half century following the 1880s) to maintain its former vitality and its dominance in the marketplace. The *Saturday Evening Post*, for example, which had enjoyed such wide appeal from the 1920s through the 1940s, floundered in the early 1960s because it could not make the transition to mass culture and could not compete with television and newer types of magazines for consumer attention. Nor was it any longer the optimal venue for advertisers.[38]

Corporate America, and especially those who controlled the mass media, became increasingly savvy about the need to "straddle" taste levels in order to maximize their audience, their sales, and their advertising revenue. We can see this trend as early as the last years of the thirties and forties when *Life* magazine strove very hard to mingle diverse stories that would appeal to as many taste publics as possible, stories ranging from classical music and ballet, as we have seen, to summer camping and the constitutional right of every American to hunt with a gun. By the fifties and sixties, major producers of popular and mass culture, like Columbia and Warner Bros., diversified their investments so that an upswing in record sales could compensate for a decline in movie attendance, and vice versa. At first those large corporations tried to shape (and even control) America's taste in popular culture. Because the moguls did not like early rock 'n' roll, they invested heavily in the promotion of folk and folk-pop music. By the later sixties, however, the corporate executives and producers were forced to acknowledge the reality of rock's mass appeal. The industry slogan was simply stated: "It smells but it sells."[39]

In the 1970s profits from record sales outstripped the net from film production. Warner Bros. soon became the largest of all the media conglomerates and recognized that traditional sources of cultural authority had no impact on the mass culture products that they needed to sell in vast quantities. Warner and similar media entities enjoyed a great deal of cultural power, but only so long as they remained sensitively attuned to the tastes and interests of a large and increasingly youthful purchasing public. Similarly, commercial imperatives forced the television networks to straddle taste levels in order to remain competitive in the ratings. Television producers sought an American vernacular as oblivious as possible to age, education, and ethnicity. They needed to satisfy audiences with programs that would appeal to children *and* adults, middlebrow *and* low. Hence the phenomenal success during the 1960s and '70s of Pete Rozelle, commissioner of the National Football League, who brought professional football from the era of the stadium to the era of television. It is germane that Rozelle began his career in public relations.[40]

Ironically, when Newton Minow, appointed by John F. Kennedy to head the Federal Communications Commission, attempted to restore hierarchies of taste to the television wasteland and "level up" the so-called Great Audience, commercial television was in the process of collapsing those hierarchies. As one expert in communications history has put it, public broadcasting (PBS) "has been forever lost in its struggle to preserve the distinction between high and low, winding up finally in the imaginary and ever narrowing 'middlebrow' in its appeals to its private donor-public." By the 1970s, integrated ownership and production of mass culture, made possible by an unprecedented concentration of cultural power, facilitated the disintegration of boundaries between various media. Consequently, a great many movies, novelized films, record releases, and television programs were all planned and produced in the same offices under the same corporate supervision. That process went a very long way toward the blurring of customary cultural levels, and rendered traditional cultural authorities increasingly irrelevant.[41]

If there is widespread agreement in the late twentieth century that clear, categorical distinctions among taste levels are largely untenable—and I believe there is[42]—we can point to at least four very different stimuli that have contributed to that outcome: the social role of media censorship (and self-censorship); the growing power of advertising in the world of entertainment (especially electronic); the antiauthoritarian counterculture of the 1960s and 1970s; and the declining public role of intellectuals in the United States.

Censorship of printed material, radio, film, and television has taken a different form for each medium, and has had variable impact at different times, almost but not quite in sequence. The overall effect, however—despite certain legal victories based upon the First Amendment that stretch from *Ulysses* and *Lady Chatterley's Lover* to the likes of *Hus-*

tler—has been to contract the role for cultural creativity and to shift respect from cultural authority to awe for cultural power. When Joseph L. Breen took over as head of the Movie Production Code Administration in 1934, he gained immense power, demanded excisions, and successfully enforced the code.

A transitional episode from the 1930s may suffice to particularize the point. During the summer of 1937 the artist Thomas Hart Benton spent a month in Hollywood on assignment for *Life* magazine. The principal work that resulted from this excursion was a large painting entitled *Hollywood*. It featured a film studio, with a scantily clad show-girl resembling Jean Harlow (who had died earlier that year) standing glamorously as the centerpiece. The stunning star is surrounded by stage sets for assorted movies (see fig. 13). Benton's painting only glossed the glamour of Hollywood, however, while concentrating on behind-the-scenes activities in the movie industry.[43]

Initially *Life* decided that it could not publish the painting because it looked too risqué for a family magazine. That was an act of cultural power based upon rational calculations about the readership's sensibilities. A year later, however, the magazine did reproduce the painting in a daring double-page spread after *Hollywood* won a prize in the Carnegie Annual, an important juried exhibition held in Pittsburgh. *Life*'s caption read, in part: "Benton says 'I know it doesn't make sense. Nothing in Hollywood does.'" In this episode, cultural authority eventually trumped cultural power.[44]

For a sense of change *and* continuity, it is instructive to recall that in 1915 the Supreme Court ruled that motion pictures were not covered by constitutional protections of freedom of speech and press. The decision declared that making films was a business, plain and simple, originated and conducted for profit, "like other spectacles, not to be regarded . . . as part of the press of the country or as organs of public opinion." That ruling capped numerous efforts on the state and local levels made ever since 1908 to establish some sort of control over the captivating commercial exhibition of films. Public authorities saw even then, in this new industry, the incipient formation of an alternative public power with a sphere of its own.[45]

A zany, nonsensical "humor of irrationality" carried over from vaudeville to radio during the later 1920s and 1930s. Because the airwaves were perceived as belonging to the public, however, humor presented through a mass medium became more subject to checks and

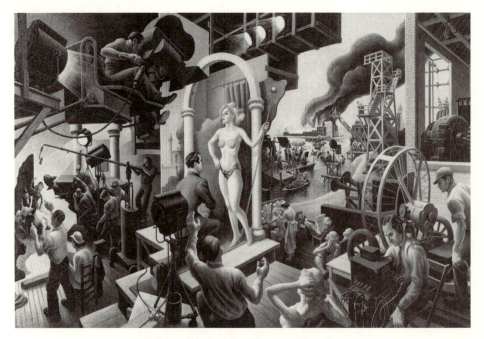

13. *Hollywood* (1937) by Thomas Hart Benton
(tempera with oil on canvas)

controls by sponsors. The sponsors feared being associated with anything smutty or distasteful, a situation of potential guilt by implicit
approval. In 1933–34, owing largely to risqué movies made by Mae
West, a production code came into being that for more than two
decades placed severe restrictions on Hollywood's ability to portray
human sexuality or to indulge in "barnyard language" that was common parlance for many Americans. As a result, numerous films from
that prudish era seem bizarre and unreal. When court cases occurred,
the mobilization of cultural expertise on behalf of the defense rarely
succeeded. Hollywood succumbed and largely regulated itself, especially in response to political pressures during World War II and the
anti-Communist anxieties that followed. Interestingly enough, in a
1954 Gallup poll, 42% of the 1,500 people asked responded that the
current degree of censorship was "about right" and another 30% felt
that it was not sufficiently strict.[46]

During the 1950s, concern became rife that children were being
exposed to excessive violence on television and in comic books. A

Gallup poll in 1954 showed that 70% of the 1,500 people asked blamed the increase in teenage crime on new and popular TV programs. An increase in juvenile delinquency was feared, and widely publicized congressional hearings took place; but the cultural authority of social psychologists was no match for the vested interests of mass media, so no enduring change occurred.* In the 1970s an intense public debate arose once again, this time sparked by the belief that television programs had contributed in a major way to criminal acts and antisocial behavior that seemed out of control. The PTA, the AMA, and other groups pleaded for regulation, such as the modest proposal for a "family hour" on TV before the bedtime of youngsters. The courts responded that such a requirement would unfairly restrain the television industry. Cultural critics dated this problem's genesis all the way back to *The Untouchables* at the end of the 1950s; but the industry fought back vigorously, and so long as viewer ratings for such programs remained high, sponsors were not about to intervene. Clearly, the position of sponsors was not consistent regarding censorship, unless the paramount importance of the "bottom line," rather than public morals, makes for consistency.[47]

Advertising agencies initially gained effective cultural power over the content of radio broadcasts between 1932 and 1937. The Crossley system of rating the size of program audiences, developed after 1931, became intensely important to sponsors and advertising agencies. The Hooper system succeeded it in 1935 and helped make sponsors a very strong cultural power during the 1940s. Norman Corwin wrote marvelous middlebrow radio programs (nonfiction) throughout the 1940s, but when his style of writing seemed inadequate for the greatly expanded audiences at midcentury, William Paley and CBS simply dumped him.[48] The very same thing happened to live drama on television during the mid- and later 1950s. Once the sponsors and networks achieved total control, by 1959, series like Rod Serling's innovative *Twilight Zone* were canceled. After 1960, the lowest common denomi-

---

* Fredric Wertham, a German-trained psychiatrist, singled out mass culture as the most important cause of juvenile delinquency. It was largely because of his influence that a U.S. Senate subcommittee spent several years exploring possible links between mass culture (comic books, film, and television) and delinquency. By 1957, when the hearings ended, little had been achieved in the way of controls. Corporate power exercised with modest prudence at appropriate moments outmaneuvered cultural authority.

nator invariably won. The networks had no use for the European system of pitching different types of broadcasts for variable taste levels. The entrepreneurial power of commerce totally crushed the recommendations of such cultural authorities as John Crosby, Jack Gould, and Gilbert Seldes—prominent television critics who pleaded for diversity.[49]

Long before the counterculture that we associate with the 1960s came into being, there were prominent individuals who attacked authority, though not cultural authority per se, as a rule. The filmmaker Mack Sennett once fondly recalled his celebration of anarchy in the Keystone comedies of the silent film era. "I especially liked the reduction of authority to absurdity, the notion that sex could be funny, and the bold insults hurled at Pretension." So did Sennett's audiences, apparently. So did the Marx Brothers from 1928 onward, and so did Fred Allen when he persistently satirized order, power, propriety, and respectability. So did Lenny Bruce and Mort Sahl a generation later. The situation became interesting and ironic in 1967 when Dr. Benjamin Spock, a cultural-authority figure for a full generation, challenged public authority by way of his active opposition to the U.S. role in Vietnam. He achieved considerable publicity for antiwar protest because of his prestige in the realm of child care.[50]

What must be grasped here is a certain complexity in American attitudes. Foreign observers have often played up an American tradition of resistance to authority going back at least to the Revolution of 1776, if not to the initial decision to emigrate from the Old World to the New.[51] But the matter is not nearly so straightforward; somehow a mysteriously invisible line seems to exist. On one side are generally acceptable occasions and ways of resisting authority—political, social, or cultural—ranging from the views of Thomas Jefferson to the comedy of Mack Sennett and Fred Allen. But then there are more controversial anti-authoritarians, ranging from John Brown to Eugene V. Debs to Jim and Artie Mitchell (who began making pornographic films in the later 1960s) to Jerry Rubin and Abbie Hoffman.[52]

Abbie Hoffman, a leader of the Yippies during the 1960s and '70s, managed to combine opposition to both political power *and* cultural authority. He cherished the coup by a Southern California chapter of Yippies who succeeded in planting a Viet Cong flag on Mount Matterhorn in Disneyland. When it came to drugs, Hoffman achieved fame for his slogan "Better living through chemistry." And when the FBI authorized a manhunt for Hoffman after he skipped bail in 1973, he thereupon disguised himself and took a tour of the main FBI building in Washington, D.C. Nothing delights those who flout cultural authority so much as irony. Hence the bemusement when the Mormon Tabernacle Choir sang "This Land Is Your Land," apparently unaware that Woody Guthrie's anthem was written in 1940 as a Marxist response to Irving Berlin's "God Bless America" (1938).[53]

Those prominent cultural authorities of the 1950s and 1960s who continued to hold a substantial audience did not convey messages that would make Americans feel better about themselves and their society. David Riesman and his colleagues told the country in *The Lonely Crowd* (1950) that it had lost its vaunted individualism and that Americans were excessively preoccupied with being the kinds of people others wanted or expected them to be. Being "other-directed" was not a compliment. Vance Packard warned the nation of sinister advertising schemes designed to persuade Americans to buy things they really did not want or need. He then added insult to insecurity by raising the ante on Riesman and company. Packard told Americans that they were status seekers—a familiar story for those who recalled Thorstein Veblen's *Theory of the Leisure Class* (1899), except that Packard's indictment included a much larger percentage of the populace. Edward R. Murrow's television programs *See It Now* and *Person to Person*, were not so insulting to their viewers, yet they conveyed messages that all was not well in the USA. Americans were either the dupes of a demagogue like Senator McCarthy or else callous toward the exploitation of migratory labor. As a critic of Cold War America, Murrow offered little comfort.[54]

During subsequent decades cultural authority has become less visible, less potent, fragmented, and among some circles even sharply criticized for failing to make any difference at all in helping the general public appreciate or understand the more complex cultural issues and challenges of our time. More often than not, the idiosyncratic reactions of audiences to cultural "products" seem to matter more than what cultural critics have to say. As Isaiah Berlin wrote to Garson Kanin, the playwright and screenwriter, in 1962: "I needn't go into 'critics versus audiences' etc., etc. you have had the same experience." Caught between the growing power of audiences as well as corporate America, the role and impact of cultural critics were greatly diminished in 1980 compared, let us say, with a half century earlier.[55]

By the 1970s it became commonplace to say that the academic disciplines customarily regarded as major sources of cultural criticism—literary studies, sociology, and anthropology—were in disarray, their discourse utterly distant from cultural clienteles in need of comprehensible guidance. The disciplines themselves were deeply divided over the merits and potential utility of poststructuralism and postmodernism. Those modes of inquiry sent messages that everyone (and therefore no one in particular) had adequate credentials for evaluating a performance or a text. As a consequence, the very concept of cultural authority was undermined even more. Books and essays began to appear in the 1980s bemoaning the failure of academic intellectuals to serve any kind of socially useful role as "public intellectuals." According to such observers, those men and women best suited by training and experience to serve as meaningful cultural critics had abdicated their potential roles, a serious neglect of their responsibility as citizens.[56]

By the 1990s the voices of such major figures as Archibald MacLeish, Mary McCarthy, Lionel and Diana Trilling, Philip Rahv, and Lewis Mumford had been stilled. Others, like William H. Whyte, either had been diverted to other concerns or had been attracted into a neo-conservative orbit that led them to direct more criticism at their erstwhile colleagues than at the changing cultural dynamics and phenomena of our time. Hence a major overview story in the *New York Times* began this way in 1990: "It has become commonplace to lament the passing of the day when thinkers like James B. Conant and Lewis Mumford played as influential a role in politics as today's media advisers. Even to those who consider themselves among the last holdouts, the question is no longer whether intellectuals are in hiding, but why." As the cultural critic Simon Frith insisted in 1997, as part of a plea for the revitalization of cultural authority in response to the real world that we live in: "popular cultural activities—like all cultural activities—depend on judgments. They are organized around patterns of discrimination and difference, through arguments about the good and the bad." Cultural criticism needed to be resuscitated and revalorized.[57]

In 1984 one of the most distinguished and wide-ranging intellectuals in the United States participated in a symposium devoted to "The Public Benefits of the Arts and the Humanities." Although his is not a familiar household name, Michael Walzer, formerly a professor of political science at Harvard, is now a professor at the prestigious Institute for Advanced Study in Princeton. The author of two books of social and cultural criticism (1988 and 1993), Walzer is also the editor of *Dissent* and a man of the left. At the 1984 symposium he offered a kind of inquiring manifesto that remains resonant in these uncertain times:

> The anti-intellectualism of populist politics is a function, in part at least, of the standard association of high culture and upper-class status. In normal times, anti-intellectualism is directed against avant-gardes, against bohemias, against radical intellectuals. In revolutionary times, it is directed against the old and established forms of high culture. It is always a dangerous passion and one to be resisted, but it won't finally be overcome until we succeed in breaking the association between high culture and high status, so that knowledge and culture and their institutions are socially autonomous, so that institutions like [the Metropolitan Museum of Art] are free from people like us [the elite] and are controlled and paid for instead by the people generally. But will the people generally subsidize greatness as we think we have done? Will high culture remain high in an egalitarian era?[58]

Most cultural institutions of the kind envisioned by Walzer are not yet socially autonomous; but perhaps cultural authority in our own time (broadly conceived from the perspective of a writer who is sixty-two) has become far more populistic than it was in 1900 or 1950. Perhaps cultural authority has shifted from being the domain of well-educated intellectuals who mainly scripted their own assessments to specialists in various spheres who are a whole lot closer to "the people" than James Gibbons Huneker was in 1890 or George Jean Nathan was in 1935. If we ask ourselves who is recognized as a cultural authority in the later twentieth century, we come up with a roster that I think would shock Huneker and his generation or Nathan and his pal H. L. Mencken.

We might list Irma Rombauer (1877–1962), the author of *The Joy of Cooking: A Compilation of Reliable Recipes, with a Casual Culinary Chat*, first published in 1936 but a book that endured in numerous editions for two full generations. And then, perhaps, Julia Child, whose star status began in 1961 with *Mastering the Art of French Cooking* and led to her own widely watched television program. Or Amy Vanderbilt's

Complete Book of Etiquette, first published in 1952, but even more enduring and pervasive than *The Joy of Cooking*. Or Alex Comfort, author of *The Joy of Sex: A Gourmet Guide to Lovemaking* (1973), another best-seller profusely illustrated with instructional drawings. Or certain disk jockeys. Or TV personality Johnny Carson. "Such was his cultural authority," according to critic Frank Rich, "that his belated inclusion of White House scandals in his 'Tonight' show monologue was the certain sign that Richard Nixon was through." Or Allan Bloom for several years following publication of his best-seller, *The Closing of the American Mind* (1987). Or those who dispense intimate advice to the millions, like Ann Landers, Dr. Ruth Westheimer, and Laura Schlessinger. Or the widely watched CBS newsmagazine *Sixty Minutes*, for those who identify exposé with cultural authority. Or Martha Stewart, professional household adviser and tastemaker to parvenu Americans. Or Oprah Winfrey when she began recommending particular books to her readers in 1996, an impact so strong that her word can sell a million copies.[59]

That is *not* a comprehensive schematization of the diverse array of contemporary cultural authorities. Many others might have been mentioned, ranging from *Consumer Reports* to those who decree what is in and out for women's wear, to those who choose the subjects for blockbuster exhibitions in museums or award major prizes for books and architectural achievement. My fundamental points are, first, that cultural authority has vastly broadened the scope of its coverage—as is only to be expected in mass culture. Second, that whenever there is a gap between attendance ratings (such as film or television) and what the critics think, the ratings matter more and they prevail. Third, as a consequence, networks, sponsors, and promoters pay much less attention to cultural critics than they once did.

Finally, also a consequence, no one person or side is any longer seen as absolutely authoritative. Television and radio producers do not as a rule produce or present a single omniscient authority. Because the public now assumes that there are at least "two sides to everything," discussion programs are set up in a dialogical manner. There is no longer an authoritative position; only divergent points of view. A 1947 survey of 3,527 Americans asked whether some agency—"either the Federal government or the radio industry itself—should see to it that . . . radio stations regularly carry programs giving both sides of public issues?" The response was overwhelmingly affirmative, with

58% assigning this responsibility to the radio industry and 23% to the federal government. (The remaining 18% responded with either "nobody" or "don't know.")[60]

Last, and important above all, cultural authority has lost considerable ground to the individuals and companies that possess cultural power. As Herbert I. Schiller wrote in 1989, "the industries that serve as the sites for the creation, packaging, transmission, and placement of cultural messages—corporate ones especially—have grown steadily as their importance and centrality to the corporate economy increases."[61]

That is one of the truly momentous shifts in American culture that has occurred over the past three decades. The sacralization of culture during the later nineteenth century may have been accompanied by an excess of cultural authority—an undemocratic and therefore not a desirable situation. But the marked decline of cultural authority during the later twentieth century, a combined consequence of corporate power and cultural democracy, may not be so entirely desirable either. With few guidelines, and with every taste considered equal to every other, an excess of mediocrity is encouraged to flourish. When the mass media seek to satisfy everyone simultaneously, excellence for anyone or anything in particular is less likely to appear. Alexis de Tocqueville did fear that a truly democratic culture could readily be afflicted by mediocrity. That remains one of his most astute insights.

7

The Gradual Emergence of Mass Culture and Its Critics

∝

I. *Mass Society and Mass Culture Are Not the Same*

During the winter of 1973 large numbers of Americans watched Senate committee hearings concerning the Watergate break-in and the possible complicity of highly placed figures in American politics. As many people, and perhaps even more, followed the televised final stages of the House Judiciary Committee proceedings in mid-1974 when it considered the impeachment of President Richard M. Nixon. Should we view those events as a mass culture phenomenon? The leading participants, investigators as well as the accused, were not themselves proletarian or invisible "members" of mass society. Nor were the commentators and analysts. The stakes, of course, could not have been higher.[1] Hence the great drama in those proceedings. Does the medium of communication alone define whether an event qualifies as mass culture? The sheer size of a viewing audience? Or does the substance of an event—in this case legal and political complexities—share equally in determining how we define it? Is it even possible to prioritize such variables as medium of communication, size of the audience, and actual content, that is, issues? These are just a few of the difficulties that we face in trying to ascertain what we mean by mass culture.

Here again, just as I have emphasized throughout, a historical perspective that is sensitive to change over time is essential if we hope to comprehend the gradual emergence of mass culture, phase by phase, during the course of the past century. For purposes of diachronic comparison, consider the quantum jump from the jukebox (ensconced in restaurants and bars during the 1930s) to MTV, from national distribution of a printed product to the globalization of images by satellite in the 1970s, from comic books to contemporary cartoons on cable networks, from the Book-of-the-Month Club to Warner Books, from Krazy Kat to Ninja Turtles, from the avant-garde to postmodernism, from *Information Please* to *Entertainment Tonight*, from the vernacular of Fred Allen to the antic vulgarity of Howard Stern and Jerry Springer. Some writers have viewed the older parts of these pairs as components of mass culture. They can do so if they choose, but should not neglect the distances that come to mind in terms of audience size, cost, marketing strategies, and behavioral effects (such as voyeurism, violence, and celebrity obsessions).

My point is simply that popular culture in the years 1930–50 (or emerging mass culture if one prefers) is quite different from mass culture as we have known it in the later decades of the twentieth century. Those who casually refer to mass culture in the context of the earlier twentieth century need to consider books like James B. Twitchell's *Carnival Culture: The Trashing of Taste in America* (1992) or Douglas Rushkoff's *Media Virus! Hidden Agendas in Popular Culture* (1994), books about our own time with their emphasis upon the ubiquitous presence of electronic media, truly vast audiences, and massive marketing campaigns for consumer novelties that are both dispensable and ephemeral. Otherwise the history of commercial culture in twentieth-century America becomes a continuous blur rather than a series of overlapping stages marked by major innovations and altered moods of consciousness.

Consider, for example, the distance between the successful performances of Charlie Chaplin in silent film early in the twentieth century and the posthumous commodification of Chaplin's persona in the 1980s, particularly in the highly effective advertising campaign for IBM micro computers. It's the distance between an audience segmented by class and ethnicity in 1915 and an audience treated as though it is virtually monolithic in 1985. It's the distance between entertainment for petty cash and the sale of a highly functional and costly product. The living Chaplin sold hearty chuckles. The Chaplin image sold access to cyberspace. The distance in time and in cultural orientation is astounding.[2]

This chapter explores some very basic issues about which there is scant agreement—in fact, about which there has been and remains considerable contestation. What is mass culture? When and how did it develop? Why do these questions exercise, even agitate, cultural critics to the extent that they do, particularly with reference to the degree of passivity or agency enjoyed by ordinary individuals in response to the attractions and dynamics of mass culture? The topic, with all of its manifestations, has been intensely disputed.

It helps to keep in mind that who uses what phrasing depends a great deal upon attitude. Critics who do not like mass culture call it just that, and their pejorative connotation comes through clearly. Other writers, who look at the very same phenomenon without disapproval, however, are likely to refer to it consistently as popular culture, thereby avoiding (they believe) any hint of disapprobation—or at least of being judgmental. They have every right to do so, I suppose; but the effect has been to make the literature on mass culture even more confusing than it would otherwise be. And to complicate matters from a historical perspective, when the Great Debate over mass culture occurred during the 1950s, polemicists on both sides basically used the same labels, but with differing inferences and implications. The emergence of populists who find agency and egalitarian benefits in mass culture has largely been a pattern in the past two decades. Consequently, that is where the terminological confusion can be most perplexing.[3]

It is instructive to notice at the outset what an extraordinary array of views we have on the question of when mass culture began. If we start with the European side, it becomes evident that for serious writers looking at the Old World, "mass culture" may be used in a casually interchangeable way with what many here would consider popular culture. Thus Benedict Anderson points to the seminal importance of Martin Luther as a popular author along with the dissemination of tracts on behalf of Reformed Protestantism, ca. 1522–46. E. P. Thompson has a similar emphasis upon the wide dissemination of inexpensive treatises in eighteenth-century England. The biographer of historian Marc Bloch casually refers to mass culture in late nineteenth-century France because "techniques of mass communication" were emerging.[4]

There are scholars who view Walt Whitman's *Democratic Vistas* (1871) as a radical document because its emphasis upon the "potential sterility and dehumanizing nature of mass culture is acute." C. Wright Mills, the dissenting sociologist, described a transformation of the nineteenth-century public into what he regarded as a modern "mass audience."[5] Richard Slotkin and Neil Harris are more inclined to date the emergence of mass culture from the turn of the century because of pulp publishing, vaudeville, silent film, pop music, and spectator sports; but I notice a significant leap in audience size and genuinely mass appeal when Harris describes the inaugural success of *Action Comics* in June 1938 and the wide syndication of Superman as a comic book hero by 1940.[6]

Cultural historians with a special interest in film commonly date the genesis of mass culture to 1915, when D. W. Griffith's epic and controversial film *Birth of a Nation* appeared, primarily because it enjoyed a broad appeal that transcended class lines. From my perspective, however, whenever *Birth of a Nation* is awarded this palm of primacy, the discussion fails to make any meaningful distinction between mass and popular culture. They simply get conflated.[7]

One other important source of confusion needs to be noted before we turn to the substantive trajectory of mass culture itself. From the later nineteenth century through World War II, the phrase "mass society" came into common usage, almost always in a pejorative way because its critics, from Nietzsche to Ortega y Gasset, thought in demographic terms and felt extreme anxiety at the rising appeal of socialism in Europe. Impressed as they were by the growth of literacy and the facile dissemination of propaganda, they worried about the ease with which a demagogue or totalitarianism might achieve dominance in a mass society where the rapidly growing populace seemed so malleable and susceptible to ideological indoctrination. Theorists of mass society like to regard themselves as realistic elitists. For purposes of clarification in our context, however, their concerns were primarily political and ideological rather than cultural.[8]

It is significant, too, that these anxieties about mass society spanned the ideological spectrum. According to the Marxist critique of mass society, especially well circulated during the second quarter of the twentieth century, mass media effectively mold the minds of people, providing them with a cultural narcotic that prevents them from realizing their common interests and joining together to overthrow their exploiters. At the time, this represented an ideological advance, a more sophisticated version of Marxism in which capitalism was joined as the arch villain by the depoliticizing implications of mass society.[9]

The word "mass," used as a modifier as well as a noun, has appeared in Anglo-American discourse for more than a century and a half. We find people as far back as the 1820s referring to society in the aggregate as a "mass." A century later, the phrase "mass society" became a heavily freighted form of shorthand for the impact of industrialization on individualism because of the large economic organizations that affected the lives of so many. To others it also meant the decline of religious values.[10] And to still others it prompted worries about the impact of propaganda, regardless of whether it came from governmental or corporate sources. In terms of validation, it should be acknowledged that many critics during the interwar years became aware of just how effective the Creel Committee on Public Information had been in 1917–19 and how innovative in manipulative ways the public relations and advertising firms were during the 1920s. It is no accident that the phrase "mass psychology" came into common usage during the 1920s and '30s.[11]

It is certainly helpful that some of the shrewdest scholars carefully avoid equating the advent of mass society with mass culture, and going even farther are careful to specify, for example, that in writing about the Book-of-the-Month Club in the 1920s and '30s, they are describing popular or middlebrow taste levels within the framework of what was just becoming a mass society. It would also be extremely helpful if we paid closer attention to the variable trajectories over time of mass production (1920s), mass consumption (accelerating after 1945), and mass education (1950s and beyond, depending upon whether one is looking at precollegiate or college education). There does appear to be a broad consensus that following World War II a major reorientation occurred from technologies of production that had been mastered so well before and during the war to technologies of distribution and consumption. The craze for Davy Crockett that Disney created in the mid-1950s, for example, was comparable in many ways to Disney's *Three Little Pigs* sensation in 1933, but with a major difference. The Crockett phenomenon became the centerpiece of an immense marketing campaign for a huge amount of merchandise. That had not been the case two decades earlier, and the Depression provides only part of the explanation. Nationwide merchandising schemes and their implementation had just begun to hit high gear by 1954.[12]

II. Commercial Culture and Proto-Mass Culture

In chapter 4 I discussed American popular culture in its prime, 1885–1935. Partially coinciding in time and partially overlapping it, developments occurred that marked an important phase in the *emer-*

gence of mass culture, yet differed from mass culture as we trace it historically after midcentury and especially from mass culture as we have known it in recent decades. For purposes of convenience, I have chosen to call these telescoped phases from the 1880s until the later 1940s "commercial culture" and "proto-mass culture." The former, especially, requires some explanation. I have borrowed the phrase "commercial culture" from the historian William R. Taylor, who uses it to describe an intermediate stage in cultural production, the antecedent of mass culture, most notable between 1880 and 1930. Taylor regards that as an era in which there was a considerable degree of collaboration, or at least mutual understanding, between producers and consumers. He coins the phrase "culture of pastiche" to designate cultural options, various types of popular culture that appealed to the diversified audiences that still proliferated during that era.[13]

I would add to that the need for us to differentiate between commercialization and commodification. Whereas the former has a long history and cannot singularly help us to differentiate between popular and mass culture, the latter is much more a post–World War I phenomenon and does help us to make some key distinctions. Minstrel shows provide a representative example of commercialized culture. The entrepreneurs tried to make them attractive, and they certainly sought a profit. But they did not make potential members of the audience believe that the show was something essential that they *had* to purchase or attend. In a commercial society one paid for something that one wanted, which is not the same as being led to believe that a major need would go unfulfilled or that a person would be socially retrograde without possessing a certain product or mode of entertainment. Major innovations stimulating the desires that we associate with commodification are mass circulation magazines, some of which first achieved prominence at the turn of the century (supplanting trading cards as an advertising medium), and then mass media such as radio, which came into its own at the end of the 1920s, although intensive advertising on the radio did not get underway until the 1930s.[14]

In my view, commercial and proto-mass culture do not mean culture intended exclusively or even primarily for the masses. Rather, they mean culture enterprisingly produced and disseminated for diverse markets with the highly potent assistance of media capable of a very broad reach. But persons of all classes and taste levels may pick and choose which aspects and objects of commercial culture they wish to have or attend. Intense pressure to consume had not yet become a major consideration; filling the needs of one's household and its members was. Thus the initial emergence of national corporations at the end of the nineteenth century meant the exploratory marketing of goods on an unprecedented scale. Montgomery Ward had its genesis in 1872, and Sears in 1897, developing a distribution system that did not become efficient and unprecedented in size until 1911. The Piggly-Wiggly stores, which introduced the concept of self-service, began in Memphis in 1916 and took off a decade later, ultimately linking 2,660 stores. Each of these systems, however, had its own regional (rather than truly national) emphasis. Moreover, they represented commercialized culture rather than commodified culture because they offered lower prices for goods that were needed but not readily available in more remote localities. Of course the Sears catalogue undeniably stimulated desires. But the primary reason for its success had more to do with filling needs than with the artificial creation of wants.[15]

It should be kept in mind that fierce critiques of mass culture did not occur until the mid- and later 1950s, when the Great Debate took place. It seems reasonable to assume, therefore, that mass culture sank roots earlier in the twentieth century, but only blossomed into full flower directly following World War II. We should note that when apprehensions were expressed during the second quarter of the twentieth century, they took forms that I call sociopolitical: What will the consequences be for political manipulation by demagogues? Will there be a standardization of ideological opinion? Will the media affect the presidential campaign of 1952 (the first to be fully covered by television)? Only thereafter did the critics' apprehensions become far more sociocultural: Will there be a degradation of taste, a decline of literacy, the fetishization of everything by means of intensified advertising, a cult of personality and celebrity?

One could date the germination of proto-mass culture to 1895, when Joseph Pulitzer's *World*, a low-cost New York daily, printed the first comic cartoon, the adventures of a street urchin of indeterminate ethnicity called the "Yellow Kid." The series, primitive by standards that prevailed twenty-five years later, proved to be so popular with the public that in 1896 William Randolph Hearst stole and hired the artist, Richard Outcault, to run his cartoons in the *New York Morning Journal*.

Outcault failed to copyright his character, so imitations swiftly sprang up in other urban papers across the country, invariably following a pattern: the adventures (and misadventures) of city youngsters from the lower social strata. In 1897 Hearst commissioned another artist to describe the shenanigans of mischievous children called the "Katzenjammer Kids." By 1913, when "Bringing Up Father" began to appear, many other cartoon strips had started to proliferate.[16]

The appeal of these comics early in the twentieth century is culturally significant, but thus far nothing distinguishes them from popular culture. Two sequential developments that emerged gradually between 1902 and 1930 place this narrative in the realm of proto-mass culture: syndication and licensed merchandising. National syndication of comic strips in newspapers originated in 1902, when Hearst started selling the right to reproduce his strips in other newspapers. He thereby opened up a national market. Every popular comic strip thereafter enjoyed this kind of regular replication, which meant that all across the country, every morning, youngsters and adults battled for first possession of the "funny papers." Comics helped to sell newspapers, and by 1910 at least nine consolidated newspaper chains existed, the largest one owned by Edward W. Scripps. Artists learned to straddle the urban/rural diversity of the United States at that time. Ethnic humor had limited appeal. Hence the "Katzenjammer Kids" eventually shifted to a semi-rural setting in order to strike a balance and maximize the cartoon's appeal.[17]

The swift spillover of that enthusiasm into an electronic medium required almost three decades before achieving a high level of technical quality. Initially, animated cartoons were not for everyone, which is why I consider the developmental stage an aspect of proto-mass culture; but the process of maturation is intriguing. Winsor McCay, the earliest animator, created *Little Nemo in Slumberland* in 1911, and then *Gertie the Trained Dinosaur* three years later. Gertie had charm and personality aplenty, a progenitor of Barney. The development of animation began to hit its stride in 1915–16, when Mutt and Jeff films, snappy and entertaining, achieved popularity. By the late teens most animated cartoons were adaptations of successful comic strips: "Bringing Up Father," "The Katzenjammer Kids," and "Krazy Kat." "Felix the Cat," always outwitted by a mouse, made his first appearance in 1921. Created by Otto Messmer, Felix had a very distinctive personality, which made him the greatest cartoon star of the silent era. Sometimes called the Charlie Chaplin of cartoon characters, Felix appeared as a loner in an indifferent world, combining resourcefulness with a touch of viciousness in order to survive.[18]

Until 1928, all animated cartoons had been derived from New York–produced comic strips. But then came an unknown named Walt Disney from California with *Steamboat Willie,* a landmark because it synchronized sound with the pictures. Next came Mickey Mouse and an amazing burst of creativity for Disney that endured without a break for more than a decade. The notion that make-believe cartoon characters could talk, sing, play instruments, and move to a musical beat seemed absolutely magical. *Snow White and the Seven Dwarfs* was a landmark in 1937 because no one imagined that a feature-length animated film might be possible. The songs from that movie became memorable hits, and the characters enjoyed immense merchandising success, which brings us to the second major sign of comics as proto-mass culture.[19]

Outcault's "Buster Brown" comic strip achieved such great appeal after 1902 that selling the right to reproduce Buster Brown's image on a wide array of products, from shoes to watches to toys and games, became far more lucrative than the income from the syndicated comic itself. That gradually turned into a normative pattern for cartoon favorites, and starting in the 1930s, with Mickey Mouse, Donald Duck, and Snow White, it would reap great dividends for Walt Disney enterprises. By 1934 Disney had fifteen people employed in his New York office to oversee the licensing of products that were either reproductions of his characters or else carried their likeness in one form or another.[20]

In the meantime, newspaper syndication of such nationally popular columnists as Joseph Alsop also became commonplace during the 1930s—a significant harbinger of mass culture. By 1925 Walter Lippmann paid close attention to the Associated Press offering news electronically and thereby having what he perceived as a pernicious effect on the responsibilities of local journalists. Prepackaged stories carried by AP helped to augment the shaping of a national culture and made the local press lazy, he believed, about intensely collecting, pursuing, and analyzing news for themselves. During the 1920s a paper like the *Emporia Gazette* accepted the need for a marked increase in national advertising, which meant some displacement of local ads. The merchants of Emporia, Kansas, a town with a population of 5,000, found themselves competing for consumers whose range of choice had been widened by the ownership of automobiles and the advent of parcel post. By the end of the 1920s, the *Gazette* no longer seemed to focus primarily on "revealing Emporia to Emporians." Small-town life had begun to be somewhat marginal even in a small-town newspaper. Celebrity photographs, national news, and comics were necessary in order to sell papers.[21]

In 1925 Walter Winchell introduced what became a revolutionary kind of column in journalism, the celebrity gossip column that focused on people in public life, ranging from movie stars to politicians to members of high society. The swift emergence of derivative Winchell imitators helped give prominence to a culture of celebrity, or fascination with celebrity, that has grown effusively and obsessively ever since. The public's hunger for that sort of news became very evident by the early and mid-1930s. Winchell thereby played an important role in shaping proto-mass culture.[22] Meanwhile, at a different level of taste, less prurient but blandly au courant, DeWitt Wallace had fashioned by the mid-1930s the first genuinely mass market magazine in the United States, the *Reader's Digest*. It developed the largest subscription sales of any magazine prior to *TV Guide* and became a household name, visible in vast numbers of American homes. The swift success of *Life* magazine in 1937–38 provides a parallel example.[23]

A cluster of significant developments, all made possible by swiftly changing technologies, accelerated the prominence of proto-mass culture during the 1930s. The standardization of nationally recognized food products was important. It meant that ethnic and regional variations in American food began to wane somewhat, with the consequence that the nation's diet became more simplified and somewhat blander. For those who wished to eat out, or did so from necessity, nationally recognized chains of eating places offered the assurance that certain dishes would always taste a predictable way and be affordable in straitened times. The standardization of products and services contributed mightily to the success of White Castle food shops in cities and Howard Johnson's restaurants on the road. For the same reasons, franchising became the key to success for national motel chains by the 1960s. The combination of local ownership and national similarity represented security and reliability to large numbers of travelers.[24]

By the later 1920s, when sound was added to film and radio broadcasts more frequently turned into national attractions, the phrase "mass-mediated popular culture" began to be appropriate.[25] Film played an important role in the emergence of proto-mass culture for two reasons. The obvious one is that during the twenties much larger "palaces" were built that could accommodate bigger audiences eager to see and discuss movies that "everyone" seemed to be talking about. But film also marked a conceptual break with the past because more than one copy of a work of art was being made. Snobbish critics were initially reluctant to categorize movies as "art" precisely because a movie was not unique—thousands of copies of any given movie could be distributed.* By the 1930s, some critics could still afford to indulge such an affectation, but fan magazines and the press could not. Besides, a general consensus developed during the thirties that Walt Disney cartoons and features were, in fact, a brand-new art form, not derived from preexisting comic strips; Disney films required the skills of real artists and astounding breakthroughs in the application of technology to art, so that industry words like "cels" suddenly entered the common lexicon.[26]

From scratchy cylinder recordings at the turn of the century to the introduction of wax recordings in 1919–20, yet another momentous shift got under way. The latter had important implications for one of the most significant aspects of American popular culture because the availability of records would gradually diminish the sale of sheet music. Therein lies a striking illustration of the transition from participatory popular culture to the more passive manifestations of mass culture. Whereas sheet music requires someone who knows how to play the piano, with others gathered around in an interactive setting to sing, anyone could play the phonograph and one or more persons could simply sit and quietly listen. By the early 1930s, on the other hand, the emergence of radio began to provide a fresh stimulus for the sale of both sheet music *and* records. Hence that decade really is noteworthy as a transitional one between popular and mass culture.[27]

Record sales increased notably in the United States after 1932, and received a tremendous boost in 1948 when the 33⅓ long-playing disc made its debut, one of several advances in technology that help to mark the transition from proto- to mass culture. At midcentury the "mobile disk jockey" had become a familiar figure at local social functions, such as teenage record hops. Shall we categorize such events as

* The photocopier was invented in 1938 by Chester Carlson. It would become an important benchmark in the transition to mass-produced images.

mass or popular culture? I am inclined to acknowledge their intermediate status. Yet another illustration from the same time frame at midcentury appears in the organizational innovations of Norman Vincent Peale, who adapted mass mailing techniques in order to distribute his messages of self-help and spiritual healing as efficiently as possible to a very broad network of people.[28]

The commercial development of radio during the interwar years began as proto-mass culture in its early phase, before NBC and CBS emerged as national networks in 1926 and 1928. By 1931, CBS had eighty affiliates; and a survey made in 1935 showed that 88 percent of American listeners preferred network to local programming. By the early 1930s *Amos 'n' Andy* had captured the fancy of the nation and helped, in the words of one scholar, to turn a "popular medium into a mass medium." Still, the process remained a gradual one. Despite the notable effectiveness of Franklin D. Roosevelt's Fireside Chats, most American politicians during the thirties disdained the radio as a means of getting their messages out. In baseball the 1934 World Series was the first to be heard nationally. When Orson Welles's startling "War of the Worlds" was broadcast on October 30, 1938, it became clear how large an audience radio now reached, and just how dramatic its impact could be. By the eve of World War II, radio had clearly moved beyond the stage of proto-mass culture.[29]

Depending upon one's perspective and criteria, however, radio listening during the 1930s was not yet a passive experience, either emotionally or functionally. "As soon as he buys his set," one observer noted, a radio listener "becomes a critic, tuning out this, tuning in that, preferring, disliking. . . . What he says is law." Many programs certainly engaged in a concerted effort to make listeners feel that they were being addressed personally. Bradley Kincaid, a popular country singer, wrote in one of his mail-order songbooks: "When I sing for you on the air, I always visualize you, a family group, sitting around the radio, listening and commenting on my program. If I did not feel your presence, though you be a thousand miles away, the radio would be cold and unresponsive to me, and I in turn would sound the same way to you." At the beginning of each episode of the daytime serial *Rosemary*, the announcer made an intimate declaration: "This is *your* story—this is *you*."[30]

Clearly, there is more than a touch of public relations if not outright falsehood in such statements. But we can turn to others that carry a stronger ring of authenticity. Don Ameche, a featured performer in radio for decades beginning in 1930, never doubted that audience involvement contributed to the effectiveness of broadcasting. "It was far and away the greatest medium of all," he remarked. "And the reason behind that is very simple. The listener had to make a contribution, and his enjoyment depended totally upon the *amount* of contribution he made." Joseph Julian, a radio actor, believed that the audience experience of radio was unique. Movie, theater, and television audiences are "essentially passive," he insisted in his memoirs. "They watch and wait for something to be 'done' to them. . . . But radio is 'Theater in the Mind,' and the audience must earn its reward. It must always expend energy, reaching out to embellish, to supply what is not there. . . . No other art form ever engaged the imagination more intensely."[31]

The era when radio truly flourished spanned the three decades following 1925, though the peak period of its popularity was even more concentrated, 1930 to 1950. After 1946, revenue from radio began to decline, and especially so starting in the early 1950s. One important consequence was the decentralization of control over affiliates, which gained greater independence from the networks. Because of the incredibly swift ascent of television, radio became a supplementary source of entertainment by the later 1950s. Unlike vaudeville, radio comedy ran through material at a "killing pace." One important result was a considerable amount of borrowing, imitation, and outright theft. Therefore, the more that one show seemed similar to another, the more this medium made the transition from proto- to mass culture. The dilution of radio's distinctiveness did not mean its death; merely that it would be taken for granted by the later fifties as a secondary aspect of mass culture in the United States.[32]

Based upon the variable phasing of these notable developments in American life, especially in the realms of entertainment and uses of leisure, I am persuaded that the full emergence of mass culture was ready to take place at the end of the 1930s. Sound tracks to accompany movies, a technology barely a decade old, had been mastered by then. Radio enjoyed unchallenged preeminence as the most accessible and affordable form of information and diversion. (The full emergence of FM technology and FCC rulings in support of FM stations meant that it did not become a major force in radio broadcasting until the 1960s.) *Time* magazine was flourishing despite a warning from Mencken to the young Henry Luce back in 1923 that a weekly newsmagazine could not possibly succeed—an absurd fantasy for the recent Yale graduate even to contemplate. Luce's next brainstorm (following *Fortune*), *Life* magazine, was also well underway, and a swift success.[33]

The democratization of attitudes toward culture had been enhanced by an array of publications, plays, murals, and sculpture made possible by the New Deal's WPA programs between 1936 and 1941. George Biddle, an American artist and member of the social elite, wrote in *Harper's* that "In the past few years mass-production media have stepped up the art audience to a mass audience, and a new or a very old conception of art is rapidly evolving. Less and less it is thought of as merely an exchange commodity on the open market to satisfy the taste of a small cultured audience. More and more it is also thought of as something of mass educational value."[34]

When *Life* took a retrospective look at popular taste in America during the 1930s, it noted a tendency that was not entirely new but surely had been accentuated by the technological advances that took place during that decade: the intense but short life of fads, short because new ones could so quickly supplant them. As *Life* put it in 1940: "Radio made song hits short-lived but epidemic while they lasted." One week later *Life* singled out Harold Lloyd's hobbyhorse as "a gratification of the national urge to have fun with gadgets." Although it had the innocent appearance of a child's hobbyhorse, it was mounted on eccentric rockers. The thing looked easy to ride, but novices invariably rocked too hard, especially when lured into a race, thereupon falling hilariously in a humiliating heap. As mass culture evolved, it seemed symptomatic that the populace could maintain an intense focus of enthusiasm only for short spurts. Few entertainment novelties had very much "staying" power.[35]

Following the war, even as family life returned to normal, as individuals reconstructed their lives and G.I.'s returned to school en masse, *Life's* coverage of American leisure highlighted anxiety and an increase in passivity. Americans flocked to beaches during the summer of 1946 to escape disturbing headlines and forget their weariness and woes. Once upon a time, according to *Life*, Americans went to the beach to swim and interact; now they were going in order to sit on the sand "trying to forget their troubles." The following summer *Life* examined "idleness" among American women and the passive pursuits that served them as "props for idle hours." In April 1948, an essay in *Life* observed that technological gadgets enabled Americans to do more and more activities in their beds: working, typing, reading—all at their fingertips, fostering a semipassive and increasingly privatized lifestyle. In 1950 a lawn mower that could be directed by remote control received comparable attention. Once energetic and bustling, Americans were becoming not merely less proactive but putatively inert in accomplishing their tasks.[36]

Life's choice of illustrative (and perhaps illustrably novel) examples may have revealed as much about the need to provide topics for conversation and sell magazines; but the publication itself, the audience that it reached, the consumer temptations that it featured, and the passivity that they were able to induce all sent signals, by midcentury, that cultural critics were eager to pick up: American culture was being coarsened, reduced to its lowest common denominators. One breakthrough after another in the realm of technology only seemed to augment the process of degradation. Critics began to chew on these matters, but could not agree upon diagnoses, not to mention remedies. Nevertheless, the problem of mass culture preoccupied them throughout the 1950s.

III. Mass Culture and the Great Debate

Critical voices had been heard for decades deploring the ways in which Americans preferred to amuse themselves. When Maxim Gorky visited Coney Island in 1906, he expressed scorn for popular entertainments because they seemed to him such an opiate of escapism. Writing a decade later in an essay titled "Trans-national America," Randolph Bourne lamented that the coming of industrialism had provided an utterly commercial substitute for the cultural core that America lacked. Culture for the masses, with its "leering cheapness and falseness of taste and spiritual outlook," had caught on so easily because there "existed no residue of pre-industrial culture to resist it."[37]

In 1961, Raymond Williams observed that for quite some time "a number of people have settled down quite happily to being critics of what they call mass culture." The sources of discontent varied, as I have noted elsewhere, but the most vociferous critics comprised a loose coalition of neo-Marxist highbrows who feared the loss or coarsening of high culture and stressed that mass culture was becoming a narcotic that left the working class docile, incapable of recognizing its own oppression, never mind taking any kind of political action to remedy it.[38] Herbert Marcuse did as much as anyone to develop the idea of mass culture as the opiate of materialistic working people and to suggest in conspiratorial terms that the problem owed much to capitalist manipulation of mass culture for self-serving purposes. He perceived Americans as passive consumers who defined themselves solely through their washing machines, automobiles, and trash compactors.[39]

According to both conservatives and Marxists at that time, mass culture is more likely to serve totalitarian rather than democratic ends because it is tainted by the worst consequences of both bourgeois ideology and industrialism. Conservatives were also inclined to view mass culture as mechanistic rather than organic (or natural), secular rather than spiritual, commercial rather than cerebral, vulgar rather than noble, appealing to the worst instincts in people rather than the best, ephemeral rather than enduring, and highly derivative rather than original. A litany like that puts T. S. Eliot in the same pew with Dwight Macdonald, which is not unreasonable when you consider that both men felt themselves besieged by mass culture. They shared the view of Theodor Adorno and the Frankfurt School that the "culture industry" was clearly pernicious. Moreover, the extension of real (i.e., traditional) culture to the masses would very likely result not in uplifting the masses but in the degradation of culture.[40]

Others who expressed vocal concern, albeit somewhat less shrill, were writers who appeared regularly in *Partisan Review*, people like co-editor William Phillips and Mary McCarthy, who speculated with some ambivalence about "the problem of equality, its consequences, and what price shall be paid for it," and then as a consequence "the spread of uniformity." In 1954 Irving Howe published an extremely controversial essay in *Partisan Review* in which he made iconoclastic charges such as the following: "Because industrialism grants large quantities of leisure time without any creative sense of how to employ it, there springs up a vast new industry that must be staffed by intellectuals and quasi-intellectuals: the industry of mass culture."[41]

In 1960 Howe looked back somewhat ruefully at the rather intense contribution he had made to an early phase of the Great Debate. "Assaults upon mass culture became an indispensable element of culture," he wrote now, "the spice for the stew." And Daniel Bell noted soon afterward that the pages of *Dissent* (edited by Howe) and *Universities and Left Review* had been filled with attacks against the excesses of advertising and the "debaucheries" of mass culture.[42] For some of these critics their most strident scorn was actually aimed at middle-brow culture, which in reality seemed even more of a threat to the traditional high culture they still valued. So they tended to write double-barreled essays that scattered shot simultaneously at both of their nemeses.[43]

Those who positioned themselves on the other side in the Great Debate scarcely had truly positive things to say on behalf of mass culture. Instead, they either warned that it was premature to pass judgment because mass culture was still in its infancy (David Riesman), or else the advocates were producers of films for educational organizations who genuinely believed that the new media could be used to level up taste (Alexander Klein), or else they were critics like Gilbert Seldes who (hopeful in the face of recent experience) argued that mass media did have some genuine achievements to show and could have even more if the Frank Stantons of this world would only stop pandering to the lowest common denominators.[44]

Edward Shils, a notably cerebral highbrow himself, "defended" mass culture in a circuitous yet thoughtful way by insisting upon the need for much greater definitional clarity, and by pointing out the unmentioned ways in which elitists did, in fact, deceitfully indulge themselves by partaking of mass culture. Shils thereby called attention quite candidly to the blurring of taste-level stratification, one of the first serious critics to do so.

> I have reservations about the use of the term "mass culture," because it refers simultaneously to the substantive and qualitative properties of the culture, to the social status of its consumers, and to the media by which it is transmitted. Because of this at least threefold reference, it tends to beg some important questions regarding the relations among the three variables. For example, the current conception of "mass culture" does not allow for the fact that in most countries, and not just at present, very large sections of the elite consume primarily mediocre and brutal culture. It also begs the important questions as to whether the mass media can transmit works of superior culture, or whether the genres developed by the new mass media can become the occasions of creativity and therewith a part of superior culture. Also, it does not consider the obvious fact that much of what is produced in the genres of superior culture is mediocre.[45]

In a conference held in Berlin in 1960, William Phillips of *Partisan Review* had a confrontation with Shils, who actually defended the benign advances made by mass culture. When Phillips attempted to challenge him, Shils wouldn't permit him to speak. Leslie Fiedler, the provocative cultural critic, was one of the few participants in the Great Debate who staunchly advocated mass culture. He published the first defense of "Superman" comics as having merit for those who read them, and he considered Russ Meyers's grade B movie *Valley of the Dolls*, which highbrows regarded as trashy, "atrociously wonderful."[46] Such positions were not widely held among the literati at that time, a configuration that would subsequently change during the 1980s.

Writing an overview essay in 1990, cultural historian Jean-Christophe Agnew asserted that historians have "deferred the arrival of mass consumer culture to the mid-twentieth century." I happen to share the substance of that position wholeheartedly, though I am unaware of any notable change in the most vocal historiographical literature that would validate Agnew's argument on behalf of a shift in the more conventional and casual chronology. Perhaps his insertion of a modifier to make the phrase "mass *consumer* culture" is key, because disposable income certainly rose to unprecedented levels after midcentury, and that trend, in turn, stimulated not merely the production of mass culture but new marketing schemes and modes of dissemination.[47] Diners Club, for example, issued the first credit card in 1950. In fact, marketing specialists soon began carving up what had been considered a large audience, stratified primarily by taste, into segments based upon age, gender, and income.

The more familiar markets for popular culture (Russell Lynes's brow levels) became fragmented so that almost no one with something to sell, except for the major television networks, tried to target everyone with a singular product. Categories had to be rearranged. The emergence of suburban movie houses, for example, meant the segmentation of film audiences by socioeconomic level and by the kinds of movies preferred by assorted age groups. The same became increasingly true of diversity within shopping malls during the 1960s and 1970s. We now appreciate that going to a mall is very much a gendered experience for adults, but less so (and more participatory) for teenagers, who regard the mall not merely as a place to shop but also as a place to "hang out."[48] Hence the paradox that although we associate mass culture with standardization, it gradually began to acquire a distinctive diversity after midcentury. Consumer patterns were not all the same, nor were taste levels. The defining attributes of mass culture must be delineated in other ways.

A Roper poll taken late in 1948 asked 3,008 Americans: "Which two or three of the things on this list do you really enjoy doing most in your spare time?" The diversity of responses and the blend of interactive and passive preferences reinforces my belief that the immediate postwar era became the final phase in the transition from proto- to mass culture. (The totals add up to more than 100% because of multiple responses.)

Listening to records	10%
Listening to the radio	53
Playing a musical instrument	5
Doing outdoor sports	14
Visiting with friends	28
Painting or drawing	2
Reading books	22
Playing cards	19
Going to movies	20
Doing needlework (sewing, knitting, crocheting)	18
Handicrafts (woodworking, metalworking)	5
Reading magazines	17
Watching sports events	16
Don't know	4[49]

How can we best particularize and substantiate the generalizations offered in the two preceding paragraphs? By specifying the most powerful manifestations of mass culture as it took shape at midcentury. Doing so will not only enable us to contrast it with what some observers have called mass culture prior to 1940, but also with differences of degree and kind that have appeared since the early 1980s. Let's begin with popular music. In the years immediately following World War II, more than four hundred new record labels came into existence. It may have been a precarious and exploratory industry, but it sold records in unprecedented numbers (the mass aspect), yet to segmented audiences (consumer diversity).[50]

The initial schemes to mass-produce cheap paperbound books emerged in the late 1930s; and the subjects ranged from Mercury Mysteries to Thornton Wilder's *The Bridge of San Luis Rey* (1927) to Shakespeare's plays. U.S. entry into World War II created a major new outlet and audience for pocket-sized books because the military commissioned more than thirty-five million copies of familiar titles to be distributed overseas to members of the armed forces. Early entrepreneurs in the paperback industry quickly learned that flashy or seductive covers helped to make books self-promoting. Moreover, Penguin and Fawcett devised an effective solution to the problem of how best to display paperback books. They developed the four-sided "Spin-it" rack that could be filled with an array of titles from assorted genres.[51]

In addition to literary classics and steamy fiction that many critics at the time considered pornographic trash, nonfiction best-sellers were carefully commissioned to suit a swiftly expanding audience that sought everything from spiritual guidance to baby care. By midcentury Benjamin Spock's *Pocket Book of Baby and Child Care* (first published in June 1946) became the second-best-selling book in American publishing history, trailing only the Bible. Within less than eight years a phenomenal growth pattern occurred. In 1946, around sixty million paperbacks were distributed; by 1953, the number more than tripled, and many new publishers entered the field. Equally striking was the expanded range of titles: not just mysteries, mayhem, sex, and science fiction, but *The Iliad* and Edmund Wilson's *To the Finland Station*. This aspect of mass culture soon became even more inclusive. The process of production and distribution may have been "mass," but the offerings were diversified.[52]

DeWitt Wallace and the *Reader's Digest*, meanwhile, a remarkable financial success during the 1930s and 1940s, looked for new worlds to conquer and took the next logical step by developing a "condensed" (abridged) book program in 1951–52. The books selected tended to be middlebrow in content, perhaps lower-middlebrow if we follow Russell Lynes's 1949 schematization—titles like *The Caine Mutiny*, or *Giant*, or *The Last Hurrah*, or works by John P. Marquand, Alec Waugh, and MacKinlay Kantor. But the extensive marketing scheme developed by Wallace's staff and the actual sales realized marked the project as highly representative of the emergent mass culture at midcentury. After just one year there were 512,000 subscribers, far more than the Book-of-the-Month Club and the Literary Guild, created late in the 1920s. When *TV Guide* emerged in 1953 as an instantaneous success (initial sales of 2.2 million copies), *Reader's Digest* bought competitive display space at the checkout counters of supermarkets. Sales promptly tripled, quadrupled, and then some. *TV Guide* and *Reader's Digest* remained staples in American mass culture for decades to come.[53] *Sports Illustrated* first appeared in 1954 and eventually became a nationwide success.

Let's notice a simple yet symptomatic sign of transition. In 1958, when John Kenneth Galbraith published *The Affluent Society*, it contained no references to television, radio, or advertising. Nine years later, when he published *The New Industrial State*, that book contained quite a few references to all three. The difference cannot be explained by the respective subject areas of the two works. It can best be understood in terms of the swift, full-scale emergence and impact of mass culture between 1958 and 1967, the very same decade in which fast-food chains and large shopping malls selling standardized brands also emerged.

The American supermarket underwent a dramatic phase of expansion between 1948 and 1963 when large chains like A&P and Safeway added many new locations. By 1956 the independent corner grocery store had not disappeared entirely, but it had become a charming relic from an earlier era. Mom-and-pop stores found it very hard to compete with the vast array of processed foods available at the supermarkets. Meanwhile, in the later 1950s Ray Kroc began his aggressive franchising of the McDonald's "speedee" system. By comparison with White Castle hamburger establishments, which had spread slowly during the 1920s and '30s on a scale characteristic of proto-mass culture, McDonald's provided a vast and very swift stimulus for the appeal of fast-food eateries during the 1960s and '70s. The standardization of both food options and services became yet another familiar characteristic of mass culture as we know it.[54]

As shopping centers developed during the 1950s and then were supplanted by the proliferation of malls two decades later—the rate of change varying from large urban areas to suburban, exurban, and more remote locations—the preponderance of chain stores and major franchises over locally owned independent stores brought shoppers the latest national trends in merchandising techniques and products. A national standardization of taste and desirability occurred: large numbers of people learning about and wanting the same things at the same time. Pepsi-Cola, for example, did not begin to advertise heavily on television until 1963–64. Blue jeans did not become the universal dress code for young people until the very end of the 1950s—and even then fraught with controversy, when worn to school, well into the 1960s.[55]

Beyond the elitist critiques of mass culture by a number of intellectuals—some from native stock like Dwight Macdonald and others coming from European crucibles of critical thought like Theodor Adorno—there were also the sensibilities of Americans who cherished older ideals of individual initiative and responsibility for choice. Their attitudes are more difficult to document because we do not have a systematic corpus of texts from them to analyze; but Gilbert Seldes spoke for such people in 1962 when he expressed the view that American individualism had been subverted by the advent of mass culture after midcentury. "As a member of a huge, undifferentiated audience," he wrote, "the individual loses importance. As a communicator, too, the individual has lost influence."[56]

For Seldes and virtually all of his contemporary critics, no other innovation marked the arrival and transforming impact of mass culture more powerfully and quickly than television (fig. 14). Initially it was considered an elite form of entertainment because most Americans could not afford sets. But ownership figures moved rapidly from 6 percent penetration of American homes in 1949 to 76 percent by 1956. The basic patterns of network oligopoly were set in motion during that time period; and by 1960 nearly 90 percent of American households had at least one receiver. It had taken radio about thirty years to achieve a comparable rate of household saturation. (In 1951, in his *Requiem for a Nun*, William Faulkner could declare that national commercial radio had so penetrated Yoknapatawpha County that the very air was "no more Yoknapatawpha's air nor even Mason and Dixon's air, but America's.") By 1988, 57 percent of American homes had two or more television sets. Consequently, parents and children became more likely to watch their favorite programs separately. Instead of promoting family unity, which occurred for a brief period during the 1950s, TV contributed to the segmentation as well as the privatization of American family life.[57]

A passage from I Corinthians, 15:33, suddenly acquired new meaning: "Be not deceived: evil communications corrupt good manners." Within less than a decade, television had become virtually addictive for a majority of Americans. In 1957 a Gallup poll asked 1,659 Americans

14. *The New Television Set* (1949) by Norman Rockwell (oil on canvas)

the following question: "If you had to give up one of these—radio, television, the newspaper, magazines—which one would be the hardest for you to give up?" Here are the responses.

radio	21%
television	46
newspaper	27
magazines	4
don't know	2

The follow-up asked which one would be the next (second) hardest for you to give up?

radio	29%
television	21
newspaper	34
magazines	12
don't know	4[58]

The spillover effects of television's ubiquitous presence were felt in countless ways. By the mid-1950s, situation comedies on TV started to command larger audiences than human interest stories in magazines. As a result *American Magazine* folded in 1956 and *Collier's* followed quickly in 1957. In the later fifties quite a few mass circulation periodicals declined and became less commercially viable. Installation of the coaxial cable in 1951 made transcontinental transmission of television possible and caused enthusiasm for certain kinds of feature and sports events to jump from primarily local to national audiences. Edward R. Murrow made his first coast-to-coast broadcast on November 18, 1951. Television had a very negative impact upon attendance at minor league baseball games once people in smaller communities could watch more distant major league teams play. Baseball became more literally the national pastime once games from other cities were visually available. Professional basketball and football, which did not enjoy an appeal at all comparable to baseball in the 1950s, would be transformed by television during the 1960s but especially the 1970s, with extraordinary consequences ranging from advertising to players' salaries to the merchandising of sports equipment and paraphernalia.[59]

In 1971 a Harris poll of 1,600 people asked for reactions to this statement: "Television has made such sports as professional football and basketball [successful], which is good." Seventy-seven % agreed, 13% disagreed, 10% were not sure. Harris also asked whether people would prefer to see baseball, football, and basketball games in person or on television. The preferences for television were 44%, 46%, and 45%, respectively, for each sport, figures that I interpret as a fairly strong inclination toward TV viewing for combined reasons involving cost, the trend toward privatization, and passivity (or inertia if you prefer).[60]

Such proportions would have been unthinkable four decades earlier, not because television did not yet exist but because being participatory in public spaces was still an essential and expected aspect of popular culture. Needless to say, those who watch a sporting event at home have no influence on the outcome of the event, whereas fans in attendance at a stadium can give the home team an advantage, especially in football but also in basketball. The term "couch potato" was coined in 1976 by Robert Armstrong, a California cartoonist. During the next two decades a series of essays on the couch-potato phenomenon appeared, ranging from serious pieces concerned with the optimal marketing strategy to increase the spending patterns of passive home consumers to satirical pieces in praise of the couch potato that provided such advice as: "Work up to big-league furniture" and "Remove distractions while the TV is on."[61]

The familiar perception, which I believe is indisputably accurate, regards television as a phenomenon that brought fundamental changes to the ways that Americans live. It meant, for example, that entertainment became not just totally accessible but fully integrated into the daily lives of Americans. TV was preeminent in home entertainment by 1960 and became the primary source of news for most adults by 1970. Less evident, at least in clear proportions, is the degree of ambivalence that Americans felt about television by the 1970s. The results of a series of polls are quite revealing here. In 1971 a Harris poll asked 1,600 Americans to respond to this statement: "Television is good because you get so much entertainment and information for free." Eighty-three % agreed, 14% did not, and 3% were not sure. Two years later Gallup asked 1,567 people for their reactions to this question: "As time goes on, do you have a more favorable or less favorable attitude toward television?" The responses ran as follows:

More	31%
Less	42
About same	23
No opinion	4[62]

In 1977 Gallup asked 1,518 Americans this question: "Thinking about how you spend your non-working time each day, do you think that you spend too much time or too little time watching television?" Here are the replies:

Too much	31%
Too little	17
About right	48
Don't know	4[63]

That apparent affirmation of the status quo appears in a somewhat different light, however, when we look at the results of a Gallup poll one year later. "Some people think that television has an effect on how they spend their time and others disagree. If you watched less television, do you think you would . . .

Read more	43%
Read less	2
Read the same amount	49
Don't know	6"[64]

Finally, a Yankelovich poll of 1,254 persons taken two months later asked: "What are the three or four things you like to do the most during your leisure time?" (The total adds up to more than 100% because people could make multiple responses.)

Camping	15%
Boating	6
Night school, continuing education, lectures	5
Hobbies such as stamp collecting	3
Volunteer work	5
Being active in things the kids are doing (e.g., sports teams, Scouts, etc.)	15
Night out at a supper club/discotheque or café	12
Skiing	2
Keeping in shape and physical exercise	9
Riding a bike	6
Going to the mountains or beach	12
Jogging	3
Playing an instrument	3
Listening to music	17
Reading a magazine	13
Being active in an organization	7
Reading a newspaper	12
Handiwork such as crocheting, knitting, needlework	13
Visiting relatives and friends	15
Taking a drive in the car	9
Going to parties	6
Shopping	8
Fishing/hunting	16

Swimming	5
Bowling	8
Playing cards	11
Going to a sporting event (i.e., ball games)	9
Going to the theater/stage shows	5
Going to the movies	7
Playing tennis	2
Playing golf	4
Reading a book	14
Going on outings with the family	11
Gardening	11
Eating out in restaurants	13
Entertaining friends	10
Watching television	24
Relaxing at home	23
Church-related activities	15
Other	6[65]

Although there is no astonishing trend apparent here, there is a pattern if one notes the top choices—watching television, relaxing at home, and listening to music—because these are comparatively passive or nonpublic pursuits rather than being notably interactive or participatory. Only when we turn to the second tier do we find much of the latter: camping, being active in things the kids are doing, visiting relatives and friends, and church-related activities.[66]

By 1978 Americans had not become exclusively interactive or passive. One would scarcely expect the balance to tip entirely to one extreme or the other. But the balance had shifted rather decisively in the direction of *more* passive and privatized activities. The validity of that conclusion has been sharply contested during the past fifteen years or so, and those contradictory views form the subject of chapter 8. We can conclude here, however, with the perspective of a prominent sociologist published in 1977, exactly when the polls just cited were being taken. The writer is Richard Sennett, and his observation appeared in the context of a book concerned with the decline of public culture.

For the spectator, the radio and the tube do not permit audience interruption; if you start reacting while the politician is on the air you miss part of what he or she says next. You've got to be silent to be spoken to. The only possible means of response is to have a TV commentator select what shall be repeated and discussed. The commentator then assumes exactly the function of the critic who interpreted for those silent audiences of the last century the performances they watched live, but the commentator has more complete control because his is instantaneous. Passivity is the "logic" of this technology. The mass media intensify the patterns of crowd silence which began to take form in the theaters and concert halls of the last century, intensify the idea of a disembodied spectator, a passive witness.[67]

Although I do not entirely share Sennett's emphasis upon creeping passivity during the later nineteenth and earlier twentieth century, my position is much closer to his than it is to those who argue on behalf of undiminished personal agency during the era of domination by mass media following the 1950s.

8

Mass Culture in More Recent Times: Passive and/or Participatory?

∞

I. The Great Debate Redivivus: An Ideological Inversion

Although scholars and critics continue to differ about when to place the genesis of mass culture and its transformation over time, no one disputes that its *full* emergence occurred more than three decades ago, and perhaps four. The 1969 moonwalk was witnessed simultaneously by more viewers, 580 million, than any previous event in history. The audience for the 1974 World Cup soccer playoff reached 600 million. On August 1, 1975, approximately one billion people watched as the United States, the Soviet Union, and thirty-three other nations signed the Helsinki Accords concerning such multilateral matters as human rights, territorial boundaries, science, trade, and environmental issues. We could endlessly enumerate the markers of mass culture. By 1992 there were almost 39,000 operational shopping centers in the United States, 1,835 of them large regional malls. Increasingly, they featured the same stores, the same consumerist environment, and the same products. Critics who worried about "standardization" back in the 1920s would be astonished, even appalled, if they could travel in a time capsule to the 1980s and '90s.

Although a consensus exists that we are now awash in mass culture, however, there is little agreement over its most fundamental characteristics and especially their behavioral consequences. Hence we have had since the mid-1980s a second "Great Debate" over the extent or degree of passivity ascribable to mass culture as opposed to contentions that personal initiative, interactivity, and self-determination have not been crushed by the overwhelming force and manifestations of mass culture. To complicate matters, moreover, there has been insufficient attention given to the palpable distinctions between mass culture in the two decades following 1960 and then in the two most recent ones. The differences between these sequential phases of mass culture matter a great deal in negotiating the conflicting positions concerning passivity and agency. Even those observers who are willing and able to view 1880 or 1920 or 1950 in historical perspective tend to treat the history of mass culture since 1960 with blurred vision. Do they acknowledge qualitative and quantitative changes that have occurred since then? Frequently they do. Does that recognition carry over into their attitudes and sweeping generalizations about the essential nature and impact of mass culture? Not very often and not very well.

To start with some fairly large categories, there does seem to be broad agreement that two crucial factors (or variables) shaping and reconfiguring mass culture are technology and advertising. Television has been the single most important feature of the former and consumerism the key consequence of the latter. Therefore, I will devote disproportionate attention to them in describing the second debate in this chapter. Needless to say, these are not discrete phenomena. They are intimately interconnected in complex ways. There is a proclivity to quote James Joyce—"Are my consumers not also my producers?"—as a pithy way to say that advertising creates or stimulates its own interactions. Too facile perhaps, even as a signifying epigram. One wonders just how many people are genuinely interactive with James Joyce. True, he did take from certain "producers," but the equation does not flow equally in both directions because ever so few of his producers subsequently became his consumers.

The most suitably representative artist for the age of mass culture may well be Andy Warhol. Warhol called the loft where he and his helpers mass-produced their images and objects The Factory (rather than "The Studio"),* and he proclaimed: "I want to *be* a machine."[1] Because his ideas and his work were collaboratively created, Warhol's mode of operation gave new meaning to notions of art that is mass-

---

* Back in the 1930s, Walt Disney's employees called his Burbank studio the "fun factory."

15. *Andy Warhol* (1975) by James Browning Wyeth
(gouache and pencil on paper)

produced. What Warhol did and achieved in the 1960s and '70s, beyond sheer notoriety, jumped well beyond what Walter Benjamin envisioned in 1935 when he wrote his subsequently famous essay "Art in the Age of Mechanical Reproduction." In addition, Warhol's capacity to connect technology with consumerism, the banality of the ordinary with the swell of celebrity, infused new meaning into the maxim of Bruce Barton, the 1920s advertising man par excellence: "Reputation is repetition." Barton had in mind maximizing the impact of commercial advertising. Warhol had in mind the commercialization of "art" redefined as repetitious products and images—the more familiar the better. Banality made millions for the Factory and its chief elf.[2]

By the later 1960s, seven out of ten Americans believed that advertising was indeed a form of art. Because it has become virtually impossible to avoid or escape it, advertising has emerged as the most common kind of art in our culture. Because ads are so pervasive, aggressive, repetitive, and intrusive, they are much more difficult to ignore than they were thirty or sixty or ninety years ago. Advertising has become one of the defining attributes of mass culture in our time, and especially so since the 1980s, when computer imaging made many ads more fun and more engaging than ever before. We have a stereotype of people using the remote control to escape ads on television. Well, many people do; but a great many others do not, especially children, who tend to love ads, along with adults who are intrigued by the ingenuity of new ads that are concocted for special occasions like athletic championships. People seek to escape stale ads that have grown wearisome; but the ad agencies work very hard to innovate and replace the narcoleptic ads with novel ones.[3]

James Twitchell has called to our attention two prescient assertions from 1915 and 1946. They are worthy of notice because their validity easily outweighs their hyperbole.

> When the historian of the Twentieth Century shall have finished his narrative, and comes searching for the subtitle which shall best express the spirit of the period, we think it not at all unlikely that he may select "The Age of Advertising" for the purpose.   —*Printers' Ink*, May 25, 1915

> These humbler adjuncts to literature [i.e., advertisements] may prove more valuable to the future historian than the editorial contents [of large magazines]. In them we may trace our sociological history, the rise and fall of fads and crazes, changing interests and tastes, in foods, clothes, amusements and vices, a panorama of life as it was lived, more informing than old diaries or crumbling tombstones.
> —Earnest Elmo Calkins, *And Hearing Not*, 1946

The central argument of Twitchell's book, although somewhat overstated in places, is significant for our purposes because it is sensitive to change over time and quite properly calls attention to the massification of advertising in recent decades. "What distinguishes modern advertising," he writes, "is that it has jumped from the human voice and printed posters to anything that can carry it. Almost every physical object now carries advertising, almost every human environment is suffused with advertising, almost every moment of time is calibrated by advertising."[4]

That observation serves as a helpful reminder that we must keep in mind not merely two debates concerning mass culture (one in the 1950s, as we have seen, and another occurring since the later 1980s, a major focus of this chapter), but long-term change over the full course of the twentieth century as well as significant alterations in the nature of mass culture just since the 1960s. The recent changes have prompted a desire on the part of cultural critics to take mass culture quite seriously as an object of analysis, and to criticize it, moreover, on less specious and less elitist grounds than its raging opponents did at midcentury. The gravitas of contemporary criticism (and appreciation) provides a secondary theme of this chapter. We have come a long way since Mort Sahl's quip about the *Playboy* centerfold: "an entire generation of American males is growing up in the belief that their wives will have staples in their navels."

The texture and thrust of serious criticism now provides specific and nuanced elaborations on Ariel Dorfman's 1975 assertion that "beyond the children's comic lies the whole concept of contemporary mass culture, which is based on the principle that only entertainment can liberate humankind from the social anxiety and conflict in which it is submerged."[5] Since the 1980s, especially, we have become aware that potent forces in the entertainment industry along with equally powerful corporations play an extremely influential role in determining the ultimate presentation and perception of our collective and mythic past. That became evident at the centennial of the Statue of Liberty in 1986 when exclusive corporate sponsorship (one sponsor per product category) became visible in vulgar ways; at the Buy-centennial of the Constitution in 1987–88; at EPCOT Center, as well as increasing numbers of theme parks in which the past is paraded as a colorful pastiche of patriotic pap; and in second-rate action films that appear to treat aspects of the American presidency, or national holidays, or military conflicts of the past half century.[6] "Treat" and "treatment" really are the operative words here. The national narrative has been telescoped, spliced, and push-buttoned to fast forward. The next logical step may very well be history rewound, a courtesy to the subsequent viewer, of course, before returning the cassette to your history-video emporium.

II. American Spectators and the Screen at Home

As we have already seen, occasional laments about the growth of passivity and "spectatoritis" appeared as early as the turn of the century. Two differences between then and now need to be acknowledged, however. First, and most obvious, is scale. Such complaints were far less frequent in 1910 or 1920, say, than in 1975. Second, and more significant, expressions of concern about passivity earlier in the twentieth century cut vertically through class lines and brow levels. Audiences for high culture events, such as theater and concerts, were expected to be attentive and silent. Jane Addams's co-worker at Hull House, meanwhile, Mary Simkhovitch, snobbishly remarked that silent film made viewers passive. That was not exactly true, in fact, but the *perception* seems to have been widely shared, mostly by people who did not go to see silent films! A generation later, though, Louis Adamic, a widely read social observer notably interested in ethnicity, insisted that consumer culture had emerged as one among several causes of passivity.[7]

As I indicated earlier in chapters 4 and 5, however, popular culture during the first half of the twentieth century flourished at various venues and in numerous ways that most certainly qualify as interactive and participatory. Let this 1927 comment by Rudolph Fisher stand for thousands of others that might be cited: "You don't just go to a cabaret and sit back and wait to be entertained. You get out on the floor and join the pow-wow and help entertain yourself." Moreover, as the historian Lewis Erenberg has noted:

> Dining, drinking, talking, and flirting at their seats with members of their own party or with those at other tables, patrons were relaxed and could see the performance in a more informal way. The tables and the floor brought audience and performer into a more intimate relationship than was possible in conventional theatres. Performers started their acts on the platform and then stepped down onto the floor and appeared among the diners. Even if the act was one that could be performed on a more formal stage, the fact of appearing in this special environment altered the nature of the interaction. The dance floor, the absence of large proscenium arch stages, and the closeness of

the audience seated at tables made the room a scene of expressive activity. The entire restaurant became the setting for performance, and customers themselves could not escape becoming involved in the action and spontaneity of the moment.[8]

Expressions of concern about the demonstrable growth of passive behavior in North America were anticipated early in the 1950s when Harold A. Innis, a Canadian historian, and sociologist Paul Lazarsfeld called attention to the passive reception of such modern media as movies and radio.[9] During the later 1950s these critical observations tended to be broadly inclusive. Singling out television as the arch-villain came a decade later. In 1957, a few months before Vance Packard's best-seller *The Hidden Persuaders* appeared, he wrote to his publisher that his research made it clear that many Americans "resent the growing conformity and sterility of their life where they are left only with the roles of being consumers or spectators." At a conference sponsored by the Tamiment Institute in 1959, historian Oscar Handlin observed: "The mass media find space for politics and sports, for science and fiction, for art and music, all presented on an identical plateau of irrelevance. And the audience which receives this complex variety of wares accepts them passively as an undifferentiated but recognizable series of good things among which it has little capacity for choice, and with which it cannot establish any meaningful, direct relationship." During the later 1950s and early '60s, critic Dwight Macdonald explicitly blamed the growth of passivity on mass culture.[10] This causal connection arose all across the ideological spectrum from right of center to considerably left of center. The diatribe had not yet become the partisan ideological dialogue that would emerge in the later 1980s.

Gilbert Seldes, invariably referred to as "the distinguished critic," shifted during the fifties from three decades of notably versatile writing to intense concentration upon film and television. At that same Tamiment Institute conference in 1959, Seldes speculated that a dramatic improvement in the quality of media programs still might not solve the immense problem of passive audiences. "A nation which is passively accepting works even ten times as good as those we have now, passively accepting them, might still be drugged and become entirely apathetic and remain emotionally immature. . . . We need an audience more active than any audience that has ever before been in the world."[11]

Because most of Seldes's career had been so supportive of popular culture, he felt quite awkward about his growing negativism during his later years. So in 1966, even while warning against making scapegoats of the mass media, he acknowledged after fifteen years of intense study that people watched television even when no program that they actually cared about was scheduled. The problem with television really went beyond passivity, Seldes said, because TV was passively addictive. He recognized that the basic objective of broadcasters "is to create a habit," which was why a weak show commonly followed a good one. The media strategy was based upon a *premise* of passivity verging upon immobility.[12]

It is necessary to notice that a nexus between mass culture and "spectatoritis" was observed persistently in realms quite distinct from television. The laments, moreover, came from conservatives, moderates, and radicals alike. We find it in the very first issue of *Rolling Stone* in November 1967. That same summer, some ultra-leftist Diggers in New York City slyly advised the press about their plans to perform guerrilla theater. Whereupon the San Francisco Diggers, founders of the movement, denounced this leak to the press as a publicity stunt, and therefore not permissible under the rules of engagement of their version of guerrilla theater because it created spectators rather than engaged participants.[13]

Richard Schickel has written a compelling passage on the passive nature of serious theatergoing during the 1960s and '70s:

> However caught up we are in the drama, we never entirely erase our consciousness of the invisible fourth wall that separates us from the players on stage. No matter how artfully they are arranged, the visible presence of theatrical conventions—the working of lights, the movement of scenery, the intermission between acts—all serve to remind us that this is not life we are witnessing, but a representation of life. . . . We remain, in the theater, in what might be termed a passive-objective state. That is to say, we enter the playhouse consciously willing to surrender ourselves to the author and actors, passively receptive to whatever delights are about to unfold, while at the same time retaining our consciousness of the formality of the setting. Above all, we will be under no illusion that we are, or could be, participants in the drama, that we have anything at stake in the proceedings other than enjoyment and, possibly, edification.[14]

197

Schickel acknowledges that by the early 1980s some leading spirits in the theatrical avant-garde had begun to rethink the problem of engagement by turning increasingly to thrust and arena staging, to entrances through the aisles, and direct address to the audience. Street and guerrilla theater carried such efforts a step further. He observes that these recent changes in stagecraft "may be seen as a practical recognition of what theater people see as a defect in their art, an inability to directly appeal to the audience's subconscious. . . ."[15]

In 1988 Christopher Lasch lamented "the transformation of politics from a central component of popular culture into a spectator sport." Looking at the low turnout of registered voters in presidential elections, the considerably smaller participation in state and local elections, and the pathetic lack of interest in meaningful schoolboard elections, Lasch concluded that "distributive democracy has been achieved at the expense of participatory democracy."[16]

Clearly, the advent of mass culture has not made *everyone* inert—that would be a specious and invalid claim—yet its overall impact is the character of a society in which proportionately more members are less active than was the case fifty or one hundred years ago. There are exceptions, of course, and each reader will supply his or her own favorite category. Tourism, for example, has reached an all-time high. More people participate in some sort of organized sport today. What young folks do at waterparks during the summer is surely participatory. There is leisure-time activity, to be sure; but not on a scale that is optimal or impressive in terms of the society as a whole. Comparisons with 1900 or even 1950 are difficult, of course, because leisure was so much less abundant then, especially for ordinary Americans.

There seems to be little if any dissent from Douglas Gomery's view that television has become the most prodigious entertainment and information machine in all of human history. Most observers would also agree with sociologist Todd Gitlin that television has done more to nationalize American life than any other single innovation or phenomenon.[17] If we ask why the social impact of television was so much greater than that of radio, multiple reasons occur. Whereas radio was and remains ideal as background "material" while one is doing other things, fewer people were inclined to turn on the television while performing tasks, especially during the first decades when each home had only one TV, a nonmobile console customarily located in the family room. Precisely because one wants to watch what is happening on the screen, a person is less likely to engage in other activities at the same time. Television has had a more profound effect than radio because it compels more of our attention. It has long been valued for its "baby-sitting" capabilities, which was much less true of radio. And it has made two full generations of Americans far more visually oriented than their predecessors—all of which, by now, is old news.

What is notably pertinent to this chapter, however, is the persistent charge—made by people with long experience in broadcasting, by advertising executives, and by a great many students of communications, sociology, psychology, and education—that television increases passivity in a wide variety of ways. Scholarly studies echo Lasch's lament by showing that television does make people politically passive. The more they watch, the less likely they are to vote. Why? Because people who depend heavily on TV for information are more inclined to believe that events are moving too swiftly and remotely to be affected by the choices of an individual citizen. By the mid-1970s, some sources wondered whether the American people had "lost the capacity for believing in the reality of events in their own lives."* Hence their sense of detachment if not despair, of being inconsequential rather than competent in their civic capacities.[18]

If we turn to public opinion polls, the findings are somewhat inconsistent and not entirely reliable. Nevertheless, some strong impressions do emerge. In May 1971 a Louis Harris poll asked 1,600 adults (nationwide) for their response to this statement: "Television is a good escape from the pressures of day-to-day living." 62% agreed, 33% disagreed, and 5% were not sure. The same people were then asked for their reactions to this assertion: "Television is bad because it turns people into watchers, not doers." 57% agreed, 37% did not, and 6% were not sure. A substantial majority thereby acknowledged the passivity-inducing effects of TV.[19]

Now let's look at three polls taken during the summer of 1978. The first one asked 1,622 adults (nationwide) what effect children's shows on television had on children's education. 55% said good, only 12% said bad, 10% said no effect, another 10% said mixed, and 13% gave

---

* Mass culture undermines civic culture in various ways. It has been observed that police-show narratives on television constantly display violations of civil liberties, thereby reducing the ordinary citizen's awareness of constitutional rights and responsibilities.

no opinion. The very same CBS poll also asked: "What effect do you think television is having on the education children now receive? In general, is it having a good effect, a bad effect, or no effect at all?" The responses to *that* question were skewed quite differently.

Good effect	23%
Bad effect	40
No effect	11
Both good and bad	20
No opinion	6[20]

Finally, in the summer of 1978, Gallup asked 1,515 people this question: "If your children watched less television, do you think they would . . .

Read more	49%
Read less	1
Read the same amount	45
Don't know	5"[21]

As I have indicated, these polls are certainly not conclusive, yet they do reveal a somewhat reluctant acknowledgment that television is conducive to passivity and provides a fairly noticeable alternative (and disincentive) to reading.

Teachers, child psychologists, authorities in the field of communications, and television personalities all expressed their concern much more emphatically. During the 1960s and '70s, teachers who remembered students who grew up without television spoke with considerable emotion about their enhanced degree of imagination, engagement, and interactive behavior. A reading specialist in the 1970s who interviewed a very indifferent student, a television watcher, reported to the boy's teacher that "he was not performing because he didn't want to. He was uninterested, passive, and uninvolved."[22]

The verdict on the PBS children's program *Sesame Street* from many perspectives has often been negative because the program encouraged passive learning, a phrase that recurs in the literature like a mantra. As early as 1960 Bruno Bettelheim expressed the view that even "instructive" television induced indolence or inertia. "My concern," Bettelheim wrote, "is less with content and much more with what persistent watching does to a child's ability to relate to real people, to become self-activated, to think on the basis of his own life experience instead of in stereotypes out of shows." Psychiatrist William Glasser, who worked extensively in elementary schools, bemoaned the inability of many TV-oriented youngsters to be engaged participants. "When asked to become actively involved in learning (to read for example)," he said, "they are passive. Used to receiving, they do not know how to put forth an effort." Spokesmen for the BBC have said that *Sesame Street* prepares kids for school but not for life, and above all, it encourages "passive box-watching."[23]

John Holt, the most widely read and respected of all authors on elementary education during the 1960s and '70s, observed that even the children seen on *Sesame Street* itself learned passively. According to Holt, "learning on *Sesame Street* means learning right answers and right answers come from grownups. We rarely see children figuring anything out . . . we rarely see children *doing* anything." Most astonishing of all, perhaps, is the testimony of Fred Rogers, host of the beloved *Mister Rogers' Neighborhood*. He, too, agrees that learning from television is a passive experience because it "invariably presents some kind of stimulation and lets viewers drink it in as they will."[24]

Two other charges against the greatest menace of mass culture appeared with some frequency during the period from the later 1960s to the early 1980s: the ultimate standardization of culture as well as its privatization. The first of those charges was succinctly conveyed in a hyperbolic blast by George Gerbner, dean of the Annenberg School of Communication at the University of Pennsylvania. "Television is the new state religion," he declared, "run by a private Ministry of Culture (the three networks), offering a universal curriculum for all people. . . ."[25]

The second charge, equally familiar, holds television responsible for the fulfillment of one of Alexis de Tocqueville's greatest fears: the privatization of social life because comfortably bourgeois people withdraw themselves from involvement in civic affairs. As one perceptive scholar has observed, television and electronic media in general have radically altered the significance of physical presence in the experience of social events. Once upon a time we assumed that physical presence and proximity were prerequisites for firsthand experience. Television has radically diminished the importance of personal presence at events of various sorts. It has become easy and convenient to view all kinds of performances without actually being there. In sum, the electronic media are seen as affecting social behavior *not* through the power of their messages but by reconfiguring the settings in which people do or do not interact and by weakening the customary bond between cultural events and specific physical sites.[26]

Perhaps one last poll is particularly apt here in support of such impressions. In 1975 the Roper Organization asked 2,007 adults a somewhat more complicated but unusually interesting question. The interviewer began by saying: "People have been talking recently about the fact that they are changing some of their living habits. I'd like to ask you about this list of things. . . . Would you go down [the list] and call off all those things you're doing less now (than a year ago/than you used to)?"

Responses:

J.	Spending time at home	10%
F.	Watching TV (television)	20
B.	Shopping in large shopping centers	19
H.	Reading books	18
L.	Buying food, beverages and other supplies in large quantities and shopping less often	6
D.	Visiting with friends or relatives who live quite nearby	22
M.	Phoning a store to see if they have an item in stock before going to buy it	15
C.	Going to take-out places for ready cooked food (hamburgers, sandwiches, fried chicken, etc.)	33
E.	Eating out at restaurants	41
A.	Entertaining friends in your home	35
I.	Shopping in stores that are not located in main shopping areas	28
G.	Going out to places of public entertainment (sports events, concerts, movies, etc.)	39
K.	Visiting with friends or relatives who do not live nearby	34
	None	18
	Don't know	4

The greatest decline or decrease occurred in eating out, going to places of public entertainment, entertaining friends at home, visiting with friends or relatives who do not live nearby, and going to take-out places. The privatization of social life does seem to have increased, and as a corollary, participatory interaction declines.[27]

We recognize that all polling results need to be read with caution, particularly those that treat matters of lifestyle and personal preferences. Nevertheless, despite flawed questionnaires and some misleading responses, polls taken by reliable organizations are useful indices of trends. Even their inconsistencies can be helpful in exposing ambiguities and "wish it weren't so" tendencies.* By the same token, of course, we now know that the rating systems designed to measure the relative success of television programs are deeply flawed. That is valuable knowledge. But from a historical perspective it is essential to recall that during the 1950s, 1960s, and 1970s, the kind of entertainment that we received from the mass media, and from television especially, was largely determined by ratings. They began in the first decade or so as nothing more than measurements of attention: what was watched and how much. After a while, however, attention got translated into "popularity" and that, in turn, into an affirmation on the part of broadcasters of the "satisfaction of wants," which, in the words of Gilbert Seldes, "in a democratic society is taken as an ethical obligation the mass media must fulfill." Give the people what they appear to want—in fact, inundate them with it.[28]

The dominance of television in American life is unquestioned. By the mid-eighties the average amount of viewing time per day had reached seven hours. By 1990, however, what began to be contested by serious observers was the quality of what appeared on TV compared to alternative modes of entertainment. Here, for example, is John J. O'Connor, television critic for the *New York Times*, comparing blockbuster movies with television:

> For decades, some of the more patronizing and printable catch phrases have been reserved for television. The pecking order of popular culture over the years settled into a widely accepted hierarchy. At the bottom, there was television entertainment—

---

* In 1979 a national poll asked: "Too often television will sensationalize the news. They'll do just about anything to make a story interesting. Agree or disagree?" 66% agreed, 21% disagreed, and 13% were not sure. (Public Agenda Foundation poll, December 1979, USPAF.80SP.R004, RCPOR.)

formula-ridden, silly, pointless, and forgettable. Far above, there was the art of film, occasionally called cinema—probing, elevated, provocative, memorable. Those distinctions never did hold up very well under close scrutiny. Now as television entertainment enters the '90s growing both more adventurous, and pointed, they are being obliterated. . . . One thing would seem certain. A significant sea change has taken place in popular culture. It is now the typical Hollywood film that is becoming pointless and forgettable. And it is television that is showing distinct signs of being provocative and, on occasion, memorable. The old pecking order is very much on the verge of collapse.[29]

The phrase "television comes of age" has by now been used too often in too many different ways. But surely a benchmark occurred late in 1997 when the Newhouse School of Public Communication at Syracuse University opened a new academic research center designated as the Center for the Study of Popular Television. The dean of the Newhouse School explained that the center would "study television entertainment programs with the same care and passion as musicologists study Mozart and Ellington, or professors of English study Melville and Pynchon."[30] Here, then, is the logical fulfillment of Seldes's unusual appeal back in 1924 that popular culture be taken seriously, especially by critics and scholars. By the 1980s and '90s the ante had been raised—or lowered, depending upon your point of view. Mass culture is now being taken quite seriously by critics and scholars.

III. Innovations in Mass Culture Since 1980

Beginning quite early in the 1980s, technological innovations enabled mass culture to undergo some highly significant changes, most notably affecting the mass media. Those changes are not only very much with us as the millennium draws to a close, they are accelerating in speed and proliferating in number. For approximately thirty years, 1950 to 1980, television underwent relatively few dramatic changes. The introduction of color mattered a lot, and program content as well as orientation shifted significantly around 1960 as sponsors and advertising agencies gained greater control over the offerings and their manner of presentation. But the networks remained few in number, virtually interchangeable in terms of what they offered and at which hours, cautious, yet powerful because of their dominance of American leisure and the dissemination of information.[31]

MTV first appeared in 1980. It not only provided young people with an alternative to the major networks in terms of content, but also of style and structure as well. MTV schedules were more flexible and fluid because the programs presented were so nonsequential. The spread of cable television during the 1980s proliferated channels, increasingly segmented the national audience, and eventually cut deeply into the viewing shares of NBC, CBS, and ABC.* Cable made the medium increasingly diverse, democratized it even more, and, many would argue, made television more participatory than it had been during its first thirty-five years. (How much more is subject to intense debate, as we shall see.)[32]

The development of a handy remote control device empowered viewers to a certain degree. If they didn't like a program or wanted to avoid commercials, it became quite convenient to switch channels. More important, however, the VCR and the prerecorded cassette took the United States by storm during the early and mid-1980s, with profound consequences for commerce and the entire entertainment industry.† Viewers could record programs and delete commercials, which radically altered the long-standing love affair between sponsors and TV. Monogamy gave way to complex (or even open) marriage. Do not believe for a minute, however, that television advertising waned as a consequence. Back in 1915 American companies spent $1 billion overall on advertising; in 1993 they spent $140 billion, and the most expensive ads appeared on television. The conglomeration and combining of advertising agencies during the 1980s became yet another sign of the times for mass culture—the massification of those who make messages for consumers.[33]

---

* It is a measure of the speed and unpredictability of these changes that when Todd Gitlin published *Inside Prime Time* (New York, 1983), his epilogue explored the emerging phenomenon of cable TV but concluded that competition would not relax the iron grip of major networks on mass culture in the United States. The potent role of CNN, Fox, ESPN, and many others apparently lay just beyond the horizon. HBO began modestly in 1972; by 1997 it had approximately twenty-three million subscribers, thereby reaching about one quarter of the viewing public.

† Many American homes now have at least two television sets, and 30% are estimated to have three. Perhaps 70% have VCR players, and at least that many have remote control devices.

Most important of all, perhaps, these and other changes in the nature of commercial television pressured the agencies to become ever more innovative and clever. Advertising acquired unexpected characteristics, such as referring to or incorporating themes from popular songs, movies, other well-known ads, and even explicit statements by and about competing products. Contemporary advertising depends upon the vast viewing audience being familiar with an array of recent referents in mass and popular culture. Consequently, mass culture has become self-referential in a way that certainly was not the case in 1925 or 1950 or even 1975. Thinking increasingly in global terms, moreover, sponsors recognize that ads will be understood, appreciated, or even disliked in various ways around the world—owing to cultural relativism. Because it is not always easy to anticipate what will work in diverse international settings, ads are constantly being tried, pulled, and remade in an ongoing process of experimentation and testing. Nevertheless, in the 1990s more than ever, the commercial remains an instrument of cultural power on behalf of free enterprise.[34]

Adding to the impact of new technologies on mass culture since the 1980s, film rentals from video stores for home use have had a very potent influence upon Hollywood and its modus operandi. The VCR made possible what authorities refer to as "time-shifting," which added extraordinary flexibility to people's leisure-time schedules because they became less dependent upon both broadcasters' and cablecasters' control of their time. In 1992 Americans rented 3.5 billion videos, and the number has leaped geometrically since then. The emergence of video games undeniably made television more interactive for some, mainly the younger generation.* By the later 1980s, television remained a passive pastime for many, but offered participatory possibilities for others, particularly youthful viewers.[35]

The intensified competition among television shows and films led to a new and symptomatic development during the 1980s: publishing reports in newspapers and journals (on a weekly basis) of the relative success of these shows in terms of box office receipts and numbers of

---

* In 1995 a double-page ad began to appear for Sony and the Game Show Channel. On the right-hand side is a futuristic cordless touchtone receiver/speaker below a single word in bold letters: **Interact.** On the left-hand page the text emphasizes "our interactive games," set in motion "simply by picking up the phone. Interact with the only network that turns your viewers into players." A Matisse-like cutout figure in four vivid colors leaps above the text in lively fashion.

viewers. Similarly, papers like the *New York Times* publish best-seller lists in at least four categories, with supplementary figures to indicate which books are advancing and which are declining. Richard Schickel has called this a "rage for quantification in the arts."[36] The implications would seem to be that the great herd of humanity will follow wherever the herd leaders go. At the very least, there is an expectation that success breeds success and that indifferent success (being only the fifth-highest-earning film that week, say) is tantamount to failure. If this pattern doesn't suggest the quantification of culture, it surely means that the massification of culture is now deemed newsworthy on a weekly basis.

The obsession with polls, ratings, and rankings that seems so pervasive in our time brings us right back to the issue of whether television has become more interactive and accessible in terms of initiative for the individual viewer. Inviting members of the studio audience or the viewing audience to "vote" on some issue is cited as an illustration of increased engagement, and it warrants some credibility.* In *People's Court*, for example, a popular legal program involving genuine cases at the small-claims level, the studio audience votes for the plaintiff or the defendant. One critic, Douglas Rushkoff, regards this as merely "a nod to interactivity" because the vote has no bearing on Judge Wapner's decision. The voting dynamic may fulfill the letter of participation, but not the spirit.[37]

Rushkoff's work is valuable because of its judicious balance. He emphasizes the generational shift that occurred during the 1980s owing to changes in technology, differences in taste preferences, and the proliferation of television sets per family. Hence this extravagant yet acute observation made by Timothy O'Leary in 1993:

> The importance of the Nintendo phenomenon is about equal to that of the Gutenberg printing press. Here you had a new generation of kids who grew up knowing that they could change what's on the screen. Upstairs, Mom and Dad are in the living room—they're baby boomers—passively watching the news or

---

* "Talk radio" started in 1970 when Boston's Eddie Andelman began to take telephone calls in order to fill dead spots on a sports program. During the 1980s and '90s, participatory programs on television grew dramatically. *Talk Back Live* on CNN, for example, is announced as "an interactive program," in which the show is primarily generated by the audience: live via telephone, fax, and the Internet.

prime time the way they passively watched Disney back when they were kids. And down in the kids' room, the kids are changing the screen . . . the ability to change what's on the screen is the tremendous empowerment.[38]

Rushkoff himself is insistent that adolescents since the 1980s "don't just receive and digest media. They manipulate it. . . . They are in a living relationship with it." The new technologies, he believes, have allowed Americans to "graduate from passive, ignorant spectators to active, informed participants." He points out that *The Phil Donahue Show* emerged during the 1970s as the very first truly participatory interview show, a revolutionary concept that made Donahue a national icon by the early 1980s and subsequently spawned literally dozens of programs with similar formats.[39]

Even Rushkoff, however, acknowledges that a basic objective of public relations firms is to create passive and manipulable audiences, and that the firms' capacity to do so has grown exponentially during the past thirty years. He recognizes that the "social, moral, and ideological intimacy this box fosters and foists is addictive." Addiction may not be quite the same thing as passivity, but there is certainly a close connection. Rushkoff notes that some MTV videos "invite interactivity"; but he subsequently acknowledges the partial and not very potent nature of the viewers' power no matter how engaged they may be. He quotes a dialogue between Beavis and Butt-head that makes the point perfectly:

> "Is this supposed to be the future?" Beavis asks. "It sucks. Change it." To which Butt-head responds with surprisingly advanced wit, "Beavis, I'm cool, but I can't change the future." More laughs. The boys understand that MTV prides itself on its ability to bend time and bring images from the past into the present, but they know how to take this all in stride. They change the channel, inflicting their will on the medium the only way they know how: channel surfing. In doing so they again demonstrate for us how to watch TV in the nineties.[40]

We could easily proliferate illustrations of the innovations that have altered mass culture and its behavioral consequences in recent years; but doing so would only gild the lily and distract us from a second major debate, which has been raging for more than a decade now and must be addressed. First, however, let's mention one more innovation, because of its apparent whimsy and because its appearance is so imminent: the VideOcart, a shopping cart with a six-by-nine screen attached where the kiddies' seat was traditionally located. Infrared sensors placed on the ceiling of the store cause the screen to flash ads, messages, and recipes as the customer passes various products. The same kind of technology that scans the Universal Product Code will now scan the shopper as he or she peregrinates through the supermarket. Intrusive, convenient, interactive (sort of), while leaving the buyer passively awaiting the next infrared zap.[41]

IV. A Second Debate: Agency Versus Passivity in Mass Culture

Although the advocates of individual autonomy and personal "appropriation" in the age of mass culture have been most vocal since the mid-1980s (when the changes just described certainly strengthened their case), the antecedents for their position actually date back to the 1950s in lesser ways and to the 1970s in more compelling ones. Historical context requires that they be noticed, even though some of them might be disputed or modified. In her study of everyday life during the 1950s, for example, Karal Ann Marling made this observation:

> Between 1947 and 1953, revenues for spectator sports and amusements showed a marked dip, despite increases in population and income and the insatiable demand for TV sets. The popular singer and CBS star Perry Como said that his favorite home pastime was "to create a still life consisting of TV set, bowl of fruit, paring knife, cigarette, and Como stretched out on the couch." But he was the indolent exception. Market research proved that it was the heaviest TV-watchers who were liable to be most interested in painting a still life or reupholstering the living room sofa. Power tools and other do-it-yourself accessories were a $12 billion industry by the end of the decade; $30 million more went for amateur art supplies. "There seems to be a major trend away from passive, crowd amusements toward active pursuits that people can carry on independently," con-

cluded a highly regarded study of this "Changed America" with plenty of time on its hands.

Marling also contends that going to Disneyland was not a passive experience because the visitor "now became an actor, a real-life participant 'face up in the rain' as a rackety little boat plowed under Schweitzer Falls." Asking rhetorically what it is like to be in Disneyland, however, Miles Orvell has offered an interpretation that I find more persuasive: "Architectural focal points capture our gaze as we move, pulling us from place to place. We travel passively through landscapes, on water, on rails, on wheels, surveying the whole of the contained space. . . ."[42]

Next, attention has been called to social scientists engaged in media research during the 1960s and '70s, scholars who pursued what is called a "uses and gratifications" approach because they believed that individuals seek to satisfy needs and consequently have specific expectations from the media. Because these researchers ascribed considerable initiative to the audience, they did not believe that effects could be inferred from looking solely at the content of programs. Their approach would thereby place an interactive model of producers and audiences at the heart of media research. Consequently, the meaning or understanding of any "text" (or media message) results from the content of the text combined with the personal interests, prior experiences, critical abilities, and values of the reader, listener, or viewer. Whatever this work eventually demonstrates in empirical ways, it certainly ascribes to audiences the attributes of active interpreters, and assigns importance to each audience member's frame of mind, legitimate motives, interests, and values.[43]

Michel de Certeau, a brilliant and influential French cultural critic, even insisted that solitary reading was not passive behavior because the very act of reading a text transforms and enhances the meaning of that text—an argument that de Certeau and his disciples eventually applied to watching television as well. Janice A. Radway, an authority in the fields of American Studies and cultural studies, has extended that argument, though less aggressively and in more nuanced ways, to ordinary middle- and working-class women who enjoy reading romances—a study that Radway made in the later 1970s.[44]

Stuart Hall, one of the founders of the cultural studies approach during the 1960s, and scholars gathered around him at the University of Birmingham and at the Open University in England, have developed emphases comparable to those of Michel de Certeau, namely: that consumers function as active respondents to their culture rather than as passive victims of media manipulation. These critics find creativity in the act of consumption and emphasize the concept of "appropriation": selecting those aspects of media messages that are meaningful to them and then "recycling" them to suit their own needs. George Lipsitz and Lawrence W. Levine have been outspoken advocates of this position in the American context, with Levine vigorously rejecting "the image of the purely passive mass audience ready to absorb, consciously and unconsciously, whatever ideological message those controlling the mass culture industry want to feed them."[45]

Perhaps the most aggressive adaptation of de Certeau and Hall's views to mass culture and television has been made by John Fiske, a professor of communication arts at the University of Wisconsin who previously taught in Australia and Great Britain. Fiske has written extensively and comparatively, drawing broadly upon in-depth studies that others have made of the television experience in various countries of the British Commonwealth. He is also one of the most explicitly ideological writers on this subject, inflecting his Marxist discourse with words like domination and resistance, polysemy (multiple meanings), cultural economy, textual space, monovocal capitalist ideology, and popular cultural capital.[46]

Let's begin with the strengths of Fiske's position. He insists upon the social diversity of the viewing audience for any given program, and then observes that people respond in different ways because of variations in class, occupation, race, and gender. Eventually, however, Fiske carries this position almost to the point of *reductio ad absurdum*, as in this sentence: "The social histories of people in societies as diverse as western capitalist democracies are constructed out of such a variety of social experiences and social forces as to provide for almost as much individual difference as any natural gene bank." He believes that viewing television customarily involves "a process of negotiation between the text [i.e., program] and its variously situated readers." The contribution of that position is to divert attention away from program content, where it usually has been, toward "the reader [viewer] as the site of meaning." The difficulty with such a stance is that it takes the spotlight away from the program, which is problematic because the program, after all, is a "given," it is what the viewer must react to.[47]

Fiske's egalitarian faith in the production of culture from the bottom up is aptly summarized in this passage:

In a mass society the materials and meaning systems out of which cultures are made will almost inevitably be produced by the cultural industries: but the making of these materials into culture, that is, into the meanings of self and of social relations, and the exchange of these materials for pleasure is a process that can only be performed by their consumer-users, not by their producers.[48]

Fiske is fully convinced that if social and economic power can take many forms, so can the modes of resistance to it. How *effective* those modes are is very difficult to demonstrate, however, and perhaps especially so in the American context. In any case, Fiske offers a stimulating observation but then spoils it with a hyperbolic conclusion.

The power of audiences-as-producers in the cultural economy is considerable. . . . But more importantly, this power derives from the fact that meanings do not circulate in the cultural economy in the same way that wealth does in the financial. They are harder to possess (and thus to exclude others from possessing), they are harder to control because the production of meaning and pleasure is not the same as the production of the cultural commodity, or of other goods, for in the cultural economy the role of consumer does not exist as the end point of a linear economic transaction. Meanings and pleasures circulate within it without any real distinction between producers and consumers.[49]

Once again at the close of this provocative work, Fiske ascribes even more power (as well as authority) to consumers than to producers and sponsors. The success of television in the financial economy, he asserts, "depends upon its ability to serve and promote the diverse and often oppositional interests of its audiences. . . . Far from being the agent of the dominant classes, [television] is the prime site where the dominant have to recognize the insecurity of their power, and where they have to encourage cultural difference with all the threat to their own position that this implies."[50]

Surely Fiske's views sustain greater validity and applicability in the altered world of mass culture that has emerged since the early 1980s, most notably because of the proliferation of television channels and the increasing heterogeneity of American society. Newcomers arriving here from all over the world do indeed have a predilection for channels that speak their language, highlight their culture, and provide news and information from their countries of origin. Nevertheless, scholars such as James B. Twitchell and Leo Bogart have quite recently provided us with abundant data on the overwhelming power (still) of the major networks, sponsors, advertising agencies, and the multinational conglomerates that increasingly own them and shape their policies. In Twitchell's extremely thorough study of contemporary advertising, for example, especially television advertising, he acknowledges that viewing audiences are increasingly diverse and segmented. Understanding that full well, sponsors custom-tailor variations on a theme for different markets; but ultimately their objective is "to be as many things to as many segments as possible." Twitchell is also persuaded that faced with the subtle (and not-so-subtle) complexities of advertising today, we tend to be passive—particularly when we simply demonize commercialism because "we see ourselves as helpless and innocent victims of its overpowering force."[51]

In 1990 John Clarke, a distinguished British social scientist who has worked closely with Stuart Hall, warned against overestimating "resistances by treating them as if they are self-evidently counterhegemonic." He added that "skeptical distance may be a foundation for oppositional and subversive practices but it is itself an inert force, a state of passive dissent." In Clarke's view, dissenting appropriations of mass culture lead nowhere unless they are connected to systematic sets of alternative meanings, oppositional practices of control, and (shared) subversive categories of "popular literacy." That skeptical alternative to Fiske's more sanguine outlook is echoed with variable emphases by sociologist Todd Gitlin and historian Jackson Lears. As Lears puts it, "ordinary people have little more control over the mass cultural products presented to them than they do over the categories constructed by opinion pollsters. In each case, managerial elites plan a menu calculated to offend the fewest people."[52]

Cultural critic Donald Lazere has addressed the larger issues raised by the overwhelming power of those who shape and dominate mass culture. "The restricted cognitive patterns induced by media in audiences," he writes, "also induce predominantly conservative attitudes, not in the sense of a reasoned conservative ideology but in the sense of an uncritical conformity that reinforces the social status quo and precludes oppositional consciousness." He subsequently adds, writing in 1989, that given the present American context, "these cognitive deficiencies comprise yet another factor contributing to conformity, authoritarianism, and passivity."[53]

Also writing in 1989, Herbert I. Schiller, the respected authority on communications industries, responds to scholars who share John Fiske's outlook, especially those who pursue the "uses and gratifications" approach.

> Yet, what is the *actual* diversity that is available over multichannel systems? To what extent is it a conglomeration of old movies, syndicated reruns, news from the same two or three press agencies, and sports of every description? Has the sponsor disappeared from cable television? Is commercialism and consumerism absent? Where are the sharply drawn social dramas? Has not cable television, no less than the networks, been swallowed by the big information-cultural combines?[54]

The most recent inquiries are equally critical. A study published in the *American Journal of Health Promotion* concluded that couch potatoes are twice as likely to develop high levels of serum cholesterol as those who rarely watch television. A survey published late in 1997 under the title "Couch-Potato Nation" has statistics for 1996 and projections for 2001 showing more Americans spending even more time in front of home screens of various sorts.[55]

COUCH-POTATO NATION*

The rise of the computer will have Americans spending even more time in front of home screens in the coming years.

Consumer media	HOURS OF USE PER PERSON		
	1990	1996	2001
Television	1,470	1,567	1,551
Radio	1,135	1,091	1,072
Home video	38	49	60
Videogames	12	26	37
Online computers	1	16	39

* "Couch-Potato Nation," *Newsweek*, Sept. 8, 1997. Projections from Veronis, Suhler & Assoc. © 1997, Newsweek, Inc. All rights reserved. Reprinted by permission.

I do not expect the divergences among these disputatious positions to disappear, or even begin to be reconciled any time soon, and for several quite different reasons. First, because some of the critics and advocates have ideological axes to grind, which makes their positions less flexible and disposes them to read all data through very particular filters. As the cultural historian and critic Morag Shiach has shrewdly observed, for example, for many theorists of cultural studies who are on the left,

> the explanation of television's power tends to be articulated in terms of conspiracies. If television is controlled by the agents of capitalism, it is argued, its representations will be ideological. The implication is that if it were controlled by the people it would provide images of "the real": but television is not so transparent, nor so easily appropriated. The only alternative to television as agent of ideological domination, therefore, lies in positing a space beyond the reach of ideology: a space of authenticity where the dominant culture will hold no sway. As we have discovered, however, such spaces are produced by the terms of cultural analysis, and have no existence outside them.[56]

Second, the remarkably expanded and enhanced use of the Internet during the 1990s—a subject beyond the scope of this book (and beyond this writer's expertise)—obviously marks the Internet as the newest and most international dimension of mass culture. Whether or not the Internet is genuinely interactive, or whether it might require us to redefine what we actually mean by interactive, is presently an issue of intense debate. Many Internet programs, in fact, explicitly advertise themselves as being interactive; but in this new age of virtual reality, are we perhaps talking about virtual interactivity? Do we need to use the word-concept "participatory" in a different way with reference to the Internet?* Those who believe that on-line chat rooms are mostly boring or bawdy take one position, while those who are attracted to "virtual communities" take a very different one. Does using the Internet achieve the ultimate in privatization, or does it lead to a specious new kind of public culture conducted from isolated stations?[57]

---

* Apple introduced the world to the Macintosh PC by means of a television ad that aired in January 1984 on Super Bowl XVIII.

From the perspective of enthusiastic educators, "the Internet reinforces the conception of students as active agents in the process of learning," says Harvard's president Neil Rudenstine, "not as passive recipients of knowledge from teachers and authoritative texts." Rudenstine goes on to declare that the Internet dovetails with a new vision of learning. "It calls upon the user to be active and engaged—following leads, distinguishing the substantial from the trivial, synthesizing insights drawn from different sources, formulating new questions."[58]

Writing in 1997, however, the Italian critic and novelist Umberto Eco, a veteran traveler in hyperreality, raised unsettling concerns that many others share, though Eco claimed to feel optimistic about the answers. We are living in a new electronic community, he observed, "which is global enough, but it is not a village, if by that one means a human settlement where people are directly interacting with one another. The real problem of an electronic community is solitude. . . . Can computers implement not a network of one-to-one contacts between solitary souls but a real community of interactive subjects?" Eco hopes so, yet he acknowledges that the jury is likely to be out for quite a while yet.[59]

To return to what I have designated the second debate, the subject of this section, my own position is clearly closer to that of skeptics like Clarke, Gitlin, Lears, Lazere, and Schiller, than to the *degree* of agency, resistance, and appropriation from mass culture perceived by de Certeau, Hall, Fiske, Levine, Lipsitz, and others. I see a significant difference between reaction or response, which may or may not occur when persons watch television, for instance, and viable, meaningful interaction within the manifold aspects of mass culture, which involves an ongoing process requiring genuine social and civic participation. To cite simply one example, and thereby acknowledge the complexity of our subject, I regard sports in the United States, overall, as being more passive at the adult level (watching rather than playing) than it was half a century ago, but increasingly participatory (and organized) for youngsters at the primary and secondary school levels. It should also be noted that during the early decades of this century Progressive educators discouraged passive spectatorship and insisted upon the importance of children's participation in sports activities.

Two important caveats are needed here concerning gender and class. Many more women are clearly engaged in organized sports as well as personal exercise programs than, say, three decades ago. When we turn to class, however, sociologists have found that persons at the "middle occupational levels" spend nearly twice as much of their leisure time in the role of passive spectators than those in either the upper or lower vocational levels, where active participation in athletics is more prevalent. The distinction is significant; but we must keep in mind that the middle class is easily the most inclusive in the United States and therefore tends to be the basis for defining "normative" behavior patterns.[60]

Finally, in order to acknowledge in yet another way that comfortable closure is impossible, we must recognize the predictable absence of any consensus about the present state of popular culture and, more particularly, how Americans feel about it. (Note that even many who write about these issues professionally continue to use the phrases "mass" and "popular culture" interchangeably.) During July 1995 the *New York Times* surveyed 1,209 adults, of whom 411 were parents with children ages two through seventeen living with them. The questions concentrated on people's perceptions of the impact on younger Americans of television, films, video games and tapes, and popular music. The responses were extremely negative, strongly emphasizing the adverse impact of mass culture in terms of violence, sexual activity, undesirable lifestyles, and so forth. The *Times*'s extensive feature story carried the headline: "Americans Despair of Popular Culture."[61]

In contrast, other reports of various sorts absolutely glow about the many high-quality programs that appear on HBO; the varied and excellent series on nature, science, and history that run on PBS; the astonishingly high visitation figures for museums of art and history, historical sites, living history farms; and community-generated arts-related activities at the grassroots level. According to many sources, the quality of popular culture in the United States is remarkably good, especially considering how inadequate the levels of financial support are.[62]

Perhaps John Fiske and others are correct when they assert that "popular culture is contradictory. It is shot through with contradictions that escape control." So if we cannot conclude with genuine conclusiveness, we should at least aspire to historical judiciousness. Much of what I have been aiming at is nicely encapsulated in the following remarks by Morag Shiach, a Scots disciple of Raymond Williams, the perceptive cultural critic from Wales (are critics who emerge from the margins less myopic about where the mainstream is headed?):

All of these judgements about popular culture, as in decline, as leading to addiction, as the last bastion of authenticity, are misleading to the extent that they are automatic. The very significant continuities from the eighteenth century to the present day, and from apologist for Victorian capitalism to theorist of revolutionary change, reveal the power of these sorts of assessments of popular culture. They represent a set of attitudes towards culture and society, but they do not represent an analysis of cultural relations at a given historical moment. If we are to be able to imagine cultural plurality, to understand the possible relations between cultural production and social power, and to see the historical dimensions of particular cultural developments, then the concepts which we bring to bear on the analysis of popular culture need to be much more carefully considered. This can only be done through an attention to the history of analyses of popular culture, a critical reappraisal of "obvious" judgements about the nature and potential of "the popular," and a constant questioning of the power and significance of the dominant culture.[63]

I concur.

9

Historians and the Problem of Popular Culture in Recent Times

∞

My particular focus in this chapter is innovation by historians (broadly defined) concerning the role of popular culture in the United States, accompanied by skepticism toward and even irritation at certain forms of innovation, especially as presented on public television and in diverse museums of history and art. I have in view artistic innovation in the presentation of American history to a broad non-academic audience accompanied by resistance from professional historians in defense of what they regard as balance, scholarly integrity, and intellectual authority. I also have in mind innovation by those who seek to clarify connections between fine art and popular culture, often responded to with staunch hostility from critics who fear the degradation of art through unbridled populism and who remain unpersuaded by the legitimacy of such connections. I will then consider innovative approaches to the acquisition and presentation of popular culture displays in history museums accompanied by resistance from some museum administrators and curators. And I will reflect upon the controversial interpretation of history in museums for a diverse public when met by negative reactions from special interest groups, politicians, and policy-makers.

Ultimately, the *problématique* of this chapter arises from two cultural dynamics, one of which surely cannot be distinctive to the United States, but a second that may have special salience in America because the very nature of the historian's vocation here seems to be publicly perceived (rather critically in recent years) as being driven by hyper-professional and political considerations—each of which involves its own perceived form of illusion or deception. The first of these two dynamics concerns the necessary act of selectiveness and *interpretation* by historians, inadequately understood by the general public as the twentieth century comes toward closure.* The second dynamic arises from a curious obsession with *authenticity*, a concern that seems conducive to a rather shallow comprehension and appreciation of history as presented in museums, historical sites, televised documentaries, films, and even books.

The centrality of this public skepticism about the inevitability of interpretation and reinterpretation (as opposed to Ranke's famous dictum that the facts, properly ascertained, speak for themselves), along with an apparent passion for a particular notion of authenticity, seem to me to lie at the heart of most recent controversies involving history as popular culture (along with popular culture as history), especially during the past decade. There appears to be a paradox in this perplexing situation. The writing of history has been democratized because it has become more inclusive. Yet inclusiveness in terms of gender, ethnicity, race, and class has not made history more accessible or popular to general readers. History still reaches a remarkably restricted audience even though it can no longer be fairly accused of elitism. Populism does not inevitably translate into popular appeal.

I. Legitimizing Popular Culture Among Historians

When Gilbert Seldes published *The Seven Lively Arts* in 1924, it appeared as a radical aesthetic manifesto. He insisted that popular culture at its best was vastly more interesting and significant than second- or third-rate highbrow culture. So he pleaded that serious attention—critical inquiry and appreciation—be devoted to jazz, to silent film

---

* See, for example, Maurice Isserman, *If I Had a Hammer . . . The Death of the Old Left and the Birth of the New Left* (New York, 1987): "What follows will not be a narrowly descriptive narrative; I see no virtue or even possibility of fashioning a historical treatment that offers 'just the facts' about the emergence of the New Left. I am offering a political interpretation of the New Left's history. . . ." (xv).

stars like Charlie Chaplin and the Keystone Kops, to ingenious comic strips like George Herriman's "Krazy Kat," to musical theater and those who composed for it, like Irving Berlin, to those who wrote poignant and amusing short stories, like Ring Lardner, to gifted circus clowns and acrobatic entertainers like the Fratellini.[1]

Although Seldes's book received a generally favorable reception, many cultural critics continued for several decades to resist his call to pay close attention to the people's culture. In 1939, for example, Clement Greenberg published his well-known screed titled "Avant-Garde and Kitsch," in which he virtually conflated popular culture with kitsch and denounced both as vulgar threats to the production of serious innovation in the arts.[2] Although this dialogue of difference persisted among intellectuals, the popularization of history remained noncontroversial so long as it did not challenge social norms and orthodox verities.

During the 1930s, a radio program called *Cavalcade of America* enjoyed wide appeal as an ongoing coast-to-coast series about U.S. history. It received numerous prizes and came as a genuine boon to history teachers, who could use it as "assigned listening." What seems notably symptomatic about this program, especially for the 1930s, was the timid conservatism imposed by its producer, the prominent public relations firm of Batten, Barton, Durstine & Osborn. Erik Barnouw discovered when he signed on with the series that "anything to do with unions, strikes, or labor relations was out of the question." African-American history was also proscribed. During its first decade *Cavalcade* never focused on a black leader. At one session Barnouw suggested that the Tennessee Valley Authority would make an engaging topic as an achievement in science and engineering. His proposal was dismissed because it might seem to endorse socialism.[3]

Nevertheless, the appearance of well-received works like Constance M. Rourke's *American Humor: A Study in the National Character* (1931) and her *Trumpets of Jubilee* (1927), along with other books prepared almost entirely by historical writers outside of academe, achieved more than a modicum of interest (if not respectability) for the study of popular culture.[4] Starting gradually in the 1950s and '60s, however, one segment of the American Studies movement, led by Carl Bode and Russel B. Nye, began to produce books and train doctoral students who reflected their mentors' enthusiasm for and commitment to popular culture. Soon the likes of Leslie Fiedler and David Grimsted added their contributions; and in 1967 Ray B. Browne of Bowling Green State University in Ohio created both the Popular Culture Association and the *Journal of Popular Culture*.[5]

Resistance remained strong among more traditional members of the academy, however, and especially so in prestigious and well-established history departments. Many professionals were astonished—in some instances even left scandalized—when Arthur M. Schlesinger, Jr., an eminent historian of politics and ideas, began to write movie reviews and comparable "ephemera" for *Esquire*, the *Saturday Evening Post*, and *Playboy*. Clio was threatened by déshabille; the discipline was losing its dignity. Raised eyebrows, frowns, even scowls of disapproval.[6]

Meanwhile, highbrow critics like Dwight Macdonald produced a series of delightfully readable but venomous essays, such as "Masscult & Midcult" (1960), attacking popular culture; and his voice was backed by a chorus that included Theodor W. Adorno, Ernest Van Den Haag, Herbert Marcuse, Harold Rosenberg, and Clement Greenberg. Popular culture, in their view, only served as a narcotic that depoliticized the masses and degraded those who aspired to create or preserve "authentic" culture. Whistle-blowers abounded among cultural critics and historians throughout the 1950s and 1960s. Where would such trash lead? When would such trends end?[7]

By the later 1960s and 1970s, however, a small though influential group (in the most casual sense—certainly not a "school") of cultural historians began to produce highly significant contributions to our understanding of popular culture in the United States, and they evoked widespread admiration rather than scorn for two reasons: first, they appeared to be dispassionate rather than parochial apologists for popular culture; and second, their work achieved a level of analytical sophistication that revealed larger truths about American thought and culture as a whole. I have in mind *Apostles of the Self-Made Man* (1965) and *Adventure, Mystery, and Romance: Formula Stories as Art and Popular Culture* (1976) by John G. Cawelti; *Humbug: The Art of P. T. Barnum* (1973) by Neil Harris; and the collected essays of Harris and Warren I. Susman, pieces that spanned several decades.[8]

Ever since the early 1980s, moreover, a steady flow of pioneering and well-received books on many aspects of popular culture has been forthcoming, primarily from academic publishers. To cite a dozen or so in the order of their appearance may seem arbitrary, yet it serves to convey a sense of the wide range of topics being respectably covered: Roy Rosenzweig, *Eight Hours for What We Will: Workers and Leisure in an Industrial City, 1870–1920* (1983); Robert W. Rydell, *All the World's a Fair: Visions of Empire at American International Expositions, 1876–1916* (1984); Kathy Peiss, *Cheap Amusements: Working Women and Leisure in Turn-of-the-Century New York* (Philadelphia, 1986); Michael Denning, *Mechanic Accents: Dime Novels and Working-Class Culture in America* (London, 1987); Robert Bogdan, *Freak Show: Presenting Human Oddities for Amusement and Profit* (1988); Lawrence W. Levine, *Highbrow/Lowbrow: The Emergence of Cultural Hierarchy in America* (1988); John F. Kasson, *Rudeness and Civility: Manners in Nineteenth-Century Urban America* (1990); Robert C. Allen, *Horrible Prettiness: Burlesque and American Culture* (1991); Charles and Angeliki V. Keil, *Polka Happiness* (1992); William R. Taylor, *In Pursuit of Gotham: Culture and Commerce in New York* (1992); Gregory D. Black, *Hollywood Censored: Morality Codes, Catholics, and the Movies* (1994); and R. Laurence Moore, *Selling God: American Religion in the Marketplace of Culture* (1994).

With few exceptions, these authors simply took for granted the legitimacy of their projects. They wrote without apologetics or defensiveness; and as validating "bookends" for their decade of proliferation they could point to two seminal and widely noticed collections of original essays, both edited by Richard Wightman Fox and T. J. Jackson Lears. The first, *The Culture of Consumption: Critical Essays in American History, 1880–1980*, appeared in 1983. The second, *The Power of Culture: Critical Essays in American History*, in 1993. In between, Paul Buhle edited a wide-ranging and useful set of essays, *Popular Culture in America* (1987).

By the 1990s complaints began to be heard from practitioners in more traditional subfields, such as military, diplomatic, political, constitutional, and economic history, that the annual meetings of the major historical organizations had become saturated with sessions devoted to popular culture—nearly to the neglect if not the virtual exclusion of older areas of inquiry. During the early 1990s only Lawrence W. Levine, who had done so much (along with his students) to achieve genuine recognition for the history of American popular culture, seemed to feel, like comedian Rodney Dangerfield, that "we still don't get no respect." As Levine lamented in a major essay in 1992: "This inability to transcend the putative aesthetic poverty of popular culture, or kitsch, as intellectuals like to call it, has made it exceedingly difficult for historians to take popular culture seriously enough to comprehend the dynamic relationships that exist between the audience and the expressive culture with which they interact. Aesthetic worth and substantive complexity are not inexorable partners." Levine's *cri de coeur*, coming as it did from a position of strength, if not triumph, seemed strangely inappropriate to some. Historical studies of popular culture in the United States were riding high.[9]

II. *Professional Historians and Popular History*

While all of those popular culture monographs were appearing during the 1980s, an aspiring director of television documentaries, enamored of American history, launched a series of productions that achieved positive recognition. Ken Burns's very first piece, *Brooklyn Bridge* (1982), received an Academy Award nomination and began a highly successful collaboration with David McCullough, a nonacademic historian who had learned his craft at *American Heritage*. Subsequent documentaries by Burns achieved broader recognition, including *The Shakers: Hands to Work, Hearts to God* (1985) and *The Congress* (1988). Popular history lovingly prepared for a discerning general audience was well launched.[10]

Throughout those same years Burns and his staff, along with a team of professional historians serving as advisers, labored on what eventually became an eleven-part documentary about the American Civil War. Roughly forty million people watched one or more segments of the series, broadcast in 1990 on consecutive nights by PBS; even more saw rebroadcasts, bought videocassettes, or viewed it as part of school classes at all levels; additional millions saw it on television in Great Britain, Germany, Japan, and many other countries. *The Civil War* may be the most successful attempt ever made to bring an aspect of American history—or perhaps the history of any nation—to a "popular" (i.e., nonacademic) audience. Consequently, the negative response of so many prominent professional historians provides a useful case study in two respects: the limits of a gifted and earnest amateur historian in attempting to understand the complexities of history as problem and process, but also the limited tolerance that professionals have for perceived omissions or misunderstandings committed by someone not formally trained in the guild. The sheer bulk of what has been written about *The Civil War* by professional historians is nothing less than astonishing. It also raises fascinating questions about the potential and the limitations of history prepared for a popular audience by nonprofessional historians, even when working with the advice of experts.

Burns takes great pride in the sheer number as well as the quality of the academic experts he consults. Nevertheless, some of the most eminent specialists on the Civil War era have rendered harsh verdicts on different aspects of the series. Leon Litwack has accused Burns of minimizing slavery as the primary precipitant of the war—what one side fought to defend and the other side shed blood to terminate. Catherine Clinton agrees and adds that Burns's "focus on military campaigns skimped those issues involving women and civilians when they *were* germane." She believes that Burns "deserves a slow painful punishment for his 'boys will be boys' coyness and his lapses concerning women." Gabor S. Boritt complains that immigrants are missing from Burns's epic, even though they provided 10 percent of the Confederate and 25 percent of the Union armies.[11]

Gary W. Gallagher, a military historian, first castigates his fellow academics for nitpicking about social, cultural, and ethnic omissions from the mammoth series—on grounds that the subject of the documentary is, after all, a vast war. Gallagher then proceeds to denounce Burns for flaws in his military presentation, particularly for misunderstanding "the impact of technology on late-antebellum American military officers" and for overemphasizing the eastern theater of the war (Virginia, Maryland, and Pennsylvania) while neglecting the western theater (Tennessee, Mississippi, and Missouri). Eric Foner joins Litwack in condemning Burns's emphasis on sectional reconciliation following the war, rather than the unfulfilled promise of genuine freedom for African Americans that Reconstruction was supposed to provide. Foner quotes William Dean Howells's observation that "What the American public always wants is tragedy with a happy ending."[12]

Burns does have advocates in the professoriat, however, among them one of the most eminent historians of the postwar South and of race relations in the United States, C. Vann Woodward. At a particularly tense planning session in 1986, when severely critical historians from academe looked at preliminary versions and offered scathing assessments, Woodward reddened and chastised his fellow scholars. Here, in his own words, is what he said:

They should realize, I admonished, that they were not addressing their usual opponents, an older generation of historians grown complacent and out of touch with new ideas and demands. They were speaking to artists, artists whose purpose was to bring to life for the present a profound national ordeal of the past, a great tragedy as it was seen, heard, felt, lamented, and mourned, or greeted as liberation by the people who went through it in the 1860s. The artists could not be expected to abandon their true role and take sides in current generational or ideological disputes among scholars. Nor should they be required to use their art to promote political, social, or moral causes and movements of the present day, however worthy they may be. Historians should be able to help artists without attempting to use them for ends quite foreign to their art.[13]

Burns is prepared to defend himself, of course, and he has done so on many occasions. He is enchanted by American history and reads it avidly. He notes that 98 percent of his respondents say, "This is fabulous"; 1 percent say that "it's a pro-black series"; and the other 1 percent? "It's only in the academic community that I found a particularly—and for me a sad—painful sort of rejection. So then one [Burns] has to say, 'Is this jealousy, is it, you know, that I'm not hewing entirely to one point of view?' That film was able to encompass *many* points of view." Later in the same interview, genuine bitterness emerged toward his antagonists. Referring to academic historians, Burns asserted that "they've failed [in] the mission to educate the people of this country, and so I'm most angry about that."[14]

If one reads carefully what Burns has to say in his own defense about all of his work, however, including an eighteen-and-a-half-hour series on baseball in American history (1994), several problems emerge that make conflict with scholars not only inevitable but unresolvable. Burns regards himself as a historian as well as an artist; but when the two roles conflict in any way, artistic imperatives take priority. For example, professional historians know that they must make their meanings explicit and clear; but Burns usually wants his major messages to remain implicit, and hence to be *felt* by the viewer.

The best letter I've gotten on *Baseball* is from a guy who said, "I just sat down in front of my TV set for nine nights, close-up on the TV set, and I have dirt and tobacco juice on me." I love the idea that my films might give off dirt and tobacco juice. And I will forever be looking for that, because I know that if he felt that, then he [absorbed] all the intellectual ideas about black emancipation and empowerment over the last century and a third since the Civil War, that all of the notions of heroism, of popular media and culture, of labor playing itself out, of the rise and decay of great cities, all of the themes that quite consciously were woven into the *Baseball* film but never once didactically said, "And now we'll have a lesson about great cities and their decay."[15]

Moreover, Burns seems most comfortable with historical facts—better yet, facts that can be documented and authenticated visually. That is why he spent so much time on the eastern theater of the Civil War and so little on the western front. Photography was young, primitive, and not very mobile in the early 1860s; not many photographers made it to the western theater. When Burns boasts about the popular appeal of *The Civil War*, his infatuation with facticity becomes apparent. "The response to the series in ordinary letters is amazing," he declares. "Thousands of people were awakened to complicated historical facts."[16] Burns is comfortable dealing with facts, even complicated ones. Interpretations are another matter, and I believe that Burns's discomfort with explicit interpretation marks him as a representative American—a point I will return to in section four.

Journalistic coverage of televised documentaries prepared by Ken Burns and his brother Ric has not only been laudatory, often lavishly so, it has frequently taken potshots at the perceived dreariness of work done by professional historians. In discussing the debate over Burns's *Civil War*, a North Carolina newspaper commented with a snicker that it's "a debate most of us missed, since most academic history, these days, is read only by other professors and a few unlucky graduate students." A few months later a letter to the *Washington Times* condemned the "ahistorical approach favored by today's grumpy academics. Both [Foner and Clinton] insist upon judging the events and Mr. Burns' coverage of them, in the light of current stultifying politically correct norms. I suspect that the series' popularity was enough to condemn it in their eyes."[17] A reviewer from Cleveland lamented that the scholars' responses to Burns, "sadly, tell us more about the current state of the history profession than about Ken Burns' *Civil War*. Some of these historians seem cast from the same mold of joyless, nit-picking pedants who recently deprived the rest of us of Disney's projected history theme park."[18]

It has to be acknowledged that advocacy and partisanship do play a part in perceptions of history presented to the general public. Burns's history of baseball emphasized racial intolerance and repression, which did not earn it positive reviews in many southern newspapers. A Norfolk writer complained bitterly that "the history of baseball becomes significant for him principally as it contributed to the racial integration of American society. . . . In 'Baseball' as in 'The Civil War,' Burns manipulated history as deftly as he manipulated the images on the screen to sanction his own values and convictions. His work assumes a self-satisfying, moralistic tone that renders the complex truths of history unimportant. . . . Burns has unwittingly revealed one of the deep afflictions of our time: the inability or the unwillingness to forgive others for the sin of not being like us."[19]

A more recent documentary (autumn 1996) directed by Stephen Ives (with Ken Burns as executive producer), simply titled *The West*, a four-part series, has similarly been caught in a crossfire between ideological extremes. According to a conservative professor of classics who wrote *Fields Without Dreams: Defending the Agrarian Idea* (1996),

After the lackadaisical reception of his subsequent epic, Baseball, Burns has attempted a return to tragic history with a new 12-hour film. . . . By hour twelve of "The West," the usual guilty suspects and their prey have been rounded up: Land-grabbing white settlers, vain and duplicitous cavalry officers, male supremacists, religious zealots, naive reformers, environmental desecrators, arrogant do-gooders, corporate thieves, barbarous buffalo hunters, polluting miners, petty murderers, and thugs all drown out the occasional noble ethnographer, photographer, and writer, who might have prevented the maltreatment of Indians, Mexicans, Chinese, and blacks. Chicano, Native American, and other supportive writers, intellectuals, and politicians . . . are brought in to trace the pathologies of modern American society back to its westward legacy of exploitation. . . . The argument can be made . . . that there was an element of unrealism and unintended selfishness among Native American leaders in thinking that the riches of the Plains were to belong perennially to the nomadic warrior culture, while millions in Europe and Asia were without any land at all and starving. . . . "The West" . . . is, alas, not an intellectually honest or comprehensive account of the West.[20]

Clearly, as the colloquial phrase goes, Burns has often been caught between a rock and a hard place, savaged by partisans of the right as well as the left for his immensely popular productions that fundamentally seek a liberal consensus about acknowledged diversities in the American experience. As a more sympathetic reviewer of *The West* has written, "What unites these contradictory stories is the film's attention to possibility, to the various dreams that brought men and women from across the oceans, from the south, and from the east to the West." That perspective helps to validate a claim by John Fiske, the sympathetic cultural studies analyst, that popular culture is inherently contradictory in its substance and in the responses that it elicits.[21]

I have used historical documentaries produced by Ken Burns as a case study to exemplify that professional historians can, indeed, become hypercritical in evaluating popularizations of the past for a large and diverse general audience. Quite often, however, their criticisms have been justified on grounds of intellectual integrity. Is there adequate attention to context, to contingency, to explanatory truth in all of its most crucial dimensions? Has the complexity of historical reality been compromised in the name of art—or to satisfy and maximize a viewing audience? Actually, Ken Burns does better by most of these criteria than many other popularized versions of the American past, such as Oliver Stone's controversial films *JFK* and *Nixon*, or televised programs that appear on the History or the Disney Channel. It is those venues that can *really* raise the hackles of professional historians and critics.[22]

III. Art and Popular Culture in Historical Context

I would now like to introduce a second "case study" arising from a historical interpretation of the impact of popular culture, this time in the realm of modern art. As with Burns's documentaries, here too we encounter heated controversy—a storm that erupted in the autumn of 1990 and persisted for more than a year. It illuminates in different ways just how problematic the historical interpretation of popular culture can be.

In October 1990 a major exhibition opened at the Museum of Modern Art in Manhattan: *High & Low: Modern Art and Popular Culture*. It was curated by Kirk Varnedoe (then the new director of the department of painting and sculpture at the Museum of Modern Art but previously a faculty member at New York University's prestigious Institute of Fine Arts) and Adam Gopnik, a former student of Varnedoe's who had become *The New Yorker's* art critic. In 1991 the exhibit (with minor alterations) moved across the continent to the Art Institute of Chicago and the Museum of Contemporary Art in Los Angeles. Because the very concept as well as the content of the show remained so controversial, the furor that it aroused percolated through the media for a full year and left a bitter aftertaste.

The basic concept of the exhibition was straightforward enough. Starting with the origins of modern art in Europe during the later nineteenth century, it sought to demonstrate not merely the presence of popular culture as artifacts and emblems in modern art, but a profound pattern of interaction and influence, especially by the former on the latter. For our purposes here, it is important to note that this blockbuster exhibit was unusual because of the *extent* to which it was driven by ideas and by serious scholarship in a specific area of cultural history.[23]

Robert Hughes, the art critic for *Time* magazine, summarized the contents of the show in one of the more temperate reviews: Varnedoe and Gopnik "have taken on a sprawling, slippery, tangled theme—a survey of the transactions between fine art and popular culture over three-quarters of a century, from Cubism to the '80s. They set out to show how some 'high' artists raided 'low' (popular and mass) culture for their own purposes. . . . Artists have always been much less snobbish about their sources than the idealizing critics who erect value systems on the back of their work. The process came to a climax in the '60s with Pop art. Moreover, since 'low' sources cycle into high products that are then cycled back, as style, into 'low' areas again, the supposedly rigid divisions between fine and popular art are more like a maze of mirrors, one reflecting the other ad infinitum."[24]

Writing for *Newsweek* one week earlier, critic Peter Plagens called attention to another major theme of the exhibition: persistence and continuity in the face of all those swift and ceaseless innovations that we associate with modernism. The premise of *High & Low*, Plagens explained,

> is that urban flotsam is to many 20th-century artists what mountains and trees were to the 19th's. And that bad-boy appropria-

tion sculptor Jeff Koons, say, is not as distant from the Monet-to-Cézanne-to-Picasso canon as one might think. Thus the show's installation of more than 250 works is garnished with little vitrines filled with specifically inspirational newspapers, comic-books and mail-order catalogues. Picasso's post-1907 work is adroitly demonstrated to have as much to do with caricature as with African masks. Caricature leads to cartoons (and Lichtenstein and Warhol), which lead to inflatable bunnies from Woolworth's which lead to a stainless steel cast of same by Koons. Voilà! Modernism and MOMA are still going concerns.[25]

Hughes and Plagens wrote wry descriptions with an occasional edge of condescension and a modicum of explanatory context. They, at least, were constructive. Other art critics fired bazookas. According to Roberta Smith in the *New York Times*, "the tale this exhibition tells is crushingly familiar, superficial and one-sided. . . . The exhibition is plagued by severe, often contradictory limits and goals. . . . This show, in which text panels announce a new heading or subheading in every gallery, is a hostage to categorization, which accounts for both its abrupt shifts in time and style and its space-devouring repetitions. . . . Beneath the prevailing veneer of timidity and conventionality lurks a breathtaking arrogance. . . . Most disappointing of all, time and time again, the promised circularity of exchange between art and popular culture is shown to go one way only: from low to high."[26]

Writing in the *Journal of Art*, historian of art Barbara Rose lamented that the museum had "abdicated its role as cultural referee by putting what used to be out in the streets inside its sanctuary." She poured scorn on what she perceived as pandering to philistine trendiness. "This shuffling of the unique icons of Modernism with the multiple reproductions of commercial culture gives those who cherish such 'collectibles' as old comics, matchbook covers, vintage movie posters and celebrity memorabilia a welcome sense of being in with the in crowd."[27]

In an essay-review for the *New Criterion*, the conservative art critic Hilton Kramer, a knowledgeable and respected observer for decades, called the exhibition a "debacle" and went on to castigate the curator in apocalyptic language: "Mr. Varnedoe has launched MOMA's most important department upon a course so disastrous that, if not promptly reversed, the very reason for the museum's existence might soon be in doubt." A little hysteria can attract a lot of attention. Even so, no consensus emerged among conservative critics. A writer for the *National Review* dissented from Kramer's critique and then offered a more reactionary logic of his own.

> In excoriating the show's curators, Hilton Kramer, the incandescent critic of the New York Observer and one of the most redoubted conservative art critics in America, damns "High & Low" as "a show in which the intellectual fashions of the academic are cynically joined with the commercial imperatives of the contemporary art market." Mr. Kramer's heart is in the right place, yet his reasoning is suspect. He is driven to this condemnation through an almost reflexive response to the mere framing of the question that the show seeks to answer: What is the nature of modernism's interaction with low culture? He knows that usually, when art types start talking about the interpenetration of high and low culture, what they really mean is that they can't tell the difference between the two, or that they can and they wish the former would just go away. Mr. Kramer attributes either or both of these prepossessions to the curators of "High & Low." Yet even if he's right, by itself that would not warrant our dismissing their research, which is generally quite useful.
>
> Elsewhere, in reviewing the curators' minute research into the aesthetics of storefronts, comics, and advertising, Mr. Kramer chastens them for adopting an archaeological approach to art. And we ask: What's wrong with that? Only where archaeology presumes upon the place of disinterested judgment does it imperil the distinctions between high and low art. Otherwise it is merely one of the many ways in which we approach the object of our affection. One does not love a woman for her furbelows, but if one loves the woman, one will come to love the furbelows too. Thus it is human, in loving modern art, to feel an emotional attachment as well to the superannuated circumstances in which that art was nurtured and grew. . . .
>
> Essentially, I do not care very much about the distinctions between high and low culture. Most of the culture worth experiencing, though surely not all of it, dates from before the Industrial Revolution. Distinctions between high and low culture become relevant only after that point.[28]

This writer, James Gardner, started his screed by proclaiming that "few critics if any will be sorry to see the Museum of Modern Art's 'High & Low' exhibition leave town." That was not entirely true, however. Commenting in *Newsday*, Murray Kempton observed that "mixed bag though it is, the purest and even some of the more dubious elements in 'High & Low' compel us to look with fresh surprise at objects so familiar that we had thought to take them for granted. And that, after all, is some of what art ought to do." Arthur Danto, an academic and the distinguished art critic for *The Nation*, praised the show as a "remarkable and valuable exhibition." Despite the generally hostile reception from critics, however, *High & Low* proved popular with the general public. As Grace Glueck reported, "even though it seems to be the show that critics love to hate, attendance has increased in the last few weeks by more than 25 percent to between 2,500 and 2,700 a day." According to a feature story in the *Christian Science Monitor*, "conversations with museum goers when the show opened in New York showed a level of satisfaction that never seemed to register in the press. Several people said that 'High & Low' was organized in a way that helped them understand the reasoning behind the exhibit." As one woman put it, "many of the exhibitions are so high brow, this [one] was fun. . . . I could understand it."[29]

The critical firestorm continued when *High & Low* moved to Chicago on February 20, 1991, and to Los Angeles on June 21. Kirk Varnedoe, meanwhile, was not surprised by the brouhaha and defended his exhibition on grounds that are germane to the focus of this chapter. His response was scholarly (in the best sense, namely, a desire to advance knowledge), historical, and educational. Had he imposed excessive order on the untidy complexity of popular culture? "I really felt this was a subject," he said, "that had been dealt with largely in terms of abstract generalizations, and that it could diffuse into thin air unless one got hold of its specifics. So I wanted to define the subject in terms of particular ideas that one could say specific things about." His operative categories became caricature, comics, advertising, and graffiti.[30] Varnedoe revealed that a month before the much-anticipated show opened in New York, he was asked whether he considered it a personal manifesto. "I didn't consider it either personal or a manifesto," he explained. "I think it's an objective piece of history." In an interview in March 1991 he remarked that art critics were "dismally unhappy" at the way he chose to interpret history. Some of them "came in feeling themselves to be specialists and didn't feel catered to. Some of the [negative] reviewers specifically say 'I'm an expert and I don't want to go to a show that's pitched for the general public.' "[31]

In June, just after the exhibition opened in Los Angeles, Varnedoe elaborated on his expectation that critics with strong ideological commitments would despise his approach. "I thought it was a given, going in, that those on the right . . . and those on the left would not like the show. [Note the parallel to Ken Burns's response.] You could certainly have written the reviews a year in advance. The vision of the left says the show is elitist, it co-opts the true energies of popular culture, it's all about class divisions. The view on the right says the show is demagogic, populist, it plays to the masses. Those are just the standardized responses, and you could see them coming." And then an arresting conclusion that does not apply to such critics as Hughes, Plagens, Kempton, and Danto. "But I don't think I was quite prepared for either how little middle ground there was or how few people were willing to stand on it and look at it. No one could have been prepared for the kind of crazy ferocity [of the criticism]. I mean, there was a weird tone: 'Let the dogs loose.' "[32]

Be that as it may, I find it fascinating that the general public was willing to stand on the middle ground, look, and learn. It was the professional art critics who became embattled, and the history-oriented professionals who were somewhat more likely to give Varnedoe and Gopnik a sympathetic hearing. In that sense, the professional alignments in this instance were somewhat different from those in the case of Ken Burns's documentaries. What remained constant? The general public's nonjudgmental curiosity about popular culture as history—and vice versa.

IV. Popular Culture and the Problem of Interpretation in Our Time

Varnedoe made one other riposte that pulls us forward to the prickly issue of interpreting the past for a heterogeneous contemporary public that claims to be extremely interested in history. Critics of *High & Low* contended either that the exhibition tried to neutralize postmodernism by pretending that it is continuous with modernism or, alternatively, that it sought to debase modernism by insisting that "recently made trash is part of high art's logical continuum." The two curators responded that they had actually sought to "describe a wheel-like motion where there's a constant interchange between the two fields [art and popular culture]." According to Varnedoe, "it's the continual inversion of hierarchies that the show is about. Hierarchies do exist. . . . It's just that they can't be defined in terms of a set of permanent rules."[33]

I believe that *High & Low* provoked so much vitriolic controversy because it was a show that propounded a thesis. All exhibitions and historical documentaries are interpretive in some way or to some degree. But *High & Low* was overtly and intensely interpretive about a topic, popular culture, that few people do not have strong feelings about, be they positive, negative, or simply idiosyncratic; and cultural critics, along with historians and art historians, have demonstrated for half a century that they are quite ardently opinionated about popular culture.[34]

Consequently, a *problématique* that really has not been examined systematically is the complex issue of popular responses to historical interpretation—the fundamental nature and reception of interpretation—in recent decades, especially in the 1980s and '90s. More particularly, I have in mind the vexed questions that have arisen when history museums choose to collect, exhibit, and *interpret* popular culture in the United States. All three functions have been controversial for several decades now, and the complexities of this saga are compounded by the changing relationship between the work done by historians in the academy and the projects undertaken by historians who function in museums, at historic sites, and other public places where the past requires explanation.[35]

Interpreting the past overtly is scarcely a new activity or phenomenon. During the 1930s Carl Becker commented that historical practice inevitably involves a combination of facts *and* interpretation. From the 1930s onward, moreover, the New York State Historical Association, located in Cooperstown, pioneered interpretive and thematic exhibits at its museums rather than merely taxonomic ones; but the displays remained patriotic, indeed uplifting, and therefore noncontroversial. By the 1970s and '80s, interpretive exhibits at history museums had become increasingly thematic yet not, as a rule, didactic. The emergence of the new social history, however, had a highly visible impact upon historians and curators working in museums, and they felt emboldened by the new scholarship to be more explicitly interpretive and explanatory. In a 1980 address to the American Association of

Museums, Neil Harris, the distinguished cultural and social historian, insisted that "if the museum's educational functions are serious, its displays must be created seriously. And that means, among other things, permitting an interpretative frame and encouraging visitors to understand more clearly the character of display as argument."[36]

In 1987 a manifesto called upon urban history museums to *interpret* the story of how the United States came to be an urban-suburban civilization. Presumably, how it happened was not self-evident; it required explanation. In a 1991 interview, Bernard Bailyn declared that the toughest part of teaching history "has been to pull together all this technical material . . . into a coherent story and at the same time explore the problems of interpretation."[37]

So far, this developmental account of historical interpretation for the public sounds uncontested and therefore unproblematic; but that has not been the case. Mike Wallace (the historian) has described certain subjects that remained taboo for museum exhibits during the 1970s and '80s because the topics were too controversial, including the war in Vietnam and the history of sexuality, especially of homosexuality. Wallace describes the dilemma of curators at a museum of labor history in Paterson, New Jersey: "Many in the community [there] believed that the great strike of 1913 had caused the collapse of Paterson, that the worker demands for higher wages led the silk mills to depart to more exploitable climes, thus bringing on the deindustrialization process. Given these bitter memories of the strike, the museum avoided confronting the question, and dealt instead with the social history of the contemporary working class communities." A new exhibition about (and in) the Statue of Liberty opened on the occasion of its centennial, July 4, 1986. "Given its location in one of the central shrines of American culture," Wallace observed, "[the exhibit's] ability to keep idolatry to the minimum is refreshing. On the other hand, it took only the most minimal risks of interpretation."[38]

We are really dealing with two distinct though closely related issues here. The first, in point of time, involves resistance by museum administrators and *some* curatorial historians to overt acts of interpretation— particularly if the subject is "sacred" to the national identity or potentially contested, and especially if it involves popular culture. It is now well documented, for example, that many in the museum world felt scandalized during the 1970s when the Museum of American History at the Smithsonian Institution put on display artifacts from the popular television sitcom *All in the Family* (1971–79). How could the studio chairs of Edith and Archie Bunker possibly be placed in the same building with the original Star Spangled Banner from Fort McHenry, the First Ladies' gowns, and George Washington's sword? Despite the hostility of more traditional curators and cautious administrators, a series of significant exhibitions concerning aspects of recent popular culture did ensue and enjoyed considerable success: *The Ruby Slippers and the Wizard of Oz* (1979 and 1991); *Black Baseball: Life in the Negro Leagues* (1981); *M*A*S*H: Binding Up the Wounds* (1983); *Hollywood: Legend and Reality* (1986); and *Sesame Street: The First Twenty Years* (1989).[39]

Resistance to the presentation of popular culture in "serious" history museums is by no means a thing of the past; but it seems to be receding now, thanks in part to the immense success of such noncontroversial exhibitions as *Red, Hot, and Blue: A Salute to American Musicals*, which appeared at the National Portrait Gallery (a history museum that is part of the Smithsonian) from October 1996 through July 1997, and *Celebrity Caricature in America*, an equally appealing exhibition at the same museum during the spring and summer of 1998.[40]

The second (and related) issue has become highly visible during the 1990s on account of several exhibitions that caused explosive controversies, most notably *The West as America: Reinterpreting Images of the Frontier* (1991) at the National Museum of American Art (note in the neglected subtitle that highly charged word "Reinterpreting," which provokes nervous anxiety) and the notoriously aborted *Enola Gay* exhibit (*The Last Act*) planned for the National Air and Space Museum in Washington, also a component of the Smithsonian. An immense amount has already been written about these and other exhibitions that caused eruptions of impassioned sentiment, pro and con.[41]

The point that I wish to make about the "lessons" those episodes teach is a little different from what has already been written, and it fits well with the focus of this chapter. By 1995, and especially owing to the *Enola Gay* fracas, the words "interpretation," "reinterpretation," and "revisionism" had become tainted in the public mind—mysterious activities that museums and historians undertake that must surely be manipulative, perverse, and highly subjective. Revisionism sounded suspiciously and unreliably Marxist rather than being a process that might be harnessed to any mode of partisanship—or to none. To the lay public today, "revisionism" apparently means meddling with conventional wisdom, otherwise known as absolute truth. In 1995 Rush Limbaugh loved to fulminate on his popular radio program against "interpretation" in history. That concern became both pervasive and highly representative. Yet it was not exactly new. Back in 1922, taking a position in his influential book *Public Opinion*, Walter Lippmann asserted that except for historians, social scientists had a much tougher time than natural scientists in persuading the general public of anything because social scientists dealt with human nature, an elusive and impressionistic subject. Lippmann made an exception for those who deal with "the historic past" because they could at least marshal facts to support their findings. Ten years later, Carl Becker explicitly acknowledged Everyman's preference for facts but implicitly indicated the perpetual inevitability of interpretation and revisionism. "In every age," Becker wrote, "history is taken to be a story of actual events from which a significant meaning may be derived; and in every age the illusion is that the present version is valid because the related facts are true, whereas former versions are invalid because based upon inaccurate or inadequate facts."[42]

Between Lippmann and Becker, two very different men, I think we have nearly enough background to understand why the American public wants to believe that, at a given time, trustworthy history consists of true facts (or else unambiguous artifacts) accurately organized and presented. No more and no less. No spin, thank you very much; and please, no revisionism. (It is hardly a secret that history gets rewritten from time to time; but "revisionism" seems to have acquired pejorative overtones through guilt by association with "radical" as well as right-wing revisionism, such as Holocaust deniers.)[43]

What, then, is the missing element or concern needed in order fully to comprehend the Americans' enthusiasm for historical facts and their anxiety about interpretation? (As far back as the 1830s the respect that Americans displayed for empirical evidence impressed Alexis de Tocqueville.) I believe that it is a curious obsession with perceptions of *authenticity*, a desire that dates back at least a century and a half. As Jackson Lears has written with reference to the later nineteenth century: "Within much of the dominant discourse of the educated classes the centrifugal spread of commercial objets d'art provoked a reassertion of familiar dualisms—deep meanings vs. superficial appearances, art vs. advertising—whether in a moralistic, aesthetic, or scientific idiom. The contrast between authenticity and artifice has persisted down to the present."[44]

Lawrence W. Levine links the assault upon diverse "inauthentic" cultural forms to a process that he calls the "sacralization of culture" in the United States and that he associates especially with the decades from around 1875 to 1915 or so. Miles Orvell has devoted an entire book to what he cleverly calls *The Real Thing: Imitation and Authenticity in American Culture, 1880–1940* (1989). William Stott's innovative study of *Documentary Expression and Thirties America* (1973) demonstrates conclusively that for the period he closely scrutinizes, authenticity served as an imperative cynosure for photographers, filmmakers, case worker studies, documentary reportage, and the informant narrative. In describing both the research and the expository strategy for his prize-winning book, *The Great War and Modern Memory* (1975), the literary historian Paul Fussell has revealed his concern about the authenticity of the many memoirs and diaries that he explored. "To what degree," he wondered, "was acute and compelling memory of traumatic occasions a dividend of a literary education?" And then, "to hint at one thing the book was about, I dedicated it to the memory [of a fellow soldier killed in World War II], and to give the proceedings empirical authenticity, to remind readers that I was alluding to a man who was once real and alive, like themselves, not an idea but an actual person. . . ."[45]

Does this ongoing concern about authenticity along with public wariness about interpretation connect with our primary concern here: American responses to historical considerations of popular culture, as well as documentary and museum presentations of popular culture? Yes, I believe that they both do. Here is a brief extract from a review written by an art critic when *High & Low* opened in Los Angeles: "Varnedoe and Gopnik signal an awareness that all is not well in the trajectory of the fine arts' alliance with popular culture by introducing a variation on Marx's aphorism, 'First time tragedy, second time, farce.' The art world's own need for fresh low-culture stock reflects recent interest in the naive authenticity of thrift-shop art."[46]

In explaining the reasons for Ken Burns's popular success in making documentary films, Robert Brent Toplin offered this observation:

One hallmark of his work concerned the rejection of fictional elements and concentration on authentic evidence from the past. In making *The Civil War*, for example, Burns did not incorporate re-enactments by modern-day figures dressed as soldiers or feature actors in period costumes or draw upon dramatic excerpts from Hollywood movies. Instead, he focused on authentic sources from the war—photographs, lithographs, paintings, newspapers, letters, signs, handbills, and other items. . . . Music also carried messages and contributed to the sense of authenticity.

Geoffrey C. Ward, chief script writer for *The Civil War* and author of the best-selling book that accompanied the televised series, had this to say in explaining his own background for collaboration with Ken Burns: "I have never taught history. But I did put in five years as editor of *American Heritage*, trying to make authentic history as widely accessible as possible on paper."[47]

Understanding why the public mistrusts the concept of interpretation and yearns for authenticity is a complex and variable matter. One reason, I believe, arises from the brevity of the public's attention span when visiting historic sites and museums, a variation on the brief attention span that Walter Lippmann noticed seventy-five years ago when Americans read their newspapers.[48] The National Museum of American History in Washington, D.C., is vast. Anyone with a genuine interest in history could easily spend the better part of two days in that huge and diverse panorama of the past. Yet we know that the average visitor (there were five and a half million in 1997) spends about ninety minutes seeing it selectively and very superficially. That person does not wish to know that multiple interpretations of an object, a phenomenon, or an event are possible. Such knowledge would only be perplexing, or even seriously discomforting.

Similarly, in terms of watching televised documentaries about the American past, that person also wants authenticity—reality or illusion—as a means of avoiding ambiguities inherent in blurred lines between fiction and nonfiction, ever more common since William Styron's wildly controversial novel *The Confessions of Nat Turner* (1967) and Alex Haley's *Roots* (1976). We even have a word now, "faction," to describe this conflation of genres that results in confusion between what was real and what is imagined, fact and fiction.

The problem exists for scholars, as well, because we have become accustomed to acknowledging the "social construction" of what we perceive to be "reality."[49] Few phenomena in the realms of culture, society, or politics have an independent, objective reality. They have been "socially constructed." Likewise, we read increasingly about "invented" or "constructed" selves, be they George Washington or Sojourner Truth, Buffalo Bill or Elvis Presley.[50] That tendency, in turn, raises concerns about *inauthentic* selves, about biographers interpreting their subjects with psychological "spin," and about invented interpretations of tradition, and thereby results in scholars sharing some of the concerns of the general public where the presentation of popular culture is involved.[51]

These reasons for (and patterns of) mistrust may help to explain the growing appeal of oral histories that present the voices of ordinary people, because they seem to be indisputably authentic and devoid of insidious interpretation or "revision." I have in mind, for example, the work of Studs Terkel, such as *Hard Times: An Oral History of the Great Depression* (1970), or *Working: People Talk About What They Do All Day and How They Feel About What They Do* (1974), or *"The Good War": An Oral History of World War II* (1984). I have in mind the steadily widening appreciation for the work of John and Alan Lomax in collecting cowboy ballads, prison songs, and music of the American folk. And I have in mind the appeal of Raymond Williams's notion that "culture is ordinary."[52] Despite the widely shared enthusiasm for Williams's populist belief that the folk create and transmit as well as receive culture, however, there still remain serious differences among historians, scholars in communications and in cultural studies, about the degrees of agency or passivity, appropriation or manipulation of popular culture by ordinary Americans, and vice versa.[53]

10

Meetings of the Minds?
Moving Beyond
Customary Categories

∞

I. Reprise and Clarification, Ambivalence and Contestation

The purpose of this final chapter is literally to complete, compare, and conclude. I would like to believe that the central themes of this inquiry are by now fully evident. Despite a large and rapidly growing body of writing, scholars and interested observers have not been sufficiently attentive to the genuine differences between mass and popular culture in the United States. One major reason results from a failure to pay adequate attention to change over time, and more particularly to distinctions worthy of note *within* phases that we blithely tend to regard as unitary, such as the generation prior to World War I, or the interwar years, or the Cold War era, or contemporary culture since the 1970s.

I have sought to indicate some major causes and consequences of the democratization of culture in twentieth-century America. Along the way we have noted the significant roles played by consumerism, American nationalism, and the partisan (even ideological) commitments of prominent observers ranging from right to left. Special notice has been given to the gradual decline of cultural authority and its displacement in recent decades by sources and stakeholders of cultural power because authority and power may occasionally coincide, but not very often in the history of popular and mass culture. Special emphasis has been placed upon the important pattern of blurred boundaries, first between mass and popular culture but eventually between high and popular culture as well, and even (in people's eclectic preferences) between high and mass culture. As the lines between taste levels have become increasingly difficult to discern, more and more phenomena, events, fads, and ideas have to be acknowledged as being "beyond category." Without stinting on the actual substance of all those phenomena, I have sought to use the views of cultural critics as open windows on the configurations of change—recognizing full well that my observers have peered through apertures that varied in size, angle of observation, and hence the potential for distortion. Being a historian myself, I have given special space in chapter nine to several kinds of historians and the problematics of popular culture.

At this point it seems incumbent upon me to revisit just a few of these matters for purposes of clarification if not, indeed, scarification—the latter in order to leave permanent markers that might indicate the particular tribal identity of this project's orientation. So let us begin, perhaps, with the relationship between taste preferences and social class. Correlations between the two that were often (though not invariably) clear during the period from the 1870s and '80s until well after World War II have become much less so since the later 1950s when most of the full force of mass culture as we know it became evident.[1]

After midcentury, such word-concepts as "taste" and "refinement" began to appear with less frequency in cultural discourse, being supplanted, for example, by new words like "lifestyle," which appeared for the first time in *Webster's Dictionary* in 1961. The term gradually replaced its predecessors, such as "way of life," and conveyed nuances of indeterminate class characteristics. Needless to say, class distinctions certainly did not disappear entirely, but direct correlations between social class and lifestyle became progressively more elusive. As late as 1948, T. S. Eliot continued to assert (just as Alexis de Tocqueville had more than a century earlier) that culture, by which he really meant high culture, and "equalitarianism" could not be reconciled.* A fair number of observers still accepted that dictum; but ever since the 1920s, and especially starting in the thirties, an increasing

---

* It surely is a wonderful irony that the longest-running Broadway musical, *Cats*, is casually based on Eliot's witty book of poems, *Old Possum's Book of Practical Cats* (1939).

number of voices called for more inclusive definitions of culture and sought ways and means to achieve what many referred to as "democratic distinction." As recently as the 1970s and '80s the National Endowments for the Arts and the Humanities continued to struggle with ways of achieving that delicate balance. Their programs sought "excellence *and* equity," quality *and* outreach to the grassroots of America. If an ideal equilibrium still has not been reached, at least many skeptics no longer read the phrase "democratic distinction" as an oxymoron.[2]

Ever since the 1960s, as increasing numbers of educated people with highbrow taste find that they also derive considerable pleasure from popular culture as well as some aspects of mass culture, the word "bicultural" has acquired special resonance—the cultural equivalent, perhaps, of "bisexual." Biculturalism really is not new, however. There has simply been a shift from certain phenomena within the society being bicultural in their audiences to much greater numbers of individuals or small groups being bicultural in our own time. When Owen Wister's *The Virginian* (1902) and W. R. Burnett's *Little Caesar* (1929) first appeared, they sold very well and enjoyed broad appeal, but not vertically to the "lower" levels as measured by income and education. Nevertheless, each book became widely imitated at all levels of access and attractiveness. Each book became a movie (several times, eventually), and each one became the prototype for a dominant American mythos and its attendant genre: the western and the gangster drama. Consequently, each book eventually had a profound impact upon popular *and* mass culture.[3]

Any given mythos might reach the public in different ways at different levels. In more recent decades biculturalism has acquired new meanings and salience because the same message is likely to reach a more homogeneous (yet highly segmented) public through the same (rather than different) media; yet individuals are increasingly likely to select their entertainments from eclectic menus. As Seldes wrote in 1950, which was a pivotal moment for our purposes, "in a democratic society there are not only many kinds of people," but each one has multiple interests, curiosities, and desires. Therefore, the inevitable function of a mass medium is to satisfy as many as possible. "When this function is well executed," he observed, "entertainment cuts across the lines of highbrow and lowbrow."[4] In recent decades that cut seems to occur whether the function is well executed or not, though it certainly bolsters the process of biculturalism if it is well done. Seldes, as much as anyone, wanted popular culture to be both democratic and distinguished.

Be that as it may, the tension between a ratings-driven desire for maximized profits and a quality-driven concern to expand horizons remained ever present during the 1980s and '90s. As one critic put it, "if broadcasters are compelled to give people what they think they want rather than what they will actually enjoy, if they have to offer what people will choose if asked, rather than what they might have chosen if they had known about it, then they will have to forget about quality."[5]

So there we have one major aspect of ambivalence and contestation in modern American cultural history. There are many others, as I have tried to indicate throughout. The Age of Anxiety following World War II—heavy clouds of potential nuclear destruction and social conformism hanging over an affluent society enjoying unprecedented leisure—seemed surfeited with anomalies. In 1948, for example, a feature story in *Life* magazine declared that the American family was atomistic and disintegrating. Why? Because of the proliferation of popular culture activities and the social nexus that they supplied— "The outward pull of movies, automobiles, bridge clubs, and Elks constantly threatens what little family unity remains." The essay actually blamed athletic teams and the Girl Scouts for the decline of family life. Hyperbolic, to be sure. A time would come when Americans would feel nostalgic about such good old days. But these were symptoms of ambivalence about cultural transition and its social consequences. *Life* obviously guessed wrong. Within a very few years television would prompt a change in attitude. Nevertheless, that is what many millions of Americans read about themselves in 1948.[6]

Yet another arena of enormous ambivalence and contestation appears when we look at attitudes toward science and technology during the 1960s and '70s. On that subject, public opinion polls are extraordinarily useful for two reasons. They reveal astonishing inconsistencies, yet it is not altogether clear whether that is because of ambiguity among the respondents or the variable ways in which the questions were asked. Here is a sampling of seven from among a great many taken at that time.

From 1971: "Modern life is much better off due to the wonders that scientific progress has brought." 81% agreed, 10% disagreed, and 9%

were not sure. Also from 1971, however: "Science is making people so dependent on gadgets and machines, people don't know what nature is anymore." Seventy-two % agreed, 22% disagreed, and 6% were not sure.[7]

From 1972: "Do you feel that science and technology have changed life for the better or for the worse?" 70% said better, 8% said worse, 11% said both, 2% felt neither/no effect, and 9% had no opinion. But in 1971, 76% agreed with this assertion: "Our scientific progress has gone far beyond our progress in managing our human problems, and it's time we concentrated on the human side." Only 13% disagreed and 11% were not sure.[8]

Turning to the end of the seventies, we have the following statement offered on a poll: "Scientific discoveries are making our lives healthier, easier, and more comfortable." 17% strongly agreed, 64% agreed, 14% disagreed, 2% strongly disagreed, and 3% didn't know. The previous year, though, another poll had presented the assertion that "people would be better off if they lived a more simple life without so much technology." 63% agreed, 33% disagreed, and 4% didn't know what to think.[9]

Perhaps the articulation of the polling instruments themselves does much to affect or even shape the responses. I do believe, however, that underlying ambiguities in American culture are just as consequential as these polls indicate. But here is one more that suggests a genuine yearning for participatory interaction: enough, already, of the couch potato syndrome. In 1977 Louis Harris and Associates put this question to 1,502 people: "If you had to choose, do you think that here in this country we might place more emphasis on . . ."

Improving and speeding up our ability to communicate with each other through better technology	15%
Spending more time getting to know each other better as human beings on a person-to-person basis	77%
Not sure	8%[10]

There does seem to be a certain yearning reflected in the overwhelming response for personal interaction. On the other hand, this poll preceded the Internet, chat rooms, and e-mail. The proportionate responses today would undoubtedly be rather different.

I've already said a great deal about the area of ambiguity and contestation concerning the passive influence of electronic entertainment versus the belief by John Fiske and others that viewers retain agency, resist domination by broadcasters, and selectively appropriate those pieces of programs that can be rendered meaningful to them and used to suit their own attitudinal or emotional needs. The most judicious comment on that divisive issue comes from a team of American researchers in journalism and communication research. "It is clear," they wrote in 1991, "that audiences should be regarded neither as passive dupes nor as active rationalists, but there is considerable territory in between."[11]

One last arena of contestation that we have not yet touched upon has received less attention, though it has not exactly been neglected. The issue involves the character and quality of journalism, both on television and in print. In his controversial book *Breaking the News*, published in 1996, James Fallows asked whether contemporary journalists (including powerful publishers and broadcasters) merely want to inform and entertain the public, or whether they actually want to engage it.

> If they want to entertain, they will keep doing what they have done for the last generation. Concentrating on conflict and spectacle, building up celebrities and tearing them down, presenting a crisis or issue with the volume turned all the way up, only to drop that issue and turn to the next emergency. They will make themselves the center of attention, as they exchange one-liners as if public life were a parlor game and make fun of the gaffes and imperfections of anyone in public life.

Fallows is most impressed by a small-scale trend that he calls "public journalism," because it can best serve what he sees as the most fundamental purpose of journalism, "making democratic self-government possible." He acknowledges that his mandate has been rejected by such large enterprises as the major networks, the *New York Times*, the *Washington Post*, and the *St. Louis Post-Dispatch*, but is advocated and practiced by newspapers in smaller and mid-size communities like Norfolk; Charlotte; Akron; Madison, Wisconsin; and Wichita. In those places, Fallows contends, reporters and editors enjoy a "natural bond to their community that will never exist between, say, Ted Koppel and his viewers around the world." Fallows is not sanguine, but he is clear about the options and their implications. He calls attention to the way the *Charlotte Observer* decided to cover North Carolina's elections in 1992. The editors did not want their reporting to be driven by those issues that each candidate believed would be tactically useful in the elections. "Instead, they began an elaborate effort to determine what issues the state's people believed were most important, and what other issues might have the greatest impact on the state's future welfare even though the public was not yet fully aware of them." If what Fallows means by public journalism ever achieves a broader scale, its impact upon our apathetic (i.e., passive) electorate could be considerable.[12]

II. Comparisons: Derivatives and Resentment Abroad

The impact of satellite technology has altered the meaning and implications of mass culture to a degree unimagined as recently as the 1970s. The speed and geographic spread of instantaneous transmission transform the implications of what is implied by "global events" because the events are not merely happening globally, they are being observed globally and simultaneously. The transformation of Eastern Europe (1989–91), the tragic events in Beijing (1989), and the Persian Gulf War (1991) come to mind immediately as examples. Sports, scientific achievements (and disasters) in space, along with an array of human interest stories, also come to mind immediately. As Michael Gurevitch has pointed out, however, global public opinion responds in diverse ways to what is reported and shown; yet the fundamental fact remains that worldwide public opinion is profoundly shaped by media practices.[13] Nevertheless, unlike public opinion polls in the United States, contradictory and confusing as they can be at times, there are no global polls. So public opinion on an international scale is even more elusive and difficult to decipher with any degree of assurance.

To survey the differences and similarities over time between popular culture in the United States and the rest of the world would require a volume considerably larger than this one and far more knowledge and information than I possess. Such a project would be exceedingly complicated, moreover, because those who investigate and write about popular culture in premodern Europe, for example, use different criteria and have some very different emphases than their American counterparts. It seems difficult if not virtually impossible to synchronize and properly compare what we have learned about popular and consumer culture in Europe prior to the mid-nineteenth century with what we know about the prerevolutionary colonies and the United States.

The historian Elizabeth Eisenstein, for example, has cast doubt on the validity of sharp distinctions between oral and literate cultures by showing that the boundaries between the two were extremely porous, and that what the illiterate peasant heard in oral culture had long since been transformed by the advent of print in the fifteenth century. Scholars who work on the Protestant Reformation in Germany or upon the genesis of mass culture in France tend to insist that mass culture, as they understand the term, began with the circulation of printed books, tracts, and treatises.[14]

Even more important, those who study popular culture in premodern Europe invariably incorporate political emphases and implications that we less frequently find developed in work done by their American counterparts. When Emmanuel Le Roy Ladurie studied carnival in the sixteenth-century French community of Romans, he found culture and popular politics inextricably intertwined, perhaps because he chose to focus on a time of bitter conflict in Romans for which the documentation is unusually rich. The same is true of Charles Tilly's work on *The Contentious French*, even though his book is broad in scope rather than a case study in depth like Le Roy Ladurie's. So Tilly looked at battles in Burgundy; Statemaking, Capitalism, and Contention; Festivals and Fights in the Ile-de-France; and so forth. When David Sabean examined popular culture and village discourse in early modern Germany, he emphasized a series of oppositional relationships in the process of looking at tensions between local power and state ideology: villagers versus regional officials, power versus conscience, and so on.[15] We have little work of that nature for the United States.

By the last third of the nineteenth century, however, popular culture along with critics' perceptions of it in Europe began to share considerably more in common with their counterparts in the United States. Highly significant differences persisted, to be sure, but they were increasingly balanced by similarities. Writing about France during this period, for example, Robert J. Bezucha uses an astute phrase, "the moralization of society," to describe the bourgeois and elitist response to the effusive growth of popular culture, a phrase that is equally apt as a succinct characterization of responses in Victorian America. Throughout Western Europe the so-called Reform Movement became pervasive: "a closer regulation of popular behavior, an [attempted] improvement in the common people's tastes and morals, a reform of their habitual vices, the instilling in them of discipline and orderliness. . . ." We call the American parallel to that the Purity Crusade. And as Bezucha summarizes the situation in Europe, the Reform Movement coincided with the breakup of traditional society: it was one of the agencies by which "the variety of local, traditional, popular cultures inherited from the past gave way before an official . . . national culture." That, too, has resonance in the American scene, though not to the same degree because ethnic, religious, and regional popular cultures were less venerable, less well established, and more malleable.[16]

When we move into the twentieth century, key differences and points of contrast still remain. The study of mass communication and culture among social scientists in the United States became heavily empirical and tough-minded. It followed Harold Lasswell's mandate to ask: "Who says what in which channel, to whom, with what effects?" European critics objected that the profusion of studies along such lines lacked "any real insight into the transmission of cultural values or concern with the growth and nature of a culture industry, seen as part of a consumer society." That phase of difference and contrast was dominant during the 1930s, '40s, and '50s. As one English scholar has observed, American research tended to concentrate heavily on Lasswell's "who," "to whom," and "with what effect," whereas European research stressed the "what" and "in what channel," "thereby, perhaps, discovering a middle-ground between the work of the sociologist and the cultural critic."[17]

By the 1950s and '60s, cultural critics in and from Europe undeniably developed more theoretical orientations, first among French and English writers, and subsequently among German and Italian ones. Eventually, of course, the European critics influenced numerous observers and critics in the United States, though staunch anti-Marxist sentiments in America placed limits upon the extent of that influence. The Europeans did cast a long shadow, but shadows get dim when skies turn heavily overcast. Anticommunism did much to spread such clouds during the 1950s and '60s.[18]

Gradually, however, beginning in the 1920s, even before the process and patterns of communication and consumerism started to proliferate, similarities in both popular culture and in the cultural critics' response began to be ever more apparent. "Standardization," for example, became a pejorative phrase in the critics' lexicon at exactly the same time in Europe and in the United States: the mid-1920s.[19]

Ever since then there has been a kind of contrapuntal relationship between derivative versions of American popular and mass culture in countries turning to free enterprise, on the one hand, and howls of outrage at American cultural imperialism from certain developing nations on the other. Evidence of the former? In Russia since 1989 the status of serious writers and intellectuals has declined, accompanied by what David Remnick calls "the general degradation of culture": the rapid rise of lowbrow mass culture in the form of pulp fiction, romances, and self-help books.[20] Evidence of the latter? This highly representative lament in 1986 from a Kenyan novelist and essayist living in exile: "The biggest weapon wielded and actually daily unleashed by imperialism against collective defiance [of the oppressed and exploited] is the cultural bomb. The effect of the cultural bomb is to annihilate a people's belief in their names, in their languages, in their environment, in their heritage of struggle, in their unity, in their capacities and ultimately in themselves."[21] So we are bitterly resented even as we are blatantly imitated—the high compliment of copying offset by flagrant violations of copyright—a pattern of ambiguity and contestation that became evident in the 1950s and '60s, but notably more manifest starting in the 1970s and intensifying ever since.

III. False Declines and Dead Ends

Ever since the critic and journalist Francis Fukuyama published *The End of History and the Last Man* in 1992, there has been a spate of apocalyptic cultural pronouncements whose labels turn out to be, in my view, considerably more alarming than their actual contents. Following the crass commercial behavior of the U.S. basketball "Dream Team" in 1992 at the Olympic Games held in Barcelona, *New York Times* journalist Robert Lipsyte proclaimed as the message of such episodes that "sports are over because they no longer have any moral resonance."[22] Such declarations bring to mind Mark Twain's eight-word cable from London to the Associated Press in 1897: "The reports of my death are greatly exaggerated." Before moving on to "The End of Mass Culture," the most pertinent of these recent assertions, let us begin with the more dire yet predictable declaration: "The Decline of High Culture." That is the leader on an essay by Robert Brustein that appeared late in 1997. By then it had become a familiar concern, floated by T. S. Eliot and Clement Greenberg in the 1940s and eventually juiced up in recurrent jeremiads in the culturally conservative journal *New Criterion.*

What Brustein bemoans is commonplace by now, yet his is a useful piece because its concerns are representative of the genre. He begins by praising Tocqueville for being so prophetic about "the problems that high culture would encounter in an increasingly massified and industrialized society." Brustein then touches base with bits of the history covered in this book, but he gets some of it very wrong. He insists, for example, that the cultural struggle of the fifties, raging in such periodicals as *Partisan Review* and *Commentary,* "not only planted wedges between high, middle, and popular culture [which is partially true], it also revived a traditional hostility against serious art and the critical intellect."[23] This last seems grievously wrongheaded because a preponderant majority of the heavyweight critics engaged in the Great Debate of the 1950s damned middlebrow and mass culture as menaces to what they really cherished and defended, namely, high culture! And a significant proportion of their readers seemed to agree. Those who did not had already staked out alternative positions.

Brustein then praises the National Endowment for the Arts (NEA) under Presidents Johnson and Nixon for being meritocratic, but blames Livingston Biddle, chairman of the NEA under Jimmy Carter, for democratizing NEA excessively by spending some of its modest budget (a small proportion actually) on "educationalists, audiences, and amateurs." I am not convinced that arts education is unworthy. Everyone *begins* as an amateur, yet yearns that greatness may eventually be thrust upon him or her. And the crack about "audiences" is too casually tossed off. Does he mean that when the Metropolitan Opera gets a major grant that helps, among other things, to hold the line on ticket prices, audiences are being subsidized? It's unclear just what Brustein means. But Livingston Biddle, who actually drafted much of the legislation that created the NEA in 1965, is on record as stating this objective: The NEA should make excellence available to the largest number of people, which is not the same thing as "trying to make everyone excellent," an unrealistic goal. Brustein's handling of recent cultural history is quirky if not capricious.[24]

Then he comes to the contemporary scene, which he finds depressing based upon a myopic nostalgia for a golden age that never was. The problem, he declares, "is that what was once a more hospitable climate for [artists'] work has turned mean and indifferent. Native talent may be as abundant as ever, but never in my memory has it been so inadequately evaluated, published, produced, disseminated, and supported." Brustein's memory is as flawed as his sense of the past. Native talent among American artists was shabbily treated—with a few exceptions, of course—in the 1830s (when Tocqueville visited), the 1880s, 1910s, 1940s, and subsequently. I rather imagine that many American impressionists, or members of the Ashcan School, or, especially, Social Realists of the 1930s and 1940s, would be staggered by today's elegant gallery shows, sumptuous catalogues, and subventions from varied sources. Not that everything is ideal for contemporary artists. Of course it isn't. But it has *never* been ideal for most, and conditions in times past were frequently a whole lot worse than they are now.[25]

Brustein eventually gets around to the mediocre know-nothing critics of today who seem to be spoiling everything.

> Finally, there is the assault on the high arts from the middle of the spectrum—more accurately, the middlebrow arbiters of culture, those vigilant watchdogs who bark at anything not immediately familiar to the middle-class public. With artistic standards being controlled by media critics, many of them incompetent, and publication and production controlled by publishers and producers hypnotized by the bottom line, the possibility of sustaining high culture in our time is becoming increasingly problematical.[26]

Just who these powerful "middlebrow arbiters" are is mysterious; presumably they are critics whose views about theater and art Brustein does not share. Robert Hughes, who writes shrewd art criticism for *Time*, or Peter Plagens for *Newsweek?* It's utterly unclear; but I do know that artistic standards are *not* being wholly controlled by media critics because the artistic standard-bearers are usually two steps ahead of the puzzled critics who may, in some instances, take years to understand what a Jasper Johns or a Robert Indiana is really doing, and why.

Surely the present situation cannot be any worse than it was in the 1940s and '50s when a critic like Clement Greenberg could wildly inflate the reputations and the prices of Abstract Expressionists at the expense, let's say, of the representational Social Realists. Is Arthur Danto a media critic because he writes for *The Nation?* Have we had very many critics as judicious or as wise as Danto? I don't believe so.[27]

Brustein does end on a note that is absolutely true: "serious and popular culture no longer coexist in their separate compartments." That has been increasingly the case for almost forty years now, as I have tried to demonstrate. There are many reasons why high culture may very well be in decline, but Brustein never mentions them. They have to do with unanticipated social changes and the increasing eclecticism of taste levels. Baby boomers prefer a more diversified cultural menu than their parents did, and as for the baby boomers' children . . . So season subscriptions for the opera, for the philharmonic, and for chamber music groups may be down; but we have more groups offering more concerts of more different kinds of music than ever before in our history. Perhaps high culture isn't in decline so much as it is being redefined—just as it was when those great, nineteenth-century classical composers incorporated folk tunes into their concert pieces, and then subsequently when the progenitors of modern art made everyday objects part and parcel of their paintings. When high culture becomes static, it hits the skids.

Leading off a lively discussion on "The End of Mass Culture," American cultural historian Michael Denning offers a radically different response to the blurring of cultural categories: he would like to dispose of them entirely. He asserts that mass culture is now ubiquitous because the cultural texts, artifacts, and performances that we witness—whether polite or popular, high or low—are almost entirely commodified. According to Denning's neo-Marxist framework, the extraordinary success of the culture industries and the new relations of cultural production have rendered the very notion of mass culture either irrelevant or meaningless. Rather than contest the distinctions between high, popular, and mass culture, Denning would simply prefer to designate all of them as "cultural commodities" as a way of acknowledging the leveling that has occurred. Having jettisoned outworn categories, he declares, let's see what difference it makes for working-class history and the politics of culture if we simply dispense with mass culture as an organizing category.[28]

From Denning's perspective, the criticisms that have been made of mass and popular culture in the United States have minimized the importance of class differences, and in turn, what has been written about class formation in America has tended to underplay the critical role of culture. Although Denning's proposal might, in some ways, seem appropriate for the close of the twentieth century, it would certainly be an unhistorical way of conceptualizing and writing about the eight or nine decades preceding—which he does not propose. His piece is prescriptive for future inquiries. His provocative essay and the conversation of which it is a part are helpful in exposing sharp differences between American and European scholars, as well as between theoreticians and those who write empirical monographs.

It is symptomatic, perhaps, that participants in that 1990–91 discussion of mass culture and the working class used variable and sometimes conflicting definitions of culture. Several references regarded culture as a variety of texts, artifacts, and performances produced by artists or craftworkers and received by audiences. Denning's own emphasis gives that foundation more commercial specificity. He insists that mass culture is all-inclusive because the texts, artifacts, and performances are virtually all commodities now. One of his respondents, sociologist and cultural critic Richard Butsch, bemoans the decline and loss of local culture. "A new mode of mass cultural production," he remarks, "has displaced community-based cultural production." Butsch wonders whether mass culture has "eaten away the institutions of collective action that are the basis of local culture, those institutions which historians of the working class have so well documented in community studies of the nineteenth century?"[29]

Perhaps because I am a historian and the historical emergence of mass culture during the course of the twentieth century has been a central theme of this project, I am not yet ready to dispense with mass culture as a category, even though I readily acknowledge that it has become too much of a convenient catchall and that the boundaries between mass and popular culture have gotten excessively obscured, like road dividers during a blizzard.[30] Still, the discussion is certain to continue because, to give just two examples, the disciples of Raymond Williams define culture in terms of practices rather than commodified objects, whereas the followers of Hilton Kramer need "mass culture" as a commodious dumpster in which to dispose of all those distasteful "products" that degrade us to the level of philistines.[31]

High culture may or may not be in decline, and mass culture may or may not be a disposable category; but I feel fairly sanguine that cultural criticism as an essential practice and contribution to our discourse is not exhausted. It functions in most of the customary places, ranging from essays in little magazines to films to television talk shows to fiction. Here, for example, is a provocative extract from Jay Cantor's *Krazy Kat*, a 1987 novel that uses as its point of departure George Herriman's quintessential comic strip from the heyday of popular culture.

Ignatz's ambitions go beyond the mere flat comic strip: the intricate plot of *Krazy Kat* encompasses Ignatz's diabolically contrived efforts to transcend the familiar two dimensions, the lowly flatland of popular culture, and attain to the roundness of high art. Ignatz explains his intentions to Offisa Pup: "Like other immigrants and their children ... I'm ready to give America a big Chanukah present back—a new image of the self. But this time why lock ourselves up in the pop-culture ghetto? Why not strut uptown to the mansion of high art, of roundness, and say that our gift to America could rank with Eugene O'Neill's or Henry James's? America *needs* a truly *democratic* high art. America needs the round comic strip!"[32]

The principal lesson to be learned, I believe, from reading such texts, along with Brustein's and Denning's and those of their respondents, is that we have come a very long way in our perceptions since Van Wyck Brooks wrote "Highbrow and Lowbrow" in 1915. Some time ago, perhaps in the generation that took me from adolescence to senescence, American leisure and taste most assuredly moved "beyond category."

This book has attempted to answer three major questions that are intimately related yet separable in terms of when they were most prominent historically, and also in order to explain the configuration of variables (or factors) needed for understanding each one.

The first query could be put this way: Why did a vexing concern about cultural stratification and differential taste levels in the United States arise around 1915 and persist for nearly half a century? At least four major factors come to mind.

- Because the intelligentsia, modest in number yet highly self-aware, especially the aspiring literati, wanted an American response to a legacy of problems raised by a bevy of European critics, such as: why did the United States seem to lack or else fail to appreciate cultural excellence, yet flourish in terms of political power, economic growth, and social stability?

- How should cultural critics in a democratic society respond to the advent of modernism and the growing presence of a cultural avant-garde? Although these phenomena could not be ignored, they only seemed to enjoy genuine appeal for a small elite. And because of intergenerational conflict among older and younger cultural critics, what did it mean if an individual or a group did not feel receptive to modernism or the avant-garde, especially when it arrived as a European import?

- How best to explain the *perceived* cultural tastes and preferences of a rapidly expanding middle class that enjoyed increasing amounts of leisure and disposable income? The swift growth of consumerism meant a visible rise in philistine taste and the augmented commercialization of culture, particularly at the middle and lower levels of the social structure. Matthew Arnold had anticipated this problem explicitly when he warned that "plenty of people will try to give the masses, as they call them, an intellectual food prepared and adapted in the way they think proper for the actual condition of the masses. The ordinary popular literature is an example of this. . . . But culture works differently. It does not try to teach down to the level of inferior classes. . . . It seeks to do away with classes." In brief, Arnold's aspiration (and challenge) had been to level up rather than dumb down.[33]

- What social implications were evident because of the proliferation of leisure-time activities and entertainments—a broader array of places to go, things to see, even books to read? And were the responsibilities of educational institutions and the media altered as a consequence?[34]

The second query can be put quite simply. Why is our understanding of the historical relationship between popular and mass culture so perplexed and confused? What characteristics and connotations should those categories convey to us, and why does it even matter? Chapter 1 is entirely devoted to that issue, but two points can be added here by way of clarification.

First, when the critical attacks aimed at mass culture began to appear in the 1940s, the object of disdain might more accurately have been recognized as *popular* culture. By the time those anxieties and charges reached their virulent peak during the later 1950s, however, television and other phenomena that we recognize as true manifestations of mass culture had in fact emerged, with the result that a considerable body of books and essays actually had two phases of cultural evolution in view and telescoped them. They have remained conflated ever since.

Second, I am persuaded that we have a certain difficulty in discerning cultural transitions accurately. What matters most, even though it eludes precision, is not when an invention or innovation first appeared, but rather when its democratization occurred. (The Selective Chronology at the start of this book unavoidably calls attention to "firsts" in order to supply at least a skeletal sense of sequence.) Wide access and popular use count for more than mere existence with uncertain potential. Consequently, the critical moments, in my view, occurred when films became popular among *all* strata of society following World War I; when the middle class could own Ford cars; when television became generally affordable by the mid-1950s; or when private possession of personal computers became commonplace in the mid- and later 1980s. The timing of major transitions in access and use tells us a lot more than the precise dates when technological breakthroughs and inventions occurred.

The third query to be addressed is why observers, starting in the 1960s, began to feel that taste-level distinctions were becoming less meaningful. On this issue the causes of transformation are genuinely multiple and complex, as we saw in the later chapters. It may be helpful, however, to summarize some of them here.

- The affluence that followed World War II enhanced social mobility as well as disposable income, which in turn made distinctions on the lower levels of the cultural scale more difficult to maintain or discern. The dramatic expansion of higher education, for example, meant that many more people had some exposure to college curricula.

- The democratic ethos that some critics had hoped for during the 1920s and others demanded during the 1930s finally became actualized as a dominant view during the 1960s. It became much less acceptable to demean the taste of ordinary men and women. Parallel with that trend, cultural critics of a populist persuasion began to insist that mass culture had some attractive or redeeming aspects, and, moreover, that intellectuals had no right to tell lowbrows what to like or dislike.

- Related to that shift, cultural criticism as a vocation began a gradual decline as an authoritative and valued social function. Looking at the final third of the twentieth century, in fact, we can watch the waning of clearly defined and widely accepted sources of cultural authority, replaced in part by the rising influence of populist sources of authority, such as opinion polls, television ratings, published statistics on movie attendance, and political preference polls. As one observer quipped, Americans became a thundering herd of individuals. (The operative phrase decades earlier had been "herd instinct.") They paid more attention to one another and considerably less to so-called experts.

The consequences? An increase in cultural populism accompanied by a decline in elitism, but also a loss of guidance unaccompanied by very much of the "leveling up" phenomenon called for ever since the 1920s in America. Although there are, indeed, some manifestations of democratic distinction to be noticed, indicators suggest that that objective occurs *for* the people but not as much *by* the people. And when most of the media and the manufacturers have their way, the goal of democratic distinction is not served at all. Cultural critics in a free society can plead for progress on the people's behalf. But the forces of cultural power have resources that vastly outweigh those of cultural authority. Amid a free enterprise ethos, power trumps authority, at least where cultural tastes are concerned. Be that as it may, the situation is considerably less attractive in unfree societies.

Appendix

Symposia on Twentieth-Century Perceptions of Culture in the United States

1. Harold E. Stearns, ed., *Civilization in the United States* (New York, 1922).
1a. "Books: 'We Want Civilization,' " a shorter symposium solicited in response to the book edited by Stearns, in *The Nation*, 114 (Feb. 22, 1922), 222–27.
2. "The Situation in American Writing: Seven Questions," *Partisan Review*, 6 (Summer 1939), 25–51.
2a. James Agee, "Some Questions Which Face American Writers Today," a contribution solicited but rejected by *Partisan Review* for its 1939 symposium. Agee then published it in *Let Us Now Praise Famous Men* (Boston, 1941), 351–57.
3. "Symposium on Characteristics of American Culture and Its Place in General Culture," held on April 19, 1940, at the American Philosophical Society and published in the Society's *Proceedings*, 83 (Sept. 20, 1940), 515–88.
4. "The State of American Writing, 1948: Seven Questions," *Partisan Review*, 15 (August 1948), 855–94.
5. "Our Country and Our Culture," *Partisan Review*, 19 (May, July, and September 1952).
6. Norman Jacobs, ed., *Culture for the Millions? Mass Media in Modern Society* (Boston, 1961), the proceedings of a symposium held in June 1959, jointly sponsored by the Tamiment Institute and the American Academy of Arts and Sciences.
7. "The Negro in American Culture," *Cross Currents*, 11 (Spring 1961), 205–24.
8. C. W. E. Bigsby, ed., *Approaches to Popular Culture* (Bowling Green, Ohio, 1976), the proceedings of a conference held at the University of East Anglia in the summer of 1973.
9. Roger Kimball, "Debating the Humanities at Yale," *The New Criterion*, 4 (June 1986), 23–33, in response to a one-day symposium on "The Humanities and the Public Interest."
10. Kirk Varnedoe and Adam Gopnik, eds., *Modern Art and Popular Culture: Readings in High and Low* (New York, 1990), a collection of original

essays by contemporary critics in conjunction with a major exhibition initiated by the Museum of Modern Art, *High & Low: Modern Art and Popular Culture*.

11. Michael Denning et al., "The End of Mass Culture," *International Labor and Working-Class History*, 37 (Spring 1990), 4–31, and additional responses in ibid., 38 (Fall 1990), 63–67, and 39 (Spring 1991), 33–34.
12. John Dean and Jean-Paul Gabilliet, eds., *European Readings of American Popular Culture* (Westport, Conn., 1996), the proceedings of a conference held at Chantilly, near Paris, in 1993.
13. Edith Kurzweil and William Phillips, eds., *Our Country, Our Culture: The Politics of Political Correctness* (n.p., 1994).

Notes

ABBREVIATIONS USED IN THE NOTES

AAAPSS   *Annals* of the American Academy of Political and Social Science
AHR   *American Historical Review*
AQ   *American Quarterly*
AS   *American Scholar*
BLYU   Beinecke Rare Book and Manuscript Library, Yale University
CS   *Cultural Studies*
JAC   *Journal of American Culture*
JAH   *Journal of American History*
JPC   *Journal of Popular Culture*
JSH   *Journal of Social History*
LCMD   Library of Congress, Manuscript Division
NEQ   *New England Quarterly*
NR   *New Republic*
NYT   *New York Times*
PAACS   *Prospects: An Annual of American Cultural Studies*
RAH   *Reviews in American History*
RCPOR   Roper Center for Public Opinion Research, P.O. Box 440, Storrs, Connecticut
SAQ   *South Atlantic Quarterly*
SEP   *Saturday Evening Post*
TQ   *Television Quarterly*
WMQ   *William and Mary Quarterly*
WQ   *Wilson Quarterly*

Introduction

1. See Raymond Williams, "On High and Popular Culture," NR, 171 (Nov. 23, 1974), 13–16; Michael Wreszin, *A Rebel in Defense of Tradition: The Life and Politics of Dwight Macdonald* (New York, 1994), 140, 287–89, 299. See also Gerald Par-shall, "The Prophets of Pop Culture," *U.S. News & World Report*, June 1, 1998, pp. 56–69, followed by Todd Gitlin, "Pop Goes the Culture" (an essay), 70–71. Although both pieces are almost entirely concerned with mass culture by anyone's definition, the term "popular culture" is used throughout.

2. Martin Jay quoted in Lawrence W. Levine, *Highbrow/Lowbrow: The Emergence of Cultural Hierarchy in America* (Cambridge, Mass., 1988), 234; Peter Burke, *Popular Culture in Early Modern Europe* (New York, 1978). For a prime example of popular culture being reshaped from "above" during the later nineteenth century, see Iain Anderson, "Reworking Images of a Southern Past: The Commemoration of Slave Music After the Civil War," *Studies in Popular Culture*, 19 (October 1996), 167–83; and for a prime example of the reverse a generation later, criteria of feminine beauty being altered from "below" by chorus girls and courtesans, see Lois Banner, *American Beauty* (New York, 1983), 115, 151–52, 180–84.

3. William Grimes, "Kirk Varnedoe in the Hot Seat as MOMA's Boy," *New York Times Sunday Magazine*, March 11, 1990, pp. 61–64; Kirk Varnedoe and Adam Gopnik, *High and Low: Popular Culture and Modern Art* (New York, 1990).

4. Roberta Smith, "High and Low Culture Meet on a One-Way Street," NYT, Oct. 5, 1990, p. C1.

5. See, e.g., Arthur O. Lovejoy, *The Great Chain of Being: A Study of the History of an Idea* (Cambridge, Mass., 1936); Diana Crane, *The Transformation of the Avant-Garde: The New York Art World, 1940–1985* (Chicago, 1987); Joan Shelley Rubin, *The Making of Middlebrow Culture* (Chapel Hill, 1992); James L. Baughman, *The Republic of Mass Culture: Journalism, Filmmaking, and Broadcasting in America Since 1941* (Baltimore, 1992).

6. See Kenneth Cmiel, *Democratic Eloquence: The Fight Over Popular Speech in Nineteenth-Century America* (Berkeley, 1990), 254; Erik Barnouw, *Media Marathon: A Twentieth-Century Memoir* (Durham, N.C., 1996), 62; Lynn Spigel, "High Culture in Low Places: Television and Modern Art, 1950–1970," in Cary Nelson and Dilip Parameshwar Gaonkar, eds., *Disciplinarity and Dissent in Cultural Studies* (New York, 1996), 327–28; Ken Ringle, "Five Stars at the Center of Their Universe," *Washington Post*, Dec. 8, 1997, pp. B1, B6; Susan Sontag, *Against Interpretation and Other Essays* (New York, 1966), 297–98.

7. Herbert J. Gans, *Popular Culture and High Culture: An Analysis and Evaluation of Taste* (New York, 1974), 32.

8. Walter Lippmann, *A Preface to Politics* (1914: Ann Arbor, 1962), 229.

9. Raymond Williams, *Keywords: A Vocabulary of Culture and Society* (New York, 1976), 78–81; Matthew Arnold, *Culture and Anarchy* (1867: London, 1960), 27.

10. For the provocative emphasis upon informalization, which I view as reciprocal to the decline of cultural authority, see Kenneth Cmiel, "The Politics of Civility," in David Farber, ed., *The Sixties: From Memory to History* (Chapel Hill, 1994), 263–84.

11. According to tradition, Ellington first heard the phrase "Beyond Category" from his longtime associate and performer Billy Strayhorn; but it appears in Ellington's autobiography, *Music Is My Mistress* (New York, 1973), 237. For a different version of the genesis of "beyond category," see David Hajdu; *Lush Life: A Biography of Billy Strayhorn* (New York, 1996), 168.

12. As a measure of perceived social change, note the following developments during the past quarter century or so: the World Leisure and Recreation Association; the International Sociological Association Research Committee on the Sociology of Leisure; the Leisure Studies Association founded in Britain in 1975 and its journal *Leisure Studies* (1982–), which publishes essays on aspects of leisure around the world; the short-lived (American) *Journal of Leisure Research*; the Quebec-based journal *Loisir et Société/Society and Leisure* (1978–); the Academy of Leisure; and the Institute for Studies of Leisure located at the University of South Florida.

Chapter 1

1. David Grimsted, "Books and Culture: Canned, Canonized, and Neglected," *Proceedings of the American Antiquarian Society*, 94 (1985), 307, 309; italics are mine. See also Tania Modleski, ed., *Studies in Entertainment: Critical Approaches to Mass Culture* (Bloomington, 1986), ix–xix; Kirk Varnedoe and Adam Gopnik, *High and Low: Popular Culture and Modern Art* (New York, 1990), 16; John Frow, *Cultural Studies and Cultural Value* (Oxford, 1995), 3, 19; James B. Twitchell, *ADCULTUSA: The Triumph of Advertising in American Culture* (New York, 1996), 41–42.

2. George Lipsitz, *Time Passages: Collective Memory and American Popular Culture* (Minneapolis, 1990), 122; Richard Slotkin, *Gunfighter Nation: The Myth of the Frontier in Twentieth-Century America* (New York, 1992), 9. Richard Ohmann contends that mass and popular culture are essentially the same—usage depending upon the writer's attitude. Nevertheless, he gives very good examples of phenomena that clearly are popular but not mass culture. He also appears to be comfortable at times conflating what mass culture was and meant in 1895 with what it meant in 1995. See Richard Ohmann, *Selling Culture: Magazines, Markets, and Class at the Turn of the Century* (New York, 1996), 13–15.

3. See Herbert J. Gans, *Popular Culture and High Culture: An Analysis and Evaluation of Taste* (New York, 1974), 3, 11; James B. Gilbert, "Popular Culture," AQ, 35 (Spring 1983), 145–46. Gilbert does, however, explicitly acknowledge that "the media in the 1950s, in their collective impact, represented something almost revolutionary in the history of mass culture and its impact on American society." *A Cycle of Outrage: America's Reaction to the Juvenile Delinquent in the 1950s* (New York, 1986), 4.

4. Harold L. Wilensky, "Mass Society and Mass Culture: Interdependence or Independence?" *American Sociological Review*, 29 (April 1964), 173–97; Russel Nye, *The Unembarrassed Muse: The Popular Arts in America* (New York, 1970), preface, and 1, 421; Lyman Bryson, "Popular Art," in Bryson, ed., *The Communication of Ideas* (New York, 1964), 278–79.

5. Oscar Handlin, "Comments on Mass and Popular Culture," in Norman Jacobs, ed., *Culture for the Millions: Mass Media in Modern Society* (Boston, 1961), 65. For a French cultural critic who does differentiate between popular and mass culture, regarding the first as considerably older and the second as dating from the 1950s, see Jean-Marie Domenach, "Popular Culture and Mass Culture: A Franco-European Dilemma," in John Dean and Jean-Paul Gabilliet, eds., *European Readings of American Popular Culture* (Westport, Conn., 1996), 222–23.

6. Slotkin, *Gunfighter Nation*, 9. See pp. 22–26, however, where Slotkin seems to use mass and popular culture interchangeably. The distinction that Fredric Jameson makes between the two is very close to the lengthy extract from Slotkin. See Jameson, "Reification and Utopia in Mass Culture," *Social Text*, 1 (Winter 1979), 134, 137, 138.

7. Jackson Lears, "Against Anti-intellectualism," *Intellectual History Newsletter*, 18 (1996), 21. Lears is notably unsympathetic to pseudo-populist defenses of mass culture.

8. See Martha Bayles, *Hole in Our Soul: The Loss of Beauty and Meaning in American Popular Music* (Chicago, 1994), 5–6. The Center for the Study of Popular Culture located in Los Angeles has a strongly conservative orientation and is most engaged by mass culture via the entertainment industry.

9. Robert Warshow, *The Immediate Experience: Movies, Comics, Theatre and Other Aspects of Popular Culture* (New York, 1962), 29, 128, 152, the quotation at 34. See also Don DeLillo's novel *White Noise* (New York, 1985), 10.

10. C. W. E. Bigsby, "The Politics of Popular Culture," in Bigsby, ed., *Approaches to Popular Culture* (Bowling Green, Ohio, 1976), 17.

11. See J. M. Golby and A. W. Purdue, *The Civilisation of the Crowd: Popular Culture in England, 1750–1900* (New York, 1984), ch. 1, esp. 17–18 and 194–95; Andrea Stulman Dennett, *Weird & Wonderful: The Dime Museum in America* (New York, 1997).

12. Constance Rourke, *American Humor: A Study of the National Character* (New York, 1931); Constance Rourke, *The Roots of American Culture* (New York, 1942); Arthur K. Moore, *The Frontier Mind* (Lexington, Ky., 1957).

13. Simon J. Bronner, *Grasping Things: Folk Material Culture and Mass Society in America* (Lexington, Ky., 1986); Robert Cantwell, *When We Were Good: The Folk Revival* (Cambridge, Mass., 1996).

14. Lawrence W. Levine, "The Folklore of Industrial Society: Popular Culture and Its Audiences," AHR, 97 (December 1992), esp. 1370; Gene Bluestein, *Poplore: Folk and Pop in American Culture* (Amherst, Mass., 1994).

15. Gans, *Popular Culture and High Culture*, vii; Michael Kernan, "Smithsonian Secretary Robert McCormick Adams Looks to New Horizons," *Smithsonian Magazine* (September 1994), 15.

16. T. S. Eliot, *Notes Towards a Definition of Culture* (London, 1948), 120.

17. Raymond Williams, "The Idea of a Common Culture" (1968), in Williams, *Resources of Hope: Culture, Democracy, Socialism* (London, 1989), 35; italics in original.

18. E. P. Thompson, *Customs in Common* (New York, 1993), 72, 83.

19. David D. Hall, *Worlds of Wonder, Days of Judgment: Popular Religious Belief in Early New England* (New York, 1989), 173, 177; Grimsted, "Books and Culture," 298–301, the quotation at 301.

20. Gary Kulik, "Designing the Past: History-Museum Exhibitions from Peale to the Present," in Warren Leon and Roy Rosenzweig, eds., *History Museums in the United States* (Urbana, 1989), 3–9; Kulik, exhibition review in JAH, 78 (June 1991), 256; Levine, *Highbrow/Lowbrow*, ch. 1.

21. Levine, *Highbrow/Lowbrow*, chs. 2–3; Paul J. DiMaggio, "Cultural Entrepreneurship in Nineteenth-Century Boston: The Creation of an Organizational Base of High Culture in America," in Chandra Mukerji and Michael Schudson, eds., *Rethinking Popular Culture: Contemporary Perspectives in Cultural Studies* (Berkeley, 1991), 374–97.

22. Daniel Walker Howe, "Victorian Culture in America," in Howe, ed., *Victorian America* (Philadelphia, 1976), 13.

23. John Tomsich, *A Genteel Endeavor: American Culture and Politics in the Gilded Age* (Stanford, 1971); Kent Ladd Steckmesser, *The Western Hero in History and Legend* (Norman, Okla., 1965), 44–45; Neil Harris, *Cultural Excursions: Marketing Appetites and Cultural Tastes in Modern America* (Chicago, 1990), 109.

24. Harris, *Cultural Excursions*, 124; Robert W. Rydell, *All the World's a Fair: Visions of Empire at American International Expositions, 1876–1916* (Chicago, 1984), 13–14, 33–35, 56–62, 64–68; James Grossman, ed., *The Frontier in American Culture* (Berkeley, 1994), 12–47.

25. Earl S. Pomeroy, *In Search of the Golden West: The Tourist in Western America* (New York, 1957), 11.

26. Charles Dudley Warner, "What Is Your Culture to Me?" *Scribner's Monthly*, 4 (1872), repr. in Alan Trachtenberg, ed., *Democratic Vistas, 1860–1880* (New York, 1970), 338, 346; Russell Jacoby, "The Decline of American Intellectuals," in Ian Angus and Sut Jhally, eds., *Cultural Politics in Contemporary America* (New York, 1989), 271–81; Thomas Bender, *Intellect and Public Life: Essays on the Social History of Academic Intellectuals in the United States* (Baltimore, 1993).

27. Eliot quoted in Stanley Edgar Hyman, *The Armed Vision: A Study in the Methods of Modern Literary Criticism* (rev. ed.: New York, 1955), 73–74. See also John Carey, *The Intellectuals and the Masses: Pride and Prejudice Among the Literary Intelligentsia, 1880–1939* (New York, 1992), 7, 9, 25, 52. Eliot's pronouncements could be quite variable and notably inconsistent over time.

28. Leslie Fiedler, "The Middle Against Both Ends," *Encounter*, 5 (August 1955), 16–23; Michael Denning, *Mechanic Accents: Dime Novels and Working-Class Culture in America* (London, 1987), 207.

29. Warren I. Susman, *Culture as History: The Transformation of American Society in the Twentieth Century* (New York, 1984), 254.

30. See Janice A. Radway, *Reading the Romance: Women, Patriarchy, and Popular Literature* (Chapel Hill, 1991); John G. Cawelti, *Adventure, Mystery, and Romance: Formula Stories as Art and Popular Culture* (Chicago, 1976).

31. Ann Douglas, "High Is Low," *NYT Magazine*, Sept. 29, 1996, pp. 175–80; Michiko Kakutani, "Common Threads," ibid., Feb. 16, 1997, p. 18; Jon Wiener, "Deconstruction Goes Pop," *The Nation*, April 7, 1997, pp. 43–44; Kakutani, "Howard Stern and the Highbrows," *NYT Magazine*, Jan. 28, 1996, p. 22.

32. John Berger, "The Cultural Snob: There Is No 'Highbrow Art,'" *The Nation*, Nov. 5, 1955, pp. 380–82.

33. E. F. Jackson to Frederick Lewis Allen, Feb. 28, 1949, Allen papers, box 4, LCMD; David S. Reynolds, *Walt Whitman's America: A Cultural Biography* (New York, 1995), 589.

34. Richard Ohmann, "Where Did Mass Culture Come From? The Case of Magazines," *Berkshire Review*, 16 (1981), 85–101, the quotations at 90, 91. For a similar emphasis upon the presence of mass culture in the United States by the end of the nineteenth century, see Rob Kroes et al., eds., *Cultural Transmissions and Receptions: American Mass Culture in Europe* (Amsterdam, 1993), esp. x, 26–27. Much of what Kroes and his colleagues identify as mass culture in that early phase I prefer to designate as popular culture—primarily because their examples of mass culture (Wild West shows, silent films, saloons, and Sunday papers) are so radically different in nature from what we consider mass culture in the last four decades of the twentieth century.

35. Susan M. Ryan, "Acquiring Minds: Commodified Knowledge and the Positioning of the Reader in *McClure's Magazine*, 1893–1903," PAACS, 22 (1997), 211–38; John Tebbel and Mary Ellen Zuckerman, *The Magazine in America, 1741–1990* (New York, 1991), chs. 7–9; Joanne Meyerowitz, "Beyond the Feminine Mystique: A Reassessment of Postwar Mass Culture, 1946–1958," JAH, 79 (March 1993), 1475.

36. Ohmann, *Selling Culture*, 23, 79.

37. Kathy Peiss, *Cheap Amusements: Working Women and Leisure in Turn-of-the-Century New York* (Philadelphia, 1986), 10.

38. Lary May, *Screening Out the Past: The Birth of Mass Culture and the Motion Picture Industry* (New York, 1983), xiv–xv, 164, 233, and ch. 6 passim.

39. Janice Radway, "The Scandal of the Middlebrow: The Book-of-the-Month Club, Class Fracture, and Cultural Authority," SAQ, 89 (Fall 1990), 714, 721, 726, 731; Rubin, *The Making of Middlebrow Culture*, ch. 3.

40. Warren James Belasco, *Americans on the Road: From Autocamp to Motel, 1910–1945* (Cambridge, Mass., 1979), 120; Meyerowitz, "Beyond the Feminine Mystique," 1476, 1479.

41. See Jeffrey N. Hyson, "The Urban Jungle: Zoos and American Society." Unpub. Ph.D. diss., Cornell University, 1999, ch. 2, 55–57; my italics.

42. James Naremore and Patrick Brantlinger, "Six Artistic Cultures," in Naremore and Brantlinger, eds., *Moder-*

nity and Mass Culture (Bloomington, 1991), 2.

43. See Pat Weaver, *The Best Seat in the House: The Golden Years of Radio and Television* (New York, 1994); William Boddy, *Fifties Television: The Industry and Its Critics* (Urbana, 1990).

44. George Ritzer, *The McDonaldization of Society: An Investigation into the Changing Character of Contemporary Social Life* (Newbury Park, Calif., 1993); John F. Love, *McDonald's: Behind the Arches* (New York, 1986); Marshall Fishwick, ed., *Ronald Revisited: The World of Ronald McDonald* (Bowling Green, Ohio, 1983).

45. Lizabeth Cohen, "From Town Center to Shopping Center: The Reconfiguration of Community Marketplaces in Postwar America," AHR, 101 (October 1996), 1050–81.

46. Randy Roberts and James Olson, *Winning Is the Only Thing: Sports in America Since 1945* (Baltimore, 1989), ch. 5, "Television, Sports, and Mass Culture"; Frank D. McConnell et al., "TV & American Culture," WQ, 17 (Autumn 1993), 56–65; David Farber, ed., *The Sixties: From Memory to History* (Chapel Hill, 1994), 92.

47. Erik Larson, *The Naked Consumer: How Our Private Lives Become Public Commodities* (New York, 1992). For a fierce yet funny critique of contemporary mass culture, see Joe Queenan, *Joe Queenan's America: Red Lobster, White Trash, and the Blue Lagoon* (New York, 1998).

48. Stuart Hall and Paddy Whannel, *The Popular Arts* (New York, 1965), 36, 47. Because their information and examples are almost entirely British, it is instructive to compare their compendium with Thomas M. Inge, ed., *Handbook of American Popular Culture*, 3 vols. (Westport, Conn., 1978–81).

49. See John A. Walker, *Art in the Age of Mass Media* (Boulder, Colo., 1994), 54–58, 71–81. Alan Swingewood's definition of popular culture is confusing because it is based on a concept of "mass" while also being part of bourgeois democratic culture. He is comfortable using a phrase like "mass-produced popular culture." See Swingewood, *The Myth of Mass Culture* (Atlantic Highlands, N.J., 1977), 107–13.

50. Clement Greenberg, "Avant-Garde and Kitsch," *Partisan Review* (Fall 1939), reprinted in Greenberg, *Art and Culture* (Boston, 1961), 10; Dwight Macdonald, "Masscult & Midcult," *Partisan Review* (Spring 1960), reprinted in Macdonald, *Against the American Grain* (New York, 1962), 3.

51. William Graebner, "Norman Rockwell and American Mass Culture: The Crisis of Representation in the Great Depression," PAACS, 22 (1997), 323–56.

52. Neil Postman, *Amusing Ourselves to Death: Public Discourse in the Age of Show Business* (New York, 1985); Douglas Rushkoff, *Media Virus: Hidden Agendas in Popular Culture* (New York, 1994).

53. See Janet H. Murray, *Hamlet on the Holodeck* (New York, 1997).

54. Neil Harris, *Humbug: The Art of P. T. Barnum* (Boston, 1973), ch. 3; Alan Trachtenberg, *The Incorporation of America: Culture and Society in the Gilded Age* (New York, 1982), 146.

55. Trachtenberg, *Incorporation of America*, 125.

56. Paul Buhle, ed., *Popular Culture in America* (Minneapolis, 1987); Anthony Smith, *Software for the Self: Technology and Culture* (New York, 1996).

57. "Vulgarity and Gentility," NYT, March 9, 1879, p. 6. See also John F. Kasson, *Rudeness & Civility: Manners in Nineteenth-Century Urban America* (New York, 1990), ch. 4.

58. Christopher Lasch, *The Culture of Narcissism: American Life in an Age of Diminishing Expectations* (New York, 1978), 33.

59. David Nasaw, *Going Out: The Rise and Fall of Public Amusements* (New York,

1993); William R. Taylor, *In Pursuit of Gotham: Culture and Commerce in New York* (New York, 1992), chs. 5–6.

60. Gallup poll, Feb. 9, 1951, Q20 (US Gallup.51-471.Q20); Roper poll, December 1975, Q R38 (US Roper.75-10.R38), both from RCPOR.

61. See Lynn Spigel, *Make Room for TV: Television and the Family Ideal in Post-war America* (Chicago, 1992); Elaine Tyler May, *Homeward Bound: American Families in the Cold War Era* (New York, 1988).

Chapter 2

1. A good summary appears in Alvin Toffler, *The Culture Consumers: A Study of Art and Affluence in America* (New York, 1964), 182–85.

2. Horace Traubel, *With Walt Whitman in Camden* (Boston, 1906), I, 455.

3. David S. Reynolds, *Walt Whitman's America: A Cultural Biography* (New York, 1995), 5, 154–55.

4. Quoted in Thomas Bender, *New York Intellect: A History of Intellectual Life in New York City, from 1750 to the Beginnings of Our Own Time* (New York, 1987), 156.

5. Michael Kammen, *Meadows of Memory: Images of Time and Tradition in American Art and Culture* (Austin, 1992), xvii; Angela Miller, *The Empire of the Eye: Landscape Representation and American Cultural Politics, 1825–1875* (Ithaca, 1993), 8.

6. Carl Bode, *The American Lyceum: Town Meeting of the Mind* (New York, 1956).

7. Lawrence W. Levine, *Highbrow/Lowbrow: The Emergence of Cultural Hierarchy in America* (Cambridge, Mass., 1988), ch. 1.

8. Russell Lynes, *The Tastemakers* (New York, 1954), 70–71, 75.

9. Stephen Hardy, " 'Adopted by All the Leading Clubs': Sporting Goods and the Shaping of Leisure, 1800–1900," in

Richard Butsch, ed., *For Fun and Profit: The Transformation of Leisure into Consumption* (Philadelphia, 1990), 89–90; italics in the original.

10. John F. Kasson, *Rudeness & Civility: Manners in Nineteenth-Century Urban America* (New York, 1990), ch. 7, "The Disciplining of Spectatorship."

11. Mark Hodin, "Class, Consumption, and Ethnic Performance in Vaudeville," *PAACS*, 22 (1997), 199; David Nasaw, *Going Out: The Rise and Fall of Public Amusements* (New York, 1993), esp. chs. 2–5; James B. Twitchell, *ADCULT-USA: The Triumph of Advertising in American Culture* (New York, 1996), 73.

12. Nasaw, *Going Out*, 94, 155–56, 159; Daniel J. Boorstin, *The Americans: The Democratic Experience* (New York, 1973), 113–15.

13. Kathryn H. Fuller, *At the Picture Show: Small Town Audiences and the Creation of Movie Fan Culture* (Washington, D.C., 1996), chs. 1–3; Darwin Payne, *The Man of Only Yesterday: Frederick Lewis Allen* (New York, 1975), 221.

14. Douglas Gomery, "The Movie Palace Comes to America's Cities," in Butsch, ed., *For Fun and Profit*, 137.

15. USHARRIS.71MAY.R28F, RCPOR; USHARRIS.71MAY.R41E, RCPOR; USROPER. 78-1. R39A, RCPOR.

16. Nasaw, *Going Out*, 230–31, 239–40; Lloyd Lewis, "The De Luxe Picture Palace," *NR*, 58 (March 27, 1929), 175–76.

17. Henry F. May, *The End of American Innocence: A Study of the First Years of Our Own Time, 1912–1917* (New York, 1959), 335; Henry Jenkyns, *What Made Pistachio Nuts? Early Sound Comedy and the Vaudeville Aesthetic* (New York, 1992), ch. 2.

18. May, *End of American Innocence*, 336–37; Randolph Bourne, "The Heart of the People," *New Republic*, 3 (July 3, 1915), 233; Andrew Walzer, "The Cultural Criticism of Randolph Bourne: A

Usable Past for Multicultural America," *Canadian Review of American Studies*, 27, no. 2 (1997), 1–22.

19. Van Wyck Brooks's "Highbrow and Lowbrow" is the first section of his *America's Coming-of-Age* (1915), reprinted in Brooks, *Three Essays on America* (New York, 1934), 15–35. See also Casey Nelson Blake, *Beloved Community: The Cultural Criticism of Randolph Bourne, Van Wyck Brooks, Waldo Frank, and Lewis Mumford* (Chapel Hill, 1990).

20. Michael Kammen, *The Lively Arts: Gilbert Seldes and the Transformation of Cultural Criticism in the United States* (New York, 1996), 6.

21. See Lynes, *Tastemakers*, 17, 35, 38, 48, 117, 165, 172, 177–78; Jennifer Scanlon, *Inarticulate Longings: The Ladies' Home Journal, Gender, and the Promises of Consumer Culture* (New York, 1995); Salme Harju Steinberg, *Reformers in the Marketplace: Edward W. Bok and the Ladies Home Journal* (Baton Rouge, 1979).

22. George M. Fredrickson, *The Inner Civil War: Northern Intellectuals and the Crisis of the Union* (New York, 1965), ch. 7, the quotation at 112.

23. Robert C. Toll, *Blacking Up: The Minstrel Show in Nineteenth-Century America* (New York, 1974), 28, 44–45; Gene Bluestein, *Poplore: Folk and Pop in American Culture* (Amherst, 1994), ch. 4; Ted Gioia, *The History of Jazz* (New York, 1997), chs. 2–4; Lewis A. Erenberg, *Swingin' the Dream: Big Band Jazz and the Rebirth of American Culture* (Chicago, 1998).

24. Robert Darnton, "Peasants Tell Tales: The Meaning of Mother Goose," in Darnton, *The Great Cat Massacre and Other Episodes in French Cultural History* (New York, 1984), 62–63.

25. Nasaw, *Going Out*, 2, 153, 236–38.

26. Robert C. Allen, *Horrible Prettiness: Burlesque and American Culture* (Chapel Hill, 1991), 246; Lary May, *Screening Out the Past: The Birth of Mass Culture and the Motion Picture Industry* (Chicago, 1983), 164, 233, 236.

27. Walter Lippmann, *Drift and Mastery* (New York, 1914), 142.

28. Albee is quoted in Nasaw, *Going Out*, 23; Barrett Wendell, *A Literary History of America* (New York, 1901), 530; May, *End of American Innocence*, 59, 64.

29. Cook is quoted in Susan Glaspell, *Road to the Temple* (New York, 1941), 225; Percy Holmes Boynton, "Democracy and Public Taste" in Boynton, *More Contemporary Americans* (Chicago, 1927), ch. 10, esp. 218–28.

30. W. C. Brownell, "Popular Culture," *Scribner's Magazine*, 82 (October 1927), 468.

31. Ibid., 468–75, the quotations at 468 and 475. See also William C. Brownell, *Democratic Distinction in America* (New York, 1927).

32. Fred Hobson, *Mencken: A Life* (New York, 1994), 264–66 and passim; Daniel J. Boorstin, *The Lost World of Thomas Jefferson* (Boston, 1948), 180–81, 211.

33. Adams is quoted in Jacques Barzun, *Of Human Freedom* (1939: Philadelphia, 1964), 65, 72, 78; Alvora quoted in Anne Brophy, " 'What of Youth Today?': Social Politics, Cultural Pluralism, and the Construction of Second Generation Ethnicity in Detroit, 1914–1943," ch. 2 (unpub. Ph.D. dissertation, Cornell University, 1999); Robert and Helen Lynd, *Middletown: A Study in Contemporary American Culture* (New York, 1929), 296.

34. See Janice Radway, "The Scandal of the Middlebrow: The Book-of-the-Month Club, Class Fracture, and Cultural Authority," SAQ, 89 (Fall 1990), 704; Steven Smith, "Personalities in the Crowd: The Idea of the 'Masses' in American Popular Culture," PAACS, 19 (1994), 252.

35. Jacob Zeitlin and Homer Woodbridge, *Life and Letters of Stuart P. Sherman* (New York, 1929), ch. 24, "Apostle of Democracy," the quotations at 521, 549; Richard Ruland, *The Rediscovery of American Literature: Premises of Critical*

Taste, 1900–1940 (Cambridge, Mass., 1967), 68–70.

36. Joan Shelley Rubin, *The Making of Middlebrow Culture* (Chapel Hill, 1992), ch. 2, esp. 52–58.

37. Jerome Mellquist and Lucie Wiese, eds., *Paul Rosenfeld: Voyager in the Arts* (New York, 1948), 324; Michael Denning, *The Cultural Front: The Laboring of American Culture in the Twentieth Century* (London, 1997); Francis V. O'Connor, *Federal Support for the Visual Arts: The New Deal and Now* (Greenwich, Conn., 1969), 28. For changing perceptions of the nature and function of propaganda in a democratic society, from World War I to the Cold War, see J. Michael Sproule, *Propaganda and Democracy: The American Experience of Media and Mass Persuasion* (Cambridge, 1997). The focal issue for Sproule is whether symbolic manipulation of people for nationalistic ends undermines democracy.

38. Gilbert Seldes, *Mainland* (New York, 1936), 34–35; Alan R. Havig, *Fred Allen's Radio Comedy* (Philadelphia, 1990), 61; J. Fred MacDonald, *Don't Touch That Dial! Radio Programming in American Life, 1920–1960* (Chicago, 1979), 47–48.

39. See "March of Mad Fads," *Life*, Dec. 26, 1960, p. 111; Rolf Meyersohn and Elihu Katz, "Notes on a Natural History of Fads," in Eric Larrabee and Meyersohn, eds., *Mass Leisure* (Glencoe, Ill. 1958), 305–15.

40. George Gallup and Saul Forbes Rae, *The Pulse of Democracy: The Public Opinion Poll and How It Works* (New York, 1940); Lynes, *Tastemakers*, 123; Robert Cantwell, *When We Were Good: The Folk Revival* (Cambridge, Mass., 1996), 32.

41. William G. McLoughlin, *Billy Sunday Was His Real Name* (Chicago, 1955), 26; Smith, "Personalities in the Crowd," 236.

42. Joe Klein, *Woody Guthrie: A Life* (New York, 1980), 184, 194; Sally Bedell Smith, *In All His Glory: The Life of William S. Paley* (New York, 1990), 91;

Stephen J. Whitfield, *The Culture of the Cold War* (2d ed.: Baltimore, 1996), 192.

43. Gilbert Seldes, "Beginnings of Popularity," in C. S. Marsh, ed., *National Conference of Educational Broadcasting* (Washington, D.C., 1936), 338–39; Joseph Wood Krutch, "The Highbrows Are Not Always Right," AS, 36 (Winter 1966–67), 14–17.

44. USGALLUP.932.QO16, RCPOR.

45. Seldes, "A Siberia for Culture," *Printer's Ink*, 234 (March 9, 1951), 57; Joseph Frank, "Our Country and Our Culture," *Partisan Review*, 19 (July 1952), 433.

46. Reprinted in Daniel Bell, *The End of Ideology* (2d ed.: New York, 1962), 30.

47. Ibid., 26, 28, 33. For a view comparable to Bell's, see Leo Rosten, "The Intellectual and the Mass Media," in Norman Jacobs, ed., *Culture for the Millions? Mass Media in Modern Society* (Boston, 1959), 71–84.

48. Stanton quoted in Gilbert Seldes, *The New Mass Media: Challenge to a Free Society* (1957: Washington, D.C., 1968), 63. For a critique of radio for pandering to the "lowest tastes" and ignoring its potential to level up, see the remarks of media critic John Crosby in *Life*, Nov. 6, 1950, pp. 147–57.

49. Gilbert Seldes, "Notes from a Traveler," SR, 37 (March 20, 1954), p. 24; Seldes, *The Public Arts* (New York, 1956), 300.

50. Toffler, *The Culture Consumers*, 60–61; Lynn Spigel, *Make Room for TV: Television and the Family Ideal in Postwar America* (Chicago, 1992), 140; John A. Walker, *Art in the Age of Mass Media* (Boulder, 1994), 68.

51. Leo Bogart, *Commercial Culture: The Media System and the Public Interest* (New York, 1995), 9.

52. Richard West Sellars, "Graceland Rivals Historic Shrines in Popularity," *Richmond Times-Dispatch*, Aug. 2, 1987, p. K2.

53. Tocqueville to Louis Kergorlay,

quoted in George Wilson Pierson, *Tocqueville in America* (Baltimore, 1997), 158–59.

Chapter 3

1. See Tim Harris, ed., *Popular Culture in England, c. 1500–1850* (New York, 1995), esp. ch. 1, "Problematising Popular Culture"; Patricia Anderson, *The Printed Image and the Transformation of Popular Culture, 1790–1860* (Oxford, 1991).

2. Alan Swingewood, *The Myth of Mass Culture* (Atlantic Highlands, N.J., 1977), Collins quoted at 104.

3. Elizabeth and Stuart Ewen, *Channels of Desire: Mass Images and the Shaping of American Consciousness* (New York, 1982), 57.

4. See Timothy B. Spears, *100 Years on the Road: The Traveling Salesman in American Culture* (New Haven, 1995); Gerald Carson, *The Old Country Store* (New York, 1954); Laurence A. Johnson, *Over the Counter and on the Shelf: Country Storekeeping in America, 1620–1920* (Rutland, Vt., 1961).

5. Daniel Horowitz, *The Morality of Spending: Attitudes Toward the Consumer Society in America, 1875–1940* (Baltimore, 1985), esp. 129–31; Susan Porter Benson, "Living on the Margin: Working-Class Marriages and Family Survival Strategies in the United States, 1919–1941," in Victoria de Grazia, ed., *The Sex of Things: Gender and Consumption in Historical Perspective* (Berkeley, 1996), 212.

6. See Daniel J. Boorstin, "Welcome to the Consumption Community," reprinted from *Fortune* in Boorstin, *The Decline of Radicalism: Reflections on America Today* (New York, 1969), 20–39; Kirk Varnedoe and Adam Gopnik, eds., *Modern Art and Popular Culture: Readings in High and Low* (New York, 1970), 205.

7. Ellen Gruber Garvey, *The Adman in the Parlor: Magazines and the Gendering of Consumer Culture, 1880s to 1910s* (New York, 1996); James B. Twitchell, *ADCULT USA: The Triumph of Advertising in American Culture* (New York, 1996), 73; George H. Douglas, *The Smart Magazines: Fifty Years of Literary Revelry and High Jinks at Vanity Fair, The New Yorker, Life, Esquire, and the Smart Set* (Hamden, Conn., 1991), 17; Susan Strasser, *Satisfaction Guaranteed: The Making of the American Mass Market* (Washington, D.C., 1989), 146–50.

8. Stephen Hardy, " 'Adopted by All the Leading Clubs': Sporting Goods and the Shaping of Leisure, 1880–1900," in Richard Butsch, ed., *For Fun and Profit: The Transformation of Leisure into Consumption* (Philadelphia, 1990), 82–83, 89; Harvey Levenstein, *Revolution at the Table: The Transformation of the American Diet* (New York, 1988), ch. 7.

9. See Daniel Horowitz, *Vance Packard and American Social Criticism* (Chapel Hill, 1994); Douglas Rushkoff, *Media Virus: Hidden Agendas in Popular Culture* (New York, 1994), 27–29, 97, 98.

10. Robert W. Snyder, "Big Time, Small Time, All Around the Town: New York Vaudeville in the Early Twentieth Century," in Butsch, ed., *For Fun and Profit*, 130–31.

11. Jackson Lears, "A Matter of Taste: Corporate Cultural Hegemony in a Mass-Consumption Society," in Lary May, ed., *Recasting America: Culture and Politics in the Age of Cold War* (Chicago, 1989), 38–57, esp. 52. See also Dick Hebdige, *Subculture: The Meaning of Style* (London, 1979).

12. Gilbert Seldes, *The Great Audience* (New York, 1950); Charles A. Siepmann, *Radio, Television and Society* (New York, 1950); Arthur M. Schlesinger, Jr., "Entertainment vs. the People," *Reporter*, Feb. 6, 1951, pp. 36–39.

13. Claude S. Fischer, "Changes in Leisure Activities, 1890–1940," JSH, 27 (Spring 1994), 453–75, esp. 456–59; Michael Lasser, "The Glorifier: Florenz Ziegfeld and the Creation of the American Showgirl," AS, 63 (Summer 1994), 441–48.

14. See Horowitz, *The Morality of Spending*, 132; Janice Radway, "The Scandal of the Middlebrow: The Book-of-the-Month Club, Class Fracture, and Cultural Authority," SAQ, 89 (Fall 1990), 729; Stuart Ewen, *Captains of Consciousness: Advertising and the Social Roots of the Consumer Culture* (New York, 1976), 28, 54; Joan Shelley Rubin, *The Making of Middlebrow Culture* (Chapel Hill, 1992), 100, 106, 108.

15. Ewen, *Captains of Consciousness*, 32–33, 37, 41; Thomas Frank, *The Conquest of Cool: Business Culture, Counterculture, and the Rise of Hip Consumerism* (Chicago, 1997); Joan Jacobs Brumberg, *The Body Project: An Intimate History of American Girls* (New York, 1997).

16. Horace Kallen, *Culture and Democracy in the United States* (New York, 1924); Adamic, "Thirty Million New Americans," *Harper's*, 169 (November, 1934), 684–94; Louis Adamic, *From Many Lands* (New York, 1940).

17. David E. Nye, *Image Worlds: Corporate Identities at General Electric, 1890–1930* (Cambridge, Mass., 1985), 133.

18. Ewen, *Captains of Consciousness*, 190–92, 206, 208; Paul Rutherford, *The New Icons? The Art of Television Advertising* (Toronto, 1994).

19. Helen and Robert Lynd, *Middletown* (New York, 1929), 88; Joseph Horowitz, *Understanding Toscanini* (New York, 1987), 190–91.

20. Dorothea Brande, *Wake Up and Live* (New York, 1936); Frederick Lewis Allen to Hildegarde Allen, May 20, 1937, Allen papers, box 2, LCMD.

21. Rachel Bowlby, "Soft Sell: Marketing Rhetoric in Feminist Criticism," in de Grazia, ed., *The Sex of Things*, 387.

22. Kenneth C. Davis, *Two-Bit Culture: The Paperbacking of America* (Boston, 1984), xii.

23. Ruth L. Maier to Frederick Lewis Allen, May 6, 1940, Allen papers, box 2, LCMD.

24. Leo Lowenthal, "The Triumph of Mass Idols," in Lowenthal, *Literature, Popular Culture, and Society* (Englewood Cliffs, N.J., 1961), 109–36; Wendy Wick Reaves, *Celebrity Caricature in America* (New Haven, 1998).

25. Lowenthal, "Triumph of Mass Idols," 116, 118, 121–122, the quotation at 123.

26. John Morton Blum, *V Was for Victory: Politics and American Culture During World War II* (New York, 1976), 95–97.

27. Ibid., 98, 100–01, 107–08; Richard Polenberg, *War and Society: The United States, 1941–1945* (Philadelphia, 1972), chs. 1, 5, 8; David Brinkley, *Washington Goes to War* (New York, 1988).

28. Warren Susman, "Did Success Spoil the United States? Dual Representations in Postwar America," in May, ed., *Recasting America: Culture and Politics in the Age of Cold War*, 32–33. See also "Family Utopia," *Life*, Nov. 25, 1946, pp. 58–60.

29. Victoria de Grazia, "The Arts of Purchase: How American Publicity Subverted the European Poster, 1920–1940," in Barbara Kruger and Phil Mariani, eds., *Remaking History* (Seattle, 1989), 250, 252.

30. Lizabeth Cohen, "From Town Center to Shopping Center: The Reconfiguration of Community Marketplaces in Postwar America," AHR, 101 (October 1996), 1051–52, 1063–64.

31. See Horowitz, *Vance Packard & American Social Criticism*, ch. 6; Paul Coates, *Film at the Intersection of High and Mass Culture* (New York, 1994), 3.

32. Erik Barnouw, *Tube of Plenty: The Evolution of American Television* (2nd ed.: New York, 1990), 132; William Boddy, *Fifties Television: The Industry and Its Critics* (Urbana, 1990), 94–95.

33. Ellen Wartella and Sharon Mazzarella, "A Historical Comparison of Children's Use of Leisure Time," in Butsch, ed., *For Fun and Profit*, 188; Rushkoff, *Media Virus: Hidden Agendas in Popular Culture*, ch. 4, "Kids' TV: Slip It in Their Milk."

34. Robert Stephen Spitz, *Barefoot in Babylon: The Creation of the Woodstock Music Festival, 1969* (New York, 1979), 99. See also Joseph Berger, "Theme Park on Woodstock Is Envisioned," NYT, April 24, 1997, p. B1.

35. Robin W. Winks, *Laurence S. Rockefeller: Catalyst for Conservation* (Washington, D.C., 1997), 150; Frank, *The Conquest of Cool.*

36. Herbert I. Schiller, *Culture, Inc. The Corporate Takeover of Public Expression* (New York, 1989), 92–93.

37. Ibid., 88.

38. Jean Evangelauf, "Academe and Business Tighten Ties," *Chronicle of Higher Education*, Nov. 6, 1985, p. 1.

39. Gustav Niebuhr, "The Minister as Marketer: Learning from Business," NYT, April 18, 1995, pp. A1, A20. See R. Laurence Moore, *Selling God: American Religion in the Marketplace of Culture* (New York, 1994), chs. 8–9.

40. Schiller, *Culture, Inc.*, 104–05. It has not commonly been noted how many of the pioneers in advertising or public relations came from intensely religious, often evangelical, family backgrounds. Bruce Barton, for example, was the son of a dynamic Baptist minister. A considerable number of "true believers" were prominent among the new advertising men. They had simply transferred the focus of their commitment to material products.

41. See John Fiske, *Understanding Popular Culture* (London, 1989), esp. 19, 24, 158; Robert Crosman, "Do Readers Make Meaning?," in Susan R. Suleiman and Inge Crosman, eds., *The Reader in the Text: Essays on Audience and Interpretation* (Princeton, 1980), 163–64; George Lipsitz, *Time Passages: Collective Memory and American Popular Culture* (Minneapolis, 1990), chs. 9–10.

42. David S. Reynolds, *Walt Whitman's America: A Cultural Biography* (New York, 1995), 319.

43. Kent Ladd Steckmesser, *The Western Hero in History and Legend* (Nor-man, Okla., 1965); Richard Slotkin, *The Fatal Environment: The Myth of the Frontier in the Age of Industrialization, 1800–1890* (New York, 1985), chs. 8, 9, 15, 20.

44. Eric Lott, *Love and Theft: Black-face Minstrelsy and the American Working Class* (New York, 1993), 16, 92–93; Ken Emerson, *Doo-dah! Stephen Foster and the Rise of American Popular Culture* (New York, 1997).

45. Lowell, "Scotch the Snake, Or Kill It?" in *The Writings of James Russell Lowell* (Cambridge, Mass., 1890), V, 243–44.

46. Rubin, *The Making of Middlebrow Culture*, 272.

47. John W. Alexander, "Is Our Art Distinctively American?" *The Century*, 87 (April 1914), 826–28; "The Point of View," *Scribner's Magazine*, 53 (June 1913), 788. The subtitle of this piece was "Expressing National Characteristics."

48. "The Point of View," 789.

49. Ibid.

50. "The Point of View," *Scribner's Magazine*, 44 (November 1908), 634. See John Carey, *The Intellectuals and the Masses: Pride and Prejudice Among the Literary Intelligentsia, 1880–1939* (New York, 1993).

51. David Nasaw, *Going Out: The Rise and Fall of Public Amusements* (New York, 1993), 151; Thomas J. Knock, " 'History with Lightning': The Forgotten Film *Wilson*," in Leila Zenderland, ed., *Recycling the Past: Popular Uses of American History* (Philadelphia, 1978), 95–115.

52. Leslie Fishbein, *Rebels in Bohemia: The Radicals of the Masses, 1911–1917* (Chapel Hill, 1982), 172–73; Edward G. Hartmann, *The Movement to Americanize the Immigrant* (New York, 1948), esp. chs. 6–7; Carol S. Gruber, *Mars and Minerva: World War I and the Uses of the Higher Learning in America* (Baton Rouge, 1976), 138–51; George T. Blakey, *Historians on the Homefront: American Propagandists for the Great War* (Lexington, Ky., 1970).

53. Brander Matthews, "American-

ism," *Harper's Round Table*, 18 (July 1897), 873–74.

54. Stuart Ewen, "Advertising and the Development of Consumer Society," in Ian Angus and Sut Jhally, eds., *Cultural Politics in Contemporary America* (New York, 1989), 89–90.

55. Karal Ann Marling, *George Washington Slept Here: Colonial Revivals and American Culture, 1876–1986* (Cambridge, Mass., 1988), 192–93, 220–21, 244, 281; Charles B. Hosmer, Jr., "The Early Restorationists of Colonial Williamsburg," in Sharon Timmons, ed., *Preservation and Conservation: Proceedings of the North American International Regional Conference . . . September 1972* (Washington, D.C., 1976), 517–18; Ron Robin, *Enclaves of America: The Rhetoric of American Political Architecture Abroad, 1900–1965* (Princeton, 1992), ch. 4.

56. Frederick P. Keppel, "The Arts in Social Life," in *Recent Social Trends in the United States* (New York, 1933), II, ch. 19, the quotations at 976–77, 979. The supporters of *Secession*, a new literary magazine created in 1922, sought a distinctively American mode of cultural and literary criticism. See Michael Kammen, *The Lively Arts: Gilbert Seldes and the Transformation of Cultural Criticism in the United States* (New York, 1996), 49–51.

57. J. H. Plumb, *The Death of the Past* (Boston, 1970), 31.

58. John Bodnar, *Remaking America: Public Memory, Commemoration, and Patriotism in the Twentieth Century* (Princeton, 1992), esp. pt. 3; Frederick Lewis Allen to Hildegarde Allen, Jan. 26, 1936, Allen papers, box 2, LCMD; Frances FitzGerald, *America Revised: History Schoolbooks in the Twentieth Century* (Boston, 1979).

59. Peter C. Rollins, "Frank Capra's *Why We Fight* Film Series and Our American Dream," JAC, 19 (Winter 1996), 81–86; Clayton R. Koppes and Gregory D. Black, *Hollywood Goes to War: How Politics, Profits, and Propaganda Shaped World War II Movies* (New York, 1987); John

Bodnar, ed., *Bonds of Affection: Americans Define Their Patriotism* (Princeton, 1996), chs. 8–10; Hans Borchers, "Myths Used for Propaganda: The Small Town in Office of War Information Films, 1944–1945," in Lewis H. Carlson and Kevin B. Vichcales, eds., *American Popular Culture at Home and Abroad* (Kalamazoo, Mich., 1996), 161–75.

60. Lippmann, *The Stakes of Diplomacy* (New York, 1915), 70–75, 77–78; Robert K. Merton, *Mass Persuasion: The Social Psychology of a War Bond Drive* (New York, 1946).

61. Raymond Fielding, *The March of Time, 1935–1951* (New York, 1978); Michael Kammen, *Mystic Chords of Memory: The Transformation of Tradition in American Culture* (New York, 1991), ch. 18.

62. Lears, "A Matter of Taste: Corporate Cultural Hegemony in a Mass-Consumption Society," 42; Roland Marchand, "Visions of Classlessness, Quests for Dominion: American Popular Culture, 1945–1960," in Robert H. Bremner and Gary W. Reichard, eds., *Reshaping America: Society and Institutions, 1945–1960* (Columbus, Ohio, 1982), 163–90; David Potter, *People of Plenty: Economic Abundance and the American Character* (Chicago, 1954), chs. 5, 6, 8, 9; Carl L. Becker, *Freedom and Responsibility in the American Way of Life* (New York, 1945), ch. 5, "Private Economic Enterprise."

Chapter 4

1. See Stuart Hall, "Notes on Deconstructing the Popular," in Raphael Semmes, ed., *People's History and Socialist Theory* (London, 1981), 227–39; David D. Hall, *Worlds of Wonder, Days of Judgment: Popular Religious Belief in Early New England* (New York, 1989); Ken Emerson, *Doo-dah! Stephen Foster and the Rise of American Popular Culture* (New York, 1997).

2. John Fiske, *Understanding Popular*

Culture (London, 1989), 27–28. See also Lawrence W. Levine, "The Folklore of Industrial Society: Popular Culture and Its Audiences," AHR, 97 (December 1992), 1373.

3. Meryle Secrest, *Leonard Bernstein: A Life* (London, 1995), 214–21; Daniel J. Singal, *William Faulkner: The Making of a Modernist* (Chapel Hill, 1997); John Edward Hasse, *Beyond Category: The Life and Genius of Duke Ellington* (New York, 1993).

4. Van Wyck Brooks, "Highbrow and Lowbrow," in Brooks, *Three Essays on America* (New York, 1934), 15–35; Lawrence W. Levine, *Highbrow/Lowbrow: The Emergence of Cultural Hierarchy in America* (Cambridge, Mass., 1988), chs. 2–3.

5. David Nasaw, *Going Out: The Rise and Fall of Public Amusements* (New York, 1993), esp. chs. 1–3.

6. Judson to William Henry Venable, April 10, 1885, quoted in Joseph Leach, *The Typical Texan: Biography of an American Myth* (Dallas, 1952), 117.

7. James L. Ford, "The Fad of Imitation Culture," *Munsey's Magazine*, 24 (November 1900), 153.

8. "The Limitations of the High-Brow," *Scribner's Magazine*, 58 (November 1915), 640–41; Brooks, "Highbrow vs. Lowbrow," 18; Lippmann is quoted in Nicholas Joost, *Years of Transition: The Dial, 1912–1920* (Barre, Mass., 1967), 247.

9. See photo-essays in *Life*, Dec. 7, 1936, pp. 50–56; ibid., Dec. 14, 1936, pp. 24–47; ibid., March 1, 1937, pp. 28–29; ibid., April 11, 1949, pp. 99–102 (esp. Winthrop Sargeant's essay "In Defense of the High-Brow," p. 102); ibid., Oct. 10, 1949, p. 16; Lionel Trilling in "Our Country and Our Culture" (a symposium), *Partisan Review*, 19 (May 1952), 314; Pound to *Hound & Horn*, March, 1, 1930, in Mitzi Berger Hamovitch, ed., *The Hound & Horn Letters* (Athens, Ga., 1982), 38.

10. Hasse, *Beyond Category*, 133; Carol Brightman, *Writing Dangerously: Mary McCarthy and Her World* (San Diego, 1992), 149; David Thomson, *Rosebud: The Story of Orson Welles* (New York, 1996), 81; Harvey Levenstein, *Paradox of Plenty: A Social History of Eating in Modern America* (New York, 1993), 223.

11. Dorothy Herrmann, *S. J. Perelman: A Life* (New York, 1986), 71, 81, 209. Perelman did the final version of the script for Todd's highly successful movie *Around the World in 80 Days* (1956), starring David Niven and Cantinflas.

12. Leonard Maltin, *Of Mice and Magic: A History of American Animated Cartoons* (New York, 1980), 63; Henry Louis Gates, Jr., "The Chitlin Circuit," *The New Yorker*, Feb. 3, 1997, pp. 53–54.

13. Alan Trachtenberg, *The Incorporation of America: Culture and Society in the Gilded Age* (New York, 1982), 231, italics in the original. See "Life Goes to a County Fair," *Life*, Sept. 26, 1938, pp. 40–42.

14. John Burke, *Buffalo Bill: The Noblest Whiteskin* (New York, 1973); Joseph G. Rosa and Robin May, *Buffalo Bill and His Wild West* (Lawrence, Kan., 1989); Robert C. Toll, *Blacking Up: The Minstrel Show in Nineteenth-Century America* (New York, 1974); Robert C. Allen, *Horrible Prettiness: Burlesque and American Culture* (Chapel Hill, 1991); Robert W. Snyder, *The Voice of the City: Vaudeville and Popular Culture in New York* (New York, 1989).

15. John F. Kasson, *Amusing the Million: Coney Island at the Turn of the Century* (New York, 1978); Nasaw, *Going Out*, ch. 7.

16. Madelon Powers, "Decay from Within: The Inevitable Doom of the American Saloon," in Susanna Barrows and Robin Broom, eds., *Drinking: Behavior and Belief in Modern History* (Berkeley, 1991), 112–31; Perry R. Duis, *The Saloon: Public Drinking in Chicago and Boston,*

1880–1920 (Urbana, 1983); Richard Erdoes, *Saloons of the Old West* (New York, 1979).

17. Kathy Peiss, *Cheap Amusements: Working Women and Leisure in Turn-of-the-Century New York* (Philadelphia, 1986), 88–89, 92, 95–99, 105–08; Lewis A. Erenberg, *Swingin' the Dream: Big Band Jazz and the Rebirth of American Culture* (Chicago, 1998), 48–54; Robert S. and Helen M. Lynd, *Middletown in Transition: A Study in Cultural Conflicts* (New York, 1937), 200, 248–49, 269; *Life*, Dec. 28, 1936, pp. 32–37; *Life*, Aug. 8, 1938, pp. 50–59.

18. Lewis Erenberg, *Steppin' Out: New York Nightlife and the Transformation of American Culture, 1890–1930* (Westport, Conn., 1981).

19. Phillip Furia, *The Poets of Tin Pan Alley: A History of America's Great Lyricists* (New York, 1990); Laurence Bergreen, *As Thousands Cheer: The Life of Irving Berlin* (New York, 1990), ch. 3; Robert S. and Helen M. Lynd, *Middletown: A Study in Contemporary American Culture* (New York, 1929), 244–46.

20. William G. McLoughlin, *Billy Sunday Was His Real Name* (Chicago, 1955); Lyle W. Dorsett, *Billy Sunday and the Redemption of Urban America* (Grand Rapids, 1991).

21. Lynds, *Middletown in Transition*, 243, their italics; Gary Cross, *Time and Money: The Making of Consumer Culture* (London, 1993), 86–87.

22. Lynds, *Middletown*, 252–53, 260, 265, 281; Lynds, *Middletown in Transition*, 269–71; Warren James Belasco, *Americans on the Road: From Autocamp to Motel, 1910–1945* (Cambridge, Mass., 1979), chs. 4–5.

23. Lynds, *Middletown*, 226; Cross, *Time and Money: The Making of Consumer Culture*, 58, 108, 173.

24. Leigh Eric Schmidt, *Consumer Rites: The Buying and Selling of American Holidays* (Princeton, 1995), 88.

25. Susan Strasser, *Satisfaction Guar-anteed: The Making of the American Mass Market* (Washington, D.C., 1989), 202, 204, 211; Robert L. Dorman, *Revolt of the Provinces: The Regionalist Movement in America, 1920–1945* (Chapel Hill, 1993).

26. Neil Harris, *Cultural Excursions: Marketing Appetites and Cultural Tastes in Modern America* (Chicago, 1990), 304–17; Richard Schickel, *Intimate Strangers: The Culture of Celebrity* (Garden City, N.Y., 1985), 50–51, 54; Michele Hilmes, *Radio Voices: American Broadcasting, 1922–1952* (Minneapolis, 1997), 59, 72–73; Garry Wills, *Reagan's America: Innocents at Home* (Garden City, N.Y., 1987), 109–11.

27. Robert Darnton, *The Forbidden Best-Sellers of Pre-Revolutionary France* (New York, 1994), 185–86; Richard Hoggart, *The Uses of Literacy: Changing Patterns in English Mass Culture* (Boston, 1961); Gary Dean Best, *The Nickel and Dime Decade: American Popular Culture During the 1930s* (Westport, Conn., 1993), ch. 3.

28. Lynds, *Middletown in Transition*, 252–53, 256–57; John Higham, *History: Professional Scholarship in America* (1965: Baltimore, 1983), 74. See also John Y. Cole, "Storehouses and Workshops: American Libraries and the Uses of Knowledge," in Alexandra Oleson and John Voss, eds., *The Organization of Knowledge in Modern America, 1860–1920* (Baltimore, 1979), 364–85.

29. Sean McCann, " 'A Roughneck Reaching for Higher Things': The Vagaries of Pulp Populism," *Radical History Review*, 61 (Winter 1995), 4–34; William Stott, *Documentary Expression and Thirties America* (1973: Chicago, 1986), 40–45; Best, *Nickel and Dime Decade*, 47.

30. Joan Shelley Rubin, *The Making of Middlebrow Culture* (Chapel Hill, 1992), 97, 106, 110; Janice A. Radway, *A Feeling for Books: The Book-of-the-Month Club, Literary Taste, and Middle-Class Desire* (Chapel Hill, 1997).

31. Janice Radway, "The Scandal of

the Middlebrow: Book-of-the-Month Club, Class Fracture, and Cultural Authority," SAQ, 89 (Fall 1990), 713, 719, 720; Lynds, *Middletown*, 271; Alvin Toffler, *The Culture Consumers: A Study of Art and Affluence in America* (New York, 1964), 47.

32. *Life*, April 26, 1937, p. 52; *Life*, Jan. 2, 1939, pp. 36–47; Best, *Nickel and Dime Decade*, 19–21; Hasse, *Beyond Category*, 199, 283, 284; Warren Susman, *Culture as History: The Transformation of American Society in the Twentieth Century* (New York, 1984), 172, italics in the original.

33. Lynds, *Middletown in Transition*, 248, 280–86, 263. For the tremendous ongoing popular appeal of women's clubs, see *Life*, June 3, 1946, pp. 137–44. For the passivity of radio listening, Cross, *Time and Money*, 58, 108, 173.

34. Leonard Maltin, *The Great American Broadcast: A Celebration of Radio's Golden Age* (New York, 1997), 15, 27–28. The man quoted was Robert E. Lee, the partner of Jerome Lawrence for more than fifty years of writing for radio and Broadway. For the contrasting perspective, however, see W. Terrence Gordon, *Marshall McLuhan: Escape into Understanding* (New York, 1997), 184, 187.

35. Maltin, *Great American Broadcast*, 292–93.

36. Hilmes, *Radio Voices: American Broadcasting, 1922–1952*, chs. 2, 6, 7; *Life*, March 7, 1938, pp. 33–36.

37. Andrew Bergman, *We're in the Money: Depression America and Its Films* (New York, 1971); Laurence Bergreen, *James Agee: A Life* (New York, 1984), 106, 284–85, italics in the original.

38. Alan Havig, *Fred Allen's Radio Comedy* (Philadelphia, 1990), 213; Arthur M. Schlesinger, Jr., "Entertainment vs. the People," *Reporter*, Feb. 6, 1951, p. 36.

39. Melvin Patrick Ely, *The Adventures of Amos 'n' Andy: A Social History of an American Phenomenon* (New York, 1991), ch. 10; Havig, *Allen's Radio Com-*

edy, ch. 9; William Boddy, *Fifties Television: The Industry and Its Critics* (Urbana, 1990), ch. 11.

40. Pat Weaver, *The Best Seat in the House: The Golden Years of Radio and Television* (New York, 1994); Michael Kammen, *The Lively Arts: Gilbert Seldes and the Transformation of Cultural Criticism in the United States* (New York, 1996), chs. 3 and 9; Marshall McLuhan, *Understanding Media: The Extension of Man* (1964; Cambridge, Mass., 1994), 248–49.

41. Ellen Wartella and Sharon Mazzarella, "A Historical Comparison of Children's Use of Leisure Time," in Richard Butsch, ed., *For Fun and Profit: The Transformation of Leisure into Consumption* (Philadelphia, 1990), 186; Lynn Spigel, *Make Room for TV: Television and the Family Ideal in Postwar America* (Chicago, 1992), 112, 134; Eduardo Galeano, "All the World's a Ball," *The Nation*, Aug. 10/17, 1998, p. 41; Richard Sennett, *The Fall of Public Man* (New York, 1977), 283–84; Robert Hughes, "Why Watch It, Anyway?" *New York Review of Books*, Feb. 16, 1995, p. 37.

42. Levine, *Highbrow/Lowbrow*, 189; William Leach, *Land of Desire: Merchants, Power, and the Rise of a New American Culture* (New York, 1993), 199–200; Gilbert Seldes, *The Years of the Locust (America, 1929–1932)* (Boston, 1933), 297–98.

43. Aldous Huxley, "The Outlook for American Culture: Some Reflections in a Machine Age," *Harper's*, 155 (August 1927), 268.

44. Spigel, *Make Room for TV*, 114–15; Gilbert Seldes, "The Gershwin Case," *Esquire*, 2 (October 1934), 108; Seldes, "Musician, Spare That Tune," *Esquire*, 26 (February 1946), 83; Erenberg, *Swingin' the Dream*, 91, 239. For Erenberg's strong emphasis upon the participatory nature of swing band audiences during the later 1930s, see pp. 36, 46–47.

45. *Life*, May 16, 1949, pp. 97–106; Allen Tate, "The Man of Letters in the

Modern World," in Tate, *Essays of Four Decades* (Chicago, 1968), 3; Dwight Macdonald, "Masscult & Midcult," *Against the American Grain* (New York, 1962), 61.

46. Toffler, *The Culture Consumers*, 10; Herbert J. Gans, *Popular and High Culture: An Analysis and Evaluation of Taste* (New York, 1974), 140–41; Janice A. Radway, *Reading the Romance: Women, Patriarchy, and Popular Literature* (1984: Chapel Hill, 1991), 205, 206, 211, 214; James B. Twitchell, *ADCULTUSA: The Triumph of Advertising in American Culture* (New York, 1996), 4.

47. Herbert I. Schiller, *Culture, Inc. The Corporate Takeover of Public Expression* (New York, 1989), 152.

48. Snyder, "New York Vaudeville in the Early Twentieth Century," in Butsch, ed., *For Fun and Profit*, 129–30.

49. *Life*, Dec. 6, 1948, p. 50; Robert Sklar, *Movie-Made America: A Cultural History of American Movies* (New York, 1975), pt. 4, "The Decline of Movie Culture." As recently as 1998, however, a Harris poll showed that "reading" ranked first among the leisure activities of Americans (30%), followed by television (21%). But reading as a category, included not only books but newspapers, magazines, even *TV Guide*, etc. Gardening ranked third, with 14%, followed by "spending time with family/kids" (13%). *Ithaca Journal*, July 18, 1998, p. 1.

50. Rubin, *The Making of Middlebrow Culture*, 269; Laurence Bergreen, *James Agee: A Life* (New York, 1984), 284–85; Richard Wightman Fox and T. J. Jackson Lears, eds., *The Culture of Consumption: Critical Essays in American History, 1880–1980* (New York, 1983), introduction, x.

51. Martha Bayles, *Hole in Our Soul: The Loss of Beauty and Meaning in American Popular Music* (Chicago, 1994), 166.

52. *Life*, May 5, 1947, pp. 46–50; *Life*, April 12, 1948, pp. 103–09; *Life*, July 19, 1948, pp. 65–71; Randy Roberts and James Olson, *Winning Is the Only Thing:*

Sports in America Since 1945 (Baltimore, 1989); H. F. Moorhouse, "American Automobiles and Workers' Dreams," *Sociological Review*, 31 (August 1983), 411.

53. Norman Cousins, *Present Tense: An American Editor's Odyssey* (New York, 1967), 65–71; "In a Second Revolution the New Role for Culture," *Life* editorial, Dec. 26, 1960, pp. 44–45; Toffler, *The Culture Consumers*, passim; Kenneth C. Davis, *Two-Bit Culture: The Paperbacking of America* (Boston, 1984), 48, 116, 166.

54. Herrmann, *S. J. Perelman*, 229, 232–40.

55. Erik Barnouw, *Tube of Plenty: The Evolution of American Television* (2nd ed.: New York, 1990), 346.

56. Abraham Kaplan, "The Aesthetics of Popular Culture," in James B. Hall and Barry Ulanov, eds., *Modern Culture and the Arts* (New York, 1967), 63, 65, 69.

57. Kammen, *The Lively Arts*, 277.

Chapter 5

1. "Highbrow, Lowbrow, Middlebrow" is reprinted in Russell Lynes, *Confessions of a Dilettante* (New York, 1966), 119–38, the quotation at 120. For a representative example of readers' responses, see Kate W. Stone, Macon, Ga., to *Harper's*, Jan. 30, 1949, Lynes papers, correspondence box 4, BLYU.

2. *Life*, April 11, 1949, pp. 99–102. For Lynes's response to the charge that he stole "middlebrow" from Virginia Woolf, see his letter to Mrs. Remsen Johnson, May 11, 1949, Lynes papers, box 4, BLYU.

3. All of these materials will be found in Lynes's papers, box 4, BLYU. See also Horace Sutton, "Low Man on the Brow Pole," *Saturday Review*, 32 (July 2, 1949), 34–35. A few years later Lynes produced a very substantial follow-up book that managed to be well informed yet wry and engaging. *The Tastemakers* (New York, 1954) became his best known work.

4. Russell Lynes, "Intellectuals v.

Philistines," NYT, July 10, 1949, sec. 7, p. 1; "The Age of Taste," *Harper's*, 201 (October 1950), 60–73; Lynes, "The New Snobbism," *Harper's*, 201 (November 1950), 40–50; Lynes, *Snobs* (New York, 1950).

5. Virginia Woolf, "Middlebrow," in Woolf, *The Death of the Moth and Other Essays* (New York, 1942), 176–86.

6. Clement Greenberg, "The Plight of Our Culture: Industrialism and Class Mobility" (1953), in Norman Podhoretz, ed., *The Commentary Reader: Two Decades of Articles and Stories* (New York, 1966), 425–37, the quotation at 432–33. See also Bernard Rosenberg and David Manning White, eds., *Mass Culture: The Popular Arts in America* (New York, 1957).

7. John A. Walker, *Art in the Age of Mass Media* (1983: Boulder, Colo., 1994), 96; see also 51, 119, 121.

8. Sidney Finkelstein, *Jazz: A People's Music* (New York, 1948); Marshall McLuhan, *Understanding Media: The Extensions of Man* (1964: Cambridge, Mass., 1994), 282.

9. Daniel Bell, "The End of American Exceptionalism" (1975) in Bell, *The Winding Passage: Essays and Sociological Journeys, 1960–1980* (Cambridge, Mass., 1980), 260.

10. See Gary Kulik, "Designing the Past: History-Museum Exhibitions from Peale to the Present," in Warren Leon and Roy Rosenzweig, eds., *History Museums in the United States: A Critical Assessment* (Urbana, 1989), 3–7; Carol V. R. George, *God's Salesman: Norman Vincent Peale and the Power of Positive Thinking* (New York, 1993).

11. Henry Nash Smith, *Democracy and the Novel: Popular Resistance to Classic American Writers* (New York, 1978), 7 and passim; William Peirce Randel, *Edward Eggleston* (New York, 1946), 175.

12. Robert C. Allen, *Horrible Prettiness: Burlesque and American Cutlure* (Chapel Hill, 1991), esp. 282.

13. George Seldes, *Witness to a Cen-tury: Encounters with the Noted, the Notorious, and the Three SOBs* (New York, 1987), 22. See also p. 38 for Seldes's sense of highbrow as a very distinct category of taste in 1912.

14. Neal Gabler, *Winchell: Gossip, Power and the Culture of Celebrity* (New York, 1994), xiii, xv.

15. Gary Cross, *Time and Money: The Making of Consumer Culture* (London, 1993), 10, 59, 127; Stephen J. Whitfield, *Voices of Jacob, Hands of Esau: Jews in American Life and Thought* (Hamden, Conn., 1984), 142.

16. See Lawrence W. Levine, "William Shakespeare and the American People: A Study in Cultural Transformation," AHR, 89 (February 1984), 34–66; Charles J. Maland, *Chaplin and American Culture: The Evolution of a Star Image* (Princeton, 1989), pts. 1 and 2; Richard Schickel, *The Disney Version: The Life, Times, Art and Commerce of Walt Disney* (rev. ed.: New York, 1985); Steven Watts, *The Magic Kingdom: Walt Disney and the American Way of Life* (Boston, 1997), 104, 115.

17. Lynes, *Tastemakers*, 206–07, 210–11; Robert Sklar, *Movie-Made America: A Cultural History of American Movies* (New York, 1975), 46, 64, 89; Steven J. Ross, *Working-Class Hollywood: Silent Film and the Shaping of Class in America* (Princeton, 1998); Miriam Hansen, *Babel and Babylon: Spectatorship in American Silent Film* (Cambridge, Mass., 1991).

18. David Glassberg, *American Historical Pageantry: The Uses of Tradition in the Early Twentieth Century* (Chapel Hill, 1990), 194, 214, the quotation at 284.

19. Herbert J. Gans, *Popular Culture and High Culture: An Analysis and Evaluation of Taste* (New York, 1974), 127–28. For a sociologist who insists that "differences are not moribund" and defends the resilience of hierarchy, yet acknowledges that "the most avid consumers appreciate *both* highbrow and popular forms," see Wesley Monroe Shrum, Jr., *Fringe and*

Fortune: The Role of Critics in High and Popular Art* (Princeton, 1996), 7–9.

20. John P. Diggins, *The Proud Decades: America in War and Peace, 1941–1960* (New York, 1988); *Partisan Review*, 19 (May to October 1952), passim; Hilton Kramer, "Cynthia Ozick's Farewell to T. S. Eliot—and High Culture," *New Criterion*, 8 (February 1990), 5–9; Kramer, "The Varnedoe Debacle: MOMA's New 'Low,'" ibid., 9 (December 1990), 5–8.

21. See Leslie Fiedler, *The Return of the Vanishing American* (New York, 1968), 15; Hayden White, "Structuralism and Popular Culture," JPC, 7 (Spring 1974), 775.

22. Robert Darnton, *The Great Cat Massacre and Other Episodes in French Cultural History* (New York, 1984), 3–4, 17; Robert Darnton, *The Forbidden Best-Sellers of Pre-Revolutionary France* (New York, 1994), 203; Donna T. Andrew, "Popular Culture and Public Debate: London, 1780," *Historical Journal*, 39 (June 1996), 405–23.

23. Peter U. Hohendahl, *Building a National Literature: The Case of Germany, 1830–1870* (Ithaca, 1989), esp. ch. 9; Reinhard Koselleck, ed., *Bildungsbürgertum im 19.Jahrhundert* (Stuttgart, 1990); Leo Lowenthal, *Literature, Popular Culture, and Society* (Englewood Cliffs, N.J., 1961), chs. 2 and 3.

24. François Furet and Jacques Ozouf, *Lire et écrire: L'Alphabetisation des Français de Calvin à Jules Ferry* (Paris, 1978); Steven L. Kaplan, ed., *Understanding Popular Culture: Europe from the Middle Ages to the Nineteenth Century* (Berlin, 1984), chs. 9, 10.

25. See George Selement, "The Meeting of Elite and Popular Minds at Cambridge, New England, 1633–1645," WMQ, 41 (January 1984), 32–48; James H. Hutson, "An Investigation of the Inarticulate: Philadelphia's White Oaks," WMQ, 28 (January 1971), 3–25.

26. James T. Flexner, *Maverick's Progress: An Autobiography* (New York, 1996), 340; Mount quoted in Lillian B. Miller, "Paintings, Sculpture, and the National Character, 1815–1860," JAH, 53 (March 1967), 701.

27. David S. Reynolds, *Walt Whitman's America: A Cultural Biography* (New York, 1995), 186, 193; Carl Bode, *The American Lyceum: Town Meeting of the Mind* (New York, 1956); Nick Salvatore, *We All Got History: The Memory Books of Amos Webber* (New York, 1996), 38–39; Ken Emerson, *Doo-dah! Stephen Foster and the Rise of American Popular Culture* (New York, 1997).

28. Reynolds, *Walt Whitman's America*, 106, 162, 311, 313, 345. It seems symptomatic that Charles Sanders Peirce, the highly cerebral "founder" of Pragmatism, would publish "The Fixation of Belief" in *Popular Science Monthly*, 12 (November 1877), 1–15.

29. Paul DiMaggio, "Cultural Entrepreneurship in Nineteenth-Century Boston," in Chandra Mukerji and Michael Schudson, eds., *Rethinking Popular Culture: Contemporary Perspectives in Cultural Studies* (Berkeley, 1991), 379.

30. Neil Harris, *Cultural Excursions: Marketing Appetites and Cultural Tastes in Modern America* (Chicago, 1990), 85.

31. David Nasaw, *Going Out: The Rise and Fall of Public Amusements* (New York, 1993), 123; Harris, *Cultural Excursions*, 42, 230–32; Harvey Green, "Popular Science and Political Thought Converge: Colonial Survival Becomes Colonial Revival, 1830–1910," JAC, 6 (Winter 1983), 20.

32. Mark Hodin, "Class, Consumption, and Ethnic Performance in Vaudeville," PAACS, 22 (1997), 203, 205; Susan M. Ryan, "Acquiring Minds: Commodified Knowledge and the Positioning of the Reader in *McClure's Magazine*, 1893–1903," ibid., 223; Charles W. Stein, ed., *American Vaudeville as Seen by Its Contemporaries* (New York, 1984), 68–77, 370–75.

33. Karal Ann Marling, *George Washington Slept Here: Colonial Revivals and American Culture, 1876–1986* (Cambridge, Mass., 1988), 215; Richard F. Bach, "Museums and the Factory: Making the Galleries Work for the Art Trade," *Scribner's Magazine*, 71 (June 1922), 766–68.

34. John W. Tebbel, *George Horace Lorimer and the Saturday Evening Post* (Garden City, N.Y., 1948), 156–57; Carl F. Kaestle, et al., eds., *Literacy in the United States: Readers and Reading Since 1880* (New Haven, 1991), ch. 7; Michael Kammen, *The Lively Arts: Gilbert Seldes and the Transformation of Cultural Criticism in the United States* (New York, 1996), chs. 2–5.

35. J. Fred MacDonald, *Don't Touch That Dial! Radio Programming in American Life, 1920–1960* (Chicago, 1979), 4–5, 17–18, 24, 26, 28; John G. Cawelti, "Popular Culture/Multiculturalism," JPC, 30 (Summer 1996), 7–8.

36. Joseph Horowitz, *Understanding Toscanini: How He Became an American Culture God and Helped Create a New Audience for Old Music* (Minneapolis, 1988); *Life*, Dec. 6, 1937, pp. 47–54; William Leach, *Land of Desire: Merchants, Power, and the Rise of a New American Culture* (New York, 1993), 320; Everett Dean Martin, "Our Invisible Masters," *Forum*, 81 (March 1929), 14.

37. MacDonald, *Don't Touch That Dial!*, 54; Michele Hilmes, *Radio Voices: American Broadcasting, 1922–1952* (Minneapolis, 1997), 218–22.

38. Sklar, *Movie-Made America*, 198; Neal Gabler, *An Empire of Their Own: How the Jews Invented Hollywood* (New York, 1988), 172–74; Alva Johnston quoted in Watts, *The Magic Kingdom*, 125.

39. Adrianna Williams, *Covarrubias* (Austin, 1994), 72; Beverly J. Cox and Denna Jones Anderson, eds., *Miguel Covarrubias' Caricatures* (Washington, D.C., 1985), 75, 78–92, 96, 106–19. Covarrubias had a great influence on Al Hirschfeld. See Wendy Wick Reaves, *Celebrity Caricature in America* (New Haven, 1998), 165, 170.

40. Reaves, *Celebrity Caricature in America*, 108, 120–21, 141.

41. James Lincoln Collier, *Benny Goodman and the Swing Era* (New York, 1989), ch. 17; Ross Firestone, *Swing, Swing, Swing: The Life and Times of Benny Goodman* (New York, 1993), 207–17.

42. Steven Watts, "Walt Disney: Art and Politics in the American Century," JAH, 82 (June 1995), 101–02.

43. Ibid., 102; Kammen, *The Lively Arts*, chs. 4–7.

44. Harvey Levenstein, *Paradox of Plenty: A Social History of Eating in Modern America* (New York, 1993), 89; MacDonald, *Don't Touch That Dial!*, 77; Robert Cantwell, *When We Were Good: The Folk Revival* (Cambridge, Mass., 1996), 190; Tim Page, "LP at 50: Waxing Nostalgic," *Washington Post*, Jan. 18, 1998, p. G1.

45. *Life*, Dec. 5, 1938, pp. 68–69; *Life*, May 1, 1950, 81–90; *Life*, March 5, 1951, pp. 95–99; *Life*, May 7, 1951, pp. 97–101.

46. Daniel Marcus, "NBC's Project XX: Television and American History at the End of Ideology," *Historical Journal of Film, Radio and Television*, 17 (August 1997), 347–66, the quotation at 355.

47. Robert Warshow, *The Immediate Experience: Movies, Comics, Theater and Other Aspects of Popular Culture* (New York, 1962), 26, 28; Lynes, *Tastemakers*, 262; Calvin Tompkins, *Merchants and Masterpieces: The Story of the Metropolitan Museum of Art* (New York, 1970), 340–41, 342, 360. In 1987, *The Helga Pictures* by Andrew Wyeth became the first art book ever chosen as a main selection of the Book-of-the-Month Club.

48. John W. Aldridge, "Highbrow Authors and Middlebrow Books," *Playboy*, 11 (April 1964), 119, 166–74; Leslie Fiedler, "The State of American Writing, 1948: Seven Questions," *Partisan Review*, 15 (August 1948), 875.

49. John Cawelti, "Beatles, Batman,

and the New Aesthetic," *Midway*, 9 (Autumn 1968), 49–70.

50. Michael Kammen, *Mystic Chords of Memory: The Transformation of Tradition in American Culture* (New York, 1991), chs. 11, 16, 18; Alvin Toffler, *The Culture Consumers: A Study of Art and Affluence in America* (New York, 1964), 152; Cantwell, *When We Were Good*, 37, 38.

51. Gilbert Seldes, "TV and the Hearings: Unfinished Business," *Saturday Review*, 37 (July 10, 1954), 27.

52. Thompson is quoted in Levine, *Highbrow/Lowbrow*, 233; Woolf, "Middlebrow," 178; Chandler to Bernice Baumgarten, Nov. 8, 1949, in Frank MacShane, ed., *Selected Letters of Raymond Chandler* (New York, 1981), 200. See also F. R. Leavis, *Mass Civilisation and Minority Culture* (Cambridge, 1930), 20–21, for a very snide attitude toward middlebrow and those who mediate with the public on its behalf.

53. *Life*, April 5, 1937, pp. 64–65; *Life*, Oct. 31, 1938, pp. 27–38; *Life*, July 12, 1948, pp. 95–113. See also Elizabeth McCausland, ed., *Work for Artists: What? How? Where?* (New York, 1947).

54. *Life*, Dec. 12, 1938, pp. 49–57; *Life*, May 15, 1939, pp. 80–81; *Life*, May 29, 1939, pp. 68–74; *Life*, June 5, 1939, pp. 47, 72–73.

55. *Life*, Oct. 28, 1946, pp. 109–17; *Life*, March 17, 1947, pp. 101–04; *Life*, March 14, 1949, pp. 120–25; *Life*, Nov. 14, 1949, pp. 93–96.

56. James T. Flexner, *A Maverick's Progress: An Autobiography*, 304–07; Cantwell, *When We Were Good*, chs. 7–9; Fred Goodman, *The Mansion on the Hill: Dylan, Young, Geffen, Springsteen, and the Head-On Collision of Rock and Commerce* (New York, 1997), chs. 1–5, esp. pp. 51–52.

57. Walker, *Art in the Age of Mass Media*, esp. chs. 2–3; Lynn Spigel, "High Culture in Low Places: Television and Modern Art, 1950–1970," in Cary Nelson and D. P. Gaonkar, eds., *Disciplinarity*

and Dissent in Cultural Studies (New York, 1996), 331; McCausland, *Work for Artists*, 14–26, 60–64, 118–22.

58. Jan Scott, et al., "Design in Television," TQ, 2 (Summer 1963), 41–57; Richard J. Stonesifer, "TV Form and TV Sense," TQ, 4 (Spring 1965), 19–27; Fred Mogubgub, et al., "Graphic Design in Television," TQ, 5 (Summer 1966), 39–64; Stonesifer, "A New Style for TV Criticism.," TQ, 6 (Spring 1967), 46–57; Barbara Schultz, "Writing and *The CBS Playhouse*," TQ, 7 (Summer 1968), 80–84; Richard W. Jencks, "Is Taste Obsolete?" TQ, 8 (Summer 1969), 7–15.

59. Spigel, "High Culture in Low Places," 331–32, 335; "Robert Saudek Is Dead at 85: A Pioneer of Culture on TV," NYT, March 17, 1997, p. B9; "The Three Tenors, Guess Who, to Sing," NYT, July 14, 1994, p. C11.

60. See Janice Radway, "On the Gender of the Middlebrow Consumer and the Threat of the Culturally Fraudulent Female," SAQ, 93 (Fall 1994), 871–93; Dwight Macdonald, *Memoirs of a Revolutionist: Essays in Political Criticism* (New York, 1957), 255; William Phillips, "Our Country and Our Culture" (1984) in Phillips, ed., *Partisan Review: The 50th Anniversary Edition* (New York, 1985), 290. In 1959 Dwight Macdonald quoted Jerry Wald, a Hollywood producer, who said: "There's no such thing as highbrow and lowbrow anymore," because college graduates watch all the best television and radio programs. Macdonald, *Discriminations: Essays and Afterthoughts, 1938–1974* (New York, 1974), 254.

61. "The *Salmagundi* Interview" in *A Susan Sontag Reader* (New York, 1982), 337. For total agreement from a different angle, see Morse Peckham, *Art and Pornography: An Experiment in Explanation* (New York, 1969), ch. 4, "Pornography and Culture."

62. Daniel Bell, *The Cultural Contradictions of Capitalism* (New York, 1976), 136.

63. Herbert Gans, "American Popular Culture and High Culture in a Changing Class Structure," PAACS, 10 (1985), 30.

64. Jim Collins, *Uncommon Cultures: Popular Culture and Post-Modernism* (New York, 1989); Nick Heffernan, "Culture at Modernity's End: Daniel Bell and Fredric Jameson," in David Murray, ed., *American Cultural Critics* (Exeter, U.K., 1995), 287; Steven Henry Madoff, ed., *Pop Art: A Critical History* (Berkeley, 1997), pt. 2; Gary Garrels, ed., *The Work of Andy Warhol* (Seattle, 1989); Carter Ratcliff, *Andy Warhol* (New York, 1983); Kynaston McShine, ed., *Andy Warhol: A Retrospective* (New York, 1989), 25–37; Lynne Cooke, "The Independent Group: British and American Pop Art," in Kirk Varnedoe and Adam Gopnik, eds., *Modern Art and Popular Culture: Readings in High and Low* (New York, 1990), 192–216.

65. John Frow, *Cultural Studies and Cultural Value* (Oxford, 1995), 23; G. Albert Ruesga, "Singing and Dancing in the Baser Manner: A Plea for the Democratization of Taste," JPC, 29 (Spring 1996), 117–35; Wilfred M. McClay, "Asking Our Questions," *Intellectual History Newsletter*, 18 (1996), 13.

66. The Senior Wrangler, "High-Brow Anxieties," *The Century*, 87 (April 1914), 970; William Prichard Eaton, "The Highbrow-Hunters: An Amusing Phase of Social Life in New York," *Munsey's Magazine*, 44 (January 1911), 527–32, esp. 527–28. See also Matthew Schneirov, *The Dream of a New Social Order: Popular Magazines in America* (New York, 1994).

67. "Doll Portraits of People Who Deserve Better," *Vanity Fair*, 33 (January 1930), p. 45; Reaves, *Celebrity Caricature in America*, 158; Alan Havig, *Fred Allen's Radio Comedy* (Philadelphia, 1990), 191.

68. Robert W. Snyder, "Big Time, Small Time, All Around the Town: New York Vaudeville in the Early Twentieth Century," in Richard Butsch, ed., *For Fun and Profit: The Transformation of Leisure into Consumption* (Philadelphia, 1990), 123; MacDonald, *Don't Touch That Dial!*, 11; Spigel, "High Culture in Low Places," 314, 328, Michael Kimmelman, "Roy Lichtenstein, Pop Master, Dies at 73," NYT, Sept. 30, 1997, pp. A1, B7.

69. Dwight Macdonald, "Masscult & Midcult," in Macdonald, *Against the American Grain* (New York, 1962), 59.

70. Greenberg, "The Plight of Our Culture: Industrialism and Class Mobility," in Podhoretz, ed., *The Commentary Reader*, 437.

71. Tad Friend, "The Case for Middlebrow," NR, 206 (March 2, 1992), 24–27, the chart on 26.

72. Tad Friend, Joan Shelley Rubin, and Lawrence W. Levine, "In Praise of Middlebrow," *Utne Reader*, 53 (September 1992), 77–83, the chart on 83.

73. Friend, "Case for Middlebrow," 24, 25.

74. Ibid., 24. For letters to the editor in response to Friend's engaging essay, see NR, 206 (March 30, 1992), p. 4.

75. Friend, "Case for Middlebrow," 24–25. A new British magazine, the *Modern Review*, founded in 1991, promoted itself as "low culture for highbrows."

76. Vladimir Nabokov had only scathing comments about the coarse and phony, which he dismissed as *poshlost*, a Russian word comparable to *kitsch*, meaning philistine vulgarity. Yet he liked American pop culture, especially comic strips and films.

77. *Washington Star* "Comment" section, Oct. 24, 1976, sec. F, pp. 1, 4; reprinted in *Wilson Quarterly*, 1 (October 1976), 158–60.

Chapter 6

1. Robert Wiebe, *Self-Rule: A Cultural History of American Democracy* (Chicago, 1995), 44.

2. David S. Reynolds, *Walt Whitman's*

America: A Cultural Biography (New York, 1995), 350, 361–62.

3. John Tomsich, *A Genteel Endeavor: American Culture and Politics in the Gilded Age* (Stanford, 1971).

4. Kathleen D. McCarthy, *Women's Culture: American Philanthropy and Art, 1830–1930* (Chicago, 1991); Ann Douglas, *The Feminization of American Culture* (New York, 1997); David J. Pivar, *Purity Crusade: Sexual Morality and Social Control, 1868–1900* (Westport, Conn., 1973).

5. Allen F. Davis, *American Heroine: The Life and Legend of Jane Addams* (New York, 1973), chs. 6, 11; Helen Lefkowitz Horowitz, *The Power and Passion of M. Carey Thomas* (New York, 1994); Susan Elizabeth Lyman, *Lady Historian: Martha J. Lamb* (Northampton, Mass., 1969).

6. Mrs. Schuyler Van Rensselaer, "American Art and the Public," *Scribner's Magazine*, 74 (November 1923), 637–40; Robert McColley, "Mariana Griswold Van Rensselaer," in *Dictionary of Literary Biography* (Detroit, 1986), vol. 47, pp. 325–30.

7. Susan M. Ryan, "Acquiring Minds: Commodified Knowledge and the Positioning of the Reader in *McClure's Magazine*, 1893–1903," PAACS, 22 (1997), 223–24; "High-Brow," *Dial*, 56 (April 1, 1914), 287–88; Lawrence W. Levine, *Highbrow/Lowbrow: The Emergence of Cultural Hierarchy in America* (Cambridge, Mass., 1988), 216, 228.

8. Stephen Hardy, " 'Adopted by All the Leading Clubs': Sporting Goods and the Shaping of Leisure, 1880–1900," in Richard Butsch, ed., *For Fun and Profit: The Transformation of Leisure into Consumption* (Philadelphia, 1990), 92; Steven W. Pope, "Negotiating the 'Folk Highway' of the Nation: Sport, Public Culture and American Identity, 1870–1940," JSH, 27 (Winter 1993), 327–40; Jonathan Prude, "Directions of Labor History," AQ, 42 (March 1990), 140.

9. Kathryn J. Oberdeck, "Contested Cultures of American Refinement: The-atrical Manager Sylvester Poli, His Audiences, and the Vaudeville Industry, 1890–1920," *Radical History Review*, 66 (Fall 1996), 40–44, 48–49, 52–53, 64, 72, 75.

10. Neal Gabler, *An Empire of Their Own: How the Jews Invented Hollywood* (New York, 1988); Steven Smith, "Personalities in the Crowd: The Idea of the 'Masses' in American Popular Culture," PAACS, 19 (1994), 254.

11. Walter Lippmann, *Public Opinion* (New York, 1922), 31, 125; see also 362.

12. James Gilbert, *A Cycle of Outrage: America's Reaction to the Juvenile Delinquent in the 1950s* (New York, 1986), 114–15; Stuart Ewen, *PR! A Social History of Spin* (New York, 1996), 183, 189–90.

13. Ronald Steel, *Walter Lippmann and the American Century* (New York, 1980), 218–19; Walter Lippmann, *A Preface to Morals* (1929; Boston, 1960), 64; National Opinion Research Center Poll, Oct. 1945, USNORC.450238.R08, RCPOR. For an explicit anticipation of Lippmann's reservations about democracy, see Aldous Huxley, "The Outlook for American Culture," *Harper's*, 155 (August 1927), 270.

14. Lippmann, *A Preface to Morals*, ch. 5, "The Breakdown of Authority." For a clear premonition of this view, see Lippmann, *Drift and Mastery: An Attempt to Diagnose the Current Unrest* (1914: Englewood Cliffs, N.J., 1961), 110–11.

15. Burton Bledstein, *The Culture of Professionalism: The Middle Class and the Development of Higher Education in America* (New York, 1976); Fred H. Matthews, *Quest for an American Sociology: Robert E. Park and the Chicago School* (Montreal, 1977); Barry D. Karl, *Charles E. Merriam and the Study of Politics* (Chicago, 1974); Maurice R. Stein, *The Eclipse of Community: An Interpretation of American Studies* (Princeton, 1960).

16. Joan Shelley Rubin, *The Making of Middlebrow Culture* (Chapel Hill, 1992), 71, 72.

17. Ibid., 123, 269; William Stott, *Documentary Expression and Thirties America* (1973: Chicago, 1986), 79–81.

18. Lynn Swarz, "The Fine Print: Diversity Within the Groups Involved in 'The Perfect Moment' Controversy and the Role of the American Press." Unpub. honors thesis in American Studies, Cornell University, 1996, 54–58.

19. David D. Hall, *The Faithful Shepherd: A History of the New England Ministry in the Seventeenth Century* (Chapel Hill, 1972); Sacvan Bercovitch, *The American Jeremiad* (Madison, Wis., 1978).

20. Alice Felt Tyler, *Freedom's Ferment: Phases of American Social History from the Colonial Period to the Outbreak of the Civil War* (Minneapolis, 1944); John L. Thomas, "Romantic Reform in America, 1815–1865," AQ, 17 (Winter 1965), 656–81; Daniel Walker Howe, *The Unitarian Conscience: Harvard Moral Philosophy, 1805–1861* (Cambridge, Mass., 1970); Daniel M. Scott, "The Profession That Vanished: Public Lecturing in Mid-Nineteenth-Century America," in Gerald L. Geison, ed., *Professions and Professional Ideologies in America* (Chapel Hill, 1983), 12–28; Rubin, *Making of Middlebrow Culture*, 14.

21. Arnold T. Schwab, *James Gibbons Huneker: Critic of the Seven Arts* (Stanford, 1963); John Henry Raleigh, *Matthew Arnold and American Culture* (Berkeley, 1957); John P. Diggins, *The Bard of Savagery: Thorstein Veblen and Modern Social Theory* (New York, 1978).

22. Michael Kammen, *The Lively Arts: Gilbert Seldes and the Transformation of Cultural Criticism* (New York, 1996), ch. 3; Casey Nelson Blake, *Beloved Community: The Cultural Criticism of Randolph Bourne, Van Wyck Brooks, Waldo Frank and Lewis Mumford* (Chapel Hill, 1990).

23. I. A. Richards, *Practical Criticism: A Study of Literary Judgment* (London, 1929), 3, 11.

24. H. L. Mencken, "Footnote on Criticism" (1922) in Huntington Cairns, ed., *H. L. Mencken: The American Scene: A Reader* (New York, 1985), 188–89. It should be noted that as a prominent cultural authority Mencken did wonders to establish the reputation of Nietzsche in the United States, and considerably raised the prestige of Joseph Conrad and, especially, Theodore Dreiser. See Fred Hobson, *Mencken: A Life* (Baltimore, 1994), 102–04.

25. Kammen, *Lively Arts*, 66, 99–100, 109; William R. Taylor, *In Pursuit of Gotham: Culture and Commerce in New York* (New York, 1992), 114; Milton Hindus, "Philip Rahv," in Arthur Edelstein, ed., *Images and Ideas in American Culture: Essays in Memory of Philip Rahv* (Hanover, N.H., 1979), 198.

26. Warren Susman, *Culture as History: The Transformation of American Society in the Twentieth Century* (New York, 1984), ch. 7; Lawrence W. Levine, *The Unpredictable Past: Explorations in American Cultural History* (New York, 1993), ch. 10; John Heidenry, *Theirs Was the Kingdom: Lila and DeWitt Wallace and the Story of the Reader's Digest* (New York, 1993), chs. 2–6.

27. Carl Becker, *Everyman His Own Historian: Essays on History and Politics* (New York, 1935), 233–55; T. S. Eliot, "Religion and Literature" in Stanley Edgar Hyman, *The Armed Vision: A Study in the Methods of Modern Literary Criticism* (1948: New York, 1955), 70–71; Stott, *Documentary Expression and Thirties America*, 178–79, 188; Gilbert Seldes, "Are People Critics?" *Esquire*, 9 (April 1937), 70, 208.

28. Phillips is quoted in Russell Lynes, *Confessions of a Dilettante* (New York, 1966), 23.

29. Ava Collins, "Intellectuals, Power and Quality Television," CS, 7 (January 1993), 28–45. For a Louis Harris poll of 1,600 people in 1971 that produced extremely positive responses to questions about the benefits of television and the

range of its news and entertainment coverage, see Harris poll, May 1971, USHARRIS.71MAY.R30F (and R30H and R32J), RCPOR.

30. Berryman in "The State of American Writing, 1948: Seven Questions," *Partisan Review*, 15 (August 1948), 858; Irving Kristol, "High, Low and Modern," *Encounter*, 83 (August 1960), 33–41; Susan Strasser, *Satisfaction Guaranteed: The Making of the American Mass Market* (Washington, D.C., 1989), 288; Dwight Macdonald, "Masscult & Midcult" in Macdonald, *Against the American Grain* (New York, 1962), 64–65n.

31. Clement Greenberg, "Avant-Garde and Kitsch" (1939) in Greenberg, *Art and Culture: Critical Essays* (Boston, 1961), 3–4; Alan Havig, *Fred Allen's Radio Comedy* (Philadelphia, 1990), 203; Irving Howe, "This Age of Conformity" (1954), in Howe, *Selected Writings, 1950–1990* (San Diego, 1990), 48; Steven Watts, *The Magic Kingdom: Walt Disney and the American Way of Life* (Boston, 1997), 401.

32. Kristol, "High, Low and Modern," 36–37; Robert W. Merry, *Taking on the World: Joseph and Stewart Alsop—Guardians of the American Century* (New York, 1996), 545–46. For the belief that mandarins of art criticism remained quite powerful through the early to mid-1960s, see Kirk Varnedoe and Adam Gopnik, eds., *Modern Art and Popular Culture: Readings in High and Low* (New York, 1990), 203.

33. Daniel Aaron, *American Notes: Selected Essays* (Boston, 1994), 188; Kammen, *The Lively Arts*, chs. 4, 5, 9; David Murray, *American Cultural Critics* (Exeter, U.K., 1995), chs. 3, 4, 6, 7, 8.

34. Laurence Bergreen, *James Agee: A Life* (New York, 1984), 117–23, 263, 272, 362–63.

35. Ibid., 398–99; Robert Fitzgerald, ed., *The Collected Poems of James Agee* (Boston, 1968), 164–65, 170–71, the extract at 170–71.

36. Susan Sontag, "One Culture and the New Sensibility" (1965) in Sontag, *Against Interpretation and Other Essays* (New York, 1966), 297; Robert F. Horowitz, "History Comes to Life and You Are There," in John E. O'Connor, ed., *American History/American Television* (New York, 1983), 83–84.

37. Herbert I. Schiller, *Culture, Inc. The Corporate Takeover of Public Expression* (New York, 1989), 109–10; Todd Gitlin, "Flat and Happy," WQ, 17 (Autumn 1993), 48.

38. Merry, *Taking on the World*, 381–82, 444, 467.

39. *Life*, Aug. 16, 1937, pp. 56–59, 81–84; *Life*, Dec. 6, 1937, pp. 13–17; *Life*, Sept. 9, 1946, pp. 80–85; *Life*, Nov. 25, 1946, pp. 125–38; *Life*, Aug. 28, 1950, pp. 53–57; *Life*, Aug. 13, 1951, pp. 102–14; Fred Goodman, *The Mansion on the Hill: Dylan, Young, Geffen, Springsteen, and the Head-on Collision of Rock and Commerce* (New York, 1997), 43, 51–52.

40. Herbert J. Gans, "American Popular Culture and High Culture in a Changing Class Structure," PAACS, 10 (1985), 23–24; Lynn Spigel, "High Culture in Low Places: Television and Modern Art, 1950–1970," in Cary Nelson and D. P. Gaonkar, eds., *Disciplinarity and Dissent in Cultural Studies* (New York, 1996), 328–36; William N. Wallace, "Pete Rozelle Dies at 70; Led N.F.L.'s Growth Years," NYT, Dec. 8, 1996, p. A62; Richard Sandomir, "Rozelle's N.F.L. Legacy: Television, Marketing and Money," NYT, Dec. 8, 1996, sec. 8, p. 3.

41. Spigel, "High Culture in Low Places," 340; James B. Gilbert, "Popular Culture," AQ, 35 (Spring 1983), 150.

42. John Frow, *Cultural Studies and Cultural Value* (Oxford, 1995), 23–24.

43. Henry Adams, *Thomas Hart Benton: An American Original* (New York, 1989), 284, 286.

44. See "Homer St.-Gaudens Runs Great Carnegie Show," *Life*, Dec. 12, 1938, pp. 72–74, with Benton's painting

in a full color, double-page spread, noting that the completed work followed more than four hundred sketches—a way of emphasizing that it really is art rather than soft pornography!

45. See Miriam Hansen, *Babel and Babylon: Spectatorship in American Silent Film* (Cambridge, Mass., 1991), 15.

46. Havig, *Fred Allen's Radio Comedy*, 118, 128–29; Leonard J. Leff and Jerold L. Simmons, *The Dame in the Kimono: Hollywood, Censorship, and the Production Code from the 1920s to the 1960s* (New York, 1990); Gregory D. Black, *Hollywood Censored: Morality Codes, Catholics, and the Movies* (New York, 1994), 1–2, 38–39; Gallup poll, Jan. 14, 1954, USGALLUP.54-525.QKO5C, RCPOR.

47. Gallup poll, Oct. 20, 1954, USGALLUP.112154.RK11C, RCPOR; James B. Gilbert, *A Cycle of Outrage: America's Reaction to the Juvenile Delinquent in the 1950s* (New York, 1986); Paul Rutherford, *The New Icons? The Art of Television Advertising* (Toronto, 1994).

48. Sally Bedell Smith, *In All His Glory: The Life of William S. Paley* (New York, 1990), 267. For Corwin's views on the various rating systems that proliferated, see his *Trivializing America* (Secaucus, N.J., 1983), 166–69.

49. J. Fred MacDonald, *Don't Touch That Dial!: Radio Programming in American Life from 1920 to 1960* (Chicago, 1979), 32–35, 59–60; Gordon F. Sander, *Serling: The Rise and Twilight of Television's Last Angry Man* (New York, 1992), chs. 12–13; James B. Twitchell, *ADCULTUSA: The Triumph of Advertising in American Culture* (New York, 1996), ch. 1.

50. Havig, *Fred Allen's Radio Comedy*, 155; Kenneth C. Davis, *Two-Bit Culture: The Paperbacking of America* (Boston, 1984), 8.

51. See Geoffrey Gorer, "The American Character," *Life*, Aug. 18, 1947, pp. 94–112; C. Vann Woodward, *The Old World's New World* (New York, 1991).

52. John Hubner, *Bottom Feeders: From Free Love to Hard Core. The Rise and Fall of Counterculture Heroes Jim and Artie Mitchell* (New York, 1993); Simon Frith, *Sound Effects: Youth, Leisure, and the Politics of Rock 'n' Roll* (New York, 1981), 7.

53. Jonah Raskin, *For the Hell of It: The Life and Times of Abbie Hoffman* (Berkeley, 1996).

54. David Riesman, et al., *The Lonely Crowd: A Study of the Changing American Character* (New Haven, 1950); Daniel Horowitz, *Vance Packard and American Social Criticism* (Chapel Hill, 1994); A. M. Sperber, *Murrow: His Life and Times* (New York, 1986).

55. Berlin to Kanin, Nov. 5, 1962, Ruth Gordon papers, box 1, LCMD; Paul R. Gorman, *Left Intellectuals & Popular Culture in Twentieth-Century America* (Chapel Hill, 1996); Michael Norman, "Diana Trilling, a Cultural Critic and Member of a Select Intellectual Circle," NYT, Oct. 25, 1996, p. A33.

56. Alvin W. Gouldner, *The Future of Intellectuals and the Rise of the New Class* (New York, 1979); Thomas Bender, *Intellect and Public Life: Essays on the Social History of Academic Intellectuals in the United States* (Baltimore, 1993), chs. 5, 7, 8; Russell Jacoby, *The Last Intellectuals: American Culture in the Age of Academe* (New York, 1987).

57. William Honan, "The Intellectual Issue for the 1990's Is Why America's Intellectuals Have Faded Away," NYT, Jan. 28, 1990, p. E6; Simon Frith, "John Keats vs. Bob Dylan: Why Value Judgments Matter," *Chronicle of Higher Education*, March 14, 1997, p. A48.

58. Michael Walzer, in *Art and Law*, 9 (no. 2, 1985), 200–201. See also Walzer, *The Company of Critics: Social Criticism and Political Commitment in the Twentieth Century* (New York, 1988), 186–87, 233–38; Walzer, *Interpretation & Social Criticism* (Cambridge, Mass., 1993).

59. See Richard Schickel, *Intimate Strangers: The Culture of Celebrity* (Garden City, N.Y., 1985); Frank Rich, "Room at the Top," NYT, Feb. 7, 1998, p. A27; Stuart Ewen, *PR! A Social History*

of Spin (New York, 1996); Margalit Fox, "In Martha 101, Even Class Anxieties Get Ironed Out," NYT, Aug. 1, 1998, p. B7; Gayle Feldman, "Making Book on Oprah," *NYT Book Review*, Feb. 2, 1997, p. 31.

60. National Opinion Research Center, Nov. 1947, USNORC.470425.R12C, RCPOR. See, in addition, the Gallup poll conducted in August 1970, USGAL-NEW.70NEWS. R07D, RCPOR.

61. Schiller, *Culture, Inc. The Corporate Takeover of Public Expression*, 30; Walter Powell, "The Blockbuster Decades: The Media as Big Business," in Donald Lazere, ed., *American Media and Mass Culture: Left Perspectives* (Berkeley, 1987), 53–63. For a prescient recognition that technology would enhance cultural power at the expense of cultural authority, see Huxley, "The Outlook for American Culture," 269.

Chapter 7

1. See Michael Schudson, *Watergate in American Memory: How We Remember, Forget, and Reconstruct the Past* (New York, 1992), ch. 6.

2. Charles J. Maland, *Chaplin and American Culture: The Evolution of a Star Image* (Princeton, 1989), 362–70.

3. See John Fiske, *Understanding Popular Culture* (London, 1989); Andrew Ross, *No Respect: Intellectuals & Popular Culture* (New York, 1989), 227.

4. Benedict Anderson, *Imagined Communities: Reflections on the Origin and Spread of Nationalism* (2d ed.: London, 1991), 39; E. P. Thompson, *The Making of the English Working Class* (New York, 1963), 711–12, 717–18, 727; Carole Fink, *Marc Bloch: A Life in History* (Cambridge, 1989), 14, 18.

5. David S. Reynolds, *Walt Whitman's America: A Cultural Biography* (New York, 1995), 483; C. Wright Mills, *The Power Elite* (New York, 1956), ch. 13.

6. Richard Slotkin, *Gunfighter Nation: The Myth of the Frontier in Twentieth-*

Century America (New York, 1992), 26; Neil Harris, *Cultural Excursions: Marketing Appetites and Cultural Tastes in Modern America* (Chicago, 1990), 123, 235.

7. Robert Sklar, *Movie-Made America: A Cultural History of American Movies* (New York, 1975), 71, 86; Michael Paul Rogin, *Ronald Reagan, the Movie, and Other Episodes in Political Demonology* (Berkeley, 1987), xviii.

8. John Carey, *The Intellectuals and the Masses: Pride and Prejudice Among the Literary Intelligentsia, 1880–1939* (New York, 1992), 3–4; Robert Wohl, *The Generation of 1914* (Cambridge, Mass., 1979), ch. 4.

9. Leon Bramson, *The Political Context of Sociology* (Princeton, 1961), 108; Edward Shils, *The Intellectuals and the Powers and Other Essays* (Chicago, 1972), 248–64.

10. Gordon S. Wood, *The Radicalism of the American Revolution* (New York, 1992), 360; John Henry Raleigh, *Matthew Arnold and American Culture* (Berkeley, 1957), 201; Peter Novick, *That Noble Dream: The "Objectivity Question" and the American Historical Profession* (New York, 1988), 243–44.

11. Steven Smith, "Personalities in the Crowd: The Idea of the 'Masses' in American Popular Culture," PAACS, 19 (1994), 225–87; Eugene E. Leach, "Mastering the Crowd: Collective Behavior and Mass Society in American Social Thought, 1917–1939," *American Studies*, 27 (Spring 1986), 99–114.

12. See Janice Radway, "The Scandal of the Middlebrow: The Book-of-the-Month Club, Class Fracture and Cultural Authority," SAQ, 89 (Fall 1990), esp. 717; August Heckscher, "The Quality of American Culture," in *Goals for Americans: Programs for Action in the Sixties. . . .* (New York, 1960), 131–32, 134; Steven Watts, *The Magic Kingdom: Walt Disney and the American Way of Life* (Boston, 1997), 314.

13. William R. Taylor, *In Pursuit of Gotham: Culture and Commerce in New*

York (New York, 1992), xviii, xxii–iii, 71, 117. Both Fredric Jameson and Stuart Hall have challenged distinctions between authentic popular culture and mass consumer culture. See Hall, "Culture, the Media, and the 'Ideological Effect'," in James Curran et al., eds., *Mass Communication and Society* (Beverly Hills, 1979), 315–48; Jameson, "Reification and Utopia in Mass Culture," *Social Text*, 1 (Winter 1979), 130–48.

14. Carl F. Kaestle et al., *Literacy in the United States: Readers and Reading Since 1880* (New Haven, 1991), 56; James Guimond, *American Photography and the American Dream* (Chapel Hill, 1991), 78; William Stott, *Documentary Expression and Thirties America* (1973: Chicago, 1986), 9.

15. Susan Strasser, *Satisfaction Guaranteed: The Making of the American Mass Market* (Washington, D.C., 1989), 212, 214, 248.

16. Bill Blackbeard, ed., *R. F. Outcault's The Yellow Kid: A Centennial Celebration of the Kid Who Started the Comics* (Northampton, Mass., 1995); Judith O'Sullivan, *The Great American Comic Strip: One Hundred Years of Cartoon Art* (Boston, 1990).

17. Rick Marschall, "100 Years of the Funnies," *American History*, 30 (October 1995), 34–45; Lisa Yaszek, " 'Them Damn Pictures': Americanization and the Comic Strip in the Progressive Era," *Journal of American Studies*, 28 (April 1994), 23–38.

18. Leonard Maltin, *Of Mice and Magic: A History of American Animated Cartoons* (New York, 1980), ch. 1, "The Silent Era."

19. Ibid., ch. 2, "Walt Disney"; Watts, *The Magic Kingdom: Walt Disney and the American Way of Life*, 33, 36, 69.

20. Richard Schickel, *The Disney Version: The Life, Times, Art and Commerce of Walt Disney* (1968: New York, 1985), 162–65.

21. Robert W. Merry, *Taking on the World: Joseph and Stewart Alsop— Guardians of the American Century* (New York, 1996), 62; Taylor, *In Pursuit of Gotham*, 114–15; Sally Foreman Griffith, *Home Town News: William Allen White and the Emporia Gazette* (New York, 1989), 213, 217, 223, 232.

22. Neal Gabler, *Winchell: Gossip, Power and the Culture of Celebrity* (New York, 1994), xii–xiii, xv; Richard Schickel, *Intimate Strangers: The Culture of Celebrity* (Garden City, N.Y., 1985).

23. John Heidenry, *Theirs Was the Kingdom: Lila and Dewitt Wallace and the Story of the Reader's Digest* (New York, 1993), 83; David Halberstam, *The Powers That Be* (New York, 1979), 98–100.

24. Harvey Levenstein, *Paradox of Plenty: A Social History of Eating in Modern America* (New York, 1993), 26–27, 30, 51; Warren J. Belasco, "Toward a Culinary Common Denominator: The Rise of Howard Johnson's, 1925–1940," JAC, 2 (Fall 1979), 503–18; Warren J. Belasco, *Americans on the Road: From Autocamp to Motel, 1910–1945* (Cambridge, Mass., 1979), 171–72.

25. I have borrowed the phrase from Richard M. Merelman, *Partial Visions: Culture and Politics in Britain, Canada, and the United States* (Madison, Wis., 1991), 36.

26. Lary May, "Making the American Way: Moderne Theatre Audiences and the Film Industry, 1929–1945," PAACS, 12 (1987), 89–124; Norman Corwin, "Entertainment and the Mass Media," in Luther S. Luedtke, ed., *Making America: The Society and Culture of the United States* (Chapel Hill, 1992), 254–71, esp. 259, 262.

27. Laurence Bergreen, *As Thousands Cheer: The Life of Irving Berlin* (New York, 1990), 169, 201; Clayton R. Koppes, "The Social Destiny of the Radio: Hope and Disillusionment in the 1920s," SAQ, 68 (Summer 1969), 363–76.

28. Fred Goodman, *The Mansion on the Hill: Dylan, Young, Geffen, Springsteen,*

and the Head-On Collision of Rock and Commerce (New York, 1997), 44–45; Carol V. R. George, *God's Salesman: Norman Vincent Peale and the Power of Positive Thinking* (New York, 1993), 166.

29. J. Fred MacDonald, *Don't Touch That Dial! Radio Programming in American Life, 1920–1960* (Chicago, 1979), 24–26; Halberstam, *The Powers That Be*, 29, 66; Gary Dean Best, *The Nickel and Dime Decade: American Popular Culture During the 1930s* (Westport, Conn., 1993), 65; David Thompson, *Rosebud: The Story of Orson Welles* (New York, 1996), 105–06, 111.

30. Joan Shelley Rubin, *The Making of Middlebrow Culture* (Chapel Hill, 1992), 269; Lawrence W. Levine, "The Folklore of Industrial Society: Popular Culture and Its Audiences," AHR, 97 (December 1992), 1378–79, 1382.

31. Julian quoted in Alan Havig, *Fred Allen's Radio Comedy* (Philadelphia, 1990), 10, 213. For comparable observations about early audiences for silent film, however, see David Nasaw, *Going Out: The Rise and Fall of Public Amusements* (New York, 1993), 152–53; Steven J. Ross, *Working-Class Hollywood: Silent Film and the Shaping of Class in America* (Princeton, 1998), 24–25.

32. MacDonald, *Don't Touch That Dial!*, 86–87; Michele Hilmes, *Radio Voices: American Broadcasting, 1922–1952* (Minneapolis, 1997), 271–90.

33. Lizabeth Cohen, whose work I greatly admire, places more emphasis than I do upon an "explosion of mass culture in the 1920s," calling attention to the expansion of chain stores, movie theaters, and radio. She does acknowledge, however, that neighborhood shops and ethnically organized leisure continued to be quite important in urban America during the 1920s, and that mass culture became far more standardized in the thirties. Even then, moreover, in a very large city like Chicago, with its notably heterogeneous population, local and ethnic tra-

ditions persisted alongside the early manifestations of mass culture. See Cohen, *Making a New Deal: Industrial Workers in Chicago, 1919–1939* (New York, 1990), 55, 97, 129, 156, 157–58, 327, 330–31, 356–57.

34. George Biddle, "The Government and the Arts," *Harper's*, 187 (October 1943), 429. Some of the federal art and theater project administrators had been openly hostile to advertising and consumer culture. See Barbara Melosh, *Engendering Culture: Manhood and Womanhood in New Deal Public Art and Theater* (Washington, D.C., 1991), 184.

35. *Life*, Feb. 26, 1940, pp. 67–79; *Life*, March 4, 1940, pp. 68–70.

36. *Life*, Aug. 12, 1946, pp. 32–34; *Life*, June 16, 1947, pp. 101–16; *Life*, April 19, 1948, pp. 139–45; *Life*, June 26, 1950, pp. 65–66.

37. Gorky quoted in John Kasson, *Amusing the Million: Coney Island at the Turn of the Century* (New York, 1978), 108–09; Randolph Bourne, "Transnational America," *Atlantic Monthly*, 118 (July 1916), 86–97; Casey Nelson Blake, *Beloved Community: The Cultural Criticism of Randolph Bourne, Van Wyck Brooks, Waldo Frank, and Lewis Mumford* (Chapel Hill, 1990), 115.

38. Raymond Williams, *Resources of Hope: Culture, Democracy, Socialism* (London, 1989), 20; and for more comprehensive coverage of the Great Debate, see Michael Kammen, *The Lively Arts: Gilbert Seldes and the Transformation of Cultural Criticism in the United States* (New York, 1996), ch. 9.

39. Herbert Marcuse, *One Dimensional Man: Studies in the Sociology of Advanced Industrial Society* (Boston, 1961); David Grimsted, "Books and Culture: Canned, Canonized, and Neglected," *Proceedings of the American Antiquarian Society*, 94 (1985), 308. Roland Barthes's *Mythologies* (New York, 1972) originated as monthly essays in 1954–56 on topics arising from contemporary events and

social phenomena. The essays, comprising a radical, antibourgeois critique of the language of mass culture, became very influential among American academics.

40. Michael Wreszin, *A Rebel in Defense of Tradition: The Life and Politics of Dwight Macdonald* (New York, 1994), ch. 15; Adorno and Max Horkheimer, *Dialectic of Enlightenment* (New York, 1991); Wilfred M. McClay, *The Masterless: Self and Society in Modern America* (Chapel Hill, 1994), 219–20.

41. William Phillips, ed., *Partisan Review: The 50th Anniversary Edition* (New York, 1985), 290; Carol Brightman, *Writing Dangerously: Mary McCarthy and Her World* (San Diego, 1992), 339; Irving Howe, "This Age of Conformity" (1954), in Howe, *Steady Work: Essays in the Politics of Democratic Radicalism, 1953–1966* (New York, 1966), 317.

42. Howe, *Steady Work*, 314; Daniel Bell, *The End of Ideology: On the Exhaustion of Political Ideas in the Fifties* (New York, 1962), 313.

43. Dwight Macdonald, "Masscult & Midcult," in Macdonald, *Against the American Grain* (New York, 1962), 3–75; Howe, "This Age of Conformity" in Howe, *Steady Work*, 342–43.

44. McClay, *The Masterless*, 243; Alexander Klein, "The Challenge of Mass Media," *Yale Review*, 39 (June 1950), 675–91; Kammen, *The Lively Arts*, ch. 9.

45. Edward Shils, "Mass Society and Its Culture" (1959), in Shils, *The Intellectuals and the Powers*, 232, 248.

46. Ibid., 234–35; Phillips, *A Partisan View: Five Decades of the Literary Life* (New York, 1983), 154–55; Leslie Fiedler, *What Was Literature? Class, Culture and Mass Society* (New York, 1982), 21.

47. Jean-Christophe Agnew, "Coming Up for Air: Consumer Culture in Historical Perspective," *Intellectual History Newsletter*, 12 (1990), 6.

48. Nasaw, *Going Out*, 250, 255. Tom Wolfe argued in the 1960s that very strong trends in mass culture moved up from the bottom, a fairly novel thing to say at that time. "Teenage culture was the wave of the future." See Wreszin, *A Rebel in Defense of Tradition*, 408.

49. Roper poll, November 1948: USROPER.48-073.R02, RCPOR.

50. George Lipsitz, *Time Passages: Collective Memory and American Popular Culture* (Minneapolis, 1990), 119.

51. Kenneth C. Davis, *Two-Bit Culture: The Paperbacking of America* (Boston, 1984), chs. 1–2; Dan B. Miller, *Erskine Caldwell: The Journey from Tobacco Road* (New York, 1995), 329–32.

52. Harrison Smith, "Culture in Soft Covers," SRL, 37 (April 24, 1954), 22; Davis, *Two-Bit Culture*, ch. 1.

53. Heidenry, *Theirs Was the Kingdom*, 223–24, 233.

54. Levenstein, *The Paradox of Plenty*, 113–14; George Ritzer, *The McDonaldization of Society: An Investigation into the Changing Character of Contemporary Social Life* (Newbury Park, Calif., 1993).

55. Lizabeth Cohen, "From Town Center to Shopping Center: The Reconfiguration of Community Marketplaces in Postwar America," AHR, 101 (October 1996), 1056; Richard Keller Simon, "The Formal Garden in the Age of Consumer Culture: A Reading of the Twentieth-Century Shopping Mall," in Wayne Franklin and Michael Steiner, eds., *Mapping American Culture* (Iowa City, 1992), 231–49; Thomas Frank, *The Conquest of Cool: Business Culture, Counterculture, and the Rise of Hip Consumerism* (Chicago, 1997), x, 175.

56. Seldes quoted in Kammen, *The Lively Arts*, 8, 341.

57. Lynn Spigel, *Make Room for TV: Television and the Family Ideal in Postwar America* (Chicago, 1992), 1, 189; Pat Weaver, *The Best Seat in the House: The Golden Years of Radio and Television* (New York, 1994), 198; Ellen Wartella and Sharon Mazzarella, "A Historical Comparison of Children's Use of Leisure Time," in Richard Butsch, ed., *For Fun and Profit: The Transformation of Leisure*

into Consumption (Philadelphia, 1990), 187. For an illustration of a disunited family watching television together yet separately, see Don DeLillo, *White Noise* (New York, 1985), 16. DeLillo, a novelist, is a keen observer of "consumer desire" in American mass culture.

58. Gallup polls April 30, 1957: USGALLUP.57-582.Q043A and Q043B, RCPOR. See Laurence Bergreen, *Look Now, Pay Later: The Rise of Network Broadcasting* (Garden City, N.Y., 1980).

59. Daniel Horowitz, *Vance Packard & American Social Criticism* (Chapel Hill, 1994), 100, 147, 155; Todd Gitlin, "TV & American Culture," WQ, 17 (Autumn 1993), 47; Frank Mankiewicz and Joel Swerdlow, *Remote Control: Television and the Manipulation of American Life* (New York, 1979), 85; Randy Roberts and James Olson, *Winning Is the Only Thing: Sports in America Since 1945* (Baltimore, 1989), 110.

60. Harris polls, May 1971: USHARRIS.71MAY.R41I, RCPOR; USHARRIS.71MAY.R28J and R28H and R28I, RCPOR.

61. John Agnew, "Targeting the Couch Potato: Marketers Learn That There Is No Place Like Home," *Marketing News*, Feb. 15, 1988; Ken Hanson, "Achieving the Zone," *Newsweek*, March 31, 1997, p. 22.

62. Philip S. Cook, ed., *American Media* (Washington, D.C., 1989), 212; Harris poll, May 1971: USHARRIS.71-MAY.R41C, RCPOR; Gallup poll, May 1973: USGALLUP.73EDUC.Q29A, RCPOR.

63. Gallup poll, December 1977: USGALLUP.990.Q5A, RCPOR.

64. Gallup poll, August 1978: USGALLUP.78ALA.R07, RCPOR.

65. Yankelovich, Skelly and White poll, October 1978: USYANK.78-FAMP.Q02A, RCPOR.

66. Ibid.

67. Richard Sennett, *The Fall of Public Man* (New York, 1977), 283.

Chapter 8

1. Richard Schickel, *Intimate Strangers: The Culture of Celebrity* (Garden City, N.Y., 1985), 237.

2. James B. Twitchell, *ADCULTUSA: The Triumph of Advertising in American Culture* (New York, 1996), 28, 203, 208, 209, 211–13. A *New York Times* editorial observed that "It is helpful to think of Warhol's blank visage—the look, he wrote, of 'basically passive astonishment'—as a mirror, and of the reflections cast by that mirror as Warhol's oeuvre." NYT, Nov. 24, 1997, p. A22.

3. Paul Rutherford, *The New Icons? The Art of Television Advertising* (Toronto, 1994), 6 and passim; Thomas Frank, *The Conquest of Cool: Business Culture, Counterculture, and the Rise of Hip Consumerism* (Chicago, 1997).

4. Twitchell, *ADCULTUSA: The Triumph of Advertising*, 229, 56.

5. Ariel Dorfman and Armand Mattelart, *How to Read Donald Duck: Imperialist Ideology in the Disney Comic* (Buenos Aires, 1972; New York, 1984), 76.

6. Mike Wallace, *Mickey Mouse History and Other Essays on American Memory* (Philadelphia, 1996); Michael Kammen, *Mystic Chords of Memory: The Transformation of Tradition in American Culture* (New York, 1991), ch. 19; Albert Boime, *The Unveiling of the National Icons: A Plea for Patriotic Iconoclasm in a Nationalist Era* (Cambridge, 1998).

7. Lawrence W. Levine, *Highbrow/Lowbrow: The Emergence of Cultural Hierarchy in America* (Cambridge, Mass., 1988), 194–95; Louis Adamic, "Thirty Million New Americans," *Harper's*, 169 (November 1934), 684–94; Adamic, "This Crisis Is an Opportunity," *Common Ground*, 1 (Autumn 1940), 62–73. For emphasis upon the participatory behavior of silent-film audiences, see Steven J. Ross, *Working-Class Hollywood: Silent Film and the Shaping of Class in America* (Princeton, 1998), 24–27.

8. Rudolph Fisher, "The Caucasian

Storms Harlem," *American Mercury*, 11 (May 1927), 398; Lewis Erenberg, *Steppin' Out: New York Nightlife and the Transformation of American Culture, 1890–1930* (Chicago, 1981), 124.

9. Harold A. Innis, *The Bias of Communication* (Toronto, 1951); Carl F. Kaestle, et al., *Literacy in the United States: Readers and Reading Since 1880* (New Haven, 1991), 35–36.

10. Daniel Horowitz, *Vance Packard & American Social Criticism* (Chapel Hill, 1994), 110; Oscar Handlin, "Comments on Mass and Popular Culture," in Norman Jacobs, ed., *Culture for the Millions? Mass Media in Modern Society* (Boston, 1961), 69; Michael Wreszin, *A Rebel in Defense of Tradition: The Life and Politics of Dwight Macdonald* (New York, 1994), 388–89.

11. Seldes in a panel discussion of "Mass Culture and the Creative Artist," in Jacobs, ed., *Culture for the Millions?*, 180.

12. Gilbert Seldes, "Public Entertainment and the Subversion of Ethical Standards," AAAPSS, 363 (January 1966), 92, 94; Michael Kammen, *The Lively Arts: Gilbert Seldes and the Transformation of Cultural Criticism in the United States* (New York, 1996), ch. 9.

13. Fred Goodman, *The Mansion on the Hill: Dylan, Young, Geffen, Springsteen, and the Head-on Collision of Rock and Commerce* (New York, 1997), 18–19; Michael William Doyle, "The Haight-Ashbury Diggers and the Cultural Politics of Utopia, 1965–1968." Unpub. Ph.D. dissertation, Cornell University, 1997, 405–06.

14. Schickel, *Intimate Strangers*, 271.

15. Ibid., 271–72.

16. Christopher Lasch, "A Response to Joel Feinberg," *Tikkun*, 3 (May 1988), 42.

17. Douglas Gomery, "As the Dial Turns," WQ, 17 (Autumn 1993), 46; Todd Gitlin, "Flat and Happy," ibid., 54. Both essays were part of a symposium on "TV & American Culture." See also Miriam Hansen, *Babel and Babylon: Spectatorship in American Silent Film* (Cambridge, Mass., 1991), 13.

18. Frank Mankiewicz and Joel Swerdlow, *Remote Control: Television and the Manipulation of American Life* (New York, 1978), 246–47; Frank D. McConnell, "Seeing Through the Tube," WQ, 17 (Autumn 1993), 60, 61. McConnell quotes Jerry Mander, Neil Postman, and Jonathan Kozol on the passivity induced by TV. See also Michael Schudson, *The Good Citizen: A History of American Civic Life* (New York, 1998), ch. 6, and Pierre Bourdieu, *On Television* (New York, 1998).

19. Louis Harris poll, May 1971, USHARRIS.71MAY.R30B and R30C, RCPOR.

20. CBS News poll, June 29, 1978, USCBS.082278.R04 and R03, RCPOR.

21. Gallup Organization, Aug. 14, 1978, USGALLUP.78ALA.R10, RCPOR.

22. Bettelheim and Glasser quoted in Mankiewicz and Swerdlow, *Remote Control*, 169, 170.

23. Ibid., 179.

24. Ibid., 180, 189–90.

25. Gerbner is quoted in Neil Postman, *Amusing Ourselves to Death: Public Discourse in the Age of Show Business* (New York, 1985), 140. For a particularly sharp critique of the standardization of modern journalism, see James Fallows, *Breaking the News: How the Media Undermine American Democracy* (New York, 1996), 149.

26. Joshua Meyrowitz, *No Sense of Place: The Impact of Electronic Media on Social Behavior* (New York, 1985), esp. 160–67.

27. Roper Organization poll, Nov. 8, 1975, USROPER.75-10.R39, RCPOR. (The total adds up to more than 100% because of multiple responses.)

28. "Study: TV Ratings Flawed," *Ithaca Journal*, March 27, 1997, p. B1;

Gilbert Seldes, *The New Mass Media: Challenge to a Free Society* (2nd ed.: 1957; Washington, D.C., 1968), 59.

29. John J. O'Connor, "Today TV Outshines the Movies," NYT, July 8, 1990, p. B1. See also Glenn C. Altschuler and David I. Grossvogel, *Changing Channels: America in TV Guide* (Urbana, 1992).

30. Lawrie Mifflin, "New Scholarly Center to Study Pop Television Culture," NYT, Oct. 15, 1997, p. E1.

31. See Pat Weaver, *The Best Seat in the House: The Golden Years of Radio and Television* (New York, 1994); Erik Barnouw, *Tube of Plenty: The Evolution of American Television* (2nd ed.: New York, 1990); William Boddy, *Fifties Television: The Industry and Its Critics* (Urbana, 1990); Jay G. Blumler, "The New Television Marketplace: Imperatives, Implications, Issues," in James Curran and Michael Gurevitch, eds., *Mass Media and Society* (London, 1991), 194–95, 198–99; Robert Metz, *CBS: Reflections in a Bloodshot Eye* (Chicago, 1975).

32. Lawrence Grossberg, "MTV: Swinging on the (Postmodern) Star," in Ian Angus and Sut Jhally, eds., *Cultural Politics in Contemporary America* (New York, 1989), 254–68; McConnell, "Seeing Through the Tube," 65.

33. Gomery, "As the Dial Turns," 45; Twitchell, *ADCULTUSA*, 2, 46, 48; Richard Butsch, "Home Video and Corporate Plans: Capital's Limited Power to Manipulate Leisure," in Butsch, ed., *For Fun and Profit: The Transformation of Leisure into Consumption* (Philadelphia, 1990), 215, 220–21, 226–27.

34. Twitchell, *ADCULTUSA*, 23–24, 246; Rutherford, *The New Icons?*, 6–7.

35. Butsch, "Home Video and Corporate Plans: Capital's Limited Power to Manipulate Leisure," 219; McConnell, "Seeing Through the Tube," 61; Douglas Rushkoff, *Media Virus: Hidden Agendas in Popular Culture* (New York, 1994), 5.

36. Schickel, *Intimate Strangers*, 248–49.

37. Rushkoff, *Media Virus*, 51.

38. O'Leary quoted in ibid., 30.

39. Ibid., 31, 39, 61.

40. Ibid., 45, 128–29, the quotation at 155. Lawrence Grossberg rejects the criticism that MTV makes its fans passive. See "MTV: Swinging on the (Postmodern) Star," 257.

41. See Twitchell, *ADCULTUSA*, 58. For a delightful but serious account of a "videoconference wedding" held at Kinko's print and copy shop in Manhattan, see NYT, Aug. 2, 1998, sec. 9, p. 8.

42. Karal Ann Marling, *As Seen on TV: The Visual Culture of Everyday Life in the 1950s* (Cambridge, Mass., 1994), 54, 93; Miles Orvell, "Understanding Disneyland: American Mass Culture and the European Gaze," in Rob Kroes et al., eds., *Cultural Transmissions and Receptions: American Mass Culture in Europe* (Amsterdam, 1993), 249.

43. Carl F. Kaestle, "The History of Readers," in Kaestle, et al., *Literacy in the United States*, 40–41.

44. Michel de Certeau, *L'Invention du quotidien* (Paris, 1980); de Certeau, *La Culture au pluriel* (Paris, 1974); Cathy N. Davidson, "Toward a History of Books and Readers," in Davidson, ed., *Reading in America: Literature & Social History* (Baltimore, 1989), 16, 17; Janice A. Radway, *Reading the Romance: Women, Patriarchy, and Popular Literature* (Chapel Hill, 1984).

45. Stuart Hall and Paddy Whannel, *The Popular Arts* (London, 1964); Hall, ed., *Culture, Media, Language: Working Papers in Cultural Studies, 1972–1979* (London, 1980); Hall, ed., *Representation: Cultural Representations and Signifying Practices* (London, 1997); George Lipsitz, *Time Passages: Collective Memory and American Popular Culture* (Minneapolis, 1990), esp. chs. 1–2; Lawrence W. Levine, "The Folklore of Industrial Society: Popular Culture and Its Audiences," AHR, 97 (December 1992), esp. 1373–74.

46. See John Fiske, *Understanding Popular Culture* (London, 1989).

47. John Fiske, *Television Culture* (London, 1987), 64, 81. For Fiske's effective use of Umberto Eco's case for diversity of response, see p. 65. For a complementary view of audience segmentation for broadcast journalism since the 1980s, see James Fallows, *Breaking the News: How the Media Undermine American Democracy* (New York, 1996), 68–69.

48. Fiske, *Television Culture*, 323.

49. Ibid., 313, 316. For a superb instance that is notably supportive of Fiske's position, see bell hooks, "The Oppositional Gaze: Black Female Spectators," in John Belton, ed., *Movies and Mass Culture* (New Brunswick, N.J., 1996), 249, 252, 254.

50. Fiske, *Television Culture*, 326.

51. See Twitchell, *ADCULTUSA: The Triumph of Advertising in American Culture*, 111, 125; Leo Bogart, *Commercial Culture: The Media System and the Public Interest* (New York, 1995).

52. John Clarke, "Pessimism versus Populism: The Problematic Politics of Popular Culture," in Butsch, ed., *For Fun and Profit*, 40, 42; Todd Gitlin, "The Politics of Communication and the Communication of Politics," in James Curran and Michael Gurevitch, eds., *Mass Media and Society* (London, 1991), 329–41; T. J. Jackson Lears, "Making Fun of Popular Culture," AHR, 97 (December 1992), 1419, 1421–25, the quotation at 1424. For skepticism about Fiske's contentions in international terms, see Michael Gurevitch, "The Globalization of Electronic Journalism," in Curran and Gurevitch, eds., *Mass Media and Society*, 190–91.

53. Donald Lazere, "Literacy and Mass Media: The Political Implications," in Davidson, *Reading in America*, 285, 292. See also Norman Solomon and Jeff Cohen, *Wizards of Media Oz: Behind the Curtain of Mainstream News* (New York, 1997).

54. Herbert I. Schiller, *Culture, Inc.: The Corporate Takeover of Public Expression* (New York, 1989), 147.

55. Quoted in Gomery, "As the Dial Turns," 43; *Newsweek*, Sept. 8, 1997, p. 12. In 1998 the National Association for Sport and Physical Education issued a report finding that American schoolchildren did not get nearly enough exercise and that many were obese. *Ithaca Journal*, Aug. 20, 1998, p. 7A.

56. Morag Shiach, *Discourse on Popular Culture: Class, Gender, and History in Cultural Analysis, 1730 to the Present* (Cambridge, 1989), 194–95.

57. Katie Hafner, "Internet: Look Who's Talking," *Newsweek*, Feb. 17, 1997, pp. 70, 72; Anthony Smith, *Software for the Self: Technology and Culture* (New York, 1996).

58. Neil L. Rudenstine, "The Internet and Education: A Close Fit," *Chronicle of Higher Education*, Feb. 21, 1997, p. A48.

59. Umberto Eco, "Gutenberg Galaxy Expands," *The Nation*, Jan. 6, 1997, pp. 35–36. See Eco, *Travels in Hyperreality: Essays* (San Diego, 1986).

60. See Allen Guttmann, *A Whole New Ball Game: An Interpretation of American Sports* (Chapel Hill, 1988), ch. 10; Thomas M. Kando, *Leisure and Popular Culture in Transition* (St. Louis, 1975), 212, 228, 241; Randy Roberts and James Olson, *Winning Is the Only Thing: Sports in America Since 1945* (Baltimore, 1989), 95–111.

61. Elizabeth Kolbert, "Americans Despair of Popular Culture," NYT, Aug. 20, 1995, sec. 2, p. 1. For variations on that theme, see the angry protests from staff and listeners in 1997 when WMAQ-TV, the NBC-owned station in Chicago, decided to hire Jerry Springer, the controversial talk show host—NYT, May 9, 1997, p. A22.

62. Warren Berger, "At 25, Excellence and Big Budgets for a Late Bloomer [HBO]," NYT, Nov. 9, 1997, sec. 2, p. 23; Michael Kammen, "Culture and the

State in America," JAH, 83 (December 1996), 805–07, 811–13.

63. Fiske, *Understanding Popular Culture*, 120; Shiach, *Discourse on Popular Culture*, 202. For a droll satire of popular and mass culture, "consumer desire," and compulsive television-watching, see Don DeLillo, *White Noise* (New York, 1985), esp. part I.

Chapter 9

1. See Michael Kammen, *The Lively Arts: Gilbert Seldes and the Transformation of Cultural Criticism in the United States* (New York, 1996), ch. 3.

2. Clement Greenberg, "Avant-Garde and Kitsch" (1939), in Greenberg, *Art and Culture: Critical Essays* (Boston, 1961), 3–21.

3. Erik Barnouw, *Media Marathon: A Twentieth-Century Memoir* (Durham, N.C., 1996), 74–77. For an emphasis upon the pervasively nonradical character of American culture during the 1930s, see Richard H. Pells, *Radical Visions and American Dreams: Culture and Social Thought in the Depression Years* (New York, 1973); and Lawrence W. Levine, "American Culture and the Great Depression," in Levine, *The Unpredictable Past: Explorations in American Cultural History* (New York, 1993), 206–230.

4. See Joan Shelley Rubin, *Constance Rourke and American Culture* (Chapel Hill, 1980).

5. Carl Bode, *The American Lyceum: Town Meeting of the Mind* (New York, 1956); Bode, *The Anatomy of American Popular Culture* (Berkeley, 1959); Leslie A. Fiedler, *An End to Innocence: Essays on Culture and Politics* (Boston, 1955), pt. 3; Russel B. Nye, *The Unembarrassed Muse: The Popular Arts in America* (New York, 1970); David Grimsted, *Melodrama Unveiled: American Theater and Culture, 1800–1850* (Chicago, 1968); Paul Berman, "Edmund Wilson—And Our Non-Wilsonian Age," *Dissent* (Winter 1997), 85.

6. Ray B. Browne, *Against Academia: The History of the Popular Culture Association/American Culture Association and the Popular Culture Movement, 1967–1988* (Bowling Green, Ohio, 1989); Schlesinger, Jr., *The Politics of Hope* (Boston, 1962), pts. IV and V.

7. Dwight Macdonald, *Against the American Grain* (New York, 1962), 3–75; Bernard Rosenberg and David Manning White, eds., *Mass Culture: The Popular Arts in America* (New York, 1957).

8. Warren I. Susman, *Culture as History: The Transformation of American Society in the Twentieth Century* (New York, 1984); Neil Harris, *Cultural Excursions: Marketing Appetites and Cultural Tastes in Modern America* (Chicago, 1990).

9. Lawrence W. Levine, "The Folklore of Industrial Society: Popular Culture and Its Audiences," AHR, 97 (December 1992), 1376. See also Levine, *The Opening of the American Mind: Canons, Culture and History* (Boston, 1996), 146–49, 167–68. And for a recent echo of Levine's concern from a different voice, see Martha Bayles, "Theory, Snobbery, and the Agony of Popular Culture," *Chronicle of Higher Education*, June 6, 1997, pp. B4–B5. For a vivid example of contestation in 1997 over the legitimacy of studying popular culture in academe, see David Buckingham, "Normal Science? Soap Studies in the 1990s," *Cultural Studies*, 11 (May 1997), 351–55.

10. Robert Brent Toplin, ed., *Ken Burns's The Civil War: Historians Respond* (New York, 1996), xvi–vii.

11. Ibid., 66, 78, 89, 127–32. See also Mary A. DeCredico, "Image and Reality: Ken Burns and the Urban Confederacy," *Journal of Urban History*, 23 (May 1997), 387–405. She contends that Burns's "images are often at odds with his narrative commentary" and that his "visuals undercut his text" regarding the urban South.

12. Foner cited in Toplin, ed., *Burns's The Civil War*, 39–59, 103–05.

13. Vann Woodward cited in ibid., 11–12. For Burns's account of that confrontational day, see ibid., 170–71. And see David W. Blight, "Homer with a Camera, Our Iliad Without the Aftermath: Ken Burns's Dialogue with Historians," *Reviews in American History*, 25 (June 1997), 351–59.

14. Thomas Cripps, "Historical Truth: An Interview with Ken Burns," AHR, 100 (June 1995), 744, 760; italics in original.

15. Ibid., 763–64.

16. Ibid., 764.

17. *Wilmington [N.C.], Sunday Star News*, May 5, 1996, p. 9D; *Washington Times*, July 27, 1996, p. A14.

18. *Cleveland Plain Dealer*, June 9, 1996, p. 11J.

19. *Norfolk Virginian-Pilot*, Nov. 7, 1994, p. 6.

20. Victor Davis Hanson in *The Weekly Standard*, Sept. 23, 1996, p. 36.

21. Stephen Aron, "*The West as America:* A Review of the Latest Ken Burns Documentary," *Perspectives* [American Historical Association Newsletter], 34 (September 1996), 1, 7–10; John Fiske, *Understanding Popular Culture* (London, 1989), 120. See also Richard Gid Powers, "The Voice of History in Popular Culture," *Perspectives*, 35 (May 1997), 23–25.

22. See William Grimes, "What Debt Does Hollywood Owe to Truth?" *NYT*, March 6, 1992, p. C15; Nora Ephron, "The Tie That Binds" (regarding Oliver Stone's *JFK*), *The Nation*, April 6, 1992, pp. 453–55; Stone's reply, ibid., May 18, 1992, p. 650; "Seeing Is Believing: History, Art and Interpretation," Max Wasserman Forum on Contemporary Art, May 14, 1992, Massachusetts Institute of Technology, Cambridge, Mass.

23. For the massive catalogue, see Kirk Varnedoe and Adam Gopnik, *High and Low: Modern Art and Popular Culture* (New York, 1990). See also an ancillary volume of original essays, Varnedoe and Gopnik, eds., *Modern Art and Popular Culture: Readings in High and Low* (New York, 1990). For an important essay (developed and revised between 1980 and 1990) that sustains the Varnedoe-Gopnik thesis, see Thomas Crow, "Modernism and Mass Culture in the Visual Arts," in Crow, *Modern Art in the Common Culture* (New Haven, 1996), 3–37.

24. Robert Hughes, "Upstairs and Downstairs at MOMA," *Time*, Oct. 22, 1990, p. 94. For a remarkably similar example of the very same enterprise in American literature and popular culture, see David S. Reynolds, *Beneath the American Renaissance: The Subversive Imagination in the Age of Emerson and Melville* (Cambridge, Mass., 1989).

25. Peter Plagens, "MOMA Takes the Low Road," *Newsweek*, Oct. 15, 1990, p. 72. Plagens actually contributed an essay on contemporary art in Los Angeles to the Varnedoe and Gopnik reader, *Modern Art and Popular Culture*, 219–29.

26. Roberta Smith, "High and Low Culture Meet on a One-Way Street," NYT, Oct. 5, 1990, p. C1.

27. Rose quoted in Paul Richard, "A Meld of Kitsch and Culture in MoMA's High and Low," *Washington Post*, Oct. 7, 1990, p. G1.

28. Hilton Kramer, "The Varnedoe Debacle: MoMA's New 'Low,'" *New Criterion*, 9 (December 1990), 5–8, the quotation on p. 5; James Gardner, "Highs and Lows, and Furbelows," *National Review*, Feb. 11, 1991, p. 57.

29. Kempton, "Finding the Art Around Us," *Newsday*, Dec. 27, 1990, p. 11; Grace Glueck, "Despite a Thrashing by Critics, Art Show Is Proving Popular," NYT, Dec. 3, 1990, p. C13; Scott Pendleton, "The Great Modern Art Conspiracy Theory," *Christian Science Monitor*, March 29, 1991, p. 10.

30. Varnedoe quoted in Glueck, "Despite a Thrashing . . . ," Dec. 3, 1990.

31. David C. Walters, "High & Low," *Christian Science Monitor*, March 29, 1991, p. 10. Attempting to explain modern art by means of a thesis-driven exhibition

was not unprecedented in 1990. A generation earlier, a television program that presented the modern art collection at the Whitney Museum announced that "modernism is born of Einstein" and the theory of relativity, thereby contextualizing modern art in terms of a scientific revolution. See Lynn Spigel, "High Culture in Low Places: Television and Modern Art, 1950–1970," in Cary Nelson and Dilip Parameshwar Gaonkar, eds., *Disciplinarity and Dissent in Cultural Studies* (New York, 1996), 336.

32. Suzanne Muchnic, "The Most Powerful Curator in the Country Did His Homework for His First MoMA Exhibit, But He Wasn't Prepared for the Reception It Got," *Los Angeles Times*, June 23, 1991, Calendar section, pp. 6, 78–81.

33. Ibid., p. 78.

34. See Paul R. Gorman, *Left Intellectuals and Popular Culture in Twentieth-Century America* (Chapel Hill, 1996); Andrew Ross, *No Respect: Intellectuals and Popular Culture* (New York, 1989); Kammen *The Lively Arts*, chaps. 8–9; Meaghan Morris, *Too Soon, Too Late: History in Popular Culture* (Bloomington, 1998).

35. Ivan Karp and Steven D. Lavine, eds., *Exhibiting Cultures: The Poetics and Politics of Museum Display* (Washington, D.C., 1991), esp. chs. 10–12; George W. McDaniel, *Hearth & Home: Preserving a People's Culture* (Philadelphia, 1982), 3–28; John Higham, "History in the Culture Wars," Organization of American Historians, *Newsletter* (May 1997), p. 1.

36. Carl Becker, "Everyman His Own Historian" (1932), in Becker, *Everyman His Own Historian: Essays on History and Politics* (New York, 1935), 248; Gary Kulik, "Designing the Past: History-Museum Exhibitions from Peale to the Present," in Warren Leon and Roy Rosenzweig, eds., *History Museums in the United States: A Critical Assessment* (Urbana, 1989), 23–28; Neil Harris, "A Historical Perspective on Museum Advo-

cacy," in Harris, *Cultural Excursions: Marketing Appetites and Cultural Tastes in Modern America* (Chicago, 1990), 95.

37. Michael Frisch, "The Presentation of Urban History in Big-City Museums," in Leon and Rosenzweig, *History Museums in the United States*, 39; Bernard Bailyn, *On the Teaching and Writing of History* (Hanover, N.H., 1994), 15.

38. Mike Wallace, *Mickey Mouse History and Other Essays on American Memory* (Philadelphia, 1996), 62, 94, 120, and passim.

39. See Ellen Roney Hughes, "The Unstifled Muse: The 'All in the Family' Exhibit and Popular Culture at the National Museum of American History," in Amy Henderson and Adrienne L. Kaeppler, eds., *Exhibiting Dilemmas: Issues of Representation at the Smithsonian* (Washington, D.C., 1997), 156–75; Lisa C. Roberts, *From Knowledge to Narrative: Educators and the Changing Museum* (Washington, D.C., 1997).

40. Wendy Wick Reaves, *Celebrity Caricature in America* (New Haven, 1998). It is worthy of note, *en passant*, that in France during the 1930s Georges Henri Rivière became very concerned about the need to break down conventional notions about taste levels and cultural strata. He eventually became the founding director of the Musée national des arts et traditions populaires in Paris, a museum with no effective counterpart in the United States. See Herman Lebovics, *True France: The Wars Over Cultural Identity, 1900–1945* (Ithaca, 1992), 163–71, 177–81.

41. See, e.g., Edward T. Linenthal and Tom Engelhardt, eds., *History Wars: The Enola Gay and Other Battles for the American Past* (New York, 1996); "History and the Public: What Can We Handle? A Round Table About History after the Enola Gay Controversy," JAH, 82 (December 1995), 1029–35; Edward T. Linenthal, *Preserving Memory: The Struggle to Create America's Holocaust Museum* (New York, 1995); Martin Harwit, *An*

Exhibit Denied: Lobbying the History of Enola Gay (New York, 1996).

42. William H. Truettner and Alexander Nemerov, "What You See Is Not Necessarily What You Get: New Meaning in Images of the Old West," *Montana: The Magazine of Western History*, 42 (Summer 1992), 71–76; Lippmann, *Public Opinion* (New York, 1922), 371–72; Becker, *Everyman His Own Historian*, 248. For a superb illustration from small-town America today, see Lore C. Banks, "The Library Censorship Issue," *Little Baldy Press* [Hot Springs, Montana, weekly], July 14, 1997, p. 3.

43. For acknowledgment that "The West as America" was intended to be revisionist, see Andrew Gulliford, "The West as America: Reinterpreting Images of the Frontier, 1820–1920," JAH, 79 (June 1992), 204. For visitor complaints about "revisionism" in a 1994 exhibition at the Newberry Library titled "The Frontier in American Culture," see ibid., 82 (December 1995), 1148. On the issue of revisionism in recent historical scholarship, see Peter Novick, *That Noble Dream: The "Objectivity Question" and the American Historical Profession* (New York, 1988), 446–52; John Higham, *History: Professional Scholarship in America* (1965: Baltimore, 1983), 255–56; Robert Maddox, *The New Left and the Origins of the Cold War* (Princeton, 1973). For the European side of the story, see Joan H. Pittock and Andrew Wear, eds., *Interpretation and Cultural History* (New York, 1991).

44. T. J. Jackson Lears, *Fables of Abundance: A Cultural History of Advertising in America* (New York, 1994), 263. For a bizarre and recent illustration of the American obsession with authenticity in historical re-enactments, see Stephen Glass, "Slavery Chic," NR, vol. 217, July 14, 1997, pp. 12–13. As part of a program called "George Washington: Pioneer Farmer," seven college students dressed as slaves at Mount Vernon and did exactly the tasks that slaves would have performed there more than two hundred years ago. They were observed by tourists and interacted with them as slaves. Because the plantation program considers only applicants who have had agricultural experience, the pool of black applicants for these internships is small. It seems to be tough to find a complete complement of African-American "slaves" in 1997!

45. Lawrence W. Levine, *Highbrow/Lowbrow: The Emergence of Cultural Hierarchy in America* (Cambridge, Mass., 1988), 164–65; Levine, "The Folklore of Industrial Society: Popular Culture and Its Audiences," 1382; Paul Fussell, *Doing Battle: The Making of a Skeptic* (Boston, 1996), 264, 267.

46. William Wilson, "High and Low Will Prove N.Y. Critics Wrong," *Los Angeles Times*, June 22, 1991, p. F1.

47. Toplin, ed., *Burns's The Civil War*, xix, xxi, Ward quoted at 148.

48. See Lippmann, *Public Opinion*, 59.

49. The Ur-text on this tendency is Peter L. Berger and Thomas Luckmann, *The Social Construction of Reality: A Treatise in the Sociology of Knowledge* (New York, 1966).

50. See Paul K. Longmore, *The Invention of George Washington* (Berkeley, 1989); Nell Painter, *Sojourner Truth: A Life, A Symbol* (New York, 1996), esp. 4–5, 30, 73–76, 79, 178, 247, and ch. 20; Greil Marcus, *Dead Elvis: A Chronicle of a Cultural Obsession* (New York, 1991); Daniel Walker Howe, *Making the American Self: Jonathan Edwards to Abraham Lincoln* (Cambridge, Mass., 1997); Robert Storr, "No Joy in Mudville: Greenberg's Modernism Then and Now," in Varnedoe and Gopnik, eds., *Modern Art and Popular Culture*, 151.

51. See David E. Whisnant, *All That Is Native and Fine: The Politics of Culture in an American Region* (Chapel Hill, 1983); Robert Cantwell, *When We Were Good: The Folk Revival* (Cambridge, Mass., 1996); Eric Hobsbawm and Terence Ranger, eds., *The Invention of Tradition* (Cambridge, 1983).

52. Nolan Porterfield, *Last Cavalier, The Life and Times of John A. Lomax, 1867–1948* (Urbana, 1996); Raymond Williams, "Culture Is Ordinary," in Williams, *Resources of Hope: Culture, Democracy, Socialism* (London, 1989), 3–18.

53. See Cary Nelson and Dilip Parameshwar Gaonkar, eds., *Disciplinarity and Dissent in Cultural Studies* (New York, 1996), esp. chs. 1, 4, 5, 9, 13; Lawrence Grossberg, Cary Nelson, and Paula Treichler, eds., *Cultural Studies* (New York, 1992).

Chapter 10

1. See Russell Lynes, *The Tastemakers* (New York, 1954), ch. 17, esp. p. 310; Lynes, *Snobs: A Guidebook to Your Friends, Your Enemies, Your Colleagues and Yourself* (New York, 1950).

2. C. W. E. Bigsby, "The Politics of Popular Culture," in Bigsby, ed., *Approaches to Popular Culture* (Bowling Green, Ohio, 1976), 11; Tocqueville, *Democracy in America*, ed. J. P. Mayer (Garden City, N.Y., 1969), 454–58; Michael Kammen, *In the Past Lane: Historical Perspectives on American Culture* (New York, 1997), 88–89, 97.

3. Richard Slotkin, *Gunfighter Nation: The Myth of the Frontier in Twentieth-Century America* (New York, 1992), 175–83 *et seq.*; Burnett, *Little Caesar* (1929: New York, 1956), foreword by Gilbert Seldes, 7. Burnett also wrote *Public Enemy* (1930) and co-authored *Scarface* (1932), a trio of masterpieces in the gangster cycle.

4. Gilbert Seldes, "Nickelodeon to Television," *Maclean's Magazine*, Jan. 1, 1950, p. 44. For a much less hopeful view than Seldes's, see Louis Kronenberger, *Company Manners: A Cultural Inquiry into American Life* (New York, 1955), 36–47, 109, 120.

5. Jay G. Blumler, "The New Television Marketplace: Imperatives, Implications, Issues," in James Curran and

Michael Gurevitch, eds., *Mass Media and Society* (London, 1991), 210.

6. "The Family in Trouble," *Life*, July 26, 1948, pp. 83–99. See Elaine Tyler May, *Homeward Bound: American Families in the Cold War Era* (New York, 1988); William Grimes, "The Camera That Came to Dinner," NYT, March 20, 1997, p. C15.

7. Louis Harris, December 1971, USHARRIS.021772.R1D, RCPOR; Louis Harris, January 1971, USHARRIS.71JAN.R58F, RCPOR.

8. Opinion Research Corp., May 1972, USORC.72NSF.R05, RCPOR; Louis Harris, January 1971, USHARRIS.71JAN.R58E, RCPOR.

9. Institute for Survey Research, December 1979, USTEMPLE.80-NSF.R24D, RCPOR; Bureau of Social Science Research, August 1978, USBSSR.78ENVR.R31, RCPOR.

10. Louis Harris, March–April 1977, USHARRIS.052377.R3, RCPOR.

11. Jack M. McLeod et al., "On Understanding and Misunderstanding Media Effects," in Curran and Gurevitch, eds., *Mass Media and Society*, 256.

12. James Fallows, *Breaking the News: How the Media Undermine American Democracy* (New York, 1996), 254–69, the quotations at 267, 255. See also "Why Today's News Is No Longer What Happened Yesterday," NYT, May 4, 1998, p. D8.

13. Michael Gurevitch, "The Globalization of Electronic Journalism," in Curran and Gurevitch, eds., *Mass Media and Society*, 185–86. See also Michael R. Real, *Mass-Mediated Culture* (Englewood Cliffs, N.J., 1977), esp. chs. 1, 2, 3, 7, 8.

14. Elizabeth Eisenstein, "Some Conjectures About the Impact of Printing on Western Society and Thought," *Journal of Modern History*, 40 (March 1968), 1–56; Priscilla P. Clark, "The Beginnings of Mass Culture in France: Action and Reaction," *Social Research*, 45 (Summer 1978), 277–91.

15. Emmanuel Le Roy Ladurie, *Car-*

nival in Romans (New York, 1979); Charles Tilly, *The Contentious French* (Cambridge, Mass., 1986); David Sabean, *Power in the Blood: Popular Culture and Village Discourse in Early Modern Germany* (Cambridge, 1984); David Underdown, *Revel, Riot and Rebellion: Popular Politics and Culture in England* (London, 1985); and for an overview, Peter Burke, "The 'Discovery' of Popular Culture," in Raphael Samuel, ed., *People's History and Socialist Theory* (London, 1981), 216–26.

16. Robert J. Bezucha, "The Moralization of Society: The Enemies of Popular Culture in the Nineteenth Century," in Jacques Beauroy, et al., eds., *The Wolf and the Lamb: Popular Culture in France from the Old Regime to the Twentieth Century* (Saratoga, Calif., 1977), 175–87, the quotations at 176; David Pivar, *Purity Crusade: Sexual Morality and Social Control, 1868–1900* (Westport, Conn., 1973); Nicola Beisel, *Imperiled Innocents: Anthony Comstock and Family Reproduction in Victorian America* (Princeton, 1997).

17. Bigsby, "The Politics of Popular Culture," 20, 22; John Carey, *The Intellectuals and the Masses: Pride and Prejudice Among the Literary Intelligentsia, 1880–1939* (New York, 1992).

18. Paul R. Gorman, *Left Intellectuals and Popular Culture in Twentieth-Century America* (Chapel Hill, 1996); David Murray, ed., *American Cultural Critics* (Exeter, U.K., 1995); Richard Pells, *The Liberal Mind in a Conservative Age: American Intellectuals in the 1940s and 1950s* (New York, 1985); Michael Walzer, *The Company of Critics: Social Criticism and Political Commitment in the Twentieth Century* (New York, 1988).

19. Harold E. Stearns, ed., *Civilization in the United States: An Inquiry by Thirty Americans* (New York, 1922), 150; Janice Radway, "The Scandal of the Middlebrow: The Book-of-the-Month Club, Class Fracture, and Cultural Authority," SAQ, 89 (Fall, 1990), 704–05, 707, 713, 720; Rob Kroes, *If You've Seen One You've Seen the Mall: Europeans and*

American Mass Culture (Urbana, 1996), 82–84, 146.

20. David Remnick, *Resurrection: The Struggle for a New Russia* (New York, 1997), 223. See also Alessandra Stanley, "On Russian TV, Suddenly the Screen Is Steamy," NYT, Nov. 13, 1997, p. A4; Jianying Zha, *China Pop: How Soap Operas, Tabloids, and Bestsellers Are Transforming a Culture* (New York, 1995). For excellent contrasts and similarities with the United States under the Soviet regime, see Richard Stites, *Russian Popular Culture: Entertainment and Society Since 1900* (New York, 1992).

21. Ngugi wa Thiong'o is quoted in Herbert I. Schiller, *Culture, Inc.: The Corporate Takeover of Public Expression* (New York, 1989), 134.

22. Lipsyte quoted in Steven W. Pope, *Patriotic Games: Sporting Traditions in the American Imagination, 1876–1926* (New York, 1997), ix. Although it could well be regarded as a part of this hyperbolic genre, much less apocalyptic is Arthur C. Danto, *After the End of Art: Contemporary Art and the Pale of History* (Princeton, 1997).

23. Robert Brustein, "The Decline of High Culture," NR, 217 (Nov. 3, 1997), 29–32. Cf. Bernard Rosenberg and David Manning White, eds., *Mass Culture: The Popular Arts in America* (New York, 1957); Harold Rosenberg, "Pop Culture and Kitsch Criticism," *Dissent*, 5 (Winter 1958), 14–19; Michael Kammen, *The Lively Arts: Gilbert Seldes and the Transformation of Cultural Criticism in the United States* (New York, 1996), ch. 9.

24. See Livingston Biddle, *Our Government and the Arts: A Perspective from the Inside* (New York, 1988), pt. 3; Michael Kammen, "Culture and the State in America," JAH, 83 (December 1996), 804.

25. Brustein, "Decline of High Culture," 30. Cf. Ellen Wiley Todd, *The "New Woman" Revised: Painting and Gender Politics on Fourteenth Street* (Berkeley, 1993); Erika Doss, *Benton, Pollock, and the*

Politics of Modernism: From Regionalism to Abstract Expressionism (Chicago, 1991); David Shapiro, ed., *Social Realism: Art as a Weapon* (New York, 1973).

26. Brustein, "Decline of High Culture," 32. See also Julia Duin, "Audio Editor Wants Christians to Be, Not Renounce, Christian Elite," *Washington Times*, Jan. 30, 1998, p. A2.

27. See Diana Crane, *The Transformation of the Avant-Garde: The New York Art World, 1940–1985* (Chicago, 1987); Christin J. Mamiya, *Pop Art and Consumer Culture: American Super Market* (Austin, 1992); Arthur C. Danto, *Beyond the Brillo Box: The Visual Arts in Post-Historical Perspective* (New York, 1992); Danto, *After the End of Art*; Berel Lang, ed., *The Death of Art* (New York, 1984), 3–76.

28. Michael Denning, "The End of Mass Culture," *International Labor and Working-Class History*, 37 (Spring 1990), 4–18, and his answer to respondents, "The Ends of Ending Mass Culture," on 63–67.

29. Richard Butsch, "Mass Culture: Terrain for Collective Action?" in ibid., 39 (Spring 1991), 33–34.

30. See, for example, Gerald Parshall, "The Prophets of Pop Culture," *U.S. News & World Report*, June 1, 1998, pp. 56–69, followed by Todd Gitlin, "Pop Goes the Culture" (an essay), 70–71. Although this feature uses the phrase "popular culture" throughout, it is almost entirely concerned in fact with the advent of mass culture. Gitlin also uses "popular" when the substance of his astute observations is actually mass culture.

31. Raymond Williams, *Culture* (London, 1981); Terry Eagleton, ed., *Raymond Williams: Critical Perspectives* (Boston, 1989); John and Lizzie Eldridge, *Raymond Williams: Making Connections* (London, 1994); Fred Inglis, *Raymond Williams* (London, 1995); Jeff Wallace and Rod Jones, eds., *Raymond Williams Now: Knowledge, Limits and the Future* (New York, 1997).

32. Jay Cantor, *Krazy Kat: A Novel in Five Panels* (New York, 1987), 60–61, italics in original.

33. Matthew Arnold, *Culture and Anarchy* (1867: London, 1960), 69–70. Arnold's most recent biographer has made a vigorous case that the author of *Culture and Anarchy* was not an elitist snob, but rather had a socially inclusive vision of culture's reach and simply wished to achieve what we would call democratic distinction by leveling up: "Arnold had no time for those who condescended to or talked down to the masses. He wanted them to enjoy the riches he himself enjoyed." His American lecture tour in 1883–84, however, did not turn out very well. One newspaper reported that Arnold "has taken a daring delight in shocking popular prejudices, jeering at popular idols, and showing contempt for the popular intellect." Nicholas Murray, *A Life of Matthew Arnold* (New York, 1997), 244–45, 319–20; the critical remark appeared in the *New York Tribune* on Oct. 22, 1883.

34. See Max Kaplan, *Leisure in America: A Social Inquiry* (New York, 1960).

Acknowledgments

The conceptualization and angles of vision observed in this book received significant feedback from engaging students who took my undergraduate seminar at Cornell each spring semester between 1992 and 1997. Fortunately for me, several of my doctoral students also chose to write their dissertations on aspects of American cultural history since the late nineteenth century, on topics ranging from urban consumerism and social envy, to American zoos, to ethnicity and intergenerational relations, to the counterculture of the later 1960s. Their own work has provided me with abundant insights and engagement.

During 1997–98 I enjoyed the good fortune of a fellowship from the National Endowment for the Humanities and a four-month stint as Guest Scholar at the Woodrow Wilson International Center in Washington, D.C., which together made it possible to bring this project to completion. A notable conference held at the Wilson Center on October 8–10, 1998, "American Culture in Global Perspective," provided me with a very significant stimulus: in the planning stages, in receiving advance copies of the papers, and in the rewarding discussions that took place during the course of those three days.

Rob Persons, research analyst at the Roper Center for Public Opinion Research, located in Storrs, Connecticut, did yeoman duty in searching through many thousands of polls for the ones most likely to be germane to the subject of this inquiry. I am much obliged to him for his acuity and perseverance. My undergraduate research assistant at Cornell, Craig W. Ginsberg, provided invaluable competence, diligence, and reliability.

I am very grateful to Ms. Mary Newman and the James Agee Trust for permission to print an extract from Agee's 1954 "Culture Song," published by Houghton Mifflin Company in *The Collected Poems of James Agee*, edited by Robert Fitzgerald (Boston, 1968). I also acknowledge the gracious permission of Mrs. Mildred Lynes to use the papers of her late husband, Russell Lynes, and to reproduce his 1976 "Commentary" at the close of chapter 5.

Chapter 9 was first presented in November 1997 at a conference on "The Historian and Public Life" held at Turin, Italy, under the auspices of the Fondazione Luigi Einaudi and the University of Turin. Professor Maurizio Vaudagna deserves warm appreciation for all of his thoughtful and meticulous arrangements.

Jennifer Evangelista and Jackie Martin prepared the manuscript with their customary skill, patience, and good cheer. At times they also needed considerable ingenuity and persistence. I am very grateful for their continued support. Ann Adelman once again did thorough and thoughtful work ironing wrinkles out of the final copy, and Knopf's astonishing production editor Melvin Rosenthal caught glitches that mere mortals would have missed. Webb Younce at Knopf also helped in countless ways, and served as an indispensable conduit to facilitate smooth transmissions. Kathryn Torgeson made the index with her customary care and deftness.

Acknowledgments

The project received considerable improvement from careful, constructive, and critical readings by James A. Hijiya, Carol Kammen, R. Laurence Moore, Richard Polenberg, and Michael Schudson. I only regret that I could not accommodate all of their thoughtful suggestions.

Jane Garrett, my astute editor at Knopf for thirty years now, and Carol Kammen once again served as midwives in bringing the book to term with minimal stress and maximum wisdom. My debt to them is great and my appreciation is appropriate in scale. I feel blessed to receive and enjoy the gifts of two such gracious editors and "long-term associates." At the beginning of this century, William Dean Howells remarked that "the man of letters must make up his mind that in the United States the fate of a book is in the hands of the women." He intended that to convey something a bit different from my meaning here. But I must acknowledge that the fate of my own books has, for quite a long time now, been in the hands of highly particular women—and that has been my very good fortune. Hence this book's dedication, for the third time in as many decades, to Carol.

October 1998

M.K.
Above Cayuga's Waters

Index

ABC-TV, 62, 205
Abstract Expressionists, 254
academics
    as cultural authorities, 134, 158
    as cultural critics, xv, 47, 103, 105–6, 109,
        165, 219–41
Acheson, Dean, 147
Adamic, Louis, 54, 195
Adams, Henry, 40
Addams, Jane, 136, 195
Adorno, Theodor, 46, 106, 183, 222
advertising
    as art form, 192–3
    early use of, 82
    media changes in, 50
    pioneers in, 274(n40)
    as profession, 54, 58
    on radio, 50, 111, 155
    role in consumerism, 66–7, 90, 145
    role in magazine sales, 51
    on television, 50, 59, 60, 205, 206, 213,
        215(n)
African Americans
    depiction in Civil War documentary, 225
    entertainment for, 76
    history of, 221
    music of, 35, 113(n), 114
    segregation of, 36
Agee, James, 91, 148–50
Age of Anxiety, The, 97, 106, 245
Agnew, Jean-Christophe, 179
Alamo, The, 63
Albee, Edward F., 31–2, 37, 138
Aldridge, John W., 117
Allen, Agnes, 55
Allen, Fred, 87, 125, 147, 156, 163
Allen, Frederick Lewis, 55
Allen, Robert C., 36, 102–3, 223
Alsop, Joseph, 170
Alsop, Stewart, 147, 148
Alvord, Edith, 40
Ameche, Don, 173–4
Americana, development of interest in, 67
American Association of Museums, 235–6
American Century, 17
American Historical Association, 10, 145

Americanism, 47–69
    promotion of, 62–9
American nationalism, role in
    democratization of culture, 242
American Renaissance, 37
American Studies movement, 221
American Tobacco Company, 141
amusement parks, 78
Andelman, Eddie, as "talk radio" pioneer,
    207(n)
Anderson, Benedict, 164
Anderson, Sherwood, 118
Andy Warhol (Wyeth), 192
Angell, Katharine, 145
Annual Exhibition of American Industrial Art
    (1922), 110
anti-Communist anxieties
    after World War II, 154, 250
    Red Scare, 43
anti-intellectualism, of populist politics, 159
architecture, cultural critics of, 142
Arendt, Hannah, 44
Armory Show of post-Impressionist art
    (1913), 104
Armstrong, Louis, 35
Armstrong, Robert, 186
Arnold, Matthew, xviii, 38, 133, 142, 257,
    303(n33)
art
    American, 120, 121–2, 131, 132
    commercial and high compared, 126
    high and low compared, 150
    mass-produced, 191–2
    popular culture and, 219, 229–34
art criticism, 41
art critics, 13, 30, 141, 142, 287(n32)
Art Institute of Chicago, 109, 230, 233
Ashcan School, 253
Associated Press, 170
Atwater Kent Program, 111
Auden, W. H., 97
audience response
    of listeners, 296(n61)
    of readers, 279(n1; n2)
authenticity, obsession with, 220, 238, 239,
    240, 300(n44)

auto-camping, 16–17
automobile, role in leisure pursuits, 17
avant-garde culture, 131, 147, 163
  convention flouting in, 13
  development of, 257
  kitsch and, 221
  music in, 116
  poetry admirers in, 29
  popular culture and, 72, 145
  theater in, 27, 198

Bailyn, Bernard, 236
Bakshy, Alexander, 110
ballets, 126, 132
  popularity of, 121
Barnouw, Erik, 221
Barnum, P. T., 22, 24
Barthes, Roland, 291(n39)
Barton, Bruce, 192, 274(n40)
baseball
  documentary on, 226–7, 228
  radio broadcasts of, 173
  on television, 185
Basie, Count, 114
Batten, Barton, Durstine & Osborn, as radio
    program producer, 221
Baum, L. Frank, 49
Beavis and Butt-head, 208
Beck, Julian, 27, 28
Becker, Carl, 145, 235, 238
Beethoven, Ludwig van, 101(n), 148
Belasco, Warren, 16
Bell, Daniel, 44–5, 101, 177
  on high art, 123
Benjamin, Walter, 192
Benson, Susan Porter, 49
Benton, Thomas Hart, xvi, 153, 154, 287(n44)
Berger, John, on art, 13–14
Berlin, Irving, 157, 221
Berlin, Isaiah, 157
Bernays, Edward L., 40, 51, 111, 112, 138
Bernhardt, Sarah, 103
Bernstein, Leonard, 73, 148, 150
Berryman, John, 146
Bethlehem, Pennsylvania, pro-labor opera
    performance in, 75
Bettelheim, Bruno, on television, 200–1
"Beyond Catgeory," xix, 21, 73, 243
Bezucha, Robert J., on reform movement,
    249–50
biculturalism, 244, 245
Biddle, George, 175
Biddle, Livingston, 252
Bigsby, C. W. E., 6
billboards, legislation against, 61
Black, Gregory D., 223
Blitzstein, Marc, 75
Bloch, Marc, 164

Bloom, Allan, 160
Bode, Carl, 221
Bogart, Leo, 213
Bogdan, Robert, 223
Bok, Edward, 35
Book-of-the-Month Club, 16, 83–4, 138, 140,
    163, 166, 181
books
  affecting popular and mass culture, 244
  best-seller lists for, 207
  on popular culture, 222–3
  role in popular culture, 57, 82, 83, 93,
    279(n49)
Boorstin, Daniel J., 50
Booth, Edwin, 63
Boritt, Gabor S., 225
Boston Public Library, 68
Bourne, Randolph, 66, 146, 176
  on cultural standards, 33–4
bowling, 92
Boynton, Percy Holmes, 38, 40
Brande, Dorothea, 55
Brandeis, Louis D., 66
Breen, Joseph L., 153
Brooks, Van Wyck, 34, 73, 74, 91, 101, 113,
    256
Brown, John, 156
Brown, Kenneth W., 27
Brownell, William C., 38, 39, 40, 41, 46, 142,
    143
Bruce, Lenny, 156
Brustein, Robert, on culture, 252–4, 256
Buffalo Bill, 11, 21, 63, 78, 241
Buhle, Paul, 223
"Buntline, Ned." See Judson, E. Z. C.
burlesque, 21, 24, 102–3
Burnett, W. R., 244
Burns, Ken, xv
  documentaries of, 224–9, 234, 239–40
Burns, Ric, 227
Burns, Robert E., 83
Bushnell, Horace, 10, 142
"business class," as higher social echelon, 81
Butsch, Richard, on local culture, 255

cabarets, 28, 80, 195–6
cable television, 205(n), 214
Cahill, Holger, 41
Calder stabile, in taste-level chart, 132
Calkins, Earnest Elmo, 51, 193
  on advertising, 193–4
Camel cigarettes, television program
    sponsorship by, 59
Canby, Henry Seidel, 16, 84, 140
Canfield, Mary Cass, 110
Cantor, Eddie, 87, 90
Cantor, Jay, 256
Capra, Frank, 68(n), 112

card playing, 81
caricatures, 112–13
Carlson, Chester, 172(n)
Carnegie Hall, 109, 113–14
car ownership, by middle class, 258
Carreras, José Maria, 122
Carson, Johnny, 160
Carson, Kit, 10
Carter, Jimmy, 24, 252
cartoons. *See* comic strips
Caruso, Enrico, 113
Cawelti, John, 118, 222
CBS, 18, 43, 45, 53, 85, 155, 173, 200, 205, 209
celebrities
    culture of, xiv, 57, 171
    obsessions with, 163
censorship, of media, 152–3, 154, 155
Center for Contemporary Art (Cincinnati),
    141
Center for the Study of Popular Culture
    (Los Angeles), 265(n8)
chain stores, 82
Chandler, Raymond, 120
Channing, William Ellery, 142
Chaplin, Charlie, 43, 104, 163, 170, 221
chat rooms, 246
Chautauqua movement, 37
Child, Julia, 159
children
    exposure to violence of, 154–5
    television ads for, 60
    television effects on, 199–201
Chitlin Circuit, 76
churches
    corporate-like management of, 62
    membership in, 88
circus, as part of popular culture, 78, 221
civic culture, mass culture undermining of,
    199(n)
civil rights movement, television's role in, 25
Civil War, 35, 109, 136
    documentary on, xv, 224–8, 240
Clarke, John, on mass culture, 213, 216
clergy, as cultural critics, 142
Clinton, Catherine, 225, 227
clubs, role in popular culture, 84–5
CNN, 205(n)
Coates, Paul, 59
Cohen, Lizabeth, 59, 291(n33)
Colbert, Claudette, 112
Cold War, 52, 67, 157, 242
Collins, Wilkie, 48
Colonial Williamsburg, 46, 67, 118
Columbian Exposition of 1893, 10, 77
Columbia Pictures, as taste arbiters, 151
columnists, newspaper syndication of, 170
Comfort, Alex, 160
comic strips, 86, 165, 168–9, 170, 221, 256

commercial culture, 47–8, 53
    proto-mass culture and, 166–76
commercialization, xiv
    of culture, 122
    of popular culture, xiv
    transition to mass culture, 55–61
Committee on Public Information, 42–3, 66,
    68, 166
Como, Perry, 209
computers, private possession of, 20, 258
Conant, James B., 158
condensed (abridged) books, 181
Coney Island (Brooklyn), 78, 176
Coney Island Beach (Marsh), 23
consumer culture, expansion of, 51
consumerism, xiv, 47–69, 89, 145, 242
    development of, 257
    promotion of, 51–5
    revisionist perception of, 62
Consumer's Research, 141
Consumer's Union, 141
consumption communities, 50–1
Cook, George Cram, 38
Coolidge, Calvin, 54, 112
Copland, Aaron, 72–3
Corneille, Pierre, 111
Cortissoz, Royal, 142
Corwin, Norman, 155
couch-potato phenomenon, 186
    poll on, 214
Council on Library Resources, 61
Covarrubias, Miguel, "Impossible Interviews"
    of, 112–13
credit cards, 179
Creel, George, 66, 68. *See also* Committee on
    Public Information
Crockett, Davy, 63, 166
Cronkite, Walter, 150
Crosby, Bing, 85
Crosby, John, 156
Cross, Gary, 103
Cross, Milton, 145
Crossley system, of rating audience size,
    155
Crowninshield, Frank, 125
cultural authority, xvii, xviii
    cultural criticism as, 141–150
    decline of, xiv, 37, 123, 150–61, 242, 259
    embodiment and exercise of, 135–41
    flouting of, 156–7
    transformation of, 133–61
    of women, 136–7
cultural criticism
    academic sources of, 134, 158
    as cultural authority, 141–50
    transformation of cultural authority and,
    133–61
    as a vocation, 259

cultural critics, xvii, 5, 12, 34, 52, 65, 72, 87, 93, 97–8, 100, 103, 126, 179, 210, 213
  decline of, xiv
  professional, 142
  standardization and, 251
cultural hierarchy, 73, 74
cultural pluralism, xvii, 53, 66, 150, 218
cultural power, 259
  definition of, 133
  increase of, 150–61
cultural stratification, xvi, xviii, 3, 11, 13, 14, 15, 29, 37
  changing perceptions of, 70–6
  deceptive increase of, 95–102
  decline of, 56
  development of, 256–7
cultural studies, 124, 210, 215
culture
  definitions of, xvii, xviii, 7
  democratization of, 27–46, 134, 242
culture of celebrity, xiv, 57, 171
"culture of pastiche," 167
"Culture Zone" column (Kakutani), 13
culturine, 74
Cummins, Maria, 102

Dalí, Salvador, 126
dance, as art, 121, 126
dance halls, 79–80
Danto, Arthur, 254
  review of modern art show by, 233, 234
Darnton, Robert, 36, 106
Debs, Eugene V., 156
Debussy, Claude, 36
de Certeau, Michel, 82, 210, 211, 216
de Grazia, Victoria, 58
DeLillo, Don, 297(n63)
democracy, cultural stratification and, 42–6
democratic change, sources and social dimensions of, 34–6
"democratic distinction," 38
democratic values, popular culture and, 28–34
democratization
  of culture, 27–46, 134, 242
  meanings of, 37–42
Denning, Michael, 12, 223
  on cultural categories, 254–5, 256
department stores, 49, 82
Depression, the, 55, 83, 115, 166
Dewey, John, 55, 146
Diggers, guerrilla theater of, 197
Diggins, John P., 105–6
dime museum (Boston), 31
dime novels, 12, 74
Diners Club, first credit cards from, 179
Disney, Walt, 76, 104, 112, 114–16, 126, 147, 166, 191(n), 227
  animated cartoons of, 170, 172, 208

Disney Channel, 229
Disneyland, 58, 156, 210
Disney World, tourist popularity of, 46
documentaries, xv, 224–9
  authenticity of, 239
Domingo, Placido, 122
Dorfman, Ariel, 194
Dos Passos, John, 143
Dostoyevsky, Fyodor, 148
Douglas, Ann, 13
Dreiser, Theodore, 118
Drucker, Peter F., 62
Durante, Jimmy, 112

Eames chair, in taste-level chart, 132
Eaton, Walter Prichard, 125
Eco, Umberto, electronic community of, 216
Edison, Thomas A., 56
Eisenhower, Dwight D., 130, 147
Eisenstein, Elizabeth, 249
Eliot, T. S., 11–12, 111, 145, 177, 243, 252
  on culture, 7–8
elite culture, 71
Ellington, Duke, xviii–xix, 35, 73, 116, 204, 264(n11)
e-mail, 246
Emerson, Ralph Waldo, 11, 37, 142
Enola Gay exhibit, 237
entertainment
  commercialization of, 70
  democratization of, 31–2
  popular, 137
entertainment discount revolution, 31
entertainment industry, role in mass culture, 194
entrepreneurs
  cultural, 30, 47, 73–4, 77, 108
  of entertainment, 137–8, 167
  of Woodstock Festival, 60
EPCOT Center, 194
Erenberg, Lewis, on cabaret entertainment, 195–6
Erskine, John, 91
ESPN, 205(n)
Europe
  high and low culture convergence in, 106–7
  mass culture in, 164
  popular culture in, 248–51
evangelical religion, as popular culture, 80–1
Evans, Augusta Jane, 102
Evans, Bergen, 97
Ewen, Elizabeth, 48
Ewen, Stuart, 48, 53, 54
Exxon, support of arts by, 61

Factory, The, as Warhol studio, 191, 192
Fallows, James, on journalism, 247–8

fast-food chains, role in mass culture, 19, 182

Faulkner, William, 73, 183

Fawcett, paperback books of, 181

FBI, Hoffman manhunt by, 156-7

Federal Arts Project, 41

Federal Communications Commission (FCC), 174
  ruling on public interest programs, 93, 116, 152

Federal Trade Commission, 141

Fern, Fanny, 102

fiction, middlebrow and highbrow, 117-18

Fiedler, Leslie, 12, 118, 179, 221-2

Fields, W. C., 113

film criticism, 34, 91

films
  animated, 76, 170
  blending of taste levels in, 112
  censorship of, 153, 154
  on contemporary events, 65, 69
  cultural authority role in, 138
  effect on proto-mass culture, 171-2
  role in mass leisure, 16, 73, 86, 87, 104, 258
  Supreme Court ruling on, 153
  television compared with, 203-4

Finkelstein, Sidney, 100-1

Fisher, Rudolph, 195

Fiske, John
  on mass culture and television, 72, 211-13, 216, 247
  on popular culture, 217, 229

Fitzgerald, Ella, xix

Fitzgerald, F. Scott, 118, 144

5-and-10-cent stores, 32, 231

Flexner, James T., 121

Flynn, Elizabeth Gurley, 66

FM technology, effect on radio, 174

folk culture, 6, 72, 106

folk heroes, in America, 10

folk music, 65, 151, 241

"folk-play," 81

folk-pop music, 151

Folkways Anthology, 116

Foner, Eric, as critic of Civil War documentary, 225, 227

food
  authorities on, 159-60
  cultural critics of, 145
  standardization of, 171

football
  role in mass culture, 19, 82
  on television, 152, 185

Ford, Henry, 17, 67

Ford Foundation, 131

Foster, Stephen, 108

Fox, Richard Wightman, 223

Fox TV, 205(n)

France
  mass culture in, 164, 249
  patrician and plebeian culture convergence in, 106

franchising, of restaurants, hotels, and stores, 19, 182

Frank, Joseph, 44

Frankfurt School, 46, 177

Franklin, Benjamin, 29

Fratellini, The, 221

Fredrickson, George M., 35

Freud, Sigmund, 112

Friend, Tad, 128, 129

Frith, Simon, 158

Frueh, Al, 113

Fukuyama, Francis, 251

Funk, Tom, 95-6, 98

Fussell, Paul, on authenticity, 239

Gable, Clark, 112

Galbraith, John Kenneth, 182

Gallagher, Gary W., as critic of Civil War documentary, 225

Gallup, George, 42, 139

Gallup polls, 25, 42, 43-4, 139, 154, 155, 183-5, 186-7, 200

Game Show Channel, ad for, 206(n)

Gans, Herbert J., xvii, 7, 105, 123

Garbo, Greta, 112

Gardner, James, review of modern art show by, 232-3

Garrett, Shelly, 76

Gates, Henry Lewis, Jr., 76

General Electric, 54

Geneva Peace Conference (1905), 56

Genteel Tradition, 136

Gerbner, George, 201

Germany, popular culture in, 249

Gershwin, George, 89, 119

Gilder, Richard Watson, 136

Gitlin, Todd, 198, 205(n), 213, 216

Glasser, William, 201

global events, definition of, 238

Glueck, Grace, on modern art show, 233

Godkin, E. L., 136

Gogol, Nikolai, 111

Gold, Mike, 101(n)

"Golliwog's Cakewalk" (Debussy), 36

Gomery, Douglas, 198

Goodman, Benny, 113, 115

Gopnik, Adam, xv-xvi, 230, 234, 239

Gordon, Jeanne, 114

Gorky, Maxim, 176

Gould, Jack, 156

Graceland (Memphis), tourist popularity of, 46

Graham, Billy, 80

Index

Graham, Martha, 112, 121
Grand Army of the Republic, veterans of, 64
Grand Opera House (New York), 32
Great Britain
  culture in, 5–6
  debating societies in, 107
  early treatises in, 164
  genesis of commercialization in, 47–9
Great Debate, over mass culture, xiv, 4, 89,
    146, 164, 168, 176–94, 252
Greenberg, Clement, 20, 103, 221, 222, 252,
    254
  on kitsch, 21, 147
  on taste levels, 97, 100, 126–7
Griffith, D. W., 104, 165
Grimsted, David, 9, 221–2
Gross, John, 123
guerrilla theater, of Diggers, 197
guidebooks
  for self-improvement, 30, 51
  for sports, 30, 51
Gurevitch, Michael, 248
Guthrie, Woody, 43, 157

Hale, Sarah Josepha, 102
Haley, Alex, 239
Hall, David D., 9
Hall, Stuart, 20, 210–11, 216
Handlin, Oscar, 4
  on mass media, 196
Handy, W. C., 113(n)
Harlow, Jean, 112, 153
Harris, Louis, 199, 246
Harris, Neil, 10, 22, 109, 165, 222
  on museum exhibits, 236
Harris polls, 32, 185, 186, 199, 246
Hawthorne, Nathaniel, 37, 102
Hays, Lee, 43
HBO, 205(n), 217
Hearst, William Randolph, 31, 168, 169
Hecht, Ben, 140
Held, Anna, 56
Hellman, Lillian, 148
Helsinki Accords, 190
Hemingway, Ernest, 118
Henry, Joseph, 30
Henry Ford Museum, 118
Hermitage, the, 122
Herriman, George, 221, 256
High & Low: Modern Art and Popular Culture
    (MoMA exhibit), xv, 229–30, 239
high art, 30, 123, 124, 253
  commercial art and, 126
highbrow(s)
  as consumers of mass culture, 72
  definitions of, 75, 100
  derivation of term, 74
highbrow culture, xiii, 13, 71, 72, 76, 93, 147

high culture
  low culture and, 119–25
  maintenance of standards of, 106
  mass culture and, 243
  middlebrow culture and, 108
  popular culture and, 6, 10, 20, 125, 243
  popular culture convergence with, 103
  role of, 26
  working class and, 11
highlowbrow culture, 129
Highway Beautification Act (1965), 60–1
Hines, Duncan, 145
Hippodrome Theater (New York), 32
Hirschfeld, Al, 144
historians
  as cultural critics, xv, 47, 103, 105–6, 109,
    165, 219–41
  professional, popular history and, 224–9
historic site museums, 118–19
History Channel, 229
history museums, popular culture displays in,
    219, 235–7
Hoffman, Abbie, 156–7
Hoggart, Richard, 82
Hollywood, Benton's painting of, 153, 154
Holmes, Mary Jane, 102
Holocaust, the, 238
Holt, John, on television for children, 201
Hooper system, of rating audience size, 155
Hoover, Herbert, 54, 67
Horkheimer, Max, 106
Horowitz, Daniel, 49
"hot rod" culture, 92
Hoving, Thomas P., 117
Howard Johnson's restaurants, 171
Howe, Irving, 147, 177
Howells, William Dean, 33, 109–10, 136, 225
Hudson-Fulton Tercentenary celebration
    (1909), 110
Hudson River school of painting, 108
Hughes, Robert, 88, 253
  review of modern art show by, 230, 231, 234
Hugo, Victor, 111
"humor of irrationality," on radio, 153–4
Huneker, James Gibbons, 142, 159
Huxley, Aldous, 88–9

IBM micro computers, advertising for, 163
Ibsen, Henrik, 111, 121
"Impossible Interviews," 112–13
Indiana, Robert, 253
industrial art, 110
Innis, Harold A., 196
Internet, the, 4, 215–16, 246
Isserman, Maurice, 220(n)
Italy, elite and popular culture convergence in,
    106–7
Ives, Stephen, 228

James, Henry, 256
Jarves, James Jackson, 30
jazz, 96, 100–1, 113, 116, 220
    as unique American music, 64–5
Jefferson, Thomas, 39, 67, 156
Jencks, Richard W., 122
Johns, Jasper, 253
Johnson, Lady Bird, 130
Johnson, Lyndon B., 252
Johnson, Nunnally, 34
Joplin, Scott, 36
journalism. *See also* Alsop, Joseph; Alsop,
    Stewart
    quality and character in America, 247–8
journalistic publishing, in America, 14–15
Journal of Popular Culture, 222
Joyce, James, 191
Judson, E. Z. C., 74
Julian, Joseph, 174
Junto, 29
juvenile delinquency, mass culture perceived
    as cause of, 155(n)

Kael, Pauline, 34
Kakutani, Michiko, 13
Kallen, Horace, 54, 66
Kanin, Garson, 157
Kantor, MacKinlay, 181
Kaplan, Abraham, 93–4
Kasson, John F., 223
Keil, Angeliki V., 223
Keil, Charles, 223
Keith, Benjamin Franklin, 31–2, 138
Keller, Frances Alice, 66
Kelley, Florence, 136
Kempton, Murray, review of modern art show
    by, 233, 234
Kennedy, John F., 19, 130, 152
Kincaid, Bradley, 173
Kingsley, Robert, 61
kitsch, 21, 30, 147, 224
    popular culture and, 221
Kittredge, George Lyman, xvi
Klein, Alexander, 178
Kohn, Morris, 32
Koons, Jeff, 231
Koppel, Ted, 147
Kornfeld, Artie, 60
Kramer, Hilton, 106, 122, 255
    review of modern art show by, 231–2
Kristol, Irving, 147, 148
Kroc, Ray, McDonald's franchising by, 182
Kroes, Rob, 267(n34)
Krutch, Joseph Wood, 43
Kultur, Germanic sense of, 38, 43, 107

labor history, museum of, 236
Landers, Ann, 160

Lang, Michael, 60
Lardner, Ring, 140, 221
Lasch, Christopher, 198, 199
    on American narcissism, 24
Lasswell, Harold, on mass communication
    and culture, 250
Lazarsfeld, Paul, 196
Lazere, Donald, on mass culture, 213–14, 216
Lears, T. J. Jackson, 5, 52, 69, 213, 216, 223
    on authenticity and artifice, 238–9
leftist politics, 124, 146
leftist scholars, definitions of culture by, xv
leisure
    American expenditures on, xix
    American preferences for, xiii
    commercialization of, 52, 70
    Gallup polls on, 183–5, 186, 200
    Harris polls on, 199, 236
    physical exercise role in, 30
    privatization of, 24–5
    reading for. *See* books; reading
    Roper polls on, 180, 282
    television's impact on, 94
    World War II's effect on, 175
    Yankelovich poll on, 187–8
leisure organizations, 264(n12)
Le Roy Ladurie, Emmanuel, 249
Levine, Lawrence W., 10, 73, 211, 216, 223,
    239
    on popular culture, 223–4
Lewis, Lloyd, 33
Lewis, Sinclair, 118
Library of Congress, 68, 109
Lichtenstein, Roy, 121, 126, 231
lifestyle, definition and usage of, 243
Limbaugh, Rush, 238
Lippmann, Walter, xvii, 7, 37, 42, 68, 74, 103,
    120, 144, 147, 170, 240
    on culture, xvii
    on public opinion, 138–40, 238
Lipsitz, George, 211, 216
Lipsyte, Robert, 251
literary criticism and critics, 40–1, 142, 145
Literary Guild, 181
literature, role in popular culture, 82, 83
Litwack, Leon, as critic of Civil War
    documentary, 225
Living Theatre (New York), IRS closing of,
    27–8
Lloyd, Harold, 175
Lomax, Alan, 241
Lomax, John, 241
Long, Huey, 112
Longfellow, Henry Wadsworth, 10
long-playing records
    development of, 172
    effect on merging of high and popular
        culture, 116

Lott, Eric, 63
Louvre, the, 122
lowbrow(s)
  definition of, 119
  derivation of term, 74
lowbrow culture, xiii, 71, 93
  definition of, 100
low culture, high culture and, 119–25
Lowell, James Russell, 64, 142
Lowenthal, Leo, 57
Luce, Henry, 120(n), 148, 174–5
Luther, Martin, 164
lyceums, 108
Lynd, Helen, 55, 81–2, 83, 84–5, 140
Lynd, Robert, 55, 81–2, 83, 84–5, 140
Lynes, Mildred, 130(n)
Lynes, Russell, 100, 105, 134, 181, 279(n2, n3)
  on brow levels, 95, 96, 97, 127, 129–32, 179

Macdonald, Dwight, 20, 21, 43, 97, 101, 103, 122, 126, 129, 145, 146, 177, 183, 283(n60)
  on passivity, 89, 196
  as popular-culture critic, 222
Macintosh computer, original television ad for, 215(n)
MacKaye, Percy, 104
MacLeish, Archibald, xvi, 158
magazines, advertising in, 50, 51, 167
Mailer, Norman, 69
mail-order companies, 49, 50, 82
Major Bowes' Amateur Hour, 42
Malina, Judith, 27, 28
Malraux, André, 122
Mapplethorpe, Robert, 141
Marble Collegiate Church, 102
Marcus, Daniel, 117
Marcuse, Herbert, 177, 222
Marling, Karal Ann, on television-watching, 209–10
Marlowe, Christopher, 111
Marquand, John P., 181
Marsh, Reginald, 23, 79
Marx, Groucho, 45, 75, 87
Marx, Karl, 239
Marx Brothers, 75, 156
Marxism, 48, 101(n), 157, 165, 177, 211, 237.
  See also neo-Marxism
"mass audience," 164–5
mass communication
  definition of, 4
  development of, 58
mass consumer culture, 179
mass consumption, 166
Masscult, 126
mass culture, 4, 15
  advertising as part of, 193
  agency versus passivity in, 209–18, 247
  civic culture undermined by, 199(n)
  commercialization transition to, 55–61
  critics of, 162–89
  development of, 17, 20, 48, 50, 53, 63, 71, 162–89, 243
  elitist critiques of, 183
  in France, 164, 249
  Great Debate over, xiv, 4, 89, 146, 164, 168, 176–89, 252
  high culture convergence with, 121
  innovations since 1980, 204–9
  juvenile delinquency and, 155(n)
  mass society and, 161
  meanings of, xiii, 3, 5, 18
  novelty role in, 12–13
  passive quality of, 77, 90–1, 209–18
  popular culture and, 3–4, 5, 13, 22, 71, 76–7, 91, 101, 257–8, 303(n30)
  proto-mass culture compared to, 49–51, 55
  in recent times, 218
  role of, 26, 49
mass education, 166
mass leisure, 16
  development of, 58
mass-mailing techniques, 173
mass media, 4, 45, 87, 189
"mass-mediated popular culture," 4, 172
mass production, 20, 166
mass society, 165
  definition of, 4, 166
  mass culture and, 161
Matthews, Brander, 33, 66
May, Lary, 16, 36
McCarthy, Joseph R., 119, 130, 157
McCarthy, Mary, 158, 177
McCay, Winsor, 169
McCullough, David, 224
McDonald's, 19, 182
McLuhan, Marshall, 87, 101
medicines and health products, misleading advertising for, 51–2
megachurch phenomenon, 62
Melville, Herman, 37, 204
Mencken, H. L., xvi, 39, 143–4, 159, 174, 286(n24)
Menotti, Gian Carlo, 116
Merriam, Charles E., 140
Merton, Robert K., 68
Messmer, Otto, 169
Metropolitan Mechanics' Institute (Washington, D.C.), 30
Metropolitan Museum of Art (New York), 73, 117, 159
  American Wing of, 67, 110
Metropolitan Opera, 114, 145, 252
Meyers, Russ, 179
"Midcult," 89, 126

middlebrow(s)
  as consumers of mass culture, 72
  Disney as, 115
  rejuvenation of, 125–32
"middlebrow arbiters," 253
middlebrow culture, xiii, 4, 12, 43, 44, 71, 72, 84
  definition of, 100
  high culture and, 108
  increase of, 92–3
Miller, Arthur, 104
Mills, C. Wright, 164
Minow, Newton, 152
minstrel shows, 35, 63, 78, 167
Mitchell, Artie, 156
Mitchell, Jim, 156
"mixed media" phenomenon, 118
modern art
  museum show on popular art and, 229–34
  popular culture influence on, 72
modernism, development of, 257
Monroe, Marilyn, 104
Montgomery Ward, 19, 48, 168
moonwalk, television viewing of, 190
Moore, R. Laurence, 223
Morgan, Joy Elmer, 64
Mormon Tabernacle Choir, 157
Morosco, Walter, 32
motel chains, 19, 171
Mother Goose tales, 36
Mount, William Sidney, 108
Mount Vernon, 46
movie audiences
  democratization of, 36
  diversity within, 91
movie fan magazines, 82
movie producers, cultural power of, 151
Movie Production Code, 153
movies. *See* films
movie stars, 36
movie theaters
  attendance at, 117, 160
  growth of, 32, 33
Mozart, Wolfgang Amadeus, 107, 204
MTV, 163, 205, 208
Mumford, Lewis, 37, 158
Munch, Edvard, 122
Muncie, Indiana, Lynds' studies on, 55, 84–5
Murrow, Edward R., 43, 157, 185
Musée national des arts et traditions populaires (Paris), 299(n40)
Museum of American History. *See* National Museum of American History
Museum of Contemporary Art (Los Angeles), 230, 234
Museum of Fine Arts (Boston), 109
Museum of Modern Art (New York), *High & Low* show at, xv, 229–35, 239

museums
  attendance at, 117, 233
  of history, 219
  popular culture exhibits of, 229–40
  popularity of, 73, 102, 118–19, 122
music
  American interest in, 120
  cultural critics of, 142
musical revues, 78, 121
Mussolini, Benito, 111, 112
myths, in the United States, 5

Nabokov, Vladimir, on popular culture, 284(n76)
Nasaw, David, 36
Nathan, George Jean, 39, 144, 159
Nation, Carry, 79
National Air and Space Museum (Washington, D.C.), aborted *Enola Gay* exhibit at, 237
National Association for Sport and Physical Education, 296(n55)
National Better Business Bureau, 141
National Endowments for the Arts and Humanities, 244, 252–3
National Gallery of Art (Washington, D.C.), 117
National Museum of American Art, American West exhibit of, 237
National Museum of American History (Washington, D.C.), popular and mass culture displays at, 7, 236–7, 240
National Portrait Gallery (Washington, D.C.), 237
National Public Radio, Popular Culture commentator of, 4
National Zoo (Washington, D.C.), creation of, 17–18
NBC, 18, 85, 111, 173, 205
NBC Radio, Red and Blue networks of, 75
NBC Symphony Orchestra, 111
NBC Television, 116–17
Nehru, Jawaharlal, 117
neo-Marxism, 176, 254
  interpretations of culture in, 47
New England, Puritan, lay and clerical thought in, 107
Newhouse School of Public Communication (Syracuse University), Center for the Study of Popular Television of, 204
New Left, 220(n)
newspapers, as entertainment source, 82
New Television Set, The (Rockwell), 184
New York Oratorio Society, 111
New York State Historical Association (Cooperstown), exhibits of, 235
nickelodeons, 32
Nietzsche, Friedrich, 165

Nintendo, 207
Nixon, Richard M., 19, 160, 162, 252
Norton, Charles Eliot, 108, 142
Nye, Russell B., 221

O'Connor, John J., on television, 203–4
Ohmann, Richard, on mass culture, 14–15
Old Sturbridge Village, 118
O'Leary, Timothy, on television, 207–8
Olmsted, Frederick Law, 22
Olympic Games (Barcelona, 1992), 251
Omnibus (TV program), xvi
O'Neill, Eugene, 112, 121, 256
oral histories, 241
Ortega y Gasset, José, 44, 165
Orvell, Miles, 210, 239
Outcault, Richard, 168–9, 170

Packard, Vance, 59, 146, 157, 196
Page, Walter Hines, 15
pageants, 104–5
Paley, William S., 43, 155
paperback books
  mass production of, 181
  sales of, 56
Paris Exposition of 1900, 36
Park, Robert E., 140
Park, Willard, 97
passivity
  growth of, 195, 196
  in mass culture, 77, 90–1, 175, 188, 191
  as response to entertainment, 88–9, 247
patriotism, manipulation of, in World
    War II, 68
Pavarotti, Luciano, 122
PBS, 200, 224
Peace Jubilee (Boston, 1869), 108–9
Peace Luncheon, Pepsi-Cola sponsorship
    of, 56
Peale, Charles Willson, 102
Peale, Norman Vincent, 102, 173
Peiss, Kathy, 16, 223
Penguin, paperback books of, 181
Penneys, 19
penny arcades, 32
Pepsi-Cola
  advertising by, 183
  Peace Luncheon of, 56
Perelman, S. J., 75–6, 93, 276(n11)
Phillips, William, 120(n), 122, 146, 177,
    179
phonographs, 80, 101, 172
photocopier, 172(n)
physical exercise, participation in, 30
Picasso, Pablo, xvi, 231
Piggly-Wiggly stores, self-service in, 168
Plagens, Peter, 253
  review of modern art show by, 230–1, 233

Planned Parenthood, as upper-middlebrow
    cause, 132
Plumb, J. H., 68
Pocket Books, as paperback publishers, 56,
    121
Poli, Sylvester, 137
Pollock, Jackson, 120(n)
Poni, Carlo, 106
Pop art and artists, 122, 124, 150, 230
popular culture
  art and, 219, 229–34
  commercialized, 21
  democratic values and, 28–34
  in Europe, 248–51
  evanescence of, 21
  high culture and, 6, 10, 103, 125
  historians and, 219–41
  interpretation of, 234–41
  magazines as purveyors of, 15
  mass culture and, 3–4, 5, 13, 22, 71, 76–7,
    91, 101, 163, 257–8, 303(n30)
  meanings of, xiii, 3, 5, 7, 38, 70
  in 1930s, 84
  participatory nature of, 22, 42, 76–8, 195
  persistence of, xv, 91–4
  phasing of, 47–69
  pivotal decade for, 83–91
  prime of, 76–83
  promotion of, 62–9
  role of, 26
  Selective Chronology on, xiii, xxi–xxvii,
    258
  studied in academe, 297(n9)
  "traditional," 6
  in transition, 70–94
Popular Culture Association, 105, 222
Popular Front coalition, 41
popular history, professional historians and,
    224–9
popular music, 64, 80, 89, 180
populism, effects on art, 219
populist politics, 159
populists, opinions of elite and popular
    culture, 124–5, 259
pornography
  films of, 156
  Mapplethorpe photographs perceived as,
    141
postmodernism, 123–4, 163, 234
  role in blurring of high and low culture,
    126
Pound, Ezra, 75
Presley, Elvis, 241
Prohibition, 28
Project XX (NBC), 116, 117
propaganda, in a democracy, 271(n37)
  See also Committee on Public Information
Protestant Reformation, 164, 249

proto-mass culture, xiv, 17, 18, 21, 50,
    291(n33)
  commercial culture and, 166–76
  increased leisure and, 53
  mass culture compared to, 49–51, 55
  pivotal era of, 59, 71
  role of, 49
  role of radio in, 85–6
  transition to mass culture, xiv, 17, 18, 21,
    50, 57, 59
public broadcasting, 152
public journalism, 247–8
public libraries, 83
public opinion
  increasing confidence of, 134
  role of, 138–9
public opinion polls, xiv, 25, 32–3, 42, 139,
    140–1, 245–6, 248
public relations, 56
  pioneers in, 40, 274(n40)
Pulitzer, Joseph, 31, 113, 168
pulp confession magazines, 83
Purity Crusade, in America, 250
Pynchon, Thomas, 204

Racine, Jean, 36
radio
  advertising on, 50, 111, 155, 167
  changing status of, 174
  critique of, 271(n48)
  cultural aspects of, xvi, 19, 64
  cultural authorities and, 160
  diversity in audiences of, 91
  effects on high and popular culture, 110–11
  effects on mass culture, 68, 80, 81, 85, 174
  effects on proto-mass culture, 171–2, 173
  humor on, 153–4
  middlebrow programs for, 155
  music on, 111
  network development in, 138
  as news source, 141
  passive reception of, 81, 196
  populist programs on, 42
  public interest programs of, 93, 116, 145
  role in American life, 85–6
  U.S. history program on, 221
  variety shows on, 126
Radway, Janice A., 16, 82, 210
"rag-time artists," 64
Rahv, Philip, 144, 158
Rand, Sally, 112
Ranke, Leopold von, 220
rare books, 110
RCA, 111
reader responses, 279(n1, n2)
reading
  as leisure activity, 279(n49)
  role in popular culture, 82, 83, 93

Reconstruction, post–Civil War, 136, 225
Reed, Edward, 110
regionalism
  decline of, 50
  in popular culture, 82
religion, popularization of, 102
religious revivals, 80–1
Remnick, David, 251
remote control device, for television, 205
Renton, Edward, 126
revisionism, 237–8, 300(n43)
Rice, Thomas D., 35
Rich, Frank, 160
Richards, I. A., 143
Riesman, David, 157, 178
Rivière, Georges Henri, 299(n40)
Rockefeller, David, 61
Rockefeller, John D., Sr., 112
rock music, 121
  movie moguls' dislike of, 151
Rockwell, Norman, 21, 184
Rogers, Fred, 201
Rogers, John, 30
Rombauer, Irma, 159
Roosevelt, Franklin D., 141, 173
Roosevelt, Theodore, 56
Roper polls, 25, 32–3, 180, 202–3
Rosenbach, A. S. W., 110
Rosenberg, Harold, 222
Rosenfeld, Paul, 41
Rosenzweig, Roy, 223
Ross, Edward A., 74
Ross, Harold, 34, 145
Ross, Steven J., 86(n)
Rourke, Constance M., 6, 221
Rozelle, Pete, 152
Rubin, Jerry, 156
Rudenstine, Neil, 216
Rushkoff, Douglas, 163, 207, 208
Russell, Bertrand, 117
Russell, Lillian, 56
Russia, degradation of culture in, 251
Rydell, Robert W., 223

Sabean, David, 249
"sacralization of culture," 239
Sahl, Mort, 156, 194
St. Louis pageant of 1914, 104
Salon of American Humorists exhibition
    (1915), 113
saloons, 79, 81
Sarnoff, David, 111
satellite technology
  film relay by, 19–20
  globalization of imaging by, 163
  news transmission by, 248
satire, of highbrow aspirations, 125
Scherman, Harry, 138

Schickel, Richard, 207
  on theatergoing, 197–8
Schiller, Herbert I., 90, 161, 214, 216
Schlesinger, Arthur M., Jr., 87
  as film critic, 222
Schlessinger, Laura, 160
Schuyler, Montgomery, 142
science and technology, attitudes toward, 246
Scopes Trial of 1925, 139
Scripps, Edward W., 169
Sears, Roebuck, 19, 48, 168
Secession, as literary magazine, 275(n56)
Seeger, Pete, 43
Seldes, George, 103
Seldes, Gilbert, 43, 44, 45, 52–3, 89, 94, 103,
    110, 115, 144, 145, 148, 178, 183
  on passive audiences, 196–7
  on popular culture, 220–1, 244–5
Selective Chronology, of landmarks in
    popular culture, xiii, xxi–xxvii, 258
self-help books, 55
Sennett, Mack, 156
Sennett, Richard, on public culture, 188–9
Serling, Rod, 155
sex, authorities on, 160
Shakespeare, William, 9, 30, 45, 63, 104, 111,
    121, 181
sheet music, 80, 172
Sherman, Stuart Pratt, 40–1, 140
Shiach, Morag
  on popular culture, 217–18
  on television, 215
Shils, Edward, on mass culture, 178, 179
shopping centers, development of, 19, 59,
    179, 182, 190
Siepmann, Charles A., 52–3
silent films, 86(n), 163, 195, 220
Simkhovitch, Mary, 195
situation comedies, on television, 185
Sklar, Robert, 68(n)
Slotkin, Richard, 165
  on American myths, 4–5
Smith, Kate, 68
Smith, Roberta, review of modern art show
    by, 230–1
Smith, Steven, 138
Smithsonian Institution, 7, 30, 236, 237
Snyder, Robert W., 52
soap operas, 18, 87
social class, taste preferences and, 243
social construction, of reality, 240–1
social dances, popularity of, 53, 80, 81, 84
Social Realists (art), 253, 254
social sciences, development as discipline,
    140
social scientists, 238
  studies of mass communication and culture
    by, 250

Sojourner Truth, 241
Sontag, Susan, xvi, 122–3, 150
Sousa, John Philip, 109
South, the, 18, 225
"spectatoritis," 89, 195, 197
Spigel, Lynn, 88, 126
Spin-it racks, for paperback books, 181
Spock, Benjamin, M.D., 156, 181
sports
  commercialization of, 30–1, 51–2, 251
  passive spectators of, 217
  on television, 185, 190
  women in, 216
Springer, Jerry, 163
Sputnik I era, 130
Stalin, Josef, 112
standardization, 190, 251
Stanton, Frank, 45, 53, 178
State of the Union address, 24
Statue of Liberty centennial, 236
  corporate sponsorship of, 194
Stern, Howard, 163
Stevenson, Adlai, 74–5, 130
Stewart, Martha, 160
Stone, Oliver, 69, 229
Stott, William, 239
Stowe, Harriet Beecher, 10
Styron, William, 239
suburbanites, shopping habits of, 59
Sunday, Billy, 42, 80
"Sunday School Circuit," 138
Super Bowl, 22, 72, 215(n)
supermarkets, development of, 58, 182
Supreme Court, ruling on movies, 153
Susman, Warren I., 12, 58, 84, 222
Swayze, John Cameron, 59
Swingewood, Alan, 47–8, 268(n49)
symphony orchestras, popularity of, 119

"talk radio," 207(n)
Tamiment Institute conference (1959), 196
taste
  for Americana, 67
  blurred boundaries between levels of,
    95–132, 243, 258
  cultural levels of, 71, 72
  Gallup poll on, 43–4
  levels and preferences of, xiv, 94
  persistence in levels of, 102–6
  social class and preferences of, 243
taste-level charts, 98–9, 127–8, 132
Tate, Allen, 89
Taylor, William R., 167, 223
technology, culture and, 289(n61)
television
  advertising on, 50, 59, 60, 205, 206, 215(n)
  cable stations, 205(n), 214
  cultural authorities and, 160

effect on views on art, 126
effects on American life, 87–8, 155, 183, 184, 186, 198–9, 214, 245, 258
history chronicles on, 69
impact on American leisure, 94
interaction with, 206, 207
legislation on, 150–1
as mass medium, 86–7, 151–2
as news source, 119, 186
passive reception of, 196, 197, 199
polls on, 199–200, 202, 203, 214
public interest programs of, 93
role in mass culture, 18–19, 20, 24, 183
taste levels for, 126
video games on, 206
violence on, 154–5
Tennessee Valley Authority, 221
Terkel, Studs, 241
Thanksgiving Day parades, 82
Thayer, William Roscoe, 22
theater, cultural critics of, 144
theatergoing, passive nature of, 197–8
theatrical and musical events, guides for behavior at, 31, 195
Thompson, E. P., 9, 164
Thompson, Frederic, 32
Thomson, Virgil, 119
Thoreau, Henry David, 142
Three Tenors concerts, 122
Tiffany, Louis Comfort, 35
Tilly, Charles, 249
"time-shifting," VCR use for, 206
Tin Pan Alley, popular music of, 65, 80
Tocqueville, Alexis de, 38, 46, 161, 201, 238, 243, 252, 253
Todd, Mike, 75–6
Tolstoy, Leo, 111
Toplin, Robert Brent, on Burns's documentaries, 239–40
Toscanini, Arturo, xix, 111, 112
Trachtenberg, Alan, 22, 77
Trilling, Diana, 158
Trilling, Lionel, 74, 146, 158
trolley parks, 78
Truth, Sojourner, 241
Tuesday Evening at the Savoy Ballroom (Marsh), 79
Turner, Frederick Jackson, 10–11
Twain, Mark, 56, 251–2
Twitchell, James B., 90, 163
on advertising, 193, 213

U.S. Embassy (Helsinki), as Williamsburg replica, 67
U.S. Sanitary Commission, 35
Universal Product Code, use with VideOcart, 209
upper-middlebrow culture, 129, 131, 132

valentines, 81–2
Van Den Haag, Ernest, 222
Vanderbilt, Amy, 97, 159–60
Van Rensselaer, Mrs. Schuyler, 136–7
Varnedoe, Kirk, as curator of *High & Low* show, xv, xvi, 229–30, 231, 233–5, 239
Vassar College, taste-level performance of, 97
vaudeville, 21, 31, 32, 37, 42, 52, 53, 73, 78, 85–6, 109–10, 126, 138, 153, 165
VCR players, 205, 206
Veblen, Thorstein, 143, 157
Verdi, Giuseppe, 109
"vernacular culture," 72
Victorian America
culture in, 9–10, 23, 70–1, 250
democratization in, 30
VideOcart, 209
video games, 206
Vietnam War, 20, 24, 156, 236
violence, in mass culture, 163
voyeurism, 163

Walker, John A., 100
Wallace, DeWitt, 171, 181
Wallace, Mike, on museum exhibits, 236
Walzer, Michael, on populist politics and museums, 158–9
Ward, Geoffrey C., on Civil War documentary, 240
Warhol, Andy, 121–2, 124, 191–2, 231
Warner, Charles Dudley, 11
Warner, Susan B., 102
Warner, W. Lloyd, 140
Warner Books, 163
Warner Bros., as arbiters of taste, 151
Warshow, Robert, 5, 117
Washington, George, 241
WASP elitism, decline of, 147
Watergate break-in, 162
Waugh, Alec, 181
Wayside Inn (Sudbury, Massachusetts), restoration of, 67
Weber and Fields, Co., 113
Welk, Lawrence, 12
Welles, Orson, 75, 86, 173
Wendell, Barrett, 37
Wertham, Fredric, 155
West, Mae, 21–2, 154
West, the, 18, 106
documentary on, 228–9
as frontier, 10–11
museum exhibit on, 237
Westheimer, Ruth, 160
Whannel, Paddy, 20
Wharton, Edith, 35
White, Hayden, 106
White, Theodore H., 69
White Castle hamburger houses, 19, 171, 182

Index

White House, tourist popularity of, 46
Whiteman, Paul, 113, 114
White Oaks (Philadelphia), 107–8
White Tower hamburger houses, 19
Whitfield, Stephen, 103–4
Whitman, Walt, 14, 28–9, 63, 108, 135–6, 164
Whitney Museum of American Art (New York), 298(n30)
Whyte, William H., 158
Wiebe, Robert, 135
Wilder, Thornton, 181
Wild West Show, of Buffalo Bill, 11, 21, 78
Williams, Raymond, xviii, 176, 217, 241, 255
    on culture, 7, 8–9
Wilson, August, 76
Wilson, Edmund, 140, 144, 148, 181
Wilson, Woodrow, 65
Winchell, Walter, 42(n), 103, 171
Winfrey, Oprah, 160
Wister, Owen, 244
Wolfe, Tom, 292(n48)
Woman's Christian Temperance Union, 79, 136
women
    in Civil War, 225
    cultural authority of, 136–7
    leisure pursuits of, 16, 210
    in sports, 216
Woodberry, George E., 37
Woodruff, Robert W., 58
Woodstock Festival (1969), 69
Woodward, C. Vann, on Civil War documentary, 225–6
Woolf, Virginia, 97, 119

Woollcott, Alexander, 103, 145
Woolworth, Frank W., 32
working class
    cultural preferences of, 12, 103
    goods consumption by, 49
Works Progress Administration (WPA), 41, 175
World Cup playoffs, 190
world fairs, in America, 10, 126
World's Fair (New York, 1939), 126
World War I, 32, 40, 42, 51, 64, 65, 68, 134, 167, 242, 258
World War II, xiv, 16, 18, 49, 52, 68, 80, 154, 165, 181, 239
    Age of Anxiety following, 245
    college attendance before and after, 119, 258
    effect on class lines of, 116
    mass culture development in, 57, 58, 71, 85, 168, 173, 180, 243
    naval history TV series of, 116–17
    popular culture persistence after, 91–2
    production advances in, 166
Wyeth, James Browning, 192
Wythe, George, 67

Yankelovich poll, on leisure activities, 187–8
Yeats, William Butler, 107
Yippies, cultural opposition by, 156
youth culture, development of, 54, 59–60, 172, 179

Ziegfeld Follies, 36, 53
Zukor, Adolph, 32

Michael Kammen was born in Rochester, New York, in 1936. He graduated from The George Washington University in 1958 and received his Ph.D. from Harvard University in 1964. He has taught at Cornell University since 1965, becoming the Newton C. Farr Professor of American History and Culture there in 1973. From 1977 until 1980 he served as director of Cornell's Society for the Humanities; and in 1980–81 he was the first holder of the chair in American history established by the French government at the Ecole des Hautes Etudes en Sciences Sociales in Paris. He has received fellowships from the National Endowment for the Humanities, the John Simon Guggenheim Foundation, the Spencer Foundation, and the Center for Advanced Study in the Behavioral Sciences at Stanford. In 1989 he was appointed Regents' Fellow of the Smithsonian Institution in Washington, D.C. He has also held the Times-Mirror Research Professorship at the Huntington Library and been a Guest Scholar at the Woodrow Wilson International Center for Scholars in Washington, D.C.

Professor Kammen has been elected to membership in the American Academy of Arts and Sciences, the Society of American Historians, the American Antiquarian Society, and the Massachusetts Historical Society. In 1976 he was elected to the Council of the American Historical Association; in 1978 to the Council of the Institute of Early American History and Culture; in 1981 to the Social Science Research Council Board of Directors; and in 1989 to the Executive Board of the Organization of American Historians (OAH). He was president of the OAH in 1995–96. In 1975–76 he served as host and moderator for *The States of the Union*, a series of fifty one-hour programs broadcast by National Public Radio.

His books include *In the Past Lane: Historical Perspectives on American Culture* (1997); *The Lively Arts: Gilbert Seldes and the Transformation of Cultural Criticism in the United States* (1996); *Mystic Chords of Memory: The Transformation of Tradition in American Culture* (1991); *A Machine That Would Go of Itself: The Constitution in American Culture* (1986), which received both the Francis Parkman Prize and the Henry Adams Prize; *Spheres of Liberty: Changing Perceptions of Liberty in American Culture* (1986); *A Season of Youth: The American Revolution and the Historical Imagination* (1978); *Colonial New York: A History* (1975); *People of Paradox: An Inquiry Concerning the Origins of American Civilization* (1972), awarded the Pulitzer Prize for History; *Empire and Interest: The American Colonies and the Politics of Mercantilism* (1970); and *A Rope of Sand: The Colonial Agents, British Politics, and the American Revolution* (1968).

Professor Kammen has co-authored and edited numerous other works, and has lectured throughout the world. In 1976 he presented the Commonwealth Fund Lectures at the University of London; in 1983 the Paley Lectures in American Civilization at the Hebrew University of Jerusalem; and in 1985 the Curti Lectures at the University of Wisconsin.

A NOTE ON THE TYPE

This book was set in Janson, a typeface long thought to have been made by the Dutchman Anton Janson, who was a practicing typefounder in Leipzig during the years 1668–1687. However, it has been conclusively demonstrated that these types are actually the work of Nicholas Kis (1650–1702), a Hungarian, who most probably learned his trade from the master Dutch typefounder Dirk Voskens. The type is an excellent example of the influential and sturdy Dutch types that prevailed in England up to the time William Caslon (1692–1766) developed his own incomparable designs from them.

Composed by North Market Street Graphics,
Lancaster, Pennsylvania
Printed and bound by Quebecor Martinsburg,
Martinsburg, West Virginia
Designed by Virginia Tan